At Twilight in the Country

By the Same Author

THE BETRAYAL OF CANADA

A NEW AND BETTER CANADA

MEL HURTIG
At Twilight in the Country

Memoirs of a
Canadian Nationalist

Stoddart

Published in 1996 by
Stoddart Publishing Co. Limited
34 Lesmill Road
Toronto, Canada
M3B 2T6
Tel. (416) 445-3333
Fax (416) 445-5967

Stoddart Books are available for bulk purchase for sales promotions,
premiums, fundraising, and seminars. For details, contact the
Special Sales Department at the above address.

Canadian Cataloguing in Publication Data

Hurtig, Mel
At twilight in the country : memoirs of a Canadian nationalist

ISBN 0-7737-2978-X

1. Hurtig, Mel. 2. Nationalists – Canada – Biography.★ 3. Nationalism – Canada.
4. Canada – Politics and government – 1935–   .★ 5. Publishers and publishing – Canada
– Biography. ★ 6. Authors, Canadian (English) – 20th century – Biography. ★ I. Title.

FC601.H87A3 1996   971.064'092   C96-931256-3   F1034.3.H87A3 1996

Cover Design: Pekoe Jones/multiphrenia
Text Design: Tannice Goddard
Computer Layout: Mary Bowness

Printed and bound in Canada

Stoddart Publishing gratefully acknowledges the support of the
Canada Council and the Ontario Arts Council in the development of
writing and publishing in Canada.

To my wife Kay

To my daughters, Barbara, Gillian, Jane, and Leslie

To my brothers, Abe and Henry, and to my sister, Goldy

and especially,
in gratitude for the courage and determination
of my mother and father,
Jennie and Julius Hurtig

Contents

Acknowledgements

THERE ARE MANY PEOPLE I need to thank, including Tony Cashman, Keith Davey, Don Bastian, Jack Stoddart, Angel Guerra, Carlotta Lemieux, Ken Battle, Doug Roche, Jim Marsh, Frank McGuire, Dalton Camp, Avie Bennett, John Robert Colombo, Denis Smith, David Bercuson, Jan Walter, Susan Kent, David Shaw, Agnes Primrose, Jean and Gordon Elbrond, Louis Melzack, Lawrence Martin, Marci McDonald, Alf Bogusky, Jim Douglas, Ivon Owen, David Perry, Scott McIntyre, Duncan Cameron, Stephen Clarkson, Ed Finn, Mietta Pagella, John Turner, Allan Fotheringham, Chris Young, Doran Chandler, Carol Martin, Bill Stephenson, Kim Stebner, Peter C. Newman, Cyril MacNeil, Victor Leginsky, Kathryn Barker, David Crane, Peter Worthington, Alan Whitehorn, Graydon Carter, Roy Megarry, Brian Patton, Jeff Simpson, Jean-Marc Hamel, Bruce Wilkinson, Mel Watkins, Hugh Winsor, David Langille, Kenneth McNaught, Anna Porter, Richard Gwyn, Christina McCall, Gillian Steward, William Neville, Joan Coombs, Carl Mollins, Erin Elder, John Beaton, Ramsay Derry, Robert Weaver, Jack McClelland, Maryan Gibson, Bob Kreiger, James Winter, and the Edmonton Public Library Reference Department.

RATHER THAN FILL THE following pages with footnotes, tables, sources, and other references, I would be pleased to answer queries from any readers who wish to follow up various matters in more detail. I may be reached in the care of the publisher. Where possible, I have obtained persmission when quoting others, but despite sustained efforts, I have not been successful in contacting some of those quoted.

Preface

IN THE FOREWORD to his fine book *Gentlemen, Players and Politicians*, Dalton Camp says he tried to write with "as much charity, compassion, and candour as an affectionate admirer of our political system could muster." Near the end of *Lament for a Nation*, George Grant writes: "But lamentation falls easily into the vice of self-pity. To live with courage is a virtue, whatever one may think of the dominant assumptions of one's age."

Sometimes it is very difficult to write with both charity and candour; sometimes it is impossible. It seems to me that, in a memoir, the author should strive to tell the truth, however he or she may view it, otherwise why would any reader find the book of value?

I am not "an affectionate admirer of our political system" and I doubt that the reborn Dalton Camp is either, anymore. He is, I believe, writing some of the finest political commentary of his life today, despite Conrad Black's vacuous criticism of him.

One of the prevailing focuses of my life has been the quest for true democracy and the reform of the political system in Canada. Throughout the pages of this book, this egalitarian thrust is a constant theme. The "dominant assumptions of one's age" in Canada now are greatly disturbing to me. Sometimes I am very disappointed and sometimes angry at the injustices I perceive, but never ever have I indulged in "self-pity." Rather than lament the developments in our country, I have chosen to fight, to the best of my ability, for what I have perceived to be our national interest. Sometimes I have been successful and often not. Along the way, there have been great adventures, extraordinary men and women, patriots and scoundrels, good luck and bad, opportunities realized and missed, wise decisions and some foolish mistakes.

For me, this book is both the end of a beginning and a beginning of the end. I wish I could write as eloquently as a Pablo Neruda in his superb memoirs, or as evocatively as Vladimir Nabokov in his, but I cannot. Nevertheless, my hope is that the reader will find value in my stories of books, people, politics, ideas, and of Canada.

Let us all "live in courage" and let us all never give in to those who would deprive us of our freedom and our country.

MEL HURTIG
Edmonton

I

THE JOYS
OF BOOKSELLING

Three Murdered Americans

OW I WANT TO begin by telling you stories of three murdered Americans, three men I met briefly, three charismatic leaders brutally gunned down in their prime, assassinated when they were beginning to change the face and the history of their country. As I sit writing these words in the summer of 1995, I believe I know what you may be thinking: "What a very strange way for a Canadian nationalist to begin his memoirs."

Perhaps. Perhaps not. You decide.

September 1956. I am swimming, swimming, swimming. The water is sparkling clean and cold. No one else is in the huge hotel pool. Eight in the morning and already it's seventy degrees Fahrenheit. In an hour I will start the long drive back north to Edmonton, up through the Nevada desert into Idaho, through the Montana passes, and into the grasslands and farmland of southern and central Alberta. I am twenty-four and my bride is twenty-one. We could just barely afford a three-day honeymoon in Las Vegas, thanks mostly to my father for lending me his Oldsmobile coupe, and Eileen's father for giving us $100. When we return to Edmonton, we will begin unpacking boxes and crates of books for the "Grand Opening!" of our tiny new bookstore.

Now Eileen is sitting under her big straw hat reading a novel at the far end of the pool. There's no one else in sight, except the fortyish, redheaded woman we saw diligently working the Desert Inn's dollar slot machines when we went to bed at midnight and who was still sitting at the same stool when we came through the almost empty lobby this morning. Now she sits by the pool, smoking, her eyes covered with big dark glasses.

Two more laps. As I touch the far end and turn back, a man comes out of the hotel, takes a chair near the edge of the middle of the pool, and unfolds his newspaper. He is handsome, his white shirt unbuttoned, the sleeves rolled up. His hair blows in the light wind as he sips his orange juice. Instead of swimming by, I impulsively pull myself out of the pool and sit dripping beside him with my feet in the water.

"Good morning."

"And good morning to you," he says and smiles.

"What do you call someone who is not a Democrat and not a Republican?"

He laughs. "A political eunuch?"

"Wrong. One more try."

He thinks, laughs again. "I give up."

"A Canadian." I feel dumb, but I want to meet him.

For the past two or three years I have been following his career closely. Now, as I sit there in the warm morning sun with him, he is friendly, relaxed, not yet forty but clearly a refreshing new political star destined for greater things, narrowly having missed becoming Adlai Stevenson's running mate in the 1956 U.S. presidential campaign. Now, as the senator from Massachusetts, he is here in Las Vegas campaigning for Stevenson.

He is already enormously popular across the country, and it takes about thirty seconds for me to see why. As we talk, he is full of smiles and energy, confident, inquisitive, charming. We talk for about twenty minutes. He asks many good questions about Canada. When I slide back into the pool, his last words are: "Come to lunch in the White House in 1960." Another big smile and a wave.

I swim over to my wife. She asks: "Who's the nice-looking man?"

"That's John Fitzgerald Kennedy."

Adlai Stevenson, a reluctant candidate, was drafted by the Democrats in 1952 and was easily defeated by war hero Dwight Eisenhower. In 1956 Eisenhower won again in a landslide and the way was open for John Kennedy. After winning reelection to the Senate by the largest margin in the 1958 midterm elections, he announced his candidacy for the Democratic nomination for president in January 1960. In the November presidential election, he narrowly defeated the Republican vice president, Richard Nixon. In January 1961 John F. Kennedy became the thirty-fifth president of the United States, the youngest president in U.S. history, and the first Roman Catholic president. From his first congressional election at the age of twenty-nine, he had moved gradually but progressively to the left, was firmly dedicated to civil rights and to labour reform, to improved conditions for the poor and to election reform. Despite the substantial forces aligned against him, he became a very popular president.

NOVEMBER 22, 1963. IT is a bone-chilling cold, miserable day in Edmonton. I am standing behind the long wooden counter at the front of my big new Jasper Avenue bookstore, talking books with one of my favourite customers, leaning on the counter, waiting to go to lunch with the director of the Edmonton Art Gallery. It's not quite noon, but the store is already full of lunchtime browsers.

Fil Fraser comes in through the double doors and walks straight to the counter. He has a funny look on his face.

"John Kennedy's been shot!"

"What?" My throat goes dry, my knees buckle.

"John Kennedy was shot in the head in Dallas. He's in hospital — they're operating."

I go to lunch, leaving the radio reluctantly. In the restaurant several people have portable radios. The mood is grim. Some women are crying. Everyone is stunned, stricken, hoping.

In fact, John Kennedy, age forty-six, was dead on arrival at Parkland Memorial Hospital. He was president for just over a thousand days. At five-thirty I close the store and go home. I cry for the first time since I was a child.

NOW IT IS JUNE 1967. For the second time I find myself at the Shoreham Hotel in Washington, D.C., as the representative of the Canadian Booksellers Association to the annual convention of the American Booksellers Association. It is scorching hot in Washington, humid, heavy, oppressive. The next day at noon the head-table guests are assembled in a room next to the giant banquet hall where the convention lunch will be held. Aside from the board and officers of the ABA, there are two special guests. I am one of them, and the other is the luncheon speaker, Martin Luther King.

A Baptist minister and civil-rights crusader, King is soon to be awarded the Nobel Peace Prize for his courage, for his long battle against segregation, and for his nonviolent campaign for better opportunities and conditions for black Americans. Imprisoned, released, imprisoned, and released again, for years he led sit-ins and protest marches across the United States. "I have a dream," he said in his famous Washington speech in 1963. His dream was the end of segregation, discrimination, racism, and violence. His riveting and inspiring speeches, his passion for his cause, his steadfast determination, gave millions of black Americans hope. Largely due to him, Congress passed the 1964 Civil Rights Act, which outlaws segregation in public accommodation and discrimination in employment, and the 1965 Voting Rights Act, which opened the door for greater participation by blacks in American elections.

A brief bookseller business session has been scheduled just before the luncheon. The directors depart, and King and I are left alone in the small room. We are to be welcomed "in a few minutes" as we wind our way through the tables in the immense ballroom. "A few minutes" turn into almost half an hour. We sit talking about our respective countries. It's impossible not to be impressed with the man. There are no smiles, but his belief in and dedication to his cause shine through. From prison he had written: "We know through painful experience that freedom is never voluntarily given by the oppressor." This is the theme that permeates his words as we sit and talk in the small, close room, waiting to be led to the head table. When we are, he gives me his card and suggests we keep in touch. And now there is a big friendly smile.

APRIL 4, 1968. IT is the tense and exciting Liberal leadership convention, and I am sitting in the jammed Ottawa Civic Centre, talking to Pierre Trudeau. There are dozens of men and women crowding around waiting to speak to him, so I take only a couple of minutes and head back down the steps to the crowded convention floor. Pandemonium reigns; everyone knows there will be at least two or three ballots. The leadership contenders and their troops are coaxing, coercing, bribing, and harassing the delegates.

As I elbow and push my way through the noisy crowd, Charles Lynch is doing the same thing, heading in my direction. As he lunges past, he shouts at me: "Martin Luther King's been shot." Stunned, I watch Lynch move through the crowd and work his way up the arena steps to Trudeau. Charles bends close, with his mouth to Trudeau's ear. I watch Pierre's face fill with pain, his eyes close, then open, then close again. Two days later he will be elected to take Lester Pearson's place as leader of the Liberal Party of Canada. In two weeks he will be sworn in as Canada's fifteenth prime minister. Now he sits in the convention centre paralysed, stricken. The people around him do not know what has happened.

Martin Luther King, thirty-nine, was speaking in Memphis, Tennessee, that day. He was hit by a bullet in the right jaw as he stood on the balcony of the Lorraine Motel; he died in hospital an hour and a half later. In his last speech he said: "Well, I don't know what will happen now, but it doesn't really matter with me now. Because, I've been to the mountaintop . . . I may not get to the promised land with you, but I want you to know that we as a people will."

THE FIRST TIME I STAYED at the Shoreham Hotel in Washington, also for the American Booksellers Association convention, was in June 1962. The night I arrived, the hotel caught fire. When the alarm went off, I quickly threw on some clothes and headed for the stairwell. So did everyone else in the hotel. It took a long five minutes to get down to only the third floor, and by this time the stairwell was packed with frantic people in various stages of dress. The doors from the corridors opened into the stairwell; panicky people pushed desperately on them, only to be confronted with a solid mass of barely moving people. By the time we reached the ground floor, there were several injuries, but none from smoke or fire. A few normally nice booksellers and publishers had become frenzied animals, shoving and trampling anyone in their way. It was a frightening experience.

The luncheon speaker the next day was thirty-seven-year-old Robert Kennedy, who had managed his older brother's senate and presidential campaigns and, to much protest, been appointed U.S. attorney general the year before. Much to the surprise and, to a certain extent, disappointment of the American press and political establishment, he became an excellent attorney general, launching a strong war against organized crime, intervening frequently to support Martin Luther King and other civil-rights leaders, and battling corruption in trade unions.

I sat next to Bobby Kennedy while he stood at the head table lectern to give his half-hour address. He spoke well, eyes on his audience, rarely referring to his notes. But I couldn't help but notice that his hands, hidden beneath the tabletop podium, were in constant motion almost the whole time, kneading, pressing, squeezing, as if shaping a ball of clay. For the audience there was no sign of anxiety. For me, at the time a chronically nervous speaker, I sat fascinated by the outward show of poise and confidence, while the hidden hands betrayed enormous pent-up tension.

I talked only briefly with Bobby Kennedy after his speech. His big friendly smile and Boston accent reminded me of the man I had met six years earlier in Las Vegas. Bobby's speech was excellent, and once again I was very impressed with a dynamic American.

Seventeen months later, President John Kennedy was assassinated in Dallas. Robert Kennedy was overwhelmed with grief and spent many months in a state of shock, often alone and staring out the window for hours. Over time, he became "a changeling," a strong critic of Lyndon Johnson's Vietnam policies, a leader very much in his own right and, in 1968, a primary-winning candidate for the Democratic nomination for president.

NOW IT IS JUNE 4, 1968, a cloudless warm summer day of bright Edmonton sunshine. I am doing boring accounting work in my office at the back of the bookstore. For some reason, for the first time in years, I haven't shaved before going to work. The office is warm and stuffy and I'm feeling tired-eyed and grubby. At three o'clock a staff member phones from the front of the store, even though I'd asked not to be disturbed. A Bill Lee "with Mr. Trudeau" wants to speak with me urgently.

"The prime minister wonders if you can meet with him privately at the Chateau Lacombe at five," he says.

Of course I can. I drive home, shower, shave, and change clothes and head back downtown. It's quarter to five when I enter the hotel lobby. Immediately I can see there's a serious problem. A big convention of mayors and municipalities has just broken up. The centre elevator is being held by plainclothes RCMP officers for the prime minister, who is speaking at City Hall. The lineups for the other two elevators stretch the length of the lobby. By five to five there is little improvement. Idea. I go through the door into the lounge and then through the swinging doors into the kitchen and head for the room-service elevator. No one stops me or even looks at me. In a minute I step out onto the twenty-first floor and proceed to 2102, the Trudeau suite. As a precaution, I knock on the door and wait, even though I suspect he's probably still at City Hall. No answer. I head for the centre elevator so I can greet him when he arrives. It is only then that a brusque RCMP officer steps in front of me and asks what I am doing. In the middle of my apologetic explanation, the elevator door opens and the prime minister bounds out of the elevator and down the hall with his entourage. When the door to his suite is opened, he sends the others away and invites me in. Off comes his suit jacket, his tie, and his shoes. For almost an hour we talk, feet up on the coffee table, and I get to know him really for the first time, although we had met several times before.

That night Lewis Hertzman, a friend from the history department of York University, is in town. My wife and I take him to Sandy Mactaggart's elegant home for dinner. We sit in the huge indoor garden by the pool, pampered by servants, warm hospitality, fine food and excellent wine. The conversation is of politics and books, music and business. I tell of my meeting with Pierre that afternoon, and everyone is anxious to hear more about the man who has been the new leader of our country for less than two months.

It is one o'clock in the morning before we are home. It's been too good a day and too good an evening to let go of. Lewis and I head for the rumpus room in the basement, each with a large brandy. I turn the radio on for some music; mostly there is only short-wave static. But as I fiddle with the dial, these words crackle through from a station in Seattle: ". . . been shot, apparently in the head . . . kitchen of the Ambassador Hotel in Los Angeles . . . more shortly." It is a good ten minutes before we learn it was Robert Kennedy the announcer was talking about.

Robert Kennedy, forty-three, had won five of the six presidential primaries he'd entered, including the key state of California that night. He spoke to and celebrated with his jubilant supporters and afterwards was guided out through the hotel pantry and kitchen by his advance men. Just after midnight, he was shot in the brain, ear and neck from only a few feet away, lying in a pool of blood on the kitchen floor only two months and two days after the death of Martin Luther King. His last words were "Is everybody all right?" He died at the Good Samaritan Hospital twenty-six hours later.

That night, lying sleepless in my bed, I thought of how easy it had been for me to go through the hotel kitchen that afternoon directly up to the prime minister's suite. I thought of the cruel violence of American society and how lucky we were to live in Canada. I thought of my three beautiful young daughters, safe and sound asleep in their beds. I remembered my time with the three dead Americans.

Albert Camus and the
Three-Hundred-Pound Woman

I know exactly when and why I decided to open a bookstore, or perhaps I should say try to open a bookstore. It proved to be far more difficult than I ever imagined. First of all, I was very young and I was very naïve. As well, there were two other small problems: I knew nothing about bookselling and I had no money.

One day when I was twenty-three, I was standing in the small book department of Esch's book-and-stationery store on the ground floor of the old Cecil Hotel. I asked the clerks about three new books I wanted, but they didn't have them, hadn't heard of them, and were not able to tell me if they were even on order. Edmonton, like most other cities in Canada, had not one single full bookstore. The stores that sold books were essentially stationery-and-office-supplies stores, with books usually a low-priority sideline. All across our huge country there were only twenty to twenty-five stores that concentrated on books.

Aside from Esch's and one other stationery/office-supply store, the best place to buy books in Edmonton was the Hudson's Bay Co.'s book department. For bestsellers and mysteries it was pretty good. But the overall staff knowledge at the Bay can be summed up in the lovely story of the lawyer who asked a clerk if the store had a copy of George Bernard Shaw's *Man and Superman*, only to be told: "Sorry we don't sell comic books." According to publisher Jack McClelland, the department stores regarded books as a "low-profit, low-volume headache. . . . Experience means a lot in bookselling and the department stores don't have it. . . . If a man does well managing the book department, he's promptly moved to dry goods."

My inability to get the books I wanted was but one factor in my decision. There were several others. I was bored, very bored, and making zero progress towards anything but stagnation. I was working at Hurtig Furs, the store my father managed for his two brothers in Winnipeg. After a couple of years of helping ladies try on fur coats, I realized this was definitely not my life's work and I had to make a change as quickly as possible. A three-hundred-pound woman helped me do so.

It happened on a sweltering, incandescent day in August. The Jasper Avenue sidewalks were baking when I went down the street to Picardy's café for an ice-cream soda. When I returned to the fur store, the first thing I saw was a huge woman, spherical in shape, with an angry look on her face. The other clerks were busy (the annual August Fur Sale was in progress) and there was no one to look after her except me.

We began with Persian lamb, moved to dropped mink, then tried sheared otter. Not only was she obese, she was also obviously wealthy and more obviously rude. Her abundent jewellery, expensive dress, and haughty manner did little to conceal the fact that her deodorant wasn't very effective that day. Now she asked to try on a muskrat coat. I went to the far end of the rack, brought out the largest coat we had, and helped her on with it. Then it happened. She stood in front of the three-way mirror, pouting, revolving slowly, then stopped, turned to me, and said: "Don't you think it makes me look heavy?" I stared at her, sucked in my cheeks in an attempt to suppress a laugh, and turned away, only to double over and burst into uncontrolled laughter.

It was my last day as a furrier.

Out of work, with almost no money, I battled off my first-ever extended depressed mood, which lasted all of a weekend, and determined that now was the time to change my life. Here, the reading I had been doing for the past three or four years was a great influence.

At nineteen I had read *The Plague*, by Albert Camus. It had first been published in France in 1947 as *La Peste*, becoming an immediate bestseller. A friend in Paris was so overwhelmed by the book that she set about doing an English translation, which she sent to me by post in 1951. It wasn't until 1960 that Penguin published the first English-language edition.

The Plague was my introduction to existentialism. While a somber book in part, its overall impact was, for me, spiritually uplifting. Here was a passion for life tied to the idea of political action. In many ways Camus was commenting on the less-than-admirable, sometimes despicable behaviour of some of the civilian population in France during the Second World War. The suffering of innocents, the despair at a lack of rational explanation for tragic events, the demand for self-dependency, the search for moral values, the struggle against evil, and the battle for human dignity are all brilliantly portrayed in what Camus described as "an attitude of solitary revolt to the recognition of a community whose struggles all must share."

In 1957, forty-four-year-old Albert Camus was awarded the Nobel Prize in literature. Less than three years later he and his good friend and publisher Michel Gallimard were killed when Gallimard's car skidded out of control at high speed and hit a tree. Camus had accepted a ride at the last minute; his unused rail pass to Paris was found in his pocket. The unfinished manuscript of *The First Man* was found in a black briefcase nearby.

Only recently did I read the words of American journalist Jack Newfield recalling how Robert Kennedy revered Camus: "He discovered Camus when he was thirty-eight, in the months of solitude and grief after his brother's death. By 1968 he had read, and reread, all of Camus's essays, dramas and novels. But he more than just read Camus. He memorized him, meditated about him, quoted him, and was changed by him."

Over the next few years I read everything else I could get by Camus, beginning with his first novel, *The Stranger*, and then I turned to Sartre and Heidegger, then back to Kierkegaard and Dostoevsky, and eventually to some Martin Buber, Karl Barth, and Paul Tillich. For me, very young, very impressionable, very determined, the stress on responsibility, humanism, aversion to conformity, and the championing of human freedom were very appealing and supportive of my own early scepticism, agnosticism, and evolving sense of political activism, social obligation, and moral rebellion.

By day I helped women try on fur coats. By night I was into sports, I went to parties, or more frequently than not, stayed home and read books. By day I was bored stiff; by night I was very happy.

After the rude fat lady acted as a catalyst, I sat down and carefully made a long-overdue, logical, existential analysis of my situation. Simplified, it went something like this: First, having spent almost every cent I ever earned, I had no money and would have to find an occupation. Second, I had already, after six years of various jobs, come to the conclusion that I would like to work for myself, be my own boss. Third, and by far the most important, I thought that if one had to work for a large percentage of one's waking hours on this earth, the key was surely obvious — find something you really like so it won't be work at all!

So, at age twenty-three what did I really like? Girls, sports, and books. I was thinking about asking Eileen, who worked in the Fashion Dress Shop next door to the fur store, to marry me. I wasn't good enough at any sport to earn a living. But I loved reading.

Edmonton was a rapidly growing university and government city with a population of over 225,000, and given that it didn't have a single full bookstore, the answer was obvious. I would open my own bookstore. To me, it seemed so logical, so perfect. After I quit the fur store, I went everywhere I could think of seeking advice about bookselling and eliciting reaction to the idea of a new bookstore. With one single semienthusiastic exception, I received no encouragement at all. None. In fact, for the most part, the idea was either flatly rejected or even ridiculed. My father thought the idea was foolish.

"*Why* would you want to open a bookstore? There's not a bookstore in the whole city."

"Exactly."

"Exactly what?"

"There is no bookstore and people will love it!"

"If it's such a good idea, how is it that no one has done it already?"

"Pa . . ."

There was little to read at the public library on the subject of bookselling. The librarians I talked to were less than excited. After all, they bought their books directly from the publishers or from the jobbers in Toronto or the U.S. Even the sales reps from the eastern publishers, who passed through town periodically, were negative. "Maybe it's a good idea, maybe, but you better work in a bookstore for at least three or four years or you will be throwing your money away," they would say. "What money?" I would reply.

Probably the greatest downer I had came from an old pro, the hard-partying, hard-drinking Bible salesman from Oxford University Press. "Sure you can do it, kid, but you better figure on being poor all the rest of your life. Bookselling is a tough, demanding, hard-nosed business, with little if any profit in it. Don't plan on raising a family if you're thinking of opening a bookstore. You won't be able to afford to do both."

Discouraged, I took the Greyhound down to Calgary. Perhaps the booksellers in the stationery and department stores there would be more enthusiastic. On the contrary, their prognosis was gloomier still. In short: "Forget it! Don't do it!" I took the bus back to Edmonton, disappointed, confused, depressed — but damned determined.

I made a list of all the people I knew who had books in their home and began to visit them in the evening. They *loved* the idea of a new bookstore, but they reminded me that most of their friends had few books. "They're too expensive. Most people don't read books."

But the more I thought about it, the more determined I became. I turned my thoughts to an interesting subject I'd been avoiding —

money. I had been in the head office of the imposing Imperial Bank in Edmonton almost every weekday for years, taking in the fur store's deposits, arranging the banking when my father became ill, flirting with the tellers, and even nodding from time to time to Mr. McDiarmid, the grim-looking manager. Once he even nodded back. Mr. McDiarmid was a typical, ominous, 1950s bank manager: an unsmiling Scot in a three-piece tweed suit and shiny black shoes, with bifocals perched on his nose. But, now, twenty-three and very nervous, I made an appointment to see him. Sitting in front of his huge desk in his office in the corner of the bank, I told him of my exciting plans and gave him a typed business plan that took me four months to put together. I explained that I was going to need at least ten thousand dollars for inventory, fixtures, rent, advertising, and so on. Mr. McDiarmid scanned the business plan, shoved it back across the desk, then stood up, narrowed his eyes, and said: "Hurtig, if your father signs the note, I'll give you $3,500 — see what you can do." End of conversation.

I walked back down Jasper Avenue with my shoulders sagging. I was sure $3,500 wasn't nearly enough, and there was no way, no way period, my father would ever sign the note. At the time, $3,500 was a great deal of money; it would probably be far too big a risk. Moreover, it wouldn't be fair to ask him and I didn't *want* to ask him.

But I did. And reluctantly he agreed, despite the fact that he didn't have $3,500, or anywhere near that amount. A week later we were both in Mr. McDiarmid's office signing the papers. The three of us shook hands, and as we went to leave the office, I turned back and, elated, said: "Mr. McDiarmid, sir, I promise to pay you back every single penny within two years." A tiny smile appeared on his face and just as quickly disappeared. "Hurtig, listen carefully. If you *are* a success, and I have my doubts, I can promise you one thing for certain. You'll owe me and the bank more money every single year you're in business."

DIFFICULT AS IT was for me to start a bookstore, it was simple compared with what my parents had gone through getting started in Canada.

If I were to take a piece of string and measure the distance on my globe between Falticeni in northeast Romania and Odessa in the Ukraine, it would be considerably shorter than the distance between Edmonton and Calgary. My father, Julius Hurtig, was born in Falticeni in 1891, only two years after the first Jewish settlers arrived in Western Canada (then the North-West Territories). My mother, Jennie

Kerschner, was born in Odessa in 1894. But my mother and father did not meet in Europe; rather, they met halfway around the world in Winnipeg.

My mother remembered the Old Country well and told us about hiding as a young child in the farthest dark corner under her bed as Cossacks waving swords rode down the streets of Odessa looking for Jews. The numerous pogroms wiped out many Jewish families. When she arrived in Winnipeg in 1909, she was fifteen, spoke no English, and had the grand total of five dollars in her pocket. Some friends of friends were supposed to meet her at the train station, but somehow they had the date wrong. One year later, my father, eighteen, having escaped to Liverpool, sailed to Quebec City, then took the train to Winnipeg where he worked as a tailor. Three years later Jennie and Julius were married in that city and a year later they moved to Edmonton with their baby boy, Abe.

My parents had very little money. My father supported his young family by jumping boxcars or, when necessary, riding the rods up to the Coal Branch in west-central Alberta, measuring the miners for suits, coming back to Edmonton the same way, where he would make up the suits in a tiny tailor shop, then head back up to Luscar, Cadomin, and Mountain Park again to deliver the suits.

My second brother, Henry, was born five years after Abe. The family was still quite poor, but my father had borrowed some money from a friend and opened up a tailor shop on 101st Street, about where Eaton Centre is today. Four years later, in 1922, my sister Goldy was born.

I was born ten years later, surely a surprise to my parents, during the height of the Great Depression. By then the family was quite middle class, living in a two-storey, four-bedroom, one-bathroom wooden house on 100th Avenue. It was quite an interesting neighbourhood. Across the street lived Friedman, the kosher butcher, and his sons Tootsie, Mooshie, and Manuel. Next door lived "Der Blinder" Cohen, the secondhand and antique dealer, so named for his bottle-thick eye glasses. Across the back lane lived the Slutker family, including four boys — Zeke, Blondie, Sonny, and David. Around the corner lived "Shifty" Shubin. Then, on the corner was the Sisters of the Precious Blood convent, and a couple of blocks away in one direction the Catholic seminary, and one block in the other St. Joseph's Cathedral. Our neighbourhood, then, was a world of Jews and Catholics. On Saturday mornings at the baseball diamond in the river valley next to where the Royal Glenora Club stands today, the Jews would play softball against the Catholics. Sometimes, afterwards, there would be a big fight.

I don't remember much anti-Semitism, but any was enough. My friend Marty Bernstein went to Alex Taylor school where he sometimes got beaten up after school was out. Another friend, Rosanna Rollingher, remembers boys (including one who is a prominent Edmonton lawyer today) throwing rocks and yelling "dirty Jew" across 114th Street at her. I also remember that when we transferred from Talmud Torah to Oliver school, for grade six, on the first day the teacher asked that "the four Jews stand up to be identified." But I don't want to make too much of this; for the most part we all got along quite well, and in junior high and high school most of my closest friends were non-Jews.

I didn't do very well in Talmud Torah; Garry Brody (now a prominent Los Angeles plastic surgeon) and I used to "compete" to see who would get the lowest Hebrew marks. When we switched to Oliver, we had to take the streetcar downtown to the Talmud Torah right after school for classes in Hebrew and Torah. Sometimes we would get home at seven o'clock with homework from both schools. I hated it. As soon as my bar mitzvah was over, I quit Hebrew school. But one thing for sure — Talmud Torah had prepared me well for public school. Until I stopped attending classes in grade twelve, my marks were high and I found the work easy.

And, I had great fun. A block from where we lived was the Central Skating Rink, on Jasper Avenue. It had a covered stand in the middle of the ice with a big coal-burning stove to help keep the four-man brass band warm. Several times a week in the winter we headed for the rink and Baxter's adjoining store for a skate, a hot dog, a Coke, and the girls. A couple of blocks down Jasper Avenue was the Sports Centre poolroom, Teddy's delicatessen, and a block further on Sly's, where they made the most delicious hamburgers and the thickest milk shakes in the entire world. In the summer, we played kick-the-can and aunty-aunty-I-over in the lane behind my house, right next to the Slutkers' chicken coop.

When I was thirteen, David Birenbaum taught me how to smoke Camel cigarettes in the attic of the barn behind his house on Ninety-ninth Avenue. From then on, from time to time, I would filch the occasional cigarette from my parents.

There were lots of family picnics down the hill in the park in the river valley, lots of trips to the lake and to Elk Island Park. On

Sundays, my father would take us out for dinner to the Royal George Hotel on 101st Street, where everyone knew him and loved him. He was friendly and unusually jovial. Our house was often full of people. Dad and his friends would play *shtook*, gin rummy, and poker in the kitchen while drinking their schnapps, while the ladies would play bridge in the dining room. There was always lots of *vursht*, corned beef, smoked meat, and *halavah*.

But when I was a child, there were very few books in our home. In the dank dark basement sat an old Yiddish encyclopedia, which I couldn't read, and an old set of the *Book of Knowledge*, which was badly out-of-date and in poor condition. Neither my mother nor my father had time to read or seemed interested in reading much more than the *Edmonton Bulletin* newspaper. But somehow, I don't know how, I became a reader. My neighbour Morris Friedman, now a very successful surgeon, says he remembers me as a voracious reader. "You had a whole lending library in your room. You were crazy about books." Strange. I am sure this is true, but I can remember very few of the books I read when I was young. I cannot explain this.

When I was seven, I remember sitting in the living room with my mother and father, my two older brothers and my sister, all of us in our pyjamas and bathrobes, reading the headline in the morning paper: CANADA AT WAR! Both my brothers announced that morning that they were off to enlist in the army. It wasn't too long before they were in their khaki uniforms and gone. My parents and my sister and I spent many hours every week huddling around the radio, listening for news of the war in Europe and of our troops overseas.

For me, the best part of school was sports. I played baseball, softball, hockey, basketball, football, and soccer. The highlight of my entire school career was undoubtedly the day in grade eleven during assembly, when the basketball coach, Arnold Henderson, for some reason pulled me out from the sidelines to centre court and, seeking to demonstrate some point, handed me a basketball and asked me to take a shot. In front of almost the entire school, I sank the shot from centre court, much to my amazement and the coach's shock. What more could any sixteen-year-old ask out of life?

At the opposite extreme was the very first day I wore a real baseball uniform as a new member of the Jasper Place Tigers. In softball I was a catcher, but in baseball I pitched. So here we were, playing a team from the Highlands. The score was one-nothing for us, it was the bottom of the ninth, and our pitcher threw four consecutive wild pitches to the first batter. After much discussion, the coach called in relief pitcher "Lefty" Hurtig, nervous, self-conscious, but thrilled. The very first pitch I threw was hit over the centre fielder's head for an inside-the-park home run. Game over. What a debut! No one spoke to me in the locker room.

Despite my height — five foot eight — I loved basketball. I survived on the school teams by practising a left-handed, over-the-head, fading-away-from-the-basket hook shot. I played organized hockey to the juvenile level, although I wasn't good enough to stick, and organized basketball for several years after high school. Even well after I married, my friend Richard Mouw and I rented a gym once a week and played one-on-one for an hour. He called me "Elbows" Hurtig, and I called him "Knees" Mouw.

By the time I was ten, my two older brothers and Goldy had married and I was the only one left at home. Only two blocks away, down in the river valley, was the Victoria Golf Course, a public course, and I used to sit on the wooden steps at the top of the hill watching for hours. When my parents asked me what I would like for a bar mitzvah gift, I asked for golf clubs, and that's exactly what I got. In front of all my friends and theirs, at the bar mitzvah reception, my proud father presented me with a canvas bag, a putter, and six clubs. One small problem. I was left-handed in *everything* — I even kicked a football with my left foot — but the clubs were right-handed. My father was beaming. I said nothing. Ever since, I have played golf right-handed.

When I was in my early teens, I became a Young Judaen camp counsellor. Once, with a friend, I hitchhiked to Regina to attend camp in the Qu'Appelle Valley. Near Lethbridge, a travelling salesman in a sleek new Hudson picked us up and drove us some eighty miles, letting us out with a wave and a smile. He said he would be turning off the highway soon and this was a good spot for us to try our luck for the next ride. The next morning in Medicine Hat we saw his picture on the front page of the *Albertan* and a picture of his mangled Hudson. The salesman had been killed at a level crossing only minutes after he had dropped us off.

This was not my first brush with death. Larry Rollingher and my father were in the front seat and Rosanna and I were in the back when our car went into a ditch and smashed into a farmer's access road when we were on the way to Calgary. I ended up in a Calgary hospital with a broken arm, wrist, shoulder, and collarbone. My father was also injured, but not seriously. Soon after, while I was still convalescing in hospital, one of my father's employees gave me a big dry-mounted map of Europe and several boxes of coloured map pins. I closely followed the Second World War on the radio from my bed, plotting the action with the map pins. From this came a great interest in geography. To this day I love maps, and can draw a very good one of the world with my eyes closed.

Stephen Leacock wrote: "I owe a lot to my teachers and I intend to pay them back some day." At Oliver school, with the exception of social-studies teacher Tom Baker, my teachers were terribly boring. By the time I got to grade twelve at the brand-new Victoria Composite High School, I was bored out of my mind. The very first day at Vic, I accidentally discovered a door closed on another door that led to steps and up to an air-conditioning room on the school roof. The next day a couple of friends and I snuck in a card table, chairs, and a deck of cards, and I spent most of my last year in school on the roof or in the Rec or Eskimo billiard rooms playing snooker. Bad! Moreover, by this time, my parents were in the habit of going south for a month during the winter, a period during which, by some strange coincidence, I would always be too sick to attend class, but not to attend lots of parties and teen dances and visit Chick's nightclub on the Calgary Trail where we would hide mickeys of rye under the table and kick them across the floor whenever the police raided, which was often.

All my Jewish friends went on to the University of Alberta, but I didn't have the faintest idea of what I wanted to do with my life. The Vic yearbook said of me: "Ambition: world travel and varsity. Activities: basketball, social committee, baseball and golf. Lots of girl-friends." At least some of it was true.

I ended up sweeping the sidewalks and dusting stock at Uncle Ben's Exchange on 101st Street and lugging pelts for buyers at the Edmonton Fur Auction Sales, and then I became a truck driver for two years for Hurtig Furs. After that I worked in the fur-storage vault, soon graduating to office work and monthly trial balances in the fur store. None of this would have happened if my father hadn't become really cross with me when I was seventeen. Searching for some career, I went to radio station CJCA and made a tape, which I sent to several rural radio stations. Much to my surprise, I was offered a job in Dawson Creek, B.C. But my father wouldn't hear of it. I would be "throwing my life away!" Dad had always been fair to me, and I was in no mood for a big fight. So that was the end of that.

Abe had gone to the University of Alberta (where they still had quotas for Jewish medical students) and become a doctor before he headed overseas in 1940. He returned from Europe a lieutenant-colonel and settled in Ottawa. Henry became an entomologist and then went to Berkeley to become a toxicologist. He had a distin-guished career in Ottawa and with the United Nations, the Food and Agriculture Organization, and the World Health Organization before his untimely death at the age of fifty-five (his heart had been dam-aged by rheumatic fever when he was a child). Goldy married Hy Estrin, one of the world's all-time sweetest men, and together they established a very successful dry-cleaning, suede- and leather-cleaning business in Edmonton.

Fate and fortune. My grandfather Mayer, whom I never met, sent his oldest son, Max, to Switzerland to avoid the draft into the Romanian army. Max was to become a watchmaker. But he didn't like Switzerland and moved on to London where he heard about Canada. With almost no money and very little English, he landed in Montreal where he washed dishes in a restaurant for two years. Then someone robbed him of all the money he had saved. Destitute and dispirited, he snuck into a boxcar and rode all the way to Winnipeg. In Manitoba he worked in a stone quarry, saved enough money to buy a wagon and a team of horses, and sold coal and wood. Now he had enough money to buy a house. In the same neighbourhood lived Sam Bronfman. Max and Sam became friends and went into the hotel business together. But they were soon in another business, as well. Prohibition was in force in the United States, and Max and Sam "ran rum" into the U.S., though most of it was rye and scotch.

Max made enough money to bring his five brothers, two sisters, and his father (my grandmother had died) to Canada. With his coal and wood money he helped pay for my father's trip to Winnipeg. My father met my mother there. Where would I be today if someone hadn't robbed uncle Max of his money in 1910? If mother hadn't fled the pogroms in the Ukraine? Do I not owe my existence to robbers and Cossacks?

AND SO, WITH MR. McDiarmid's money in place, I spent about a month walking through the downtown streets to find a store I could afford to rent. One day a For Rent sign appeared in a shop window.

Opposite the west entrance of the Bay, just north of Jasper Avenue on 103rd Street, a tiny record shop, formerly (you could tell!) a pet store, was going out of business. The store was only 425 square feet, but the rent was right and the location was pretty good. I signed a one-year lease and set to work contacting publishers, amassing catalogues, discount schedules, and the other paraphernalia necessary to the trade. I also began planning the store layout. I painstakingly built a scale model in balsa wood and then began building our shelves, counters, window-display area, and so on, all in my parents' garage. Since I am to carpentry as Jean Chrétien is to syntax, we got help from a carpenter friend. We did all the painting and staining ourselves, and when the inexpensive, tough cocoa-mat carpet was in and the shelves installed, we began unpacking the first boxes of books.

All of this was interrupted by our small wedding in the basement of the Beth Shalom synagogue. Even though Eileen, a Protestant, had gone through the extensive, lengthy, and demanding training sessions and the naked Mikvah immersion ritual of conversion to Judaism, the synagogue officials refused to allow us to be married in the main shul auditorium on the ground floor. Eileen's parents and my parents were disappointed; I was angry. I rarely went back.

When we returned from Las Vegas, we filled the store windows with big signs announcing opening day, October 4, 1956. We publicized a contest whereby opening-day customers had numerous chances to win new fiction and nonfiction titles. We hand-delivered flyers door to door, and every day we hoped that we knew what we were doing. A few days before the opening, we were dead broke. Several sections of the store had so few books that we had to turn them face out to make the shelves look full.

Hurtig Books became the first books-only bookstore between Toronto and Vancouver, and in Vancouver there was only Ireland and Allan, and the Marxist People's Co-op bookshop run by Binky Marks. We were also the first bookstore anywhere on the Prairies to carry a large selection of Penguin paperbacks, as well as Anchor, Vintage, Scribner, Evergreen, and other quality nonfiction trade paperbacks.

At eleven o'clock the night before the store was to open, I was still at work, sitting on the floor in my jeans, unpacking newly arrived boxes of books. There was a loud banging on the front door. I opened it to find the one individual who had given me even the slightest encouragement, a droll, book-loving travelling salesman for

Macmillan and McClelland and Stewart. He had a bottle of Remy Martin with him, along with two snifters and some flowers. His name was Bill Duthie. He knew more about books than anyone I had ever met, and his advice was enormously helpful. A year later I was able to return the favour. Bill knew little about the business end of retailing, and I was able to be of much assistance to him when he planned his first store in Vancouver. I convinced Bill that he *must* have a cash register, something he had resisted strenuously. But more importantly, when Bill saw the young, inexperienced Mel Hurtig, who knew almost nothing about bookselling, doing what he himself had wanted to do for years but just hadn't quite got around to, he went to work and opened his superb, soon-to-be-famous Robson Street store in 1957.

Opening day for Hurtig Books! At eight in the morning Eileen and I trudged up the steep Third Street hill from our small walk-up apartment down in the river valley near John Ducey Park. I swept the sidewalk in front of the store and took down the signs in the window announcing the opening. Everything was in place; Eileen dusted books that didn't need dusting. At nine we unlocked the front door. Nothing happened. Five after nine, ten after nine, twenty after . . . nothing. We were embarrassed, standing there looking at each other, me nervously clearing my throat, she pacing the floor. Finally I broke the tension and asked if she would mind walking down to the fur store to get some change for the till, which we didn't really need.

Eileen wasn't out of the store more than a minute when the first two customers walked in. Then two more, then another and another and another. When Eileen returned, there were a dozen people in the tiny space. The rest of the day, until closing, the store was crowded with customers. The television station CFRN sent in their cameras for the suppertime news. An *Edmonton Journal* reporter requested an interview for her story. Friends from all over the city brought flowers. But the overwhelming majority of the customers were people I didn't know — some who were simply curious, but others who loved books and wanted to see the new store.

When we closed at nine, we counted the cash and cheques. First-day sales were $435! We were amazed. We were rich! Even in our most optimistic dreams we never expected such a marvellous response. In 1956, $435 was a lot of money, especially for a young couple who were eating macaroni pretty regularly and had a bank payment due in a few days.

I cannot leave opening day without recounting a story that shows how deep my knowledge of books was. Bobby Dyde, the prominent wife of prominent lawyer Sandy Dyde, asked if I had the new novel by Taylor Caldwell. I said, "I don't believe he's written anything recently." Mrs. Dyde scowled, brusquely informed me that if I didn't know that Taylor Caldwell was a woman I didn't have much hope of surviving as a bookseller, spun around and walked out of the store. It was at least four years before I saw her again.

Even though the bookstore was a success from day one, the net profits were small, and we had trouble paying both our bank loan and our bills. The Musson Book Company, one of the biggest wholesale publishers in Toronto, representing, among others, Simon and Schuster and Harper and Row, cut us off promptly when we didn't pay our opening invoices in exactly thirty days. It was embarrassing. Here we were, promising good service and a splendid selection, and we couldn't supply books from a number of important American and British publishers. However, all our other suppliers were very helpful, and we managed to pay almost all our invoices within sixty days. And the publishers were most impressed by how many books we were ordering and selling.

We were constantly expanding our modest inventory, buying more and more new and backlist titles and broadening our selection in response to customer demand. Every month, as word of mouth and a bit of advertising did the job for us, our sales increased and the store became more crowded with people and new books. It wasn't long before we began looking for a larger facility, and we soon found vacant space in the old wooden Campbell Furniture building on 100 A Street. The uneven linoleum floors sloped in every direction, the long deep street windows meant we were cooked in the summer, and we shared inadequate, dingy bathroom space with the furniture store, but once again the run-down building was the right rent and had a pretty good downtown location, and now we had three times the space. We used cash flow to pay for new shelving, new counters, and more books, and strained the patience of publishers and wholesalers by paying many of our bills in ninety days.

Our new larger store soon became much more successful than the first. Sales more than doubled, from $36,000 our first year to $80,000 in 1959. I was working ten to twelve hours a day, often seven days a week, but it didn't seem like work at all. In fact, it was great fun. By this time Eileen was at home, looking after our first child, Barbara, who was born on Christmas Day 1957, and Gordon Elbrond was my right-hand man and an excellent young bookseller with a great sense of humour.

Unfortunately we couldn't afford air-conditioning, and the awnings we bought only managed to capture the warm air and make the situation even worse. One of Gordon's daily mid-afternoon jobs in the summer was to head for the Selkirk Hotel and return with ice-cold beer for the two of us — and frequently our customers. According to Gordon, "when our favourite customers, the nuns, came in, with their school book lists, we would go around the store sucking in our breath and popping Clorets."

Business boomed. Every quarter we established new sales records. Within three years the second store was also too small. This time we took a big gamble; in the summer of 1962 we moved to a huge, bright new store in the prime shopping area on Jasper Avenue, with a huge rent to match and a five-year lease. Ironically the store was right across the street from the old Cecil Hotel, the location of the Esch store, which no longer occupied the corner space, their book department having closed down some years earlier. Was I nervous about this bold plunge? You bet. But for the most part, I was so busy planning and stocking the new premises I didn't have much time to think about what a giant leap we were taking, although at night I sometimes lay in bed wondering if I wasn't being too optimistic in risking everything we had built up over the past five years.

By the time we had knocked out some walls and converted a dirt-floor warehouse at the back into retail space, we had the largest bookstore in Canada, some seven thousand square feet. And it soon became the best bookstore in the country. Nathan Cohen, the distinguished *Toronto Star* critic, wrote: "Who would expect Edmonton to have the best classified and most up-to-date bookstore in Canada?" The noted British publisher André Deutsch said: "Mel Hurtig's bookstore is certainly the finest in Canada and one of the best I've seen anywhere." Lord Allan Boyd, who would soon come to play an important role in my life, wrote that our store was "one of the great bookshops of the world." Toronto historian William Kilbourn described it as "a superb bookstore and even something of a phenomenon in the social history of Canada."

We had, in fact, turned the bookstore into something much more — a friendly, social, intellectual meeting place. Dianne Woodman, a longtime respected member of Canada's book trade, recently said: "It was an exciting time . . . there were so many fascinating people. . . . Whenever they came to town they came straight to the bookstore and they stayed and stayed and stayed." Marshall McLuhan, William Kurelek, Frank Underhill, Tommy Douglas, Margaret Laurence, Al Purdy, Farley Mowat, W.O. Mitchell, Peter Gzowski, Pierre Berton, Harry Golden, Leonard Cohen, Mordecai Richler, Irving Layton — almost every day a well-known writer, entertainer, or politician spent much of a morning or afternoon in the store. Often we ended up taking them to lunch or bringing them home for dinner.

By all standards for the time, the store was huge, but we made it comfortable and easy to use. We served free coffee and doughnuts, and had tables and chairs with chess sets and Japanese GO boards at the back of the store. On the walls were large relief maps, author photos, colourful posters, and paintings. And at the back of the store there was space for an easy-to-assemble portable stage and curtains. From time to time, we presented original plays, author readings, lectures, and informal talks by visiting and local writers, critics, social and political commentators, and others, with crowds of as many as 350 seated comfortably on fold-up chairs. These free events became immensely popular.

We innovated in many ways. There were cork bulletin boards on which people could leave messages for friends, family, and lovers. In the middle of the store was a giant loose-leaf index to help customers find the books they were looking for, with over 1,000 category listings. Every week we added more. Each section of the store was clearly identified and numbered, and the index told the customers exactly where to find books on rocks and minerals, engineering, sex education, the Inuit, the economy, the Holocaust, Arctic exploration — you name it; it was almost certainly to be found in the store index. Not only was this a great help to customers, it was also a wonderful training tool for our new employees and a huge time-saver for the staff. As well, we had copies of *Books in Print* and the *Subject Guide to Books in Print* exclusively for customer use, so books could be looked up by title, author, or subject.

We developed our own unique shelving units and section-identification system. The shelving (some of which is still in use today at Audrey's Books in Edmonton) allowed for both face-out or spine display and was adjustable in height. The section signs had snap-in white lettering, so that sections could be easily moved around for space or seasonal needs.

We had what was probably the best children's book section in North America, with tiny colourful tables and chairs for the kids. Gillian, our second daughter, was born just before we moved into the big new store, and our third daughter, Jane, was born two years later. So, not only did our children benefit from the huge selection of juvenile fiction and nonfiction, but so did their father. As Eileen or I read *Winnie the Pooh*, *Anne of Green Gables*, *Little Women*, *Wind in the Willows*, or *Black Beauty* to the children, I was reading them or hearing them for the first time, since during my own childhood, my parents never had the time to read to me and we had very few children's books in our home.

Reading modern classics like *Charlotte's Web* or *Charlie and the Chocolate Factory* to my own children helped me stock the store with interesting well-written books and give advice to parents constantly in search of good reading for their kids. Over the years I sold thousands of copies of books such as *Stuart Little*, *The Secret Garden*, *Paddle to the Sea*, and *Alligator Pie* to appreciative mothers and fathers who would gratefully soon return for more suggestions.

The store was so big we needed library-style book trucks and an intercom system. And, it was big enough to add spoken recordings, globes, bookplates, and other book-related items, all of which broadened the store's appeal. Soon our annual sales topped half a million dollars and they were headed higher. Many professors in the English, Sociology, and History departments at the University of Alberta were unhappy with the service they then received from the university bookstore and began ordering the texts for their students through us. Not only did this provide an enormous boost in sales, but it also introduced thousands of students to our bookstore for the first time. Many became regular customers upon graduation, and more than a few became lifelong book lovers and close friends.

By May of 1967 *Maclean's*, exaggerating greatly, called me "the literary conscience of the prairies . . . Hurtig Books is the only bookstore in Canada that puts Barry Goldwater's *Conscience of a Conservative* on the fiction shelves." And it was about this time that my political activities began costing me a fair number of conservative and Conservative customers. A number of prominent local Tories stopped shopping in the store, and a fairly substantial amount of provincial-government business disappeared. We hardly noticed. Business was so good that we opened two branch stores, and we were often able to give ourselves and the staff good bonuses at year end.

The first day that the big new Jasper Avenue store opened, my father walked the three blocks from the fur store to see what was happening. To this day I can clearly see him sitting in the wicker chair near the front entrance with a big grin on his face, watching the lineup at the cash register, chatting with customers, and very proud of his youngest son. Soon Dad was heading for the bookstore every morning for a coffee and picking up our daily deposit to take to the Imperial Bank.

My father died in 1964 at the age of seventy-three. One story he often told was about how he and three friends tried to buy several corner lots in downtown Edmonton, but they couldn't raise the money. The price was $500; the best they could manage was $385, so the deal was never consummated. The lots are where Edmonton Centre is today.

Mr. McDiarmid was right. Every single year I was in the retail book business, as our inventory and capital costs and receivables all increased, as we became more and more successful, as without fail we established new annual sales records, we also owed the bank more and more money.

Glimpses of Overwhelming Mysteries

WHAT A GOOD THING that I ignored all the gloomy advice I received and became a bookseller! The stores were a financial success, and the eclectic education I received on a daily basis from books and from many of the people I met and worked with was wonderful. My years as a bookseller were exciting and stimulating and they changed me in a thousand ways.

In the store every day was like Christmas or Hanukkah. Every day we would unpack boxes of new books from around the world and put them on display. And every evening, almost without fail, I took some of the books home to read at night or on the weekend. When I read a new book I liked, I could easily sell a hundred or more copies. Bookstore customers constantly ask for suggestions and a good bookseller's enthusiasm is rarely ignored.

But it was very much a two-way street; almost every day I learned something from my customers. Being on the floor, that is, actually selling books instead of being squirrelled away in an office, provided a splendid opportunity to learn about both people and books. For the first ten to twelve years of my bookselling career I was almost always at the front counter, meeting customers, discussing, listening, and selling books; the paperwork could wait for the late-evening or early-morning hours.

When I entered bookselling, my education was sparse. When I left bookselling sixteen years later, my knowledge and interests had expanded enormously. Let me give you a few diverse examples. Before I opened my store, I had never read a single mystery. I wasn't interested in them at all. But early in my bookselling career I noticed that many of my best and brightest customers read and enjoyed mysteries, mostly, in those days, in the form of the dark green Penguin paperbacks. After a while I began asking the numerous mystery aficionados what their favourite mysteries were. For weeks I kept a list tucked away under the front counter. Then I picked two books that had been mentioned often, *Trent's Last Case*, by E.C. Bentley, and *The Daughter of Time*, by Josephine Tey. I was immediately totally hooked. I read nothing but mysteries for months.

The same thing happened with science fiction, which I had never read. Again, I made a list of customer favourites over a period of several weeks. This time I started out with John Wyndham's *The Day of the Triffids* and once again became totally addicted.

In high school my marks in social studies and English were always in the nineties, my marks in trigonometry and algebra always in the twenties. Math bored me completely. One day one of my best customers strongly recommended Clifton Fadiman's anthology *Fantasia Mathematica*. After reading this superb collection, I was fascinated by math, and my developing interest in politics and my new interest in numbers helped lead me to a subsequently intense interest in economics.

When I was unpacking boxes of books with Bill Duthie on the night before my first bookstore opened, I remember hauling out a copy of Peterson's *A Field Guide to Rocks and Minerals*, which I had ordered on the advice of John Allen. I remember thinking, Now *who* would likely buy *that*? It wasn't long before I found out, and it wasn't long before my own interest in nature dominated my reading.

By and large, I hadn't read that much fiction. But a beautiful woman customer, who was a voracious reader, suggested *The Heart of the Matter* and *The End of the Affair*, by Graham Greene. I devoured these and subsequently read almost all of Greene's fiction. Lawrence Durrell's *The Alexandria Quartet*, with its four contrasting interpretations of the truth, became the first novel (or novels) that I felt compelled to read twice. William Golding's *Pincher Martin*, with its surprise ending, was the next. Later, such novels as *Catch 22*, by Joseph Heller, and *The Watch That Ends the Night*, by Hugh MacLennan, captured me, made me enormously envious of the authors' writing skills, and helped produce a lengthy period in my life where I averaged a novel a week.

But this was only the beginning of my expanded reading adventure. The philosophy department at the University of Alberta began ordering texts and other reading requirements from our store. And many members of the department became close personal friends. Soon I was regularly monitoring philosophy courses at the university and reading and arguing philosophy late into the night with Richard Mouw, Herman Tennessen, Richard Price, and other professors and graduate students, more often than not accompanied by ample quantities of Ne Plus Ultra scotch.

My bookstore and my customers opened the doors of art, history, and biography for me for the first time. Several years after I sold my three bookstores, I read Pablo Neruda's *Memoirs*, now my favourite autobiography, partly because as a bookseller I had become fascinated by Neruda's poetry, just as I had become interested in Constantine Cavafy's poetry when I read *The Alexandria Quartet*.

Early in his memoirs Neruda writes: "Little by little, life and books give me glimpses of overwhelming mysteries. . . . All the while I was moving in the world of knowing, on the turbulent river of books, like a solitary navigator." I, too, was swept away on the same turbulent river, to unforeseen destinations.

Many of my best customers were doctors. One of these doctors, whom I shall tell you more about in a moment, was fascinated by psychiatry even though professionally he focused on body parts considerably lower down in the human anatomy. This doctor cast almost a hypnotic spell over a large group of other doctors, and they all read and intensely debated psychiatry, though only two of the group were psychiatrists. Of course I began reading psychiatry, too, and not long after began planning a novel based in a mental home. I had much of the plot and characters worked out when Ken Kesey's *One Flew over the Cuckoo's Nest* appeared and immediately soared to the top of the bestseller lists. I abandoned the idea forever, but not before I had learned more about psychiatry and mental institutions than I really wanted to know.

My growing interest in Canadian politics soon led me backwards to an interest in Canadian history and a friendship with several of Canada's leading historians: Donald Creighton, William Morton, Arthur Lower, and later to publication of historians Desmond Morton, Hugh Dempsey, and many others. Early in my "public life," Donald Creighton wrote from his home in Brooklin, Ontario:

> The copy of your address to the Institute of Chartered Accountants arrived yesterday and I read it at once with growing interest and excitement. I think it is a masterly effort. It combines comprehensive and detailed knowledge with passionate rhetorical skill. That combination, when dedicated to a subject so technical and complicated as the American takeover of Canadian industry and natural resources, is both rare and wonderful. I congratulate you warmly on a superb performance. It seems a great pity to me that the vast distances of our country seem to have prevented us from meeting each other so far. It would be a great pleasure to have a long talk with you.

Such a generous letter from such a distinguished historian was a great thrill for me. Only a few weeks before, I had finished reading Creighton's impressive, award-winning biography of Sir John A. Macdonald and was well aware of and supported his nationalist positions and opposition to continentalism. Unfortunately Donald Creighton died before we could arrange a meeting.

As I previously mentioned, I was constantly taking inventory home, and books filled my library, the living room, and other areas of the two-storey house we'd bought, an old renovated farmhouse on a ravine in Crestwood. It had cost $18,500, financed by both a first and second mortgage. We weren't by any means wealthy, far from it, but I could provide my family with a decent standard of living. And a lot of books.

Book People

A BOOKSTORE IS A SUPERB place to learn about people — their character, their interests, their idiosyncrasies, strengths, and weaknesses. I have never met a good bookseller who didn't have a barrelful of funny and frequently sad stories about customers, about publishers and sales reps, about visiting authors. You meet them all — the geniuses and the psychos. Sometimes it's hard to distinguish between the two.

Let me start my anecdote list with Leonard Cohen. In the mid-sixties Leonard arrived in Edmonton on a McClelland and Stewart book tour for his latest book of poetry. We got along well, and that evening he came to the house for dinner. After dinner, we sat talking in the living room. Suddenly, without a word, Leonard pulled his feet up off the floor, crossed his legs on the sofa, pulled his turtleneck sweater well up over his head, and disappeared into some other world. My wife and I sat looking at each other. Should we say anything? Was it the supper? Drugs? Should we leave the room? Almost half an hour went by before he rejoined us. No one mentioned what had happened. On the way back to the hotel Leonard turned to me. "Mel," he said, "I very much want you to publish my new novel."

I was speechless. My new publishing company was still in the planning stage, and I was still at least a year away from publishing our first book. Furthermore I immediately recognized a problem. Jack McClelland had been very helpful to me over the years. How could I steal away one of his star authors? I couldn't and very reluctantly I explained this to Leonard.

Well, of course, authors change publishers all the time, always have and always will. But I felt a strong sense of loyalty to Jack. While I was a bookseller we spent quite a bit of time together. I remember one night that began with Nathan Cohen, Farley Mowat, Hugh Kane, Bill Duthie, Jack, and I downing scotches at the King Edward Hotel in Toronto. By midevening Nathan, cape and all, had departed into the night, and Farley, Hugh, and Bill had all become quite incapacitated. Jack and I left for more drinking and partying. We ended up at ten the next morning, sitting on counter stools in some dive on Spadina, eating corned beef sandwiches.

For reasons I cannot explain, drinking and the book trade went hand in hand. Publishers, booksellers, authors, and sales reps were frequently heavy drinkers. In Toronto the standard was two martinis before lunch. One Toronto printer was known to order a carafe of gin martinis at lunch. One well-known bookseller opened the shop with a full bottle of rye underneath the counter and, without fail, when the shop closed at five-thirty, the bottle was empty. A Bible salesman for a staid Toronto publishing house was the champion boozer and womanizer on the road. Call it what you will — conviviality, entertainment, hospitality, relaxation — drinking was an accepted fact of life.

Like the rest of us, Jack McClelland is not perfect. Once I was in charge of a public lecture series at the University of Alberta, and I invited Jack to be the featured speaker. For weeks in advance I told friends and customers about this dynamic, charismatic, articulate publisher. The night of the speech we had a packed auditorium. I picked Jack up at the Macdonald Hotel and drove him to the university. There were two problems: first, Jack had had a couple of drinks; second, Jack clearly had not prepared for his talk. He gave an awful speech; the crowd left shaking their heads, greatly disappointed.

This story is in strong contrast to the very appealing, energetic, gregarious, charming Jack McClelland. Time after time I would see him at conventions speaking to each bookseller or librarian as if he or she was his special friend and very important in his life. He was full of laughter, stories, and blarney. Women adored him. Men were in awe of him.

I don't believe Jack McClelland has received anywhere near the honours and recognition he deserves. For years Jack did more for Canadian authors, booksellers, and readers than all the other publishers in the country combined. He supported and encouraged his developing authors in a manner unequalled in the publishing history of our country. He stuck with authors he believed in, even if their early books were financial or critical failures. He became close friends with many writers, often at crucial points in their careers, when they needed his friendship and support the most.

Back, for a moment, to Leonard Cohen. The day after I turned down the offer to publish *Beautiful Losers*, and in the middle of his book tour, he disappeared for eight days. McClelland and Stewart was frantic. Television and radio shows and heavily advertised autographing parties had to be cancelled. Booksellers with a large inventory of Cohen's books were furious. Eventually we found him in Edmonton in a seedy hotel on Ninety-seventh Street. He had spoken to Eli

Mandel's English class at the university in the morning, connected up with poet Jon Whyte, headed to the Army and Navy surplus store to buy thermal underwear, and that was that for the tour. Cohen and Whyte became involved with a couple of sisters on skid row. One result was Leonard's song *Sisters of Mercy*.

Mordecai Richler was something else again. He visited the store and our home often. At first I found this brilliant and prolific writer very appealing, full of great satirical stories, acerbic but funny, astute but often moodily laconic. He chainsmoked his small cigars and began drinking heavily in midafternoon. There was a side to Mordecai that was dark, deeply negative and, as the alcohol consumption mounted, frequently bitterly hostile. Moreover, his eighteen years in England had left him quite out of touch with what was happening in Canada and with a warped political, economic, and social perspective of our national affairs. Unfortunately several influential American magazines considered him an authority on Canadian affairs. Many of his articles published in the U.S. were blatantly anti-Canadian and badly distorted events in our country.

At first I accepted Mordecai's visceral antinationalism with casual amusement. But finally a couple of trips together ended our friendship. Mordecai wrote from England that he was doing an article for *Maclean's* on the Canadian Rockies; would I like to come along? Since I love the mountains and know them well, I volunteered to be his chauffeur and guide. Off we went in my old Ford station wagon headed for Calgary, Banff, Lake Louise, then up to Jasper. But the weather turned sour, and Mordecai's disposition soon matched it. For most of the trip the rain clouds were so low we could never see above the treeline. We ate dinner in the cavernous dining room at the Banff Springs Hotel almost alone. The food was bad, the singer worse.

The Banff-Jasper highway is probably the most beautiful stretch of paved road anywhere, but the rain continued in torrents, barely allowing us to see the road ahead. When we got to Jasper, instead of making our planned visits to Mount Robson, Edith Cavell, and Maligne Lake, we ended up spending much of a day and an evening in a pool hall where we were easily twenty years older than anyone else in the room. That was the best part of the trip. The worst part was Mordecai's subsequent dreadful article about Banff and Jasper in *Maclean's*. It was grossly unfair, distorted, and ignorant. For several months afterwards I received letters and phone calls whose basic message was, Hurtig, if you don't like it here, why don't you just get the hell out!

Sometime later Stu Hodgson, the commissioner of the Northwest Territories, invited Mordecai and me to tour the Arctic with him. Mordecai and I flew to Yellowknife where we were, much to our astonishment, ensconced in a luxurious penthouse suite at the top of the only high rise in town. The furniture was expensive, the carpets deep, the Inuit sculpture magnificent, and the stereo system marvellous. If we took a drink from the numerous full decanters set out for our use, the container was always filled to the brim in our absence. Not exactly what we had expected!

From Yellowknife we flew in a Fairchild F-27 east across the Arctic and made many fascinating stops along the way. We ended up on Broughton Island on the east coast of Baffin Island in Davis Strait, where we were marooned by a severe snowstorm for three days. Mordecai's mood, not great to begin with, became ugly. He called the Inuit "stupid people" for living as they did and where they did. He attacked his host and the officials who accompanied us. Finally, when the weather cleared, he abandoned the tour and headed back to Montreal. I was happy to see him leave. What a contrast with the public image of the man who wrote *The Incomparable Atuk*!

Before I leave the story of our trip to Baffin Island, I must tell you about a small incident that occurred shortly after we landed on isolated Broughton Island. After a late dinner of reindeer and red wine, we went for a long walk with our interpreter. It was one in the morning, but still very light out, and almost everyone, including children, was still up. The interpreter knocked on the door of a tiny tarpaper shack, not much larger than a big outhouse. Inside were two seventeen-year-old girls. On the floor a huge dead seal oozed blood. And on the table was the only book in the place, a copy of Xavier Hollander's *The Happy Hooker*.

My store had so many fascinating customers over the years it's difficult to single out only a few to write about. Let me start with one of my favourite stories about books. One of my best customers was Anthony Mardiros, the chairman of the Department of Philosophy at the University of Alberta. A great reader with an extraordinarily wide range of interests, Tony was usually in the store at least once a week to browse among the newly arrived titles or order the books on his want list. We soon became good friends.

At about the same time another of my best customers was Joe Kaziuk, a garage mechanic in Vilna, Alberta. But I had never met Joe; he was for years and years a wonderful customer, but all our business was done by mail. Joe would regularly send in a want list, and we would ship him our catalogue and his parcel of books. Month after month, year after year, in would come Joe's lists and out would go his reading.

One summer afternoon, something quite remarkable happened. Tony Mardiros was in the store with his list and we stood at the front counter talking. While we talked, a short, unshaven man, dressed almost entirely in black, entered the store and stood near the front entrance, glancing uncertainly at me and then at the store. After a few moments he approached the counter and took a list from his pocket.

"Are you Mr. Hurtig?"

"Yes, sir, I am."

"Mr. Hurtig, I am Joe Kaziuk."

"I don't believe it. How wonderful to finally meet you!"

We both laughed, talked for a few minutes, and then Joe handed me his book list. I looked at it with amazement. There were four books on his list. One was a new novel by William Golding. The second was a book on Australian aboriginal art. The next was an obscure book on aesthetics published by Blackwell, in Oxford. I can't remember the fourth book. What was so remarkable was that Tony Mardiros, standing at the counter a few feet away, also had come in with a list of four books; three of them were identical to Joe's. I showed Tony Joe's list and showed Joe Tony's list. I remember they both blinked, broke into big smiles and then warm laughter. The garage mechanic from Vilna and the chairman of the philosophy department headed out the door for coffee at the Caravan café and frequently corresponded thereafter.

One thing I discovered over my years of bookselling was this: while it is true that most people never ever set foot in a bookstore (they say that sixty percent of Americans never buy a book in an average year), it is also true that many of those who frequent bookstores tend to be voracious readers with a wide range of interests and an unending thirst for knowledge. The level of reading among book lovers is remarkably high, much higher than I think most people realize.

I can't leave Tony Mardiros without telling you an appalling story. One day I flew to Toronto for some meetings and to visit friends. The plane, full except for one seat beside me, was late taking off. Finally a man came down the aisle, removed his jacket and sat in the remaining seat. The plane took off immediately. Now, over the years I had developed a habit of not talking very much on planes. Because

I was with people almost constantly, I valued the time alone to read, to write, to think, or to get some work done. Usually I buried my face in a newspaper as soon as I boarded. On this trip, the man next to me spoke not a word until lunch was served as we approached Winnipeg. As soon as the trays were down, he introduced himself and persisted in conversation. He asked my occupation and as soon as I told him, he asked me if I knew a man named Tony Mardiros.

"I certainly do. Tony is one of my best customers."

He immediately began asking questions about Tony. I quickly became uncomfortable. Could what was happening actually be what I thought was happening? I asked him for his business card. Sure enough, RCMP. While we talked I pondered two choices: I could explain that Tony was not only a customer but a friend and I wouldn't answer any more questions; or I could listen carefully and get more information about exactly what was going on. I chose the latter.

By the time I got off the plane in Toronto my head was spinning. I couldn't believe it. The RCMP was asking me to spy on Tony Mardiros. Lewis Hertzman met me at the terminal and I immediately told him exactly what had happened. He was astonished. I asked Lewis, for some possible future use, to make a record of what I had told him.

The RCMP officer had indicated that he would contact me again later in Edmonton. Day after day, week after week, nothing happened. Of course I had already alerted Tony and we had agreed to wait to see what would happen next. And what came next was even more disconcerting. Late one Friday afternoon RCMP inspectors Byrne and Kushniruk showed up in the store, one of them my airplane companion, and the other a handsome, young, redheaded man. The two sat in my office at the back of the store, trying to get me to give them information about Tony. During the course of their remarks, they explained that they regularly tapped the phones at the University of Alberta and that "Red" was there posing as a student so that he could infiltrate campus student groups and keep a close eye on the faculty.

This was a time in my life when many faculty members were personal friends of my family. It was also a time when I was spending many hours sitting in on the courses they taught. I had enormous respect for the university then as I do today. When the store was set to close, I asked the two RCMP officers to leave. That night I visited the university president, Max Wyman, at his home, took him for a long walk along Valleyview Drive, and told him his phones were being bugged. He was horrified.

I'm not certain what action Max took. I had no further visits from the RCMP, although one ex-commissioner years later confided to me that the force had been engaged in similar activities at campuses all across the country, often at the request of the CIA.

Not all the men and women who frequented the bookstores bought books. Some merely hung around and read them on the premises. One such was Tom, a personable fellow in his middle fifties, the senior vice president for Northern Alberta for one of Canada's largest banks. About twice a month, usually on a Friday, Tom would come into the store around twelve-thirty and stand or sit reading a book and drinking our coffee until the store closed at five-thirty.

"Sorry about that, Tom," I'd say, "but it's closing time."

"No problem. See you soon."

And off he would go. Never once, over a period of several years, did Tom ever buy a book.

Another interesting "customer" was the wife of a prominent Edmonton surgeon. Every Saturday morning, almost without fail, she would come into the store, pour herself a coffee, plunk herself down in the wicker chair by the front door, and read the *New York Times Book Review*, making notes as she turned the pages. Then, she would ask for two or three novels that had caught her interest and charge them to her account. And then, every following Monday morning, soon after we opened, her maid would return the books since Mrs.— either (1) didn't like them or (2) hadn't had time to look at them. At first I was annoyed, especially when we discovered jam stains, but after a time the whole charade became so regular and so blatant we were more amused than annoyed.

Another person who rarely bought a book but spent countless hours standing and reading in the store was the young Joe Clark. I had no problem with this whatsoever; Joe was an underpaid reporter at the *Edmonton Journal* and he obviously loved reading. Almost always he was in the Canadiana section, completely lost in the pages of the book he held, seemingly oblivious to the time. Historian Tony Cashman remembers this well: "Mel Hurtig subsidized Joe Clark's education, simple as that." Perhaps. If so, it was a pleasure.

Earlier I mentioned the doctor who was immersed in psychiatry and very influential with many other doctors. Tall, handsome, and square-shouldered, he was always well dressed, wore a bow tie, and kept his hair in a brush cut. When I was very young he intimidated the hell out of me with his brusque, demanding manner. But as I got to know him and learned more about him, we became friends. The doctor had three great passions in life: books, gardening, and booze, not necessarily in that order. During the spring and early summer, I hardly saw him; he was in his garden when he wasn't at the office or the hospital tending to his patients. However, for most of the rest of the year he was in the bookstore every few days.

If Dr.——— ordered a book I didn't have in stock, I never ordered only one copy. Usually I ordered twenty or thirty, because I knew that shortly after Dr.——— had finished reading the book, a steady stream of other doctors would come into the store looking for copies. I never met another man whose love of good books was so easily and so enthusiastically communicated to a peer group. Unfortunately alcohol got the better of him. Much to our dismay, he killed himself one Christmas Eve.

On Banning Short Skirts

B EING A BOOKSELLER in Canada has never been easy, for many reasons. First, a lot of customers read British and American, as well as Canadian, newspapers and periodicals. They expect you to stock the books they read about. This means sorting through some 65,000 new English-language titles every year. Title selection is an enormously important, time-consuming job, but it is *the* key for any bookseller who expects to survive.

A major problem we faced, especially in Western Canada, was poor service from the Toronto publishers and the wholesalers who called themselves publishers, but were simply agents for imported foreign books. Often it would take several weeks or months for orders to be filled. Even books on the bestseller lists took ages to reorder. McClelland and Stewart and Macmillan did a pretty good job representing their foreign publishers, but some of the Toronto agents were hopelessly inept. Of course it was the bookseller who faced the angry customer who had to be told week after week: "No, I'm sorry. It's still not in. We'll phone again." Inevitably, due to poor service from Toronto, we lost customers who opened or reopened accounts at Scribner's or Brentano's in New York, or Foyle's in London.

Another serious problem was pricing. Many of the Toronto agents marked the imported book prices up in an unconscionable manner. Into the store would come your devoted customer with a clipping from the *New York Times Book Review* for an American book retailing at $20. But we had it priced at $29.95, even though the exchange rate at the time was almost even and there was no tariff. The customer wasn't happy, especially when multiple-copy orders were involved. Simply put, some Toronto agents took advantage of their agency and gouged the booksellers and the public.

After a while Bill Duthie and I said enough is enough. Where publishers and agents did a reasonable job, we supported them faithfully. Where service and pricing were terrible, we ordered our foreign books from U.S. or U.K. wholesalers. Invariably this meant we had inventory when our competition did not. On the plus side, this put pressure on Toronto for better service and fairer prices.

Yet another problem was that our suppliers were often in direct competition with us. A corporation might ask for a quote on one hundred copies of a book to use as a promotion, or Christmas or anniversary gift. We would sharpen our pencils to the best of our ability. Later we would learn that the Toronto publisher or agent had underbid us and made the direct sale. The year I opened my first store, Roy Britnell, then the dean of Canadian booksellers, said: "I should not be surprised if Canadian publishers cream off in the neighbourhood of fifty percent of book sales before booksellers get a chance at what is left." No wonder there were so few bookstores in Canada.

The list of problems goes on. Frequent postal strikes created havoc in an industry so dependent on the mails. Freight costs have to be absorbed; the bookstore customer in Vancouver or Halifax expects to pay the same price as the customer in Toronto. With the expansion of Coles, Classics, and W.H. Smith stores across the country, price-cutting began to hurt independent booksellers. In most countries publishers offer booksellers a graduated discount schedule. Most independents would buy a $20 book for $12. But the big chains, with their huge buying power, would pay $10 for the same book and frequently use their extra margin and large volumes to offer traffic-creating discounts at close to or even below cost. Independent booksellers had to rely on good service, knowledgeable staff, broad inventories, and customer loyalty. Unfortunately, with poor service and exorbitant pricing from Toronto, customer loyalty was not always easy to sustain.

Then there's the enormous number of publishers to contend with, all with different terms of trade, different discount schedules, different return policies. The paperwork is a tremendous burden. At my store we dealt with hundreds of publishers, government agencies, think tanks, associations, and self-published authors from many countries. It would take me most of a day every month just to approve and sign accounts-payable cheques the bookkeeper had spent the month preparing.

As I began to travel more and more for political or trade meetings, or on speaking engagements, I found it more and more difficult to keep up with the required bookselling reading. When I returned home from a trip, my desk would invariably be piled high with publishers' catalogues, trade magazines, galleys, and a steadily increasing volume of political correspondence.

Except for my first few months as a bookseller, I always relied on my own instincts for doing the buying. Some of the publishers' sales reps (all men at the time) like Bill Duthie, Jim Douglas, and Jim Hogg were great. You could rely on their judgement and know they would never try to oversell a title. Unfortunately others were incompetent and poorly informed. All the reps would travel by train, lugging their heavy trunks up to their hotel sample rooms. Boozing and partying often followed the day's selling of the new spring and fall titles and the backlist.

The good reps were treasures. Jim Hogg not only knew his catalogue backwards and forwards, but all the other reps' catalogues as well, simply because he loved books so much. Jim Douglas was also a book man through and through. (He and Scott McIntyre went on to found the successful Vancouver publishing house, Douglas and McIntyre.) I would always try to make time for Jim Douglas's semiannual visits. In turn, Jim would always look forward to his visits to my bookstore, because usually I had a great book laid aside for him.

Bill Duthie was in a class by himself. He was by far the most respected and loved book salesman I have ever encountered, with the possible exception of Gordon Garner. Later Bill became a "bookseller's bookseller," incredibly generous, helping even his competition. Over the years his belt buckle wore a deep groove into the front counter of his own excellent Vancouver store. When you walked through the front door, you knew Bill would be there, full of his lovely wry sense of humour, dispensing reading advice and comment — and sometimes the contents of a bottle of rye. He knew books well, he read them, and then did what a great bookseller does best — matched his books to his customers. One of the greatest pleasures of bookselling is creating pleasure for others. He did this with huge success. Sadly, Bill died far too early, in 1984, one day short of his sixty-fifth birthday.

Knowing your inventory and knowing about forthcoming titles is basic to good bookselling. In Canada we had roughly twice as many titles to contend with as our counterparts in the U.S. Not even the wisest, most experienced bookseller could avoid mistakes and abundant unsold inventory. I remember once ordering 250 copies of a new William Golding novel that only sold about fifty copies. Conversely, I remember turning my nose up at a book by Farley Mowat and Jack McClelland called *The Boat Who Wouldn't Float*. Who, I asked, would want to read about two old boozers floating down the St. Lawrence River together? Apparently quite a few. I ordered five copies of the book and eventually sold some three hundred, although I could have sold many more if I hadn't been out of stock so often. Go figure.

There are few things in less demand than last season's bestselling novel. Stocking fiction is always a minefield. Then there are the bestsellers whose paperback rights are sold prematurely because the publisher didn't expect the book to do well. Suddenly, often with no prior warning, the poor bookseller is faced with a mountain of unsold hardcover inventory. Yes, the books are returnable, but the time involved in looking up invoice numbers, requesting permission to return books in writing, eliminating store pricing stickers, taping torn jackets, packing the books up for return, and paying freight costs back to the publisher is a perpetual hassle.

We came up with a better idea. Rather than returning our unsold inventory, we had a giant, once-a-year, one-day, fifty-percent-off sale. We would rent a large vacant Jasper Avenue store and haul in rented tables, extra cash registers and coffee urns, pile the books on the tables and prepare for the deluge. It was not uncommon for there to be a block-long lineup an hour before the store opened. The sale became so successful we didn't need to advertise; we simply put a sign up in the main store a month in advance. By 1963 we needed a vacant 8,000-square-foot store for the sale; hundreds of people poured in as soon as we opened and we had to lock the doors for an hour. Every year we added bestsellers, staple backlist titles, and carefully selected high-quality imported remainders, especially art books, to the tables to create an even better bargain selection. As I explained in *Publishers Weekly*, "We're much better off selling the excess inventory at half price instead of returning the books to the publisher. It gives us instant cash flow, and makes many friends for the bookstore." Our customers loved our annual sale, and so did our bankers.

There were lots of other problems we had to contend with. Nutcases who came into the store with razor blades to cut out pictures of naked ladies — Rubens, Manet, Renoir, and Ingres — and one deranged individual who sliced photographs of Julie Andrews as Mary Poppins out of every book in which they appeared. There were characters who came in daily to read a particular book, cover to cover, dog-eared the page at the end of each day's reading, and then complained when "their" book was sold. There were customs officials who delighted in holding back eagerly awaited special-order shipments because there were pictures they liked to look at or words they never encountered in school to contend with, and then there was censorship. Two detectives arrested Gordon Elbrond in the store one day because he sold them a copy of Hubert Selby's *The Last Exit from Brooklyn*. In court I pointed out: "The third volume of the Kinsey Report made a very important point. . . . They concluded, as did the U.S. president's commission, that it was clear that such things as women's stockings, perfume, short skirts, and earrings have a far greater tendency to excite. Consequently, if you consider banning literature, you had better consider banning short skirts as well."

At the time, unlike people, books were often judged guilty unless proved innocent. And those who made the decision were frequently detectives or customs officials whose reading experience was, to put it politely, virtually nonexistent. Invariably, if we asked what guidelines or standards were employed in deeming a book obscene, we received no reply whatsoever. The only alternative was to proceed to court, but what bookseller can afford expensive lawsuits battling the Crown? Of course the publisher would usually chip in, but still the costs were prohibitive. In the early 1970s, *Playboy* magazine, the *Georgia Straight*, Andy Warhol's screenplay *Blue Movie*, and scores of other books and magazines came under attack. And of course fundamentalist vigilantes patrolled the bookstores looking for "smut," like the backsides of naked women on the cover of a book about Doukhobors. Few if any of the books under attack at that time would encounter the slightest problems today.

In retrospect, compared to the pleasures of bookselling, most of these problems were really quite minor and had to be accepted as part of the normal life of a retail bookseller. However, one problem, by far the biggest problem of them all, used to drive me to the use of a long list of bad words I rarely employed.

Who Steals Books?

ALAS, A LOT OF different people. Over the years I narrowed the list down to the following categories: ministers, priests, and rabbis; doctors, dentists, lawyers, engineers, and architects; students, teachers, and professors; clerks, farmers, and homemakers; men, women, and children.

Just as I cannot explain why so many men in the book trade drink so much, I cannot, for the life of me, explain why so many normally law-abiding citizens steal books. At my store businessmen with briefcases, mothers with baby carriages, and students with clipboards had to be asked to step back into the store after departing with books they hadn't paid for.

One day the long and eagerly awaited *Webster's Third International Dictionary* arrived. It was huge, selling for $79.95, the equivalent of well over $300 today. We had ordered ten copies. I asked the staff to put nine copies in the storage room at the back of the store and to put one copy on display near the cash register. Fifteen minutes later, I went to show the new dictionary to a teacher-librarian; it was gone. I called the police and told them to look for someone walking down Jasper Avenue listing heavily to one side. No luck.

We had in the store a magnificent four-volume boxed set of the nature writings and art of Ernest Thompson Seton, *Lives of Game Animals*, published in Boston and selling for $150. It was one of my prized book sets, one I wished I could afford for my own library. One day a staff member glumly reported to me that the first volume in the set was missing. Blast! I asked Gordon Elbrond to get on the phone to Boston and order a replacement. No luck again. The publisher advised that they sold only the four-volume set.

Two weeks later volume two was gone. I was furious. Now, nothing else mattered; I was determined to catch the rotten son of a bitch, no matter what! The next morning I called a meeting of the staff. "I don't care what else you do, I want you to keep a close eye on the nature section. Don't leave the floor without passing the responsibility on to another member of the staff!" Ten days later volume three was gone. That night when the store closed, I did something I had never done before and have never done since. I gathered the staff together in the alley behind the store and burned a book — volume four. There was no bloody way in the world I was going to allow the thief a crack at the last volume.

On another occasion a staff member phoned back to my office from the front of the store. "Mel, we've just caught a man going out of the store with eleven books on archaeology under his raincoat."

"Send him back here," I said.

In all the years I was a bookseller, I never once called the police when we caught someone stealing books. However, I usually tried very hard to scare the heck out of him or her. Theft was a great problem for us; it cost us lost sales and had a substantial impact on our fragile bottom line. Dozens of times I would walk to a particular bookshelf in response to a customer inquiry, reach for a book, only to find it wasn't there even though I knew it hadn't been sold. So not only had the book been stolen, but the sale had been lost and it was often weeks before a replacement arrived.

Back to the office came the man, the raincoat, and the eleven books on archaeology. Immediately one thing became apparent. This was one very big man — perhaps six foot four, 240 pounds. As he climbed the four steps up to my office, he banged his forehead on the top of the door frame. If he had been unhappy as he was escorted back to my office, now he was bridling with hostility. I asked him to have a seat. As I put my hand on the telephone, here's how the conversation went:

"Is there any reason why I shouldn't call the police?"

"No."

(Wait a minute, this wasn't what I expected. That was the wrong answer. What do I say now? I stuttered and improvised.)

"Have you ever been charged with a crime before?"

His eyes narrowed. "Yes, I have."

"Do you mind my asking what for?"

His eyes narrowed further, he leaned closer, fixed me with his gaze, and growled: "Assault with a dangerous weapon."

"I see." Gulp.

What I almost said was, "Are there any other books you'd like to have, sir?" We let him go and he never came back. However, I can still see his scowling, menacing face today.

Many of the books stolen from our store turned up in a local used-book store that actually employed the book thieves. Unfortunately it was years before we discovered this. Audrey Whaley, one of our clerks who would later open the excellent Audrey's Books, remembers that, one by one, gorgeous Ansel Adams books went missing from the store's photography section. After a couple of weeks she found them all in the used-book store. This time the police were called.

LOUIS MELZACK, ALONG WITH Roy Britnell, were the deans of trade bookselling in Canada when I opened my first store. Louis was always generous with advice and encouragement. When I began publishing, he became a wonderful supportive customer. Louis, whose father, like my father, had been a tailor, started off in 1928 at the age of twelve with his fourteen-year-old brother selling secondhand magazines in a small store on Bleury Street in Montreal, but along came the Great Depression and the rent, $55 a month, proved to be too much. The older brother headed off to New York, and Louis had to choose promptly between returning to school or trying to keep the store open. He kept the store and gradually, very gradually, Universal Books, as it was then known, looked like it might just survive. Louis thought the name Universal somewhat pretentious and changed it to Classic Books. He bought books from the Salvation Army for fifty cents and sold them for a dollar. Stephen Leacock, who taught economics at McGill, began coming into the store and lent young Louis books to read from his own library. He introduced Melzack to, among others, Sherlock Holmes. The secondhand book and magazine store slowly began carrying new books. In 1938 Melzack gathered up his courage, borrowed $3,000 from a friend, and moved to a store on St. Catherine's Street (rent $150 a month). The business took off. In 1980 Louis Melzack sold his sixty-seven bookstores to his son Brian, who later merged the 149 Classic stores with W.H. Smith.

Like Jack McClelland, Louis Melzack was a remarkable pioneer who has not received even a shadow of the recognition he deserves. This scholarly, self-educated patriot gave the University of Montreal his extraordinary collection of priceless rare Canadiana, a multimillion-dollar collection that took a lifetime to assemble. Louis opened the first all-paperback bookstore in the world and the first airport bookstore in Canada, persuaded New York mass-market publishers to sell to bookstores direct at a forty percent discount, instead of the booksellers' having to go through local magazine wholesalers who offered a paltry twenty percent discount, and he operated excellent bookstores. By the time he retired and sold his stores to Brian, he had never once had to take out a bank loan. Amazing.

I asked Louis what it was like when he was a poor boy, twelve years old, with no money, sitting in the back of the dingy, secondhand bookstore. "It was wonderful! There were no customers to disturb me. I read a book a day."

On one visit to my store Louis prevailed upon me to have the honesty of my staff checked by a security firm, something he suggested all major retailers do on a regular basis. I resisted strenuously. "There's no way any of my staff would steal money from the store," I declared. But Louis persisted and finally I caved in.

The very first day the store was professionally "shopped," one of my best longtime employees was caught pocketing the money from three different sales. I was heartbroken. Not for a moment did I really believe something like this would ever happen. I called her into the office the next morning and let her read the written report. She burst into tears and I almost did, too. I told her she could keep her job, but the next day she resigned and we never saw her again. In her letter of resignation she admitted that she had been stealing money from the store for more than five years.

Well, such a sad tale was most certainly the exception. But the more I began to travel, the more "shrinkage" became a problem. Absentee management and bookselling don't work.

I can't leave my tales of book theft without telling a W.H. Smith story someone told me last year. Outside one of their Montreal stores the staff had parked a book cart loaded with dead remainders. A sign saying Any Book $1.00 protruded from the pile. A security-firm employee watched the following sequence of events. First, a furtive-looking character showed up, glanced around several times, and then quickly slipped a book under his jacket and departed. A few minutes later a woman arrived, browsed through the books, selected one, tossed a loonie into the cart, and left. In less than five minutes another sidewalk browser appeared. After a couple of minutes he, too, selected a book, looked around carefully, put the book in his briefcase, picked up the loonie, and headed off down the street.

Goodbye to Bookselling

In 1966 I opened a branch store in Sandy Mactaggart's Campus Towers, adjacent to the University of Alberta. A young student, an attractive brunette named Noel Cameron, with a couple of young kids and a husband working on a PhD in English, talked herself into the job of running the store. We allowed students charge accounts, frequently helped graduate students with discounts, and gradually built a profitable store. Noel worked hard to make the store a success and to impress her "patriarchal" boss.

One Saturday night she and her husband, Jack, invited my wife and me for dinner at their home. They were a struggling student family, but they both knew food and how to entertain. When we arrived, the dining-room table was covered with a colourful cloth and beautifully decorated with flowers. There were candles, baskets of breads, cheeses, wine bottles, goblets, and containers for sauces and a several-course meal. Obviously it had taken much care and planning. It was a great evening and a fine dinner until Noel got up to bring the dessert and Jack got up a few moments later to grind the coffee. The table, piled high with dishes and food, was a simple picnic table. When Noel got up, there was no problem. But when Jack got up, Eileen and I immediately saw the opposite side of the table slowly begin to rise in the air. We didn't have a chance. Over we went, crashing on our backs on the floor, our feet in the air. And over came all of the plates, candles, wine, flowers, gravy, and food on top of us in one spectacular mess.

The delightful, book-loving Noel and her second husband, Andrew, now live in a magnificent home, Raven Hill herb farm, perched atop a hillside on the Saanichton Peninsula north of Victoria. Noel is the author of four books, including two bestselling cookbooks, and owns a mystery bookstore.

In 1969 I opened another branch in the new, then fashionable McCauley Plaza. Only three stores away, my second wife-to-be, Kay, operated her upscale and trendy Image Ladies Wear, although we didn't meet until twelve years later.

By 1971 I was travelling more and more as national chairman of the Committee for an Independent Canada, and Keith Davey and other Liberals were putting a considerable amount of pressure on me to run for Parliament in the upcoming 1972 federal election. With all the travel and the expansion of the business, which now included the three bookstores and Book Order Service, a separate company designed to handle special orders, I found myself increasingly bogged down with paperwork, personnel matters, and other aspects of retail bookselling that were a lot less appealing than being on the floor selling books.

By this time the bookstores were allowing me to make both the first and second mortgage payments on our beautiful new home on what is now called Alexander Circle, and support my family, including daughter number four, Leslie, who was born in 1970. Lest anyone harbour the impression that the stores provided a lavish income and opulent lifestyle, my take-home pay in my last year of bookselling was all of $21,750. But in those days it was more than enough to provide a comfortable living.

I was becoming convinced that it was time to sell the bookstores. In 1967 I had begun publishing Canadian books, as well as selling them. Almost immediately I realized that I loved publishing as much or even more than bookselling. Moreover, it seemed to me that publishing would give me more time to pursue the other activities I was involved in.

In January 1972, after stipulating that I would sell only to a Canadian company, I sold my retail business to the Vancouver book wholesaler Julian "Buddy" Smith. (Buddy almost bought the Duthie stores at the same time, but at the last minute Bill changed his mind.) By the time I sold the bookstores, our sales from our new publishing division already exceeded those of the entire retail operation. I took out an ad in the *Edmonton Journal* that began with a big THANK YOU and ended by saying:

> The best part of bookselling is found in the good people one meets, the interesting people, the genuinely nice people. Most Canadians never go into a bookstore . . . ever! I happen to be prejudiced — I think people who make the time to come into a bookstore on a Saturday with their kids, or who value and love books, or who understand that there's more to life than "The Beverley Hillbillies" and "O'Hara of the U.S. Treasury" — those people who are lucky enough to have discovered the riches to be found in books, are among the wealthiest people anywhere.

There was one other reason I sold the stores. As I explained to Dianne Woodman in an interview for *Quill and Quire*, "I find it exciting to be a publisher. I've found it creative and profitable. But, in order to continue publishing I need more money. Our fall '71 publishing program cost us $176,000, we have a very ambitious list lined up for 1972, and the logical and inevitable way to raise this money was to sell the stores." Mr. McDiarmid, the bank manager, continued to be prophetic. Every year, as we continued to expand, we continued to owe the bank more and more money.

Aside from the pleasure of serving so many fine customers and meeting many bright authors and publishers from around the world, perhaps one of the nicest things about my years as a bookseller was working with fellow booksellers on the board of the Canadian Booksellers Association, where I eventually became vice president and then chairman. Bill Duthie, Mary Scorer, Evelyn DeMille, Barry Britnell, Bob Pittam, Don Quick, Harald Bohne, to mention only a few, all had two things in common. First, they loved books. Second, they were excellent dedicated booksellers.

The Albert Britnell bookstore on Yonge Street has now been in business for more than one hundred years. Sadly, one of Canada's best booksellers, Barry Britnell, fell ill with leukemia in 1980. In June of that year he wrote to me: "Mel, I'm feeling much better and seem to be holding my own. I'm still not a hundred percent, however, but we're all working on it and are optimistic." Much to our dismay, Barry died that fall.

Many young men and women on our bookstore staff have gone on to great success as authors, booksellers, and publishers. John Falconer, Audrey Whaley, and Gordon Elbrond all have enjoyed long careers as successful booksellers; Myrna Kostash became a fine author, and Jan Walter, who started with us as a young untrained bookseller, has gone on to become one of Canada's most respected publishers. Jean Elbrond, who met her husband as a fellow clerk in the bookstore, wrote: "I learned more in a year at Hurtig's than I did in thirteen years at school. I am indebted to you in so many ways." Audrey Whaley said: "Your staff taught me everything I know. It was a great atmosphere with wonderful customers."

The circle goes round. Mel Hurtig as a young bookseller thinks Taylor Caldwell is a man. The young clerk in Helene Hogg's Seymour Books in North Vancouver, when asked for a copy of Margaret Atwood's *The Edible Woman*, returns from the fiction section holding aloft a book. "Do you mean this?" she asks, earnestly offering William Burrough's *The Naked Lunch*. And last year, my daughter Leslie, already a superb bookseller at twenty-five, tells a customer in Greenwood's bookstore that she didn't think they had an Evelyn Waugh book because they haven't stocked many of her titles lately.

Bookselling provided all of us with a great education, a lot of good laughs — even if many of them were at our expense. One day while I was a struggling bookseller, my seven-year-old daughter, Jane, appeared on a popular local television show. She was asked by the interviewer, "Now, how would you like to tell us all about what your favourite books are?" Without a moment's hesitation Jane answered, with a great big bright smile on her face, "Library books!"

II

THE LURE OF
POLITICS

I Join the Liberal Party

ANADIAN POLITICS FIRST captured me in the mid-sixties. For months, through much of 1964, the House of Commons was mired in vicious dogfights between Prime Minister Lester Pearson and former prime minister John Diefenbaker. The floor of the Commons was deep in ugly accusations and counteraccusations. As day after day of bitter debate turned into week after week and month after month of government paralysis, Canadians became fed up to the teeth, disgusted by the behaviour of their political leaders.

Keith Davey reports a beleaguered Mike Pearson calling him into his East Block office early one morning to ask for advice after reading a harsh *Globe and Mail* editorial criticizing the behaviour of the two party leaders. Davey remembers screwing up his courage and telling the prime minister: "Sir, the reason they are writing that is because that is exactly what has happened. Mr. Diefenbaker has brought you down to his level."

If things were bad before, the June 1964 flag debate worsened them considerably. John Diefenbaker was furious about the proposal to replace the Red Ensign and the Union Jack with Pearson's three-maple-leaves flag. When the new single red maple leaf flag was finally raised on Parliament Hill on February 15, 1965, after a ferocious, prolonged debate in the House of Commons ending in closure being invoked, John Diefenbaker wept.

In November 1965, at Walter Gordon's suggestion, the Liberals, in an attempt to escape a minority-government situation, again went to the people in a federal election, but fell two seats short of a majority. Walter Gordon took responsibility and resigned from the cabinet, much to the dismay of many of his colleagues. Soon after, the Liberals moved to the right, with the likes of Paul Hellyer, Mitchell Sharp, and Bob Winters very much in control. When Gordon returned to cabinet as president of the Privy Council in 1967, he himself was in a minority situation, and his influence both in the cabinet and with Mike Pearson had diminished considerably.

After the centennial celebration and Expo 67, much to the surprise of virtually everyone, Pearson announced his intention to resign and called for a spring 1968 leadership convention. When I visited Montreal during Expo, many of my friends in Quebec told me that Canada was going to fall apart. Quebec, they said, inevitably would leave Canada, and then, sometime later, other parts of the country would assuredly opt to join the United States.

The more I thought about these dire predictions, the more I travelled across the country and fell in love with it, and the more I read and listened, the more convinced I became that I should try to do whatever I could to see that the right person became the next prime minister. And the more I saw of him on television and the more of his writings I read, the more I became convinced that the forty-eight-year-old Minister of Justice Pierre Trudeau was the right person.

While I had followed politics closely, beginning first with a fascination with U.S. politics, like the vast majority of Canadians I knew next to nothing about the inner workings of political parties, constituencies, leadership conventions, and the behind-the-scenes operations of the local, provincial, and federal Liberals. Nevertheless, late in 1967, green and naïve as could be, I led the formation of a small group in Northern Alberta in an attempt to support Trudeau's as-yet-unannounced candidacy to replace Pearson.

When I phoned Ottawa for the first time seeking information about Trudeau's intentions, an old friend, Ivan Head, who had been working in Ottawa as associate counsel on the Constitution, answered the phone. No, Trudeau had not yet made up his mind. No, there was no indication as to when he would. Trudeau was on his way to Tahiti. We went ahead anyway. It wasn't until late in the winter that Trudeau announced his decision to run. By then, Mitchell Sharp, John Turner, Paul Hellyer, Bob Winters, and Paul Martin all had well-organized national campaigns under way and had many potential delegates already committed to support them.

This would be the first time in the history of Canada when a group of people would get together at a convention to elect a prime minister. Day after day the interest in the April convention heightened.

The competition among the leadership candidates was intense.

The first Liberal meeting I went to with my friend Ralph MacMillan was a disaster. Someone gave a very boring, poorly delivered, and very long talk. Then a group of middle-aged lawyers began debating some remarkably mundane and parochial issues. Nobody talked to us. I left the meeting thoroughly discouraged.

Nevertheless, we went ahead and developed an excellent energetic organization to back Trudeau. Suddenly, one day, something dawned on me. I had no idea whatsoever how we could become delegates to the convention. I phoned Ralph; he had no idea either, but promised to call back. When he did, the news was not good. Each constituency was entitled to six delegates. One had to be a "youth delegate" and one had to be a "woman delegate." The president of the Edmonton West constituency association wanted to be a delegate, and so did the past president. So did the secretary, the treasurer, the other members of the executive, the bagman, and all their predecessors. We didn't stand a chance.

How disappointing. We had been working many hours every day organizing; now it appeared we would not even be able to attend the convention. I went home from the bookstore that night quite disconcerted. In the middle of the night a light went on. Wait a minute! Very early the next morning I phoned Ralph. Exactly *how* were these delegates chosen, and by whom? Ralph didn't know either, but phoned me back in a few minutes. Fancy that — they were elected. Elected by whom? By members of the Liberal party who lived in the constituency. Fancy that!

The mid-February meeting to select the six delegates was held in the Glenora school auditorium. There were full slates of Sharp, Turner, Hellyer, Winters, and Martin delegates. The constituency executive, anticipating a big turnout, had prepared five hundred printed ballots. One small problem. After we had learned about the election rules, Ralph and I, along with Swede Liden, Bonar Bain, Una Evans, Roger Belzil, and a host of others, had gone out and sold some eleven hundred new Liberal memberships. A thousand of them showed up at the meeting.

Pandemonium reigned. The auditorium was too small, there were only 350 chairs, it was boiling hot inside and freezing cold outside, the microphone at the front of the auditorium broke down, the chairman did not know the rules of order well, the constituency executive was in a state of panic. By midnight, although most of the crowd had left, we had elected three Trudeau delegates, including Ralph and me. Previously, of the eighty-four delegates elected in all of Alberta, only two supported Trudeau.

Now, when I speak to university political science students about the 1968 West Edmonton meeting to select the delegates to the convention, I say that what we did is called "participatory democracy" when you win; when you lose it's called "packing the meeting."

The leadership convention in Ottawa was certainly one of the most exciting events I have ever attended. Pierre Elliott Trudeau was elected, but only after a fourth ballot. He would be our first prime minister born in the twentieth century.

It didn't take very long after the convention for me to learn more about how the Liberal party operated. Where not too many months ago the Liberal membership in our constituency had amounted to less than one hundred, now it was close to two thousand, thanks to the hotly contested delegate race. Yet not one single constituency meeting for members was held during the next fifteen months. Almost two thousand new members of the Liberal party were totally ignored. Incredibly, when finally the executive was forced by the constitution to hold an annual meeting, there was no mailing to notify members. All those enthusiastic men and women who had heard so much about participatory democracy didn't even hear about their constituency's annual meeting.

Now, *why* would this be? Wouldn't you think that the party hierarchy would want to take advantage of the huge influx of new members to build a strong, vibrant organization and to help prepare for the next election and for future elections?

Hardly. The Liberal party was made up largely of professional people who dominated the executives of the constituency associations. And patronage dominated the decision-making process in the party. Lawyers wanted NHA mortgages and other government legal work, appointments to government boards and to the bench; car dealers wanted to sell cars to the RCMP; architects, contractors, and engineers wanted government contracts for new buildings and renovations. When the Liberals were in power in Ottawa, the last thing in the world the local executive would want was other people horning in on their patronage territory. Grassroots? Grassroots meant workers every four or five years during election campaigns. Period. No wonder the Liberal party in Alberta that I joined had been decaying and moribund for years.

Soon after the leadership convention, a strange thing began to happen. Lawyers I didn't know, or hardly knew, began inviting my wife and me over for dinner. They were an incredibly friendly bunch. And they all had one thing in common — they wanted bench appointments and believed I had influence with the new prime minister.

It wasn't long too before I began to learn about fundraising in the Liberal party. At the time, the election laws were almost a joke; there was no effective mandatory disclosure, as well as no limits on campaign expenses and poor control over expenditures. One Edmonton bagman used to head to Toronto and Montreal once a year and literally return with a black satchel full of cash. Cash, not cheques. Why cash? Because most of the money represented undisclosed corporate funds, and at the time there were no donation tax credits. One day I asked the bagman how I would know if when he returned, say, with $100,000 in cash that he hadn't been given $200,000? Without hesitation he answered: "You *wouldn't* know." One $100,000 cash donation from a Montreal grocery chain had shrunk to $25,000 by the time it reached Ottawa!

As far as Liberals in Western Canada in general went, Keith Davey summed them up quite nicely: "In October 1966, the Liberal National Policy Conference found Liberals from Western Canada, sensing that the party focus was running in their direction — and obviously delighted with the fall from grace of both Walter Gordon and me — better organized than ever before. They brought with them a determined right-wing agenda which sought to delay medicare and to reject economic nationalism." Keith, as long as I have known him, is rarely given to understatement, and I mean that as a compliment. But in this case, his description of the 1960s western Liberals was restrained. In short, many western Liberals were conservatives or should have been Conservatives. They happened to be in the Liberal party not for ideological reasons, but because it was to their pocketbook's advantage to do so.

Politics: Exhilarating — and Disillusioning

T HE FIRST IMPORTANT EVENT in a postelection reborn federal Liberal party's efforts at participatory democracy was a "thinkers' conference," an attempt to revive the grassroots spirit of the very successful 1960 Kingston conference. The new conference was scheduled for Harrison Hot Springs, in British Columbia, in November 1969.

I had become a member of the federal party's National Policy Committee in 1968, chairman of a new Liberal task force on international affairs, and Alberta policy chairman. By the summer of 1969, I was getting fed up with the right wingers who dominated the party on the Prairies. In an article in the *Toronto Star*, I wrote:

> The Liberals on the Prairies, for the most part, are not liberals at all, nor even Liberals. Not a real alternative for the voters, but simply more Conservatives under another name. Most of them have failed to fight for medicare, failed to interpret government policies to their constituents, and failed to think and act in terms of the national interest.
>
> Pierre Trudeau's inability to democratize the structure of the Liberal party is his single most significant failure since his election.

This was the first time I had criticized Trudeau. Ross Thatcher and other right-wing members of the western Liberal establishment were furious. But many rank-and-file party members were delighted. In a lead editorial about the upcoming provincial leadership convention, the *Red Deer Advocate* had this to say: "If delegates want any advice they would be well advised to push their policy papers aside and take a good look at the chairman of their policy committee: Mr. Mel Hurtig, Edmonton publisher, progressive thinker, engaging human being, would give the Liberal party a contemporary lustre, appeal to emerging voter groups and distinctiveness, from the Social Credit and Conservative parties."

Soon after there was much pressure on me to run for the leadership of the Alberta Liberal party. A delegation from Calgary and Southern Alberta came up to see me, and another delegation of young Liberals also offered their support. While I was very flattered, there was no chance I would accept, even though I was assured the leadership would be mine if I wanted it, an optimism I did not share. My interest was in Canada as a whole and in federal, not provincial politics. Besides, my publishing company was just nicely under way and needed my attention.

Not long after, the leader of the Alberta Liberal party, Jack Lowery, embarrassed the party by suggesting it should merge with the sinking Social Credit ship of former premier Harry Strom — and that lost the Liberal party most of the slim credibility it had with Albertans. I led the attack on Lowery at a party convention in Red Deer, and that was pretty well the end of it. Again the pressure was on me to run for the leadership. Among the many nice letters that arrived over the next weeks was Elaine Verbicky's. "I don't know if you realize how much of a spark plug you are," she wrote. "As someone said after the meeting in Red Deer, 'That's the first time I've met any older person in the Liberal party with that much idealism.'" I was all of thirty-eight at the time and, yes, despite being an older person, still very idealistic.

During the crisis that had erupted in the party as a result of Lowery's merger suggestion, I gave a widely reported speech in which I said: "The province needs a Liberal party that is not a club, but a real Liberal party interested in people and issues — not just in bench appointments. The patronage system should be abolished and the party should open itself up to more participation by the rank-and-file members. I'm sick and tired of going to secret Liberal meetings."

A few days later there was another secret Liberal meeting at the Macdonald Hotel, chaired by former Social Crediter, then Liberal Agriculture Minister Bud Olson from Medicine Hat. The press had caught wind of the meeting, and there were three television cameras and several reporters standing outside the meeting room waiting to hear what we had decided to do about Lowery.

The meeting went on and on. There was only one topic — patronage. Who was going to build the new government building in Yellowknife? Which law firms would get Department of Justice work? Which architects would design the new government building in Calgary or Red Deer? Which insurance agents would get government contracts? Finally I could wait no longer. I interrupted.

"Bud, aren't we going to talk about anything other than patronage?"

Olson scowled at me and said: "What else did you have on your mind, Mel?"

I looked at him, looked around the room, then got up and left.

Lowery's support eroded quickly, and he chose not to enter the up-coming leadership contest and quickly vanished from Alberta politics.

Around this time I began to speak out increasingly about reform of the electoral system to make it much more democratic. Two years in the Liberal party had taught me that the system was corrupted by the way money dominated the decision-making process. I suggested that all donations, including nonmonetary contributions, be open to public scrutiny, that there be strict limits on campaign spending, including spending on nominating meetings and leadership conven-tions, and that constituency officers accept no form of business dealings with government. It was increasingly clear to me that patronage worked diametrically in opposition to the best interests of participatory democracy.

My colleagues in the hierarchy of the Alberta Liberal party, mostly lawyers, were not very happy with my speeches and interviews on the subject. But once again, rank-and-file party members whole-heartedly agreed with what I was saying.

By the time of the Harrison policy conference I was beginning to feel pretty disillusioned. It seemed to me that the participatory democracy and grassroots policy process was largely window dressing. The major theme of my own policy paper for the conference was Canadian sovereignty. The expert ten-person foreign-affairs task force I had assembled for Harrison expressed similar concerns. One oft-repeated theme was that in an era of dangerous nuclear confrontation, Canada wasn't doing enough to try to deescalate tension between our superpower neighbours, to support detente, and to work towards the reduction of the buildup of the "nuclear balance of terror." As well, how could Canada ever have an independent foreign policy dedicated to peace if day by day we were losing our ability to decide our own future as more and more of our country and its resources were con-trolled by non-Canadians? Shortly before the conference there was pressure from Ottawa for me to modify my paper. I didn't. About this time, I told the *Edmonton Journal* that I found politics "easily the most exhilarating thing I have ever done, and also the most disillusioning."

In my Harrison paper I said that Canada's foreign and defence policy was that of a colonial nation: "Is it likely that because of our economic domination by our giant ally we have already lost our opportunity for an independent foreign policy? Is our foreign and defence policy in fact the policy of a colonial nation, and is our sovereignty a myth?"

Since it was already clear that neither the External Affairs Department nor the Liberal-dominated House of Commons committee on foreign affairs were receptive to any important changes in policy, I called the much-trumpeted government foreign-policy review "an exercise in rhetoric." Mr. Trudeau was not pleased.

In a lead editorial titled "Hurtig's initiative," the *Toronto Star* suggested: "The questions Mr. Hurtig asks are grave and urgent. If the Harrison Hot Springs conference is to be a real policy-making meeting, it must come to grips with them and not rest content with easy assurances from ministers or External Affairs functionaries." But, in fact, the Harrison conference proved not to be a real policy-making event. Rather, it turned out to be an image-making meeting meant to present a facade of participatory democracy in the Liberal party. Many of the hardworking organizers left disillusioned and embittered.

The conference, supposedly intended to be a grassroots "thinkers.'" conference to help shape future government policy, was very much controlled by the prime minister's office and Mitchell Sharp's office. Both did their best to avoid contentious issues such as the heavy degree of American ownership and control of the Canadian economy, and foreign-policy issues relating to Canadian independence. According to University of Toronto political scientist Stephen Clarkson, all the hard work and detailed preparation that had gone into advocating a more independent and nationalist position "turned out to be so much wasted effort for the militants who had squandered energy on the participatory exercise from its high-spirited start in 1968 to its dismal finish in 1971."

Andy Snaddon, editor of the *Edmonton Journal*, wrote: "Perhaps the most interesting panel in many was the one on International Relations organized by Edmonton publisher Mel Hurtig." He also wrote that clearly, more than anyone else, I had the prime minister's ear. Not quite. What happened to mislead Snaddon was this. The evening of the conference's opening day all the delegates and government people were, drinks in hand, assembled in a large banquet room that had been cleared of all furniture save four tables in the corners for the bartenders — which was where almost all the crowd was gathered. I was crossing the floor when Trudeau entered from the opposite end; we met in the middle. The two of us stood there talking in low voices for some five minutes. It was clear to everyone that we were talking about important matters given the facial expressions, gesticulations, and obvious intense nature of the discussion. But rather than talking about important matters of state, the prime minister was giving me hell for a book we had just published, a book that had immediately climbed to the top of the bestseller lists. The book was by Alberta native leader Harold Cardinal. Its title — *The Unjust Society*. Trudeau, having run on the slogan of "the Just Society" was displeased, to say the least.

ANOTHER INTERESTING MEETING at Harrison was with Senator Paul Martin (who at that time did not have to be referred to as Paul Martin, Sr.). A Franco-Ontarian of humble origins, Martin was trained in the law and in international affairs, and became an outstanding Canadian politician. He was first elected to the House of Commons in 1935. Early on he was a delegate to the League of Nations. He guided the Citizenship Act through the House of Commons. He spent much of a decade helping prepare Canada for medicare and developing the required health-care legislation. He was instrumental in Canada's peacekeeping role in Cyprus and ably assisted prime ministers Mackenzie King, Louis Saint-Laurent, Lester Pearson, and Pierre Trudeau in many areas. He had run unsuccessfully for the leadership of the Liberal party in 1948 and 1958. Martin was an early and enthusiastic champion of Canada's universal social programs, a strong proponent and defender of medicare, family allowances, and unemployment insurance. He was also, in many ways, a consummate politician. But again, like all of us, he had his flaws.

I had never met Paul Martin but was aware of his accomplishments in the Liberal government. I had also heard, on several occasions, a legendary story about him that went like this:

> Every year he would hold an all-day summer picnic for his constituents in Windsor. One morning he was introduced to a young man at the picnic.
> "Nice to meet you," said Martin. "How's your father?"
> "I'm sorry, Mr. Martin, but my father died last year."
> "No. I don't believe it! Why didn't someone tell me? I can't understand how I could have missed it. I'm very sorry to hear the news. Your father and I were good friends."
> Later in the day, Martin was in a different part of the picnic grounds, and was introduced to the same young man again.
> "How's your father, lad?"
> "He's still dead, Mr. Martin."

Late in 1967 Martin called me from Ottawa. "Mel, this is Paul Martin," he began. "We've never met but I've heard a great deal about you and I admire you greatly."

"Well, thank you, Mr. Martin. What can I do for you?"

"Mel, as you know, I'm running for the leadership of the Liberal party. I need your help."

"Well, you know I'd love to help, but I'm working for Pierre Trudeau and have been for some time."

"Mel, forget it. He's not going to run. Anyway, I'm going to be in Edmonton next month. I must have you as a key person in my campaign. I hope you will do me the honour of meeting with me."

"Paul, may I call you Paul? I would love to meet you, but I'm afraid it would be a waste of your time. I really am committed to Pierre."

After another ten minutes I reluctantly agreed to meet him. When he arrived in Edmonton in January we sat nose to nose in his room in the Macdonald Hotel for more than an hour. Finally he was convinced that I would be supporting Trudeau. We shook hands, had a quick drink, and I departed.

On the final day of the Harrison conference I was walking down a long corridor in the hotel with a lawyer from Halifax. We came to a right-angle turn in the corridor, and around it came Paul Martin. My companion immediately said: "Hi, Paul. Paul, this is Mel Hurtig."

Martin warmly shook my hand and said: "For goodness' sakes, Mel Hurtig! I've heard a lot about you. I've been wanting to meet you for quite some time."

IN THE SPRING OF 1970 a group of Liberal cabinet ministers and members of Parliament invited me to Ottawa to speak to them about the future of the party and the government. It seemed to me that both were in big trouble and in serious danger of losing the next federal election. I called for dramatic reforms, a highly ethical approach to government, a much fairer tax system, and other fundamental changes. The talk was very well received, but nothing of consequence happened.

Once again I was under heavy pressure to run, this time federally. I wanted to, but the more I saw of the Liberal party in action, the less certain I was that I wanted to be part of it. There was another important consideration. Trudeaumania was turning to Trudeauphobia all across the country, but more so in Western Canada and even more so in Alberta.

I talked the decision over with my family and staff. Keith Davey kept calling, offering enthusiastic encouragement. Calls came in every week from Liberal members of Parliament. Finally in June I announced that I would seek the Liberal nomination in the Edmonton West riding held for many years by Progressive Conservative Marcel Lambert.

The Harrison conference had been preparation for a formal Liberal policy conference the next year in Ottawa. In late November the conference was held at the Chateau Laurier in Ottawa, attended by over a thousand delegates from across Canada. Pauline Jewett, a former Liberal MP, and I co-chaired the International Relations session. There were some twenty-five resolutions to be debated and a long lineup at the floor microphones all evening. When it looked as if several key resolutions that clashed with government policy might be passed, several Liberal MPs and executive assistants sent for help. And help soon arrived in the form of Prime Minister Trudeau, Minister of External Affairs Mitchell Sharp, and Minister of Defence Donald Macdonald.

As soon as Pierre Trudeau entered the room (he stood at the back without taking a seat), there was much commotion. Many of the delegates gathered around him, and the noise level made continued floor discussion impossible. Pauline Jewett solved the problem, striding to the stage mike, staring directly at the prime minister, and very firmly saying: "Would the persons at the back of the room who are causing a commotion either leave immediately or sit down and be quiet?" There was a stunned silence in the room, then Pierre and his entourage took seats. Subsequently, after interventions by Trudeau, Sharp, and Macdonald, most of our key policy resolutions were defeated.

Allen Linden and several other key policy committee chairpersons told Stephen Clarkson after the convention that we'd been had. It was true. Once again the prime minister and senior ministers managed to squelch any significant deviations from government policy. Liberal activists were dismayed. Spirit in the party sagged right across the country.

So much for participatory democracy. It wasn't long before Pauline Jewett left the Liberal party.

The longer I was in the party, the more time I spent in Ottawa, the more disappointed I became. In 1971, in a speech, I returned to the theme of money in politics:

> Canadians would demand the resignation of many of their gov-
> ernments if the truth of political financing were revealed. Big
> business funds the political process, and as a result government

often legislates in ways which can only startle the imagination of someone interested in the well-being of the majority of Canadians. Our current government, which is supposed to believe in participatory democracy, has done little to improve the situation. The "bagman" is invariably the most powerful figure in every province.

How many people know that each Liberal cabinet minister in Ottawa has in his office a filing cabinet with an A-list, a B-list and a C-list, and those lists determine which faithful Liberal lawyers get government work, which architects and engineers get jobs, who gets appointed to government boards, who gets radio and television licences, etc., and etc., and etc.?

And who exactly are the persons on those lists? For the most part, they are men who donate large sums of money to the Liberal party. The result is an undemocratic, antiquated system run by an elite in the best interests of an elite.

Again, not exactly words meant to endear me to the party, the prime minister, and the cabinet. And the election had not yet begun.

In the spring of 1971 Eric Kierans, the Liberal MP for Duvernay, resigned his seat in the House of Commons. Kierans, who is unquestionably one of the most intelligent men I have ever met, had been director of the School of Commerce at McGill, president of the Montreal Stock Exchange, a minister in the Quebec Lesage government, and minister of communications and postmaster general in the Trudeau cabinet from 1968 to 1971. In 1968 he ran against Trudeau for the Liberal leadership with a very strong economic platform, which was head and shoulders above those of all the other leadership contenders.

Kierans and Trudeau had a long lunch prior to Eric's resignation. Eric made it clear that on the issue of tax reform alone he would have to quit. "We've lost every bit of tax reform . . . I can't vote for the budget," he told Trudeau. "Well, perhaps you can be away," was Trudeau's suggestion. "No, I can't duck out," Eric replied.

Kierans stood up in the House of Commons and voted against his own government on a matter of principle. And that was that. He had spent three frustrating years in Ottawa and resigned principally because of the Trudeau government's economic policies. Now the warnings he began delivering across the country were very similar to my own and to Walter Gordon's. This was highly ironic, since Kierans had led the attack on Gordon's nationalistic June 1963 budget while Kierans was president of the Montreal Stock Exchange. At the time he charged that it was "utter nonsense" to worry about the nationality of a corporation.

A decade later Eric Kierans was saying that he would "go even further than Gordon did" and "the day is going to come when people are going to ask, 'Why were you so stupid? Why did you give it all way?'"

Eighteen years later Canada was to sign an agreement giving its resources away in a manner no other developed nation in the world ever would have agreed to.

Today Kierans says there is no question that Trudeau understood economic issues well, but they were not of primary importance to him. He was preoccupied with other issues. When economic matters came to the cabinet table, it was always the Department of Finance and the Bank of Canada that prevailed. Bob Bryce, the deputy finance minister, and Louis Rasminsky, the bank governor, always controlled the agenda.

Kierans left the cabinet in April 1971, although he had intended to resign in October 1970. Then the Quebec crisis arose, and Kierans and others did not want his resignation to be misinterpreted, so he agreed to stay on temporarily.

Eric Kierans had previously reconciled with Walter Gordon in 1967, after having attacked and embarrassed him when Gordon was finance minister. But after Kierans had confronted René Lévesque, while they were both in the Quebec Liberal party, and forced Jean Lesage to take a stand for Canada in opposition to Lévesque, Gordon called Kierans at Montebello, and the two were in frequent friendly contact thereafter.

Often supportive of Kierans's economic positions was Pauline Jewett, an intelligent, courageous person of great integrity, and one of the strongest Canadian patriots I have been privileged to know. She had been a nationally respected member of Parliament in the Pearson government, attracted to the Liberal party by the exciting Kingston conference and the progressive political agenda it produced. She was elected vice president of the Liberal Party of Canada, serving from 1966 to 1970, having been narrowly defeated by Conservative George Hees in the 1965 federal election. Soon after the Chateau Laurier policy conference, she rejected an offer to run for the Liberals in Ottawa Centre and an almost certain cabinet position if the Liberals were reelected.

When she quit the Liberal party, she cited three reasons: first, Liberal economic policies, which failed to address unemployment; second, the failure of the party to reform the bagman approach to party financing; and third, the failure of the government to do anything about the growing American ownership of industry and resources in Canada.

Pauline went on to head the Institute of Canadian Studies at Carleton University from 1971 to 1974 and later became the first woman to head a major Canadian university when she was appointed president of Simon Fraser University in 1974. After joining the NDP, she was elected to Parliament in 1979, 1980, and again in 1984 from the British Columbia riding of Westminster-Coquitlam.

Pauline and I worked very well together in the Liberal party, and then in the Committee for an Independent Canada, where she had been scheduled to succeed me as chairperson before the SFU appointment. After the disappointing Chateau Laurier session, she wrote to me that "we were dumb to have given Mitchell Sharp such a glorious opportunity, even though listening to him would surely have convinced many in the audience that he avoids all the main issues."

So, two good allies in the House of Commons, two people I admired a great deal, were gone from Parliament and gone from Ottawa. I believe Trudeau was threatened by Kierans, who was the only one in the entire caucus who was his intellectual equal, and whose grasp of economics was far greater. In any event Trudeau treated him shabbily, giving him the post office portfolio. What a waste of great talent.

In later years, when Trudeau, Turner, or Chrétien Liberals wanted me to run for Parliament and promised me virtually certain cabinet posts, I would remember Eric Kierans and say: "No way. Turner would give me the post office," or "Chrétien would give me veterans affairs." In either case I was likely being optimistic.

Running for Parliament

B Y MARCH OF 1972 I was increasingly unsure about whether I belonged in the Liberal party. But the more I voiced my doubts and expressed my concerns to my friends and supporters, the more they urged me to run. Not without many misgivings, I made the final commitment.

When I announced the decision, I said: "I'm running for Parliament because I'm very worried about the future of our country. I believe that if we continue to allow others to buy up Canada, our children will at best be tenants and servants in the country we've given away. Most Canadians agree with me, but our politicians have done nothing." Soon after, I appeared before the House of Commons committee studying the government's proposed legislation relating to foreign investment. I was appalled by the poor knowledge of economics and foreign direct investment displayed by most of the MPs on the committee. Liberal Bob Kaplan chaired the committee; I wrote to him when I returned to Edmonton:

> Do you know the story about the man who stood on the sloping deck of the *Titanic*, just before it sank beneath the waves? He stood there raving about how good the food was in the restaurant. That's what your committee reminded me of on Tuesday afternoon.
>
> I thought that the level of questioning was unbelievable. It was obvious that several members of your committee hadn't even bothered to read *Foreign Direct Investment in Canada* or any of the other important reports that have come out.

In 1968 Pierre Trudeau had promised that reform of election spending would be a "top priority." But nothing of significance was done. While the Canada Elections Act required each candidate to fully disclose the source of his or her financing, there was no such disclosure requirement for the party at the national or the constituency level. Hence, candidate-disclosure provisions were meaningless. The Elections Act was full of holes, the wording vague, and much of it had no effective legal status. Most constituencies ended up channelling all donations to a single source and then reporting only a single donation. There were no campaign limits. In the previous election in 1968, more than a quarter of all the candidates had failed to even file the minimal returns relating to campaign funds required under the Election Act. While the act provided for penalties, not one of the 267 candidates who violated the legislation was prosecuted. In short there was no enforcement at all.

I decided to voluntarily disclose all contributions to my campaign, cash or in kind, to put a limit of $1,000 on the size of any single contribution, and to refuse to accept funds from foreign corporations.

Of course this meant that I also had to refuse money from the Liberal party, which gladly accepted large sums from foreign firms. The Liberals offered my campaign some $7,000, then some $13,000 when the press began saying I had a good chance to win. I turned them down. We would likely have to run our campaign with less than half the funds my Conservative opponent Marcel Lambert would spend, but we would try to overcome the disadvantage by running a people-intensive campaign instead.

Globe and Mail columnist George Bain wrote a column on the editorial page entitled "All by Himself." It resulted in more than a hundred favourable letters from across Canada. The column read in part:

> Perhaps Mr. Hurtig will be able to run, pointing with pride to the position taken by his leader and government on the issue that has been uppermost in Mr. Hurtig's mind — foreign ownership. Perhaps not.
>
> But what is certain is that he is not going to have to dwell long upon the government's record in the area which he has chosen as the other base for his candidacy. That is political reform, and particularly, reform of the law relating to the raising and spending of campaign funds. On this the Trudeau government had done nothing, notwithstanding early promises.

I challenged Marcel Lambert to reveal the sources of his campaign funds. He replied that it was not an issue, since he "was not aware of the direct sources of any of the money." According to Lambert, there was "nothing nefarious in not disclosing my sources of campaign funds. I don't even know who gave what. It's up to the donor, not the candidate, to make such disclosures."

If there is any one thing I have learned about politics, it is this. If any politician, federal, provincial, or municipal, tells you that they do not know who has put up the money for their campaign, your reply, no matter how reserved or proper you are, should always be: "Bullshit!"

Marcel Lambert, stodgy, pudgy, out of shape, and out of new ideas, was no easy opponent. Quite the contrary. He had been a Rhodes Scholar, was an admired war hero who was captured at Dieppe, a successful lawyer, and an MP who paid careful attention to births, deaths, anniversaries, birthdays, passport problems, and the like.

Though much of the first half of 1972 I criticized the Liberal government, saying that the prime minister was "using cosmetics to cover up his lack of firm policy to deal with foreign investment." I had a steady stream of leaks from Ottawa that indicated that the forthcoming policy statement on foreign investment, foreign ownership, and foreign control would be weak and ineffective. While I derived no great joy from criticizing Trudeau, I could think of no other way to try to get the public to put pressure on the government. Since all the public-opinion polls strongly supported my position and had for quite some time, I felt justified in trying to move the government to some meaningful action.

Of course, I was challenged often about running as a Liberal while at the same time frequently criticizing the government. My answer was always the same: "If I thought the Liberal government was doing a perfect job, I would have no need to run for Parliament."

In March we arranged a huge campaign-style rally at the Jubilee Auditorium in Edmonton. All of the Alberta candidates were gathered on the stage with the prime minister in front of a jam-packed auditorium. After Mr. Trudeau's speech, there was a question-and-answer period. The Tories had arranged for one of Marcel Lambert's people to occupy a floor microphone, and the first question for the prime minister was how he liked all the criticism he had been receiving from one of his own candidates, Mel Hurtig. Pierre replied by calling me "a thorn in my flesh," but said he very much hoped I would be elected so I could argue my views in caucus. But the thorn in my flesh comment made all the headlines. As soon as the rally was over, *Toronto Star* columnist David Crane asked if I had planted the question, since it was obvious that Mr. Trudeau's response would get me thousands of extra votes. At the time I was startled by the suggestion, but as the evening wore on and several others made the same one, I realized that with Trudeauphobia rampant across the land, particularly in Alberta, the prime minister had unintentionally given my campaign a big boost. For some reason the Conservatives kept pounding home Trudeau's thorn in my flesh comment. They raised it at every public forum. Each time they did, I got more supporters.

According to the Liberal party headquarters in Ottawa, the prime minister's prairie tour was an unqualified success. "The warmth and enthusiasm with which Prime Minister Trudeau was received in the West has given encouragement and confidence to all Liberal candidates and supporters throughout Canada." Talk about living blindfolded in an impenetrable cocoon! It would have been a pleasure to take whoever wrote those lines on one of my daily door-to-door excursions. Time after time as I knocked on doors, I heard almost the identical words: "Hurtig, I'd *like* to vote for you, but there's no damn way I'm going to vote for that bastard."

In April I again attacked what I saw as a corrupt system of political financing, describing our election laws as "among the least effective of any of the Western democracies" and promising to work for "a much more open political system allowing for greater participation by Canadians of all income levels . . . The average Canadian would be appalled by the manner in which campaign funds are normally obtained." Both Pauline Jewett, who the same week announced her candidacy for the NDP in Ottawa West, and Flora MacDonald, who was running for the Conservatives in Kingston, picked up the same election-reform theme.

At about this time, it was revealed that some wealthy Tories were in secret negotiations to provide Quebec Judge Claude Wagner with a $300,000 fund to challenge Bob Stanfield's leadership.

The Trudeau government's policy on foreign investment was released on May 2. It proved to be even weaker than many of us had feared. I described the government's legislation in my speeches and in the press as a "Mickey Mouse policy" and a "tissue-paper proposal," the disappointing result after sixteen long years of study. I pointed out that France, Great Britain, Japan, Australia, and even countries like Peru and Liberia screened foreign takeovers.

Charles Lynch wrote in his Southam column that I was getting so much mileage out of the issue of foreign ownership in Canada that my political opponents would demand equal time if they could only think of something to say. Marcel Lambert and his Tory colleagues vigorously opposed screening foreign investment. However, despite the contrary image, western Canadians were strongly with me on the issue. Seventy-five percent were in favour of screening; sixty-nine percent said there was enough U.S. investment in Canada already. Only sixteen percent said there should be no screening.

Soon after the government announced its policy, I wrote to Walter Gordon:

> The answer is that Trudeau has betrayed us all. Having per-
> sonally been forced to accept compromise after compromise
> along the way, I cannot accept this ultimate sellout on the
> part of Pierre and his cabinet.
>
> For my own part, I must carefully weigh my political

future. I have been knocking on doors every day and I now think that with a few breaks we could win. We've managed to put together a tremendous campaign team . . . even quite a few Conservatives and some people from the NDP and a large number who have never been involved in politics before. It's a rather remarkable bunch with everything from a few old backroom boys to three football coaches!

Twice during the run-up to the 1972 election campaign, Trudeau announced that he was "browned off" with the "Canada firsters." When the press asked me for a response, I said for my own part I was sick and tired of the Canada lasters who were selling out our country as quickly as they could.

I was not alone in the Liberal party on the issue of foreign ownership. In June 1972, urged on by the Committee for an Independent Canada, thirteen Liberal MPs published an open letter calling for stronger and more comprehensive controls on foreign ownership in Canada, and condemning the government's proposed legislation.

The government ignored the plea. From then, until the federal election later in the year, I was in constant touch with the thirteen MPs and many other Liberal candidates who shared my views. All of them strongly endorsed my tough criticism of the government's token legislation.

The Edmonton West Liberal nomination was contested by me, a young woman, and a man who withdrew shortly before the nominating meeting. Henry Kreisel kindly agreed to nominate me, and Lois Hole agreed to be the seconder. Henry, the distinguished author of *The Rich Man*, was, as both a writer and teacher, one of the most loved and widely respected men I have had the pleasure of knowing. He won many literary awards and later became vice president of the University of Alberta. His list of accomplishments fills pages — all this from a man who fled the Nazis in Austria, came to Canada in 1940 at the age of eighteen, only to find himself held with his father in an internment camp. (Anyone who spoke German was deemed a threat.)

On the night of the nomination Henry gave a superb speech, praising my career as a bookseller, publisher, and activist. Lois Hole, one of the most respected women in Alberta, was very generous. "Mel Hurtig is a man of outstanding ability, sincerity and great humility," she said. "He understands and cares about people. . . . When a man of this calibre offers himself for the public service, we must seize the opportunity and give him our wholehearted support."

In my own speech I spoke again about the need for the reform of democracy, elections, the House of Commons, and other political institutions. I quoted several Canadian politicians and also John F. Kennedy: "Every man can make a difference and every man should try." I said I *would* try to make a difference and I quoted Louis Riel: "One spark can start a prairie fire."

I also spoke about nationalism and other themes that would be constant during the rest of my public life: the dominance of big business in the public decision-making process, excessive corporate concentration, unfair tax policies, poverty, poor fiscal and monetary policy, and then I launched into a strong attack against Marcel Lambert. A new poll had just come out showing that seventy-nine percent of Canadians believed that both politicians and political parties should be compelled to reveal the sources of their political funds, and eighty-four percent said there should be strict limits on campaign funds. I said: "I can tell you that my campaign is not financed by Imperial Oil, Shell Oil, or Gulf Oil. I owe no favours. My campaign books are open for your inspection." I challenged Marcel Lambert to follow my example and make all financial contributions to his campaign public. The packed auditorium gave me a long standing ovation and I won the nomination easily. Now came the hard part.

Ultimately, although I talked about many different issues, my campaign narrowed down to two: the need for a radical reform of democracy and the need for more Canadian control over our own economy. I hammered away at these at every opportunity. Edmonton Liberal lawyer Mike MacDonald said in a press interview: "Every time he speaks we get more volunteers." It was true. But Marcel Lambert derided my campaign of "two little issues."

Increasingly my stand received support from the Liberal caucus in Ottawa. At least four cabinet ministers and some forty Liberal MPs now shared my views.

While Edmonton West had been a Tory stronghold for the past fifteen years, an important factor in our favour was that the voting age had been lowered to eighteen from twenty-one, so we had seven years of young voters who had never voted in a federal election before. Harvey Scott, my wonderful campaign manager, and twenty-two-year-old David Margolus, Harvey's right-hand man, had done a superb job of organizing the lawn-sign campaign, the canvassing, the poll captains, voter transportation, the telephone campaign, and the like.

We were fortunate to have so many terrific volunteers. I would come back in from my door-to-door calls about nine-thirty each evening, and the office would be packed with people, often until midnight, despite the fact that the election was weeks away. Thanks to Harvey (who was also coach of the University of Alberta football team), David, Sandy Watson, and others, the spirit in the campaign headquarters was great. We didn't have the newspaper, radio, and billboard campaigns of our Conservative opponent, but we certainly had the enthusiasm of a big, cohesive, fun-loving campaign team dedicated to the task.

Our campaign literature stressed a much more open political system, less secrecy in government, full disclosure of all political financing, more women in the House of Commons, a fairer tax system, a *real* war on poverty, full-employment policies, a united Canada with stronger representation from the West. And, of course, an end to the growth of foreign ownership. On our brochure, Johnny Wayne and Frank Shuster said: "We'd vote twice for Mel Hurtig!" and Peter Newman, then editor of *Maclean's* magazine, said: "Mel Hurtig is one of those rare Canadians more concerned with issues than politics." Well-respected Edmonton businessman Henry Singer said: "Who says politics doesn't attract dedicated and aggressive young men?" and Hugh MacLennan said: "Mel Hurtig is a man of dynamic imagination who has served this country well."

In 1972 the Edmonton West voting list had a staggering 76,800 names. It was an enormous riding, including all of St. Albert and extending east and north to Griesbach and farther, to the new subdivisions along the city's eastern boundary. All in all, I knocked on some nine thousand doors. And all in all, I encountered numerous negligees (black and otherwise), vicious dogs, and equally vicious Trudeauphobes. On our very first day of canvassing, my campaign companion, Keith Wakefield, was badly bitten by a ferocious little dog and off we went to Emergency.

All those thousands of homes were a great education for me. The terrible poverty and the hungry and poorly dressed children I encountered in several parts of the constituency were in sharp contrast to the relative affluence of much of the riding and the ostentatious wealth in some of it.

The first time I did an open-line radio show, one of the questions was: "Mr. Hurtig, what do you intend to do about the warble flies?" I knew nothing about warble flies and next to nothing about agriculture.

It was part of a lifelong learning process. In later years I frequently spoke to agricultural conventions.

The Liberal party's slogan for the campaign, somehow, was The Land Is Strong. Good Lord! How they could have come up with such an awful slogan given the country's poor economic performance was beyond me. As soon as the billboards and brochures appeared, comedians, cartoonists, and editorial writers across the country, not to mention the Conservatives and the NDP, went to work.

In 1968 Pierre Elliott Trudeau had, in the words of Gordon Donaldson, "arrived like a stone through a stained-glass window." In contrast, in 1972 the candidates were often running on their own, downplaying Trudeau the millstone, and even the Liberal party. Across the country perhaps the only issue that seemed to capture the voters, aside from Pierre Trudeau, was NDP leader David Lewis's "corporate welfare bums" campaign, which accused large corporations of not paying their fair share of taxes while ripping off the people to the tune of hundreds of millions of dollars annually in new lobbied tax concessions, soft government loans, and cash grants.

The Liberals lost much of their own Liberal support. Eric Kierans wrote Trudeau that he intended to vote NDP because of a host of "damaging Liberal economic policies." In a signed editorial, longtime Liberal supporter *Toronto Star* publisher Beland Honderich endorsed the Conservatives, the first time in fifty years the *Star* had backed the Tories. Early in August, I wrote Walter Gordon:

> It seems to me that there are only three possibilities for the future of Canada. One is that we continue as present and that we soon exist as a sovereign nation in name only. Unless one of the two things I'm going to suggest in the following happens, I think this is most likely.
>
> So what are the alternatives? I think there are only two. First is a strong effort to take over the Liberal party as McGovern was successful in doing with the Democratic party. I do not think that this is impossible.
>
> Second is the formation of a new Canadian Party. I am personally in favour of this. Obviously the formation of a new party would take place after the coming election. My feeling is that you and I and Eric and one or two others should get together and talk about this. My reading of the country is that past history and the failure of new parties is not important. My

feeling is that the country is ready for a Canadian Party. My feeling is that the CIC has been effective, but not nearly effective enough.

By the end of August Walter Gordon had told *Maclean's* that "if Pierre Trudeau does not announce some major changes in his policies, I expect some of us will decide, on the day of the election, that we must put the future of our country first."

After a long campaign, it was increasingly clear that I had chosen a very tough riding. Even in 1968, with Trudeaumania at its peak, Lambert had won by a comfortable margin against an excellent and well-respected Liberal candidate, Tevie Miller, and Lambert had won the riding six consecutive times. According to Nick Hills of Southam news service, "Hurtig began as a three-to-one underdog against Lambert, a former House of Commons speaker. Three weeks ago Hurtig had apparently narrowed the gap to only three percent, and now there is an *Edmonton Journal* poll which actually shows him ahead." Nevertheless, Hills went on, if I were to win it would be "perhaps the greatest upset of this 1972 election." Yet again, "In a dull and colourless election, Hurtig is a beacon of individualism."

The riding was the second-most populous west of Toronto. While Edmonton at the time was solidly Tory provincially and while Alberta Premier Peter Lougheed was out campaigning for Lambert, it didn't take long for our well-organized, people-intensive campaign to scare the heck out of our opponents.

Halfway through the campaign, something astonishing happened. At a large University of Alberta forum, Marcel Lambert said that women wouldn't need abortion reform "if they kept their legs together." The audience was momentarily stunned, and then there was a long period of loud, abusive catcalls. My campaign manager Harvey Scott turned to me. "We've just won the election," he said. "I think you might be right," I replied. Neither of us could believe that Lambert had made such a stupid remark. It was all over the media across the country the next morning. Women were outraged and showed up at forums with signs saying, "Lambert is an insult to women," and "Lambert unfit to represent the people of Canada." Speaking in Vegerville, John Diefenbaker tore a strip off Lambert, calling his fellow Conservative's comments "disgusting."

During the campaign the Conservatives spread the rumour that I had sold my bookstores to an American company. At first I ignored the claim, but the Tories persisted. Finally I had to call a press conference to deny the "despicable, unadulterated, complete utter garbage." It was my first taste of gutter politics. There were many more to come.

One of the reasons the Conservatives had to resort to these tactics was the strength of our campaign and the fact that we were setting the agenda for debate. Kevin Peterson of the *Calgary Herald* wrote:

> Mr. Hurtig appears to have Mr. Lambert running harder than ever before. The strong Hurtig campaign has left Mr. Lambert rattled. . . . The Lambert organization is also stunned by the type of people Mr. Hurtig has drawn to his campaign, which now includes more than 500 extra workers. "We expected he would have lots of kids and young people," one of Lambert's key workers said. "But it's the people in their late 20s and 30s, the war babies, that are doing the real work . . . Hurtig's stolen the initiative."

With three weeks to go an *Edmonton Journal* poll showed me leading Lambert thirty-two to twenty-five percent, with the NDP at four percent, but with a huge forty percent undecided. Only in Edmonton West was there "an indication that many of those voting Conservative in 1968 intend to switch to the Liberal candidate this time."

Five days before the election the Liberals had a huge rally in Toronto. According to Trudeau, "the issue is one of confidence in Canada and the Canadian people have the clearest choice that has been given to them in years." He asked for "support for the kind of economic management" his government had provided, somehow ignoring the rise in unemployment since 1968, the sharp increases in inflation, in poverty, and a steadily worsening balance of payments.

Just before the election, *Toronto Star* writer Walter Stewart wrote to me: "This is the damndest election I ever saw . . . with the exception of Himself, there is no issue central to all regions, and if Himself doesn't get the pickle out soon, all you chaps with the red and white signs are going to be in deep trouble."

On October 11 Trudeau wrote to all the candidates: "The campaign is going well for us and I look forward to working with you in the 29th Parliament."

It was not to be. Lambert won Edmonton West by some 8,000 votes. Our headquarters were full of glum campaign workers, and the tears flowed freely. Across the province my fellow Liberal candidates all fell within an hour of the polls closing. When all the votes were counted, I had received the strongest support of any Liberal in Alberta, some 21,000 votes. I pulled 3,000 more votes in the Tory stronghold of Edmonton West than cabinet minister Pat Mahoney managed in Calgary South, 5,000 more than Liberal incumbent Hu Harries in Edmonton, and 8,000 more than Nick Taylor in Calgary. In percentage terms, we led all other Liberals in Alberta by a wide margin, with almost thirty-six percent of the vote. However, as I have said often, before and since, statistics like these are for losers.

It was a slaughter. The Liberal party in Western Canada was nearly wiped out. Most of the western Liberal elite blamed the government for leaning too far to the left. The same Liberals in Western Canada who had supported Mitchell Sharp and opposed Walter Gordon and sought the delay of the introduction of medicare were still in charge of the four western party organizations after the election. Ontario Liberals, meanwhile, blamed Trudeau's lack of action on foreign ownership and reported that many of their supporters had voted NDP to rebuke the prime minister for being far too conservative.

Without question, the prime minister was the biggest factor in the loss. Such statements as his "Why should I sell your wheat?" or "Where's Biafra?" or "Fuddle-duddle" were repeated back to me over and over on the doorsteps. The last thing in the world the electorate wanted was an arrogant politician, and their perception of Trudeau was one of insolent, contemptuous, defiant arrogance.

By the time the last results were in from British Columbia, the Liberals had lost forty-six seats, their majority was gone, and Robert Stanfield and the Conservatives had ended up with 107 Commons seats, only two behind the Liberals. The Liberal representation in the House of Commons from Western Canada had plunged from twenty-eight seats to seven.

Not only were the Alberta federal Liberals wiped out in 1972, but the animosity towards them continued through the federal elections in 1974, 1979, 1980, 1984, and 1988. Not one single Liberal was elected in Alberta until 1993, when hatred for Brian Mulroney was a key factor. In the 1980 election, only two Liberals were elected west of Ontario.

After the election Andy Russell wrote to me: "From an old hand who has fought alone for better environmental management for many years, taking a licking is not something new, but just the same I would have liked to win this fight. The current running against us was just too strong." And so it was.

Now I was faced with many questions about my future. Because of the minority government, it was likely that there would be another election within a year or two. There were offers to contest two different "safe" Toronto seats for the Liberals. The NDP talked to me about another "safe" Ontario seat. Meanwhile, I was under pressure to assume the chairmanship of the Committee for an Independent Canada. Then, too, there was my publishing business, which I had all but ignored for much of a year. I was forty, had tasted politics, found the campaign exhilarating, loved the people I had worked with during the election, but was disgusted by much of what I had seen.

I joined the Liberal party because of Pierre Trudeau, and he was one of the principal reasons I left the Liberal party the following year.

Goodbye to the Liberals

THE TRUDEAU GOVERNMENT, instead of making election reform "a priority," didn't pass legislation responding to the recommendations in the 1966 Barbeau Royal Commission report until 1974. During the six years I was in the Liberal party I had pressed the prime minister and the government hard on the issue. Poll after poll showed that I was on the right track. Consistently an overwhelming majority of Canadians, mostly in the eighty percent range, supported full disclosure of election revenues and expenses, and tough limits on campaign spending.

As you already have gathered, watching the patronage system at work in the party disgusted me. While the press reported it from time to time, no one seemed to make it an important issue. Most members of the press gallery in Ottawa seemed to take it for granted, something to be accepted. The way patronage worked was simple. Of course there was never anything in writing, but almost everyone who had been in the party for even a relatively short period realized that when you made donations, you would get on the lists, and when you received government work, you were expected to pay up again. And when you paid up again, you were in line for more government work, or perhaps a board or bench appointment.

There was an irony in all this for the Liberal party. Not only did patronage create a corrupt system of rewards, it also robbed the party of many of its most active and experienced workers, who now headed for the bench or for one of the long list of government appointments.

In any event I had had enough. When I made my decision to leave the party in August of 1973, I wrote to Keith Davey:

> I have many good friends in the Liberal Party, and there are many Liberals I admire and respect. With others from across Canada for six years I tried to work within the Party for the ideas and policies we believe in. For two years I served on the National Policy Committee, I chaired the Task Force on International Affairs and held local and provincial Party offices. I worked very hard, learned a great deal, met some fine friends and have few regrets. But I did not join the Liberal Party for social reasons.
>
> Any modest hopes that I might have had to work successfully for new policies within the Liberal Party have been clearly misplaced. Status quo reigns and status quo I cannot accept.
>
> I would like to thank you for your own support and encouragement. Personally I wish you the very best and hope we might continue to have a friendly relationship.
>
> Keith, I would like to urge you in the strongest possible terms to press for prompt passage of the proposed election-expenses bill. It's by far the most important legislation the Trudeau years have produced and it would be a tragedy if it went the same route as the tax reform, the competition act and foreign ownership legislation.

The Liberal party I left was still dominated by an entrenched party hierarchy, an establishment of wealthy entrepreneurs and lawyers, tired senators, patronage-hungry party hacks, aging backroom boys, and MPs who rarely had much impact on public policy. That said, some of the finest Canadians I have ever met were loyal, dedicated, altruistic Liberals. Unfortunately they were never in control of the party in the years that I was a member.

Patronage was, of course, hardly exclusive to the Liberals. The Conservative party, when in power in Ottawa, had always been at least as corrupt in this respect. And during the Mulroney years, as has been well documented, it descended to new depths of impropriety.

In 1974 Keith Davey tried very hard to get me to run in the

Toronto riding of Don Valley. In 1968 Liberal Bob Kaplan had beaten Dalton Camp in the riding by some 5,000 votes. In 1972 Conservative James Gillies beat Kaplan by 6,000. Keith's wife, Dorothy, was sure that if I ran in Don Valley I would win. Keith felt we would need about $50,000, and if I ran the party would put up much of the money and there would be no trouble raising the rest. Davey said there would be no difficulty getting the support of the *Toronto Star* and he would be willing to put a full-time organizer to work the next day. Dorothy said she thought we could have the services of Royce Frith for the campaign and many others. Keith said it was a guaranteed cabinet seat.

I was very grateful to both Keith and Dorothy for their confidence. But I could see no way that I could return to the Liberal party or accept money from them.

Trudeau's Failed Promises, Missed Opportunities

WITHOUT QUESTION, Pierre Trudeau is the most charismatic man I have ever met and certainly one of the most brilliant. Compared to the men and women who followed him as prime minister, he was a giant. I doubt that I have ever encountered more than a handful of men who possessed such a sharp, analytical mind. Curiously it was also a mind that was not as constructive as one would have expected.

Despite the prevalent image to the contrary, Trudeau's economics, by the time he arrived in the House of Commons in November 1965, were conservative, and he was moving gradually but steadily farther to the right. Whatever other talents and knowledge he possessed, in both cases considerable, he knew relatively little of the people and values of Canada outside the Montreal-Ottawa-Toronto triangle. He came to Ottawa primarily to see that French-Canadians had a fair opportunity to play their deserving role in the nation, and his preoccupation was national unity and constitutional reform. In 1971 Walter Stewart wrote in *Shrug, Trudeau in Power* that Trudeau's government had been more conservative than any since that of William Lyon

Mackenzie King "and less successful, in terms of the mandate it received, than its much-harried, much-abused predecessor, led by Lester B. Pearson." He went on to say that under Trudeau, we were more than ever distant from anything that could be called a Just Society. "The economy is neither prosperous nor fairly distributed; Parliament had not been so much reformed as emasculated; the politics of participation has turned out to be, not to put too fine a point on the matter, a fraud . . . while our economy and national integrity are still on the auction block to the United States."

After the gruelling years of wrangling between John Diefenbaker and Lester Pearson, the nation was crying out for strong leadership. Trudeau promised new politics, yet he never delivered. Nevertheless, I believe that any objective assessment of his remarkable career would have to conclude that he was one of Canada's outstanding prime ministers.

Trudeau joined the Liberal party and was elected to Parliament in 1965. Three years later he was prime minister, much to the shock of the right-wing Liberal elite who had dominated the party after Walter Gordon's departure. At the 1968 leadership convention Judy LaMarsh was overheard pleading with Paul Hellyer: "Don't let the bastard win it, Paul. . . . He isn't even a Liberal."

In the 1968 federal election the Liberals swept to victory on a wave of Trudeaumania, winning 155 seats in the House of Commons, while the Conservatives dropped to 72, the NDP 22, and the Créditistes 14.

Soon after the election I received a warm thank-you letter from the new prime minister, saying that my efforts "were instrumental" in his success and promising ongoing and increased consultations and involvement. It was a generous and cordial letter, which I appreciated. The following month Ralph MacMillan and I were invited, with a handful of others from across the country, to dinner at 24 Sussex Drive. It was a pleasant, interesting evening.

In August of 1968 I was at 24 Sussex again for a meeting with the prime minister. Late in the conversation I asked him if it was fair for me to ask what he intended to do about the recently released Watkins report on foreign ownership. Trudeau paused, half mumbled one or two inarticulate sentences, paused again, and said, "No, Mel, in fact, it's not fair for you to ask at this time." I looked at him and he looked at me; we both cleared our throats and that was the end of it. It was also the beginning of my doubts that he would bring in adequate legislation to deal with the problem of foreign ownership.

I must stop here and tell you a little story. During our earlier talk in the Chateau Lacombe, Trudeau had asked me to advise him on matters relating to the plight of Canada's native peoples. I'd felt greatly honoured. It was the first time a prime minister had ever asked me for any advice, and it was an area of concern I had much knowledge of. I took the request very seriously and went to work, skipping my planned summer holiday on Vancouver Island with my wife and children and cutting short a long-planned hiking expedition in the Rockies. Over a period of four months I worked on average six or seven hours a day on the document, which I couriered to Trudeau's "Personal and Confidential" attention early in September.

About a month later I visited the prime minister's office on the third floor of the Centre Block. Trudeau greeted me warmly, closed the door to his office, and we settled in for a talk. Soon I asked him what he had thought of the report.

"What report?"

"The report you asked me to do on Canada's Indians."

"Mel, I haven't seen it. When did you send it?"

I explained that he should have had it a month ago. He called his assistant Gordon Gibson into his office and asked him what had happened to the report I sent in. Gibson didn't know, but promised to find out. A few minutes later, Gibson was back in the office. "Prime Minister," he said, "Mel's report was sent to the Department of Indian Affairs."

The very first line of my report called for the abolition of the Department of Indian Affairs. Before Trudeau ever saw my document on its own, the department had prepared a hundred-page attack on my report, which was sent to the prime minister, along with a copy of my document.

Just after I left the prime minister's office that day, Trudeau came rushing down the hallway calling to me. "Mel, Marc wants to see you before you leave."

I had only a vague idea who "Marc" was, but was soon ushered into Principal Secretary Marc Lalonde's office. We sat across the desk from each other, exchanging small talk for a few minutes. Then Lalonde came to the point. "Mel," he said, "who would you like to see appointed chief justice of the Trial Division of the Supreme Court of Alberta?"

"Pardon?"

He repeated the question while I sat there with a stunned look on my face. At last I said, "Marc, I'm sorry, but I'm just not capable of answering such a question."

Lalonde looked at me as if I was a creature from another planet.

When I walked back down the marble corridor, it was clear to me that I had had the opportunity of at least helping to choose the next Trial Division chief justice. The more I thought about it, the more I was appalled that I should have ever been asked such a question. To say I was politically naïve would be a colossal understatement.

In 1969 I again visited 24 Sussex Drive and was surprised to see the near-empty bookshelves in the library. At the next meeting of the board of directors of the Canadian Booksellers Association, I suggested that the CBA make an annual presentation of new Canadian books to the 24 Sussex library. For a few years after that, leading booksellers from across Canada made the presentation on behalf of the CBA, most of them quite thrilled to see the prime minister's residence and meet Trudeau at the reception that followed.

In May 1958 Trudeau had written in *Cité libre* about "the hold of the U.S.A. government" on Canadian public policy because of the heavy degree of control of the Canadian economy by U.S. corporations. He'd said that

> in key sectors of the Canadian economy non-residents are in a position to make decisions contrary to the well-being of Canadians . . . Foreigners will decide if our oil wells are to be worked or closed, if our ore is to be transformed here or elsewhere, if our factories are to be automated or not, if our products are to be put on the world market or not, or if our workers are to be free to exercise their right of association or not. Foreigners will decide . . . and will collect the profits.
>
> Either we shall passively suffer our situation of economic domination, and then it would be better to be annexed out-right to the United States, rather than to be a colony exploited without limit. Or else, we shall intervene vigorously by adopting economic policies. . . .

But was Trudeau really an economic nationalist? Hardly. Not long after his election in 1968, the PMO began to work hard to suppress the nationalists in the party. Trudeau so disliked the eternally loyal Herb Gray's nationalism that he removed him from the cabinet and shunted him off to the back benches in 1974, where he languished for more than five years.

Trudeau's upbringing and education in Quebec and abroad had

made him into an internationalist, and he despised Quebec nationalism. His lack of knowledge of the rest of the country weakened the possibility that he would embrace pan-Canadian economic nationalism. Moreover, nationalism for Trudeau meant the kind of conflict that had led to two world wars. According to Trudeau, "The glue of nationalism must become as obsolete as the theory of the Divine Right of Kings."

Until Trudeau's "resurrection" in 1980 the nationalists in the Liberal party had little influence. Nationalist legislation during the first twelve Trudeau years came primarily as a result of pressure from the NDP during the minority government after the 1972 election. Meanwhile, the bureaucracy in Ottawa was becoming increasingly continentalist.

As might be expected, Trudeau disliked people who criticized him. After I left the party, I stepped up my criticism. In a talk to a large crowd at the University of Alberta, I again went after the prime minister for his failure to take meaningful action to curb the growth of foreign ownership and foreign control in Canada. The talk, entitled *The Defeat of Canadian Nationalism*, pointed out that more of the same in the future would mean "Canada will haemorrhage to death; your children will have a backbreaking debt to pay." It was the first of many warnings I would give in years to follow about Canada's growing internal and external debts.

It wasn't long before I began hearing from the prime minister's office that they were displeased with my criticisms. In some instances the reaction was volcanic, but I wasn't concerned, since I had little confidence in the judgement of most of the overblown functionaries in the PMO.

While the business press and his political and philosophical opponents accused Trudeau of being ignorant about economics, nothing could be further from the truth. There has not been a prime minister before or since with better training in economic theory. Of Canadian prime ministers, he easily had by far the best understanding of monetarism and Keynesian theory. However, while he studied if not mastered the many cabinet briefs dealing with economic matters, he rarely demonstrated economic leadership in cabinet. In fact, he often seemed uninterested. Certainly he seemed to have little concept of how he wanted Canadian-American economic relations to change or evolve in the future.

Along with increasing American domination of the economy came "cultural baggage" and pressure relating to foreign policy. Yet the

Trudeau governments took few aggressive steps relating to Canadian cultural sovereignty, and the major foreign-policy review he commissioned after he became prime minister somehow managed to virtually ignore the United States.

Someone who worked closely in Ottawa with Trudeau for years described the prime minister's tepid approach to economic policy:

> While he spent astonishing long hours working at his job, economics was not a priority, although he did pay attention.
>
> Yes, Eric Kierans is right; he was impatient with economics. His entourage — Joel Bell, Jim Coutts, Jack Austin et al. — were highly suspicious of Ottawa's economic establishment and even paranoid about Finance. With some justification. Finance ministers Macdonald, Turner, etc., whatever their predilections, were moved inevitably to Finance's straight and narrow.
>
> To his credit, the Thursday cabinet meetings often went on into the late afternoon and evening. The table was always piled with books and books of briefing documents . . . a staggering number from the PMO and PCO [Privy Council Office] and the departments. Pierre liked to go to bed at ten. But he would always arrive Thursday morning having, beyond doubt, read them all. It was intimidating. He often knew the briefs better than the minister who was presenting.

No one whose opinion I respect has suggested that Trudeau did not understand economic theory. But as Duncan Cameron has written, "The younger Trudeau spent much time giving seminars on economic problems to trade unionists, yet he ended up a prisoner of neoclassical economics."

Nor was Trudeau preoccupied with issues of tax reform. After Lester Pearson, under heavy pressure from big business, had abandoned Kenneth Carter's recommendations for progressive tax reform, the Liberal party showed little interest in reviving the debate and antagonizing their financial backers, especially with the party's financing in such a sorry state.

When Finance Minister Edgar Benson produced a relatively modest white paper on tax reform, once again the business community strongly attacked the proposals. Benson et al. were socialists if not communists, and the Liberal government was planning a massive confiscation of wealth. Entrepreneurs deserved all their tax holidays, their special rates, incentives, and write-offs, and woe to the politician who wanted to change even a dollar of the enormous tax concessions so long entrenched in the system.

Trudeau claimed that the government would not be bullied by threats from the business community. But, in fact, most of the reform measures Benson proposed were withdrawn. If friends and supporters and financial backers such as Paul Desmarais and Charles Bronfman explain to you the benefits of a tax system that assists with wealth accumulation over dinner or at their Palm Beach estate where you are their guest, there is little likelihood you will seek to antagonize them.

Whatever Trudeau's concerns may have been about the Department of Finance in his early years in Ottawa, after an initial period of apprehension and estrangement, Finance progressively became more powerful in the Ottawa decision-making process, in fields of social and other policy, and in resource development and all other areas of economic significance.

Walter Gordon and Simon Reisman had battled each other for years in Ottawa. Now Trudeau appointed the continentalist Reisman to the crucially important position of deputy minister of finance.

By January of 1970 relations between Trudeau and me had deteriorated. I could still see him when I wanted, but we were both growing impatient with each other. On January 7 I wrote to him:

> I believe, Prime Minister, that you may be missing the most important thing that is happening now in our country. Almost everywhere, there is a new sense of Canada; not chauvinism, not xenophobia, not isolationism so much as a genuine sense of purpose, confidence and identity.
>
> Yet, when you tell Canadians that the limits of our independence may only be in the range of ten to fifteen percent, many or most Canadians are saying in response that that isn't good enough; we must take steps to retrieve our independence.

I went on to say how disappointed many of us had become in his failure to see that participatory democracy in the Liberal party was more than a slogan, that patronage still dominated the party and worked diametrically in opposition to democracy, and that "young Canadians are not only *not* joining the Liberal party now, they are leaving by the thousands. Ask the president of the Canadian Student

Liberals. They are leaving because the system makes meaningful participation largely an illusion." At the end of the letter I apologized for the tone. "Will you remember the spirit in which my comments are intended? You said to me at Harrison, 'Mel, you are supposed to help *before* we make policies, not after.' It seems to me that the best way I can help is to be as frank and honest as possible, and this is what I have done."

On March 6, 1971, the headline in the *Toronto Daily Star* reported the marriage of Pierre Trudeau and Margaret Sinclair. Below it was an equally large headline: "Gordon predicts tough laws to halt U.S. domination." According to the *Star* reporter:

> The federal government will bring in tough legislation to stop the growth of U.S. domination of Canada's economy and keep Canada independent for at least another 100 years, Walter Gordon predicted yesterday. Gordon . . . said the government is too aware of the public mood to take any other course.
>
> Earlier, at a McMaster University teach-in, Edmonton book publisher Mel Hurtig said he was confident that a report on foreign ownership being prepared by Revenue Minister Herb Gray would take a "real tough" approach. But Hurtig, a foreign policy advisor for the Liberal party, told the spirited student-faculty gathering that he feared the government would "emasculate" the recommendations in the report.

So, as he had been in the past, Walter was much more optimistic than I about Pierre Trudeau and the Liberal party bringing in the type of legislation we both felt was urgently needed. And from 1968 to 1972 the prime minister's arrogance, uncaring image, the deteriorating economy, the downgrading of Parliament all resulted in a substantial loss of respect. In Western Canada, well before the national energy program, a substantial feeling was growing that Trudeau didn't know or care about the West.

After the disastrous 1972 election Peter Newman wrote in *Maclean's*: "What happened to the magic? Or more important, what happened to the man? Did he ever possess the qualities we endowed him with? Had he been altered by power? Why didn't he turn into the leader we had been yearning for and so many of us were sure he really was?"

And what was Newman's answer to these questions? Trudeau, he said, "wouldn't listen to his critics in the Commons. He paid no heed to the MPs in his own caucus. He stifled the dissenters in his cabinet. He ignored the spoken and written pleas of citizens who sought to focus his attention on their concerns." Newman went on: "As the circle of isolation grew around him, it was almost as though he was alienated . . . from the very purpose that had catapulted him into power . . . surrounded by courtiers whose chatter he mistook for the sound of reality."

Many of the key men around Trudeau were educated abroad, had spent much of their working lives outside Canada, came from well-to-do Ottawa and Montreal families, and, in Newman's words, "treated people who existed outside the Ottawa-Montreal axis as though they belonged in colonial outposts . . . [They were] an elite with little obligation to spend time on or with lesser people."

Amazingly, prior to the 1972 election, one of Trudeau's key right-hand men, Jim Davey, forecast that the Liberals would win 172 seats. Another, Dave Thomson, head of the prime minister's western regional desk, forecast 170 seats. Was it any wonder Pierre Trudeau was out of touch with a reality that was obvious to so many others?

On June 9, 1974, the prime minister wrote to me. This time the letter was to "Dear Mr. Hurtig." Fair enough. In four pages he defended his record relating to foreign ownership. The letter could have just as easily been written by a Mitchell Sharp or a Paul Hellyer, or for that matter, Robert Stanfield. For the most part it was full of clichés and rhetoric. The letter listed various steps the government had taken over the past six years to stem the growth of foreign ownership and promised more announcements in the future. But it entirely missed the key point I had often raised with Trudeau in relation to the government's previous legislation. Foreign corporations in Canada, which already dominated dozens of key industries, were still allowed to expand in a virtually unlimited manner. While the government was at last somewhat concerned with the entry of *new* foreign investment, the huge tumour already inside the national body was growing unchecked every day.

On May 22, 1979, a disgruntled electorate opted for a Joe Clark minority government. The Tories won 136 seats, the Liberals fell to 114, the NDP won 26, and Social Credit gained 6. Trudeau and the Liberals lost for several reasons. First, Trudeau had been prime minister for eleven years, and the electorate had grown disillusioned with his leadership. Moreover, the Liberals had formed the government of

Canada since the election of Lester Pearson in 1963. After sixteen years the voters wanted a change. Second, Trudeau's perceived arrogance had once again turned off many who had previously been attracted to him. As well, many Liberals felt betrayed by what they saw as an abandonment of principles, at best, and deception, at worst. And third, there was an ever-growing perception across the land that Trudeau and crew had no idea about how the Canadian economy should be managed, that their economic policies were ad hoc and without consistency, innovation, or direction.

After the election defeat Pierre Trudeau pondered his future. Late in 1979 he announced that he would resign as Liberal leader. But the new Joe Clark government was weak, ill prepared, and inexperienced. It lasted only seven months before it was brought down in the House of Commons on a sloppily prepared-for vote on John Crosbie's first budget. The defeat came only three weeks after Trudeau announced his retirement; the prospects of a new election and pressure from Jim Coutts, Keith Davey, and Allan MacEachen changed his mind. Some three months after his retirement, he was once again prime minister.

This time, he came back as a resurrected Canadian nationalist, promising a much stronger Foreign Investment Review Agency and a national industrial strategy. In a piece in *Today* magazine, Toronto writer Heather Robertson suggested that although "Trudeau once opposed nationalism, now he sees it as a 'practical necessity.'" Robertson summarized what was to become a brief period of "new nationalism" in the Liberal party:

> The Liberal Party of Canada, the party of reciprocity, free trade and internationalism, the party of C.D. Howe, who sold our economy to foreigners cheap, and of Lester Person, who nestled us under the wing of the American eagle, the party that crucified Canada's gentle patriot, Walter Gordon, and humiliated his disciple Herb Gray, transformed itself into the champions of Canadian nationalism.
>
> The born-again Liberal Party, wrapped in the flag and flourishing the most aggressive national policy since Sir John A. Macdonald . . . galumphed triumphantly back into power. . . . Nationalism, once condemned by the Liberals, is now respectable, even chic.

And what about the new Pierre Trudeau, who had been "Canada's fiercest critic of nationalism"? After his reelection he advised: "I am not adverse to interventionism to protect the public good . . . there is a point at which too much foreign investment becomes enough."

According to Robertson, "The Liberals had stumbled on the political secret of the century: the Canadian people wanted to remain Canadian. Independence now reflected the majority opinion; nationalism had become the conventional wisdom."

The Committee for an Independent Canada had played an important role in helping to produce "the majority opinion." Amazed as we were by the change in Trudeau, we were delighted, though wary.

Despite the win in the 1980 election, the Liberal party itself was a mess. Soon after the election, the polls began to show a decline in Liberal support, dropping below thirty percent. Financially the party was sinking deeper and deeper into debt. Soon party morale had taken another dive, and the focus of animosity was the prime minister's office. Meanwhile, in cabinet, grateful ministers who had been so quickly and so unexpectedly returned to power, provided no challenges for Trudeau. Many of his strongest opponents had left and few had the courage, the talent, or the desire to enter even into private policy disputes with the leader.

Party discipline and patronage kept the rest in line. Backbenchers were fortunate if they had a few minutes to say their piece in caucus once a week. Dissent was rarely tolerated, and Trudeau's aggressive, analytical debating style frightened cabinet ministers, backbenchers, and party officials alike. Activism in the party virtually ceased entirely. The idea of participatory democracy vanished. The idea of policy conferences was considered a joke.

And once again the Liberal party changed. During the last years of the Trudeau government, the continentalists were again the dominant force. Herb Gray and Lloyd Axworthy found themselves constantly losing cabinet debates to the likes of Donald Johnston and the new trade minister, Ed Lumley, a strong free-trade supporter. At the same time, poor fiscal and monetary policies produced larger and larger deficits and an accumulated debt over $170-billion. Liberal popularity across the country fell even further.

Late in his career as prime minister, Trudeau embarked on his international peace initiative, travelling the world, warning of the dangers of the increasing proliferation of nuclear weapons. Ronald Reagan was angry with the Canadian "peacenik," and Margaret Thatcher was dismissive. In the rest of Europe and in India there was little response. The Chinese showed no interest at all. Throughout this period I thought of how very disappointed so many of us were, how surprised I had been, when, despite his deep-felt beliefs on the subject and his clear understanding of all the reasons he should not do so, Pierre Trudeau nevertheless buckled under American pressure and agreed to test the cruise missile. This was the man who in 1968 had suggested that he would soon be ready to channel the defence budget into helping Canada's Indians and the world's poor. Instead, that budget had spiralled from less than $2-billion to over $7-billion in 1983.

And how did Washington react to Trudeau's 1983 peace initiative? U.S. Undersecretary of State for Political Affairs Laurence Eagleburger described it as "akin to pot-induced behaviour by an erratic lefty."

What did Trudeau accomplish besides the long-overdue integration of Francophones into the federal bureaucracy, greater bilingualism in Ottawa and across the nation, and his efforts towards national unity? Certainly the patriation of the Constitution and the Charter of Rights were important. His strong leadership was the decisive factor in the defeat of the separatists in the 1980 referendum and was a key factor in the defeat of the Meech Lake and Charlottetown accords. As well, his government made progressive changes to the justice system and to immigration policies.

But while he battled the premiers and his fellow Québécois in their never-ending efforts to take more and more power for themselves away from Ottawa, he was blind to the continuing erosion of national sovereignty that came with the American domination of the Canadian economy. When American businessmen visited the prime minister's office, Trudeau often made it clear that he was "not an economic nationalist." Only when his government was in trouble, and when the polls showed he could expect strong public support, did he take steps to curtail the growth of foreign ownership.

Ultimately Trudeau's anti-Quebec nationalism overwhelmed his ability to understand the powerful threat that excessive foreign ownership and economic integration with the United States represented. His preoccupation with the Constitution and national unity dominated his actions, and years later he was mostly silent during the crucial national debate about free trade in the period 1985 to 1988.

When on February 29, 1984, Pierre Trudeau again announced his decision to resign, he had been prime minister longer than any prime minister other than John A. Macdonald and William Lyon

Mackenzie King, and had served longer in office than any other western leader of the same period.

The Trudeau years left Canada in poor economic condition. Some one and a half million Canadians were unemployed, four million men, women, and children were living below the poverty line, the annual federal deficit had reached $35-billion, adding to the rapid buildup of debt, the trade deficit in labour-intensive finished products was increasing sharply, while Canada's international-services deficit continued to escalate and the secondary sector of our economy had been operating at well below capacity for many years. One 1984 study showed that Canada had finished fortieth among the nations of the world in its economic performance during the nine-year period 1974–1982.

The first few times I met Pierre Trudeau, I had the impression that he was a shy man. His image was the opposite: a straight-on, thumbs-in-the-belt-loops speaker, aggressive, a swinger, a tough guy. He was indeed all these things. But like many men whose image is one of arrogance, there was another side to the man, especially during the 1960s and 1970s. Once I took my four awestruck young daughters into his Centre Block office to meet him. When we came out, I asked them what they'd thought. Almost in unison they said: "Gee, Dad, how come he's so shy?"

He is certainly the most private man I have ever met, rarely confiding in friends, austere in most of his male personal relationships, yet carefree and abandoned with very young women. Many of his supposedly close friends and colleagues were never once invited to dine at 24 Sussex, nor at his home in Montreal.

He is also one of the most gracious and elegant human beings I have ever encountered.

III

Deeper into the Fray

Something Is Going on Out There

IN 1965 GEORGE GRANT said that matters had reached the point where it was now too late to hope for an independent Canada. The next year, in *A Choice for Canada*, Walter Gordon said that unless important decisions were made very quickly, it would indeed be impossible to ever turn the country around.

In 1968 my publishing house released *The New Romans*, which the *Calgary Herald* called "probably the worst collection of Canadian writing ever to appear under the covers of one book published in Canada." The *Ottawa Citizen* had a different view, saying, "*The New Romans* is probably the most important Canadian book published in this country during the past decade. It could well change the course of the future of this country." *The New Romans* was a strong warning about further Canadian integration with the United States.

In his 1968 book, *The Discipline of Power*, former U.S. under-secretary of state George Ball wrote:

> Canada, I have long believed, is fighting a rearguard action against the inevitable.... I wonder, for example, if the Canadian people will be prepared indefinitely to accept, for the psychic satisfaction of maintaining a separate national and political identity, a per capita income less than three-fourths of ours. The struggle is bound to be a difficult one and I suspect over the years, a losing one.... Sooner or later commercial impera-tives will bring about free movement of all goods back and forth across our long border; and when that occurs, or even before it does, it will become unmistakably clear that countries with economies so inextricably intertwined must also have free

movement of the other vital factors of production — capital, services and labor. The result will inevitably be substantial economic integration, which will require for its full realization a progressively expanding area of common political decision.

Mitchell Sharp, Walter Gordon's longtime opponent, became finance minister after Gordon's resignation late in 1965. Gordon agreed to return to the cabinet, but only after Lester Pearson consented to a new government task force that would specifically study foreign direct investment in Canada and its impact on the Canadian economy. The *Watkins Report*, published in 1968, was the first comprehensive study of the activities of foreign multinationals in Canada, and it clearly demonstrated the negative impact of excessive foreign ownership and control.

Later, in 1970, Montreal economist Kari Levitt produced her important book about foreign ownership, *Silent Surrender*. *Montreal Star* associate editor Boyce Richardson wrote: "If the facts revealed by Mrs. Levitt in her book were generally known to the Canadian public, there would be an explosion of anger which would change the social framework in this country." My *own* anger had begun long before, as I watched more and more of Canada being bought up by foreigners every day, every week, every month, and in increasing amounts every year.

The late 1960s and early 1970s were described as a period of "new nationalism" in Canada. There was a great deal of student activism on the campuses, a positive feeling that meaningful political change could be achieved, the feeling that people should and could take charge of their own futures. The atmosphere of self-determination and community participation had, in the words of University of Toronto economist Abe Rotstein, "a compelling quality." It was also a time of war in Vietnam, of the shootings at Kent State University, of the atrocities at My Lai, and of increasing violence in U.S. inner cities.

On February 3, 1970, Abe Rotstein and then *Toronto Star* editor-in-chief Peter Newman invited Walter Gordon to lunch at the King Edward Hotel. (Ironically, in those days, the hotel was American owned.) By the time lunch was over, the idea of a new national organization to promote Canadian economic and cultural independence had been born. The first important planning meeting of the Committee for an Independent Canada was held in the third-floor offices of a nondescript building in downtown Toronto in the spring of 1970. Walter Gordon chaired the meeting. Among those present were Rotstein, *Le Devoir* editor Claude Ryan, Jack McClelland, Keith Davey, advertising executive Jerry Goodis, activist Dorothy Petrie, Bill Kilbourn, architect John Parkin, and lawyer Eddie Goodman. It was the first time I had met many of them.

By the early fall, plans were well under way for a national campaign to bring the issue of foreign domination of the Canadian economy to the attention of more Canadians and to put pressure on the Trudeau government for legislative action. But the October crisis in Quebec intervened, just as the new national organization and campaign were about to be launched.

By early 1971, the CIC was active across the country. Meetings were attracting good crowds and lots of volunteers. Membership was growing and the press was beginning to pay attention. Richard Nixon's hostile and aggressive economic policies angered millions of Canadians and bolstered support for the committee.

Just how bad was foreign ownership in Canada when the CIC was formed? Of the 362 companies in Canada with assets of $25-million or more, seventy-six percent were foreign-controlled. No other major developed country had foreign control exceeding sixteen percent. Some sixty percent of all manufacturing and mining in Canada was controlled by foreigners, ninety-nine percent of petroleum refining, eighty-three percent of the oil-and-gas industry, eighty-five percent of the primary metal-smelting-and-refining industries, ninety-seven percent of the automobile industry, seventy-eight percent of the chemical industry, seventy-seven percent of the electrical apparatus industry, ninety-six percent of the computer industry, ninety-two percent of the aircraft-and-aircraft-parts industry, and so on, and so on.

And every single year hundreds of Canadian companies were being taken over by nonresidents, mostly Americans: sweater manufacturers, hockey-stick companies, distilleries, movie theatres, funeral homes, forestry companies, dairies, pipe manufacturers, magazine distributors, bus lines, snowmobile companies, burglar-alarm firms — you name it. By 1969, foreign insurance companies took forty-two percent of all insurance premiums in Canada. This percentage was the highest of nineteen countries surveyed in a Swiss study. Second, behind Canada, stood Pakistan at twenty-four percent.

In November of 1970 I spent more than three hours with Revenue Minister Herb Gray, who had been charged by the prime minister with the job of producing a report for the government on the question of foreign investment, ownership, and control. I came away from the meeting reassured and convinced that Gray's report would be at least as tough as that of the all-party External Affairs committee headed by Ian Wahn had been. I reported to my colleagues that "the homework has been done and the conclusions will be valid ones."

Gordon, who had become the CIC's first honorary chairman, intended the organization to concentrate on the single issue — a tough screening agency whose impact would be to stem the growth of foreign ownership. In his 1977 book *A Political Memoir* he wrote: "It was not intended originally to keep the CIC going for any extended period." The press conference that announced the formation of the new committee was held at the Granite Club in Toronto on September 17, 1970. At the end of the meeting a reporter pointed out that, quite appropriately, we had been meeting in the Colonial Room.

Many well-known Canadians became members and also served on the CIC's national steering committee. Along with those I have already mentioned, the list included: artists Harold Town and Molly Lamb Bobac; former Conservative cabinet minister Alvin Hamilton; Doris Anderson, the editor of *Chatelaine* magazine; John Archer, the head of the Regina campus of the University of Saskatchewan, and Henry Hicks, president of Dalhousie; Lloyd Axworthy, who was the director of the Institute of Urban Studies at the University of Winnipeg; authors Pierre Berton, Earle Birney, Al Purdy, Dorothy Livesay, and Alden Nowlan; native leader Harold Cardinal; Donald Chant, head of Pollution Probe; broadcasters Adrienne Clarkson, Betty Kennedy, Max Ferguson, Jack Webster, and Laurier LaPierre; Ed Finn, the trade union activist; *Toronto Star* publisher Beland Honderich; Edmonton surgeon Dr. Harry Hyde; Pauline Jewett, director of Canadian Studies at Carleton; Liberal senators Harry Hays and Maurice Lamontagne; Judy LaMarsh; Stan Little, president of the Canadian Union of Public Employees; authors Hugh MacLennan, Eric Nicol, Robin Mathews, Christina Newman, and Farley Mowat; historians Hugh Dempsey, W.L. Morton, and Kenneth McNaught; Allan O'Brien, the mayor of Halifax; lawyers Yves Fortier and Michael Meighen; Eamon Park, the national past president of the NDP; political scientists Norman Ward, Denis Smith, and Hugh Thorburn; Jack Biddell, president of the Clarkson Company; businessmen Lloyd Shaw, Jake Moore, Malim Harding, and Leon Weinstein.

And in the true tradition of Sir John A. Macdonald's Conservative party, there were lots of Red Tories involved, including Flora

MacDonald, farmer Bruce Pallett, and philosopher George Grant. Among the Conservative members of Parliament who joined later were Ron Atkey, Jim Gillies, Terry O'Connor, Reginald Stackhouse, Paul Dick, Gordon Fairweather, Robert Coates, Joe Clark, Angus Maclean, and David Macdonald.

One of the key founding members was the energetic Edwin A. Goodman. He had been vice president of the Ontario Progressive Conservative Association for seven years and of the National Conservative Association for ten. He was the Tory national campaign chairman in the 1965 and 1968 federal elections, and national chairman of organization from 1968 to 1971.

Jack McClelland was named first chairman of the new organization, while Claude Ryan accepted the responsibility for organizing the CIC in Quebec. However, when the FLQ crisis broke out, the whole Quebec organization fell apart. Ryan resigned from the CIC a year later.

While those who first organized the committee had limited objectives and limited expectations, few of those who joined (including me) realized this. It wasn't long before the members were looking for broader long-term goals, and a permanent democratic structure of decision-making.

The CIC had some trade-union support, but also major opposition. We raised the issue of autonomy for Canadian unions, and several of the big union leaders were outraged. The steelworkers, in particular, were very hostile. Of course, the term "international union" was a euphemism. More correctly, international unions were branches of American unions, headquartered in the U.S. One national union president from Ottawa told me: "Mel, I can't even order a typewriter ribbon for my office unless I get permission from Cleveland."

In October 1979, even when asked a grossly unfair loaded question by Gallup — would you be willing to accept "a big reduction in your standard of living as the price of buying back control of foreign-owned industries?" — forty-six percent of Canadians said yes, and only thirty-two percent said no. As Sandy Ross wrote in the *Financial Post*, "Apparently an astonishing number of Canadians are willing to make sacrifices to remain Canadian. . . . Something new is happening in this country. The people who run it would be smart to listen."

Perhaps in Name Only

A T THE LIBERAL PARTY of Canada's 1970 national policy conference, the following resolutions were approved by lopsided margins:

- we must repatriate more control of our economy;
- we must gain majority control of our industries;
- we must prevent Canadian capital being used to finance increased foreign control;
- we must ensure that foreign corporations operating in Canada follow guidelines for good corporate citizenship;
- we must require full disclosure with respect to the operations of foreign-owned corporations in Canada.

But in case there was any doubt in anyone's mind after reading his *Lament for a Nation*, George Grant made it clear, at a McMaster teach-in in 1971, who the real culprits had been all along: "The Liberals have been selling our Canada for the last thirty years." And so they had been. Would they now change?

During the 1960s, even though I much respected Donald Creighton, Walter Gordon, and George Grant, I thought that the portrait they were painting might be somewhat darker than need be. But gradually, late in the decade and more so throughout the 1970s, I changed my mind. The more I learned, researched, and studied, the more I became convinced the nation was in great peril.

I hoped that the CIC would become a broad-based, nonpartisan, patriotic organization. We had Liberals, Conservatives, and NDP supporters in the CIC, and a great many members who had no party affiliation. My hope was that I could help turn the organization into a democratic grassroots group. Without question the CIC had started out dominated by a Toronto elite. But gradually the members across the country, much at my urging, began to take control.

It wasn't long before a rivalry developed with the Waffle wing of the NDP, led by Mel Watkins and Jim Laxer. For the Waffle, socialism was the only answer, and in battling for greater Canadian independence we were deemed to be on their turf. As far as they were concerned, the issues of foreign ownership and control could only be resolved through left-wing strategies, an independent socialist

Canada. According to Mel Watkins, "Socialism and only socialism can lead the way to Canadian independence." In 1971 Jim Laxer unsuccessfully challenged David Lewis for the leadership of the NDP. The following year the Waffle was purged from the Ontario NDP, and it disintegrated two years later.

The CIC's Statement of Purpose was succinct, advocating greater Canadian independence, less dependence on imported foreign capital and foreign-manufactured goods, more upgrading of resources before export, much less foreign ownership, the promotion of Canadian culture, greater trade union autonomy, the protection of Canadian jurisdiction in the Arctic, more Canadian content in education, and a more independent Canadian foreign policy. Over and over again we stressed a number of fundamental points: most members of the CIC are strong internationalists; an independent Canada could play a much more effective role among the world community of nations, but an independent foreign policy could not emanate from a branch-plant country. We did not support "ultranationalism," chauvinism, jingoism, or anti-Americanism. Our fundamental aim was to preserve Canada as a separate country in control, to as great an extent as possible, of its own decision-making processes.

From the outset I had grave reservations that the Liberals would adopt nationalist policies. In April 1971, prior to our board meeting in Toronto, I circulated an eleven-page document titled "On the Future of the CIC." I pointed out that the current Liberal government had been debating the issue of foreign control for three years and had done nothing, and I forecast it would do little in the future. As well, I asked, "Can anyone look at the Conservative party today and imagine they would be much better? And if anyone believes the NDP will gain power soon, well, as Rotstein says, 'choose your illusions.'" After urging that the CIC hold a national conference in September, with delegations from every province, I came to the most important and contentious part of my paper.

> There is an enormous paradox in the Canadian political system. On the one hand it is open and available and democratic in theory and to a much lesser degree in practice. On the other hand it is very much dominated by an economic and political elite.
>
> Good political strategy by a dictator in Canada would encourage groups like the CIC, "community action groups," "politics of the streets," "participatory democracy," so long as

more people didn't get directly involved in the political process. Stop and consider all the massive energy devoted across the entire country by (as only one example of many) pollution control groups. Then, stop and think about how many people were at your last constituency meeting.

The CIC is dedicated to change. Urgent change. Such change can only be effected via the political process. That simply means electing the right people . . . people who will truly represent the best interests of Canada. Bluntly, if the energy that the CIC has expended were to be directly mobilized into the political process, the results would be a thousand times more significant. . . .

Sure, the CIC with a quarter of a million signatures on a petition may draw the attention of a few politicians and a few newspaper editors. But, the power to make the decisions that have to be made lies in elected office. I grow dubious about the ability of Canadians to ever learn this lesson when I see so many experienced politicians in the CIC ignoring it.

The "new politics" (will it ever come?) is not the politics of charismatic visits to shopping plazas or proper television make-up or elites gathering at window-dressing policy conferences. The real new politics will arrive when somehow citizens realize the power that they would actually have if they would learn how easy it is to use it. And this is where the CIC, if you stop and analyse, fails. . . .

The CIC could become a political party. Who wants it? Not very many. Who would leave the CIC if we became a party? Probably a good many of our political elite. Who would come to us? The people. I arrive at my conclusions about the CIC becoming a political party reluctantly. My decision in this respect is motivated by a genuine belief that for Canada to survive there is much urgency in the decisions that have to be made.

The CIC, as now intended, is a "pressure group." But pressure whom? Pierre Trudeau? Mitchell Sharp? One would have to be terribly politically naive to imagine any important success. Are we interested in success, or are we just fooling around, and fooling ourselves?

I had thought carefully before throwing out the idea of a new party. I knew it would bring strong negative reaction from those who had started the organization. Yet I persisted and did so principally because my sources in Ottawa told me there was little chance the Liberals would adopt a nationalist agenda.

As I had suspected, there was zero support from the CIC's founders to even think about a new political party. I did get my way, though, concerning a founding national convention, which was scheduled for Thunder Bay in December. In the meantime, the CIC would organize chapters and send speakers across the country, distribute information to the media, to members, and to the public, organize a petition campaign, and seek a meeting with the prime minister to present our concerns, our suggestions, and the petition.

While many other nations had screening agencies, limits on domestic loans to foreign corporations, voting share limits, land-sale controls, takeover controls, key industry controls, director regulations, and so on, Canada, with by far the greatest foreign ownership and control, had by far the greatest absence of legislation to deal with the problem.

The Watkins report and the Wahn report had both recommended a strong screening agency. A tough effective agency would be one of our principal goals when we met with the prime minister. The petition we hoped to present to Mr. Trudeau read: "I believe that the survival of Canada as an independent nation is one of the most urgent issues facing Canadians today. The time for mere talk is past; action is urgently needed. I join with other citizens of many political persuasions and backgrounds to urge our elected representatives to make Canadian independence a top priority."

But by the spring of 1971, something important had begun happening. Alexander Ross, writing in the *Financial Post*, spelled it out:

> There are several hundred letters arriving every week at the CIC's national headquarters. . . . The people are sending money, as little as 25 cents, as much as $50. The committee's name, apparently, is enough to induce hundreds of people to find out more about the organization. Many letters contain offers of help.
>
> *Something is going on out there.* . . . The letters pouring into the CIC indicate that in every part of English Canada, people are deeply and decently concerned by foreign takeovers, by Americans gobbling up cottage land, by politicians and businessmen who not only defend the sellout, but actually subsidize it.

Flora MacDonald says: "I've never seen anything like this in politics. . . . The interest! The emotion! It's as though people had been looking for something for years, something that none of the parties are offering."

Then Flora said something that rather astounded me. "You know, you can almost imagine this thing replacing the old parties."

By the time we met Mr. Trudeau in his Centre Block office in June, we had active CIC branches in forty communities across the country and in every province except Newfoundland. Included in our brief to the prime minister was a three-page appendix of national public-opinion polls supporting our petition: seventy-one percent said they were opposed to more U.S. investment in Canada, ninety-two percent supported government action to increase Canadian owner-ship, eighty-eight percent thought that the nation's growing concern over Canadian nationalism "was a good thing."

Trudeau was originally scheduled to meet with a large delegation of CIC members from across Canada, but just before the meeting Jean Marchand was sent from the PMO to inform us that the dele-gation would be limited to five, and then a last-minute concession was made to allow seven delegates into the prime minister's office for an hour-long meeting. Jack McClelland, Walter Gordon, Eddie Goodman, Flora MacDonald, Pierre Berton, a university student (whose name escapes me), and I were selected to form the delega-tion. Trudeau welcomed us warmly. Then Jack McClelland and Flora MacDonald described our work and raison d'être.

The prime minister complimented the CIC for doing a fine job of focusing public attention on the issue of foreign ownership and said he very much hoped that the CIC would continue its work in the future. There were over 170,000 signatures from across Canada on the petition we presented to Mr. Trudeau.

We had separate meetings with Herb Gray, Robert Stanfield, and David Lewis. They were friendly and seemed supportive of our goals. We came away from the meetings elated, believing that the govern-ment was about to announce strong new measures designed to deal with the problems we were addressing. Trudeau asked us to "stay in being so that there would be voices throughout the country" that would support the government's new policies.

However, much to our disappointment, month after month went

by and still the government had not even released the Gray report. But someone, perhaps Herb Gray or more likely someone from his office, then leaked the full draft of the report to Abe Rotstein, who was then the editor of *Canadian Forum* magazine. In December 1971, *Forum* published much of what was an excellent report.

The Trudeau government took another four months to finally release the actual report and then introduce legislation in the House of Commons. And what a disappointment it was! We immediately attacked the bill as hopelessly inadequate and began an intense lobby of Liberal MPs. Soon more than a dozen Liberal MPs were publicly calling on the government to produce stronger legislation. But not one of the MPs had the courage to vote against the legislation at the first or second reading in the House.

By late summer, the CIC was quickly running out of money and heading for a big deficit. Walter Gordon, Eddie Goodman, and Jack Biddell, who had all made very generous financial contributions, were ready to close the committee down, but the general membership was upset by the proposal. The mood was "try and stop us" from continuing. Pierre Berton donated $5,000 in fundraising seed money to keep the organization going, which made a huge difference. Plans for a founding convention proceeded.

We had a splendid organization in Edmonton. Abe Rotstein wrote: "Your Edmonton operation is undoubtedly the best in the country." And in Calgary Joe Clark served as acting chairman and my advance man, returning the favour of his bookstore education.

Flora MacDonald, the indomitable, enthusiastic, energetic, sixth-generation Cape Breton redhead, a longtime powerful backroom Conservative, was accurately described by *Toronto Star* writer Tom Hazlitt shortly after she became the CIC's first executive director: "She's the kind that drinks martinis, works all night, will talk politics rather than eat, who loves her friends and makes excuses for her enemies — and does it all with the kind of intensity that makes liars of those who say Canadians are dull.

"She has taken on the job of making Canada independent with all the mystic passion of a Highland woman sworn to protect the hills of home." Flora had worked in the Ottawa Conservative headquarters for more than ten years before John Diefenbaker fired her in 1966, and she subsequently managed Robert Stanfield's election as Tory leader and then went to work in the political-science department at Queen's University. Flora's enthusiasm was contagious. For her, the

CIC "could change the whole political fabric of Canada."

Gordon, Goodman, Biddell, and others continued to be incredibly generous in putting up much of the money needed to run the CIC. But now, in mid-1971, all three were increasingly convinced that the organization had served its purpose. I strongly disagreed. In all the years I was to know and work with Walter Gordon, this would be the only time we had a strong disagreement. Walter, Eddie, and I had a tense meeting in Toronto. I said the coming convention, and only the coming convention, could determine the fate of the committee. Reluctantly they agreed.

Our first national conference was held in Thunder Bay in December 1971. Jack McClelland stepped down as chairman and Eddie Goodman and I were elected co-chairmen. Over four hundred delegates from nine provinces attended the conference; about half of them had no formal political affiliation.

It was ironic that we chose to hold the founding convention in Thunder Bay, the home of C.D. Howe, the man who had become all-powerful in the Louis Saint-Laurent government. As Gordon put it, "If it hadn't been for C.D. Howe, there would have been no occasion for the committee to come into being. . . . His whole philosophy was continentalism." And his basic policy was to let Americans buy up whatever they wanted of Canada.

The day before the Thunder Bay conference opened, the Ontario government released a report showing that more than forty-nine percent of corporate taxable income in Canada went to foreign-controlled firms, and in Ontario the figure was over fifty-four percent. In his opening speech to the conference, Walter Gordon said:

> We the members of the committee and others, especially the young, do not want to be absorbed into the U.S.A. more or less by default. We believe we can have a better life if we are left to develop our sense of values in our own ways — ways that can differ perceptibly from those of our American friends. . . .
>
> The committee has done a most useful job in the past twelve months in focusing attention on this issue. Now our organization must be strengthened all across the country. We must keep going until we are satisfied that Canada will first recover and then retain her independence economically, culturally, politically. Let us never forget our responsibilities to future generations of Canadians.

Walter received a long standing ovation. The delegates were unanimous in their enthusiasm for and dedication to the CIC. We now had a very mixed group of men and women, professionals, white-collar and blue-collar workers, farmers, and academics. I was delighted.

The Bay Street Boys
and a Bunch of Socialists

THROUGHOUT 1970 AND 1971 public-opinion polls continued to back us. When asked by Gallup whether or not they thought the nation's growing concern over Canadian nationalism was a good thing, fifty-nine percent said it was a good thing, and only eight percent said it was not. When asked whether they would like to see more U.S. capital invested in Canada, sixty-two percent said there was enough now, and twenty-six percent said they would like more.

By early 1972 fifty-five members of Parliament (twenty-six Conservatives, thirteen Liberals, and sixteen members of the NDP) had joined the CIC.

While Walter Gordon, Eddie Goodman, Jack Biddell, and now Bob Blair from Calgary gave the organization sizable donations, by mid-1972, it was smaller contributions from across the country that provided most of the committee's revenue.

I was always surprised by the oft-repeated statements by our opponents that a reduction in foreign investment automatically meant a big reduction in the Canadian standard of living. There was no evidence whatever to support that contention. On the contrary, the few available studies on the subject showed that, at best, foreign investment brought a very tiny net benefit to the Canadian standard of living. At worst, there was a large negative impact, not to mention loss of control of the vital decision-making processes.

According to Liberal Party President Senator Richard Stanbury, Canadians would have to "give up their high standard of living" to become more independent. Soon after Stanbury made this unqualified statement, a new study appeared showing that the *maximum possible* benefit of foreign investment was one-third of one percent of GNP.

After we again raised the issue of Canadian banks' using Canadian savings to finance the foreign takeover of Canadian assets, Earle McLaughlin, chairman of the Royal Bank, told an Empire Club audience that his bank and other chartered banks would continue to finance such takeovers if the loans are profitable. For the next quarter century, the Royal Bank would continue to be in the forefront of continentalism in Canada.

In May 1972 at a CIC executive meeting, Abe Rotstein, with the blessing of Walter Gordon, said: "The nonpartisan status of the Committee for an Independent Canada will have to be seriously reconsidered at our fall convention in September. After the debacle of the Gray report, I can only conclude that the reelection of the Trudeau government will mean an end to an independent Canada. . . . The decision to take a stand against the Liberal party under its present leadership will have to become a major item of debate at our conference."

I was very pleased, even though I was running for the Liberals in the election. To me, the Rotstein–Gordon statement constituted a long-overdue breakthrough.

When we appeared before the House of Commons standing committee on finance, trade, and economic affairs in June 1972, Walter Gordon, who a year before had felt the Canadian government was about to tackle this vital issue, commented on his disappointment. "Finally at the beginning of last month, it was announced in effect that the prime minister no longer thought it was important to do anything at all significant to contain the increasing control of our economy by foreigners or, in other words, to do anything meaningful about the Canadian independence issue."

In my presentation I took the bill apart piece by piece. Afterwards, one of the Commons committee members told the press that we were "a bunch of socialists," while another called us "the Bay Street boys." A fine balance.

In any event, much to our delight, our strong presentation, support from a number of Liberal MPs, and growing public support for our position helped kill the bill, which died on the order paper at the close of the session.

Eddie Goodman, my co-chair, had been particularly effective in his attack on the Trudeau government. Alas, Robert Stanfield, the Conservative leader who had almost become prime minister in the 1972 election, proved weak on the issue of Canadian independence.

Stanfield had sent us a telegram that presented some modest proposals dealing with the problem of foreign ownership, but at the same time most of his Conservative members of Parliament were doing everything they could in the House of Commons to block second reading of the government's legislation, Bill C-58, dealing with the special status of *Time* magazine and *Reader's Digest* in Canada. Moreover, the Tory attacks were blatantly dishonest and clearly designed to deceive the public about the nature of the legislation. As well, it was clear that most Conservatives in the House of Commons supported the U.S. group that formed a key part of the Mackenzie Valley pipeline consortium, and only a minority of Tory MPs would support strong regulations designed to curtail the growth of foreign ownership.

The CIC's second national conference was held in Edmonton in September 1972, just before the federal election. Key speakers were Eddie Goodman, Pauline Jewett (who was running for the NDP in Ottawa West), and (are you ready for this?) Pat Carney. We came out strongly against the proposed Mackenzie Valley energy corridor, citing a long list of economic, social, and environmental concerns. Nonresident ownership of Canadian land and Canadian content in education, the media, and the arts were all key conference topics. The results of a survey of federal-election candidates were released. When asked whether or not the extent of foreign-equity investment in Canada was a matter of serious concern, ninety-eight percent of NDP candidates, seventy-eight percent of Liberal candidates, and fifty-four percent of Conservative candidates agreed. Most candidates felt there was insufficient Canadian content in the schools, and most opposed existing special tax exemptions for *Time* and *Reader's Digest*.

Much to our surprise, David Lewis attacked the CIC just before the conference. According to Lewis, Canadian independence was not much of an issue in the election campaign. But according to Peter Desbarats, Ottawa editor for the *Toronto Star*, "Far from being a non-issue, nationalism is the dominant issue in the campaign."

On the surface Lewis's statement seemed bizarre. Since he was up against Pierre Trudeau ("an unabashed critic of nationalism," according to Desmond Morton) and Robert Stanfield, who would never dream of bringing in strong nationalistic legislation, and since the polls clearly showed increasing public concern about foreign influence in all regions of the country, and since his own candidates supported our concern, one assumed that Lewis would have seized the issue with enthusiasm. But just as Ed Broadbent would fumble away the NDP's opportunities during the 1988 free-trade election, David Lewis made a serious error in 1972.

Those who tried to explain Lewis's action cited the terrible struggle Lewis had had with the Waffle faction in his party, the dominant position of the international unions in the NDP and the CIC's call for more union autonomy, and the fact that many prominent members of the CIC were Liberals or Conservatives. Pauline Jewett was furious and scolded Lewis publicly.

By December of 1972, although CIC membership had increased to almost eight thousand, the organization was again short of money. Eddie Goodman made a special appeal to members. Publication and distribution of our national newsletter was only made possible because *Saturday Night* magazine agreed to pay the postage if we agreed to enclose a brochure about the magazine, which we did.

From 1973 on the CIC was constantly short of money; we were doing a great many things and needed to do a great many more. By January we had a $30,000 loan outstanding. Again we made an appeal for money to our members. The same month, the government produced Bill C-132, the new foreign-investment legislation. While it was a modest improvement over the previous effort, it also fell far short of steps that would properly address the problem of foreign ownership and control.

Increasingly the issue of the proposed Mackenzie Valley pipeline occupied our attention. Early in 1973 more than six hundred people packed a CIC meeting in Toronto to hear Eric Kierans debate Energy Minister Donald Macdonald and two petroleum-industry executives. Kierans came away the clear victor in the debate, calling for a pipeline moratorium, government hearings on future Canadian energy and industrial policy, and greater Canadian control of our natural resources. He called the proposed pipeline "a fifty-fifty deal with the Americans . . . the old 'roads to resource syndrome'; we build the road and they take the resources."

Early in 1973 the *New York Times* asked me for an article. I agreed, and wrote that Americans would never dream of accepting anywhere near the degree of foreign control that already existed in Canada, and that Americans would be unwise to think they could continue to buy up our country. I said that for all the intimidating blustering from John B. Connally (then special adviser to Richard Nixon) the U.S. was doing extremely well in its dealings with Canada, including a $15-billion current-account surplus over the past seventeen years.

And I also said that most of the money Americans were using to buy up Canada came from Canada, not from the U.S.

The article prompted lots of good calls and letters from Canadians living in the U.S. and lots of hostile mail ("Who do you think you are? Where do you think you'd be without us?") from Americans.

At the March 1973 annual conference of the CIC, this time in Ottawa, I was elected chairman. I was now clear of any attachments to the Liberal party and felt I could manage my publishing and still continue my pro-Canada activities. In my acceptance speech I spoke about what I believed was "a heightened sense of urgency" relating to the issue of Canadian sovereignty. John Trent, Ottawa political scientist and CIC research-and-policy-committee chairman, attacked all three major parties for failing to address the issues of foreign ownership and control. My old friend Pauline Jewett became deputy CIC chairman. Jack Biddell continued as treasurer, and Barbara Daprato was elected CIC secretary. Eddie Goodman succeeded Walter Gordon as honorary chairman.

At the conference I again informally and very gently raised the question of a new political party. By the time of our October Western Regional Conference in Calgary, there was substantial support for the idea. After board meetings the idea was invariably discussed over drinks in hotel rooms and bars. Walter Gordon, Peter Newman, and Abe Rotstein were all very negative. According to Walter, "There was no thought of starting a new political party, which could never have been successful."

Soon after the Ottawa conference I was scheduled to go to Trail, B.C., to speak to a Canadian Workers Union rally. Doug Swanson, president of the Trail local of the CWU, had spoken at our convention's closing banquet. His attempt to get steelworkers in British Columbia to desert the United Steelworkers of America had put Swanson and his colleagues in a bitter battle with the huge international union. The CIC agreed to back Swanson, and we called upon B.C. Premier Dave Barrett to allow a certification vote.

I stopped overnight in Edmonton before heading for Trail. At three in the morning my wife and I were awakened by a phone call. Eileen answered.

"Is this Mrs. Hurtig?"

"Yes."

"Mrs. Mel Hurtig?"

"Yes."

"Mrs. Hurtig, please tell your husband this. If he goes to Trail tomorrow, he's a dead man, and tell him we're not kidding."

I went to Trail, not without some trepidation, and gave a rousing speech promoting autonomy in the Canadian trade-union movement. Following my appearance in Trail, the United Steelworkers of America took out a large ad in local newspapers attacking me for my "anti-union record." The ad also bitterly attacked Walter Gordon and Eddie Goodman who "have never demonstrated a sincere concern for the working people in Canada."

Lynn Williams, Canadian director-elect of the United Steelworkers of America, attacked me and the CIC for being "millionaire business-men and corporation lawyers who don't have much in common with wage earners." Yet most of our CIC members and almost all of our board were wage earners, homemakers, farmers, or students. Williams accused us of financing Canadian unions opposed to the "international" unions (which, as I've said, were American unions with a Canadian branch, or "district," as they called them). I wish the accusations had been true, but we didn't have enough money to finance our own organization properly, let alone breakaway trade unions.

In April we continued to do our best to pressure the three political parties to have Bill C-132 substantially strengthened to include the screening of the expansion of existing resident foreign corporations, to allow government to closely monitor intercorporate pricing arrangements between parents and subsidiaries, and other measures designed to halt the growth of foreign ownership.

Jack Biddell produced an excellent long list of suggestions that would strengthen Canadian companies, but Finance Minister John Turner responded with only a polite acknowledgement. Ironically, while the left continued to attack the CIC for being a capitalist business organization, we had a difficult time raising money in the business community.

My friend philosopher Richard Mouw invited me down to Calvin College in Grand Rapids, Michigan, to speak to students and faculty. I told them that Canadians were getting tired of hearing threats from John Connally that we had better sell the U.S. our resources or there would be "flak." I said U.S. subsidiaries in Canada were contributing to high unemployment by importing goods and services that should be produced in Canada, that Senator Vance Hartke's suggestion that the Auto Pact was "a form of foreign aid" was laughable, and that every time Herman Kahn said that the U.S. was doing Canada a favour by buying our resources, the CIC was flooded with new applications for membership. I said I was considering sponsoring Connally, Hartke, and Kahn on cross-Canada speaking tours.

By the end of May 1973, after a Liberal caucus meeting, which was immediately reported to me in every detail, it was clear the government had no intention of doing anything more. Walter Gordon wrote to me: "I expect I shall decide to come out against the Trudeau government." Bravo, I said.

Also in May, Donald MacDonald, president of the Canadian Labour Congress, launched an ugly ignorant attack against us, saying the CIC had "a record of being anti-labour" and was "anti-union." By this time we had a large contingent of trade-union members in the organization. Moreover, as I wrote MacDonald, "I number among my close friends quite a few rank-and-file union people, and several union officials, and have always been a supporter of the trade-union movement." I challenged MacDonald to produce a shred of evidence to back up his claims. He never criticized us again.

On June 21, 1973, we again appeared before the Commons standing committee on finance, trade, and economic affairs. We called Bill C-132 "a smokescreen" and the proposed screening agency "a toothless jellyfish." Pauline Jewett, Abe Rotstein, and John Trent spelled out the weakness of the proposed legislation. The bottom line: "The bill will in no way reduce the current disastrously high levels of foreign economic control in Canada, let alone stop continued annual growth of foreign ownership and control."

After we appeared before the Commons committee, the *Windsor Star* lead editorial said: "The most cogent, sophisticated, knowledgeable and pragmatic contributions to the crucial Canadian debate on foreign economic control continue to come not from the Canadian Chamber of Commerce, not from any of the political parties, not from the revised Waffle, but from the much-maligned and frequently ignored Committee for an Independent Canada."

In introducing the new legislation, Industry, Trade and Commerce Minister Alastair Gillespie said the government had improved it beyond what the earlier bill on foreign investment had contained, because obviously "the people had been ahead of the politicians." Far ahead. And the government had nowhere near caught up.

While we were being attacked from the left for being a capitalist organization, the vituperative Conservative MP Don Blenkarn wrote to Eddie Goodman: "It disturbs me that the New Democratic Party seems to be taking over the Committee for an Independent Canada."

And I wrote to NDP MP Lorne Nystrom that in failing to take a strong stand on Bill C-132, the NDP "botched an important opportunity to turn our country around." As I mentioned before, in 1972 the NDP had failed to make the issue of Canadian sovereignty anywhere near a priority, despite the fact that the polls clearly showed it was of vital concern to an overwhelming majority of Canadians. Now, holding the balance of power in Parliament, they had failed to pressure the Liberals to ensure legislation to deal with an issue that so many felt would affect the very survival of our country. Mel Watkins called the NDP's performance "a complete cop-out."

There was no question in my mind that the international unions were the key factor in the NDP's dismal performance. The steelworkers, the autoworkers, machinists, and food workers were all branches of big U.S. unions, and the union hierarchy in Canada were all under the thumb to oppose movements for greater autonomy and, God forbid, independent Canadian unions.

Ed Finn, a superb union researcher and labour writer for the *Toronto Star*, and a strong proponent of more independent Canadian unions, remembers David Lewis at the time inviting him to lunch in the parliamentary restaurant and Lewis vehemently berating him for calling for more union autonomy. Finn was shocked.

When Jim Laxer mounted a strong campaign against Lewis in his bid for the NDP leadership, the steelworkers bused in some two hundred delegates to support Lewis. Enough said.

The response to my leaving the Liberal party was beyond my expectations. I received a great many letters of congratulations from across the country. And I wrote to Walter Gordon: "It seems to me that it is no longer possible for anyone who deeply cares about the survival of Canada to belong to a party that continues to allow the sellout of our country."

From 1970 to 1973 I crossed the country dozens of times, speaking in church basements, high school auditoriums, to service clubs, in hotel ballrooms, at universities and colleges, to national conventions of business leaders and trade unionists, to teachers and professors, to women's organizations and resource-management groups, and to many others from St. John's to Victoria, from Yellowknife to Windsor.

Over and over again I stressed that "you don't have to be anti-American to be pro-Canadian." Then I would often tell Peter Newman's story about the lavish dinner Lester Pearson had given at the Canadian High Commissioner's in London. U.S. Secretary of State Dean Rusk sat across from Mr. Pearson, and many State Department officials were present. The night before there had been a particularly grizzly murder in Hyde Park. A prim *London Times* reported the story as follows: "The body of the girl was found decapitated and dismembered, but not interfered with." Pearson leaned across the table and pointed at Rusk. "You know, that's the way we Canadians feel about you Americans. You can decapitate us and you can dismember us, so long as you don't interfere with us!"

I often spoke about what I felt was an extraordinarily undemocratic electoral system: "More than ninety percent of all funds raised by politicians and political parties in this country comes in donations in excess of a thousand dollars. This means that big business and big unions support the political parties. Political parties form governments. Now stop and consider the ramifications of the fact that most big business and big industrial unions in Canada are American controlled."

In December of 1973 the Liberals' Bill C-132, the Foreign Investment Review Act, was passed in the House of Commons. For the CIC it was both a modest victory and a huge defeat.

Prophets Without Honour

B Y EARLY 1974, the CIC had expanded its activities. We appeared before the National Energy Board, presented mounds of research material relating to tar sands and heavy oil development, organized an expert task force on energy use in Canada, gave detailed suggestions concerning trade in oil and natural gas, and made an excellent presentation to the House of Commons standing committee on privileges and elections relating to the reform of election regulations and improvements to the government's Bill C-203, An Act to Amend the Canada Elections Act. As well, we actively campaigned for increased Canadian content in education and fewer appointments of non-Canadians in our postsecondary institutions (incredibly during the 1968–69 year more than seventy-five per-cent of positions in Canadian universities and colleges went to non-Canadians while many highly qualified Canadian graduates were finding it impossible to find jobs).

Meanwhile, CIC speakers were visiting schools, churches, service clubs, speaking at lunches and dinners and universities and colleges across the country, and mail was pouring in from across Canada. Membership was up about 2,300 from a year earlier and our financial situation had improved. We moved our national office from Toronto to Ottawa and hired an outstanding young man, Daryl Logan, from Vancouver, as our new executive director.

By the summer, I would have been chairman of the CIC for a year and a half, and I had been co-chairman for more than a year previously. I decided to step down in June to give more attention to my publishing house. Once again the Liberals were pressuring me to run in the anticipated federal election, and once again some lavish promises were coming from Ottawa and Toronto, but I was not interested.

I spent much of the first six months of 1974 working on CIC matters and speaking across the country. In Port Colborne some two thousand people gave me a long standing ovation after a very tough antigovernment speech, much to the embarrassment of two federal cabinet ministers who had to sit on the stage throughout my talk.

My schedule was ridiculous, from province to province, city to city, town to town, and then more of the same all over again, day after day after day: speeches, meetings, receptions, interviews, open-line shows, debates, panel discussions, and television shows. Meanwhile, there were newspaper and magazine articles to write, research to be done, and tons of letters and phone calls to answer. There were always a million things to be done and always not enough time to do them.

I hoped Pauline Jewett would agree to run for chairman and be elected to take my place after the June 1974 national conference. I also hoped to spend more time with my family and in my publishing company. In a speech in North York in February I announced I would step down as chairman. My pictures in the newspapers and magazines of the time show I certainly needed a rest. I looked haggard and drawn, with big bags under my eyes.

In April I received a cordial letter from Tommy Douglas announcing his intention to renew his membership in the CIC and asking me to lunch next time I was in Ottawa. At the same time, B.C. Premier Dave Barrett agreed to speak at our June convention in Toronto. Along with Pauline Jewett's key role, we were definitely making headway in our efforts to involve the NDP in the committee.

On May 21, 1974, I sent the prime minister the following telegram:

In 1974 despite the passage of the Foreign Investment Review

Act, without the takeover of a single Canadian company, and without the entry of a single new non-resident firm, foreign ownership in Canada will grow by at least 4 to 5 billion dollars STOP The Committee for an Independent Canada would very much welcome a reply from you indicating what measures you are prepared to recommend that will halt the growth of foreign ownership in our country STOP We would be most grateful if you could respond at your earliest convenience so that your reply may be passed along to our chapters across Canada for their consideration STOP At the same time the CIC strongly urges that during the course of the present election campaign you clearly spell out to the people of Canada your position re the growth of foreign ownership, the solutions you advocate, and the priority you intend to attach to the issue STOP Lastly, we most respectfully wish that in your reply to this telegram you indicate whether or not you feel that our current level of foreign ownership is proving detrimental to the Canadian economy, contributing both to inflation and unemployment STOP The annual convention of the Committee for an Independent Canada will be held beginning June seventh STOP A reply from you before that date would be very much appreciated STOP

Similar telegrams were sent to Robert Stanfield and David Lewis. Neither Trudeau nor Lewis had replied by the time of our convention. Stanfield's reply promised tax credits for Canadians investing in small business and a resources program designed to help Canadians achieve majority ownership. Pauline Jewett was again furious that David Lewis hadn't responded. Trudeau's reply arrived Sunday night after the convention was over. Just as well; it was noncommittal and of little interest.

While I was stepping down as chairman, I would continue to be active in the organization as honorary chairman. In my final report I said that "for the second time in 21 months a federal election will be held apparently without the issue of foreign ownership considered a priority by any of the party leaders. Just as no other nation in the world would have tolerated the sellout of their country as Canadians have, similarly no other country would allow their politicians to so completely abdicate their responsibilities. Sadly, despite all of our activities to date, 'silent surrender' still best describes Canada in 1974."

By the time of our convention, the CIC had become an increasingly important factor in the debate over Canada's future. Throughout 1974 we continued to work on national-unity projects, continued to appear before the National Energy Board, the Alberta Energy Resources Conservation Board, Mr. Justice Tom Berger's Mackenzie Valley pipeline commission, House of Commons and Senate committees relating to corporate concentration and magazine legislation, and other provincial government boards and committees relating to education and energy.

On July 18, 1974, Alastair Gillespie tabled in the House of Commons a new toothless code of guidelines for good corporate citizenship by foreign corporations in Canada. Meanwhile, Finance Minister John Turner was assuring the Investment Dealers Association that they would have "complete freedom to obtain capital" since it was clear that in the future Canada would require "substantial foreign debt and equity capital."

When, in 1974, Statistics Canada finally published the 1971 foreign-ownership figures, the list was again appalling. The extent of foreign ownership of firms in Canada was: manufacturing, fifty-eight percent; mining, sixty-nine percent; oil and gas wells, coal mines, eighty-one percent. In many industries foreign ownership stood at eighty percent or more. Some seventy-five percent of foreign ownership in Canada was American. Some ninety-three percent of all the expansion capital employed by U.S. firms in Canada came from Canadian sources.

We now know that just before the 1974 federal election was called, there was a fierce battle in cabinet on the issue of foreign ownership. Herb Gray and other cabinet nationalists had produced a highly confidential document containing strong proposed new legislation. The document was leaked to me in advance. It was well beyond my most optimistic hopes.

And the prime minister, in an unexpected telegram, promised me announcements on the issue of foreign ownership in the near future. Nevertheless, throughout the election campaign, neither Mr. Trudeau nor any of his cabinet colleagues made foreign ownership an important issue. According to the *Montreal Gazette*, "Nationalism has, in fact, become unfashionable in Ottawa."

In the election Pierre Trudeau and the Liberals were returned, this time with a majority government. Robert Stanfield had run a poor campaign and fumbled the football. This time the Liberals increased their Commons seats from 109 to 141, the Conservatives dropped from 107 to 95, and the NDP fell from 31 to 16.

Later in the year after I delivered a speech in London, Ontario, the *Windsor Star* editorialized that "the frustration and the urgency felt by Mr. Hurtig and the other members of the CIC are readily apparent. . . . They are, in a special way, prophets and, being in their own land, they are prophets without honour . . . and that is Canada's loss."

Peter Newman put it somewhat differently in the *Toronto Star*:

> When we started the Committee for an Independent Canada to believe in Canadian independence was like being a part of some goofy cult, such as collecting butterflies or old match covers.
>
> Every time an American journalist came up here to do his big take-out on Canada, he'd earnestly interview one of us and then we'd appear for a couple of paragraphs in his story or for 60 seconds in his TV show — like those obligatory glimpses of twitching witch doctors they used to have in documentaries about emerging African states.
>
> But now partly as a result of the committee's missionary efforts, nationalism has raised collective consciousness so that wanting to retain our independence has become an accepted part of nearly every Canadian's thought process.

The Fervour of a Fanatic, the Patience of a Saint

THE CIC WAS ACTIVE until it closed down in 1981. Our 1975 conference was in Vancouver, where Daryl Logan, in his annual report, thanked "Mel Hurtig, who did not let up one bit." Unfortunately it was true. For the next couple of years after my "retirement" as chairman, my pace was almost as active as before. Gradually, very gradually, there were signs we were having a greater impact. Alastair Gillespie had promised legislation to require new natural-resource development to be majority-Canadian-owned, and Minister of Indian Affairs and Northern Development Judd Buchanan announced that future development in Canada's North would have to have ninety percent Canadian content or show just cause for not doing so.

The conference's Saturday-night banquet speaker was Herb Gray, who attacked recent Economic Council of Canada proposals for free trade. According to Gray, with free trade, unemployment and foreign ownership in Canada would increase, and Canadian culture and political independence would suffer. Gray was also critical of his government's proposals in part two of the Foreign Investment Review Act, pointing out major loopholes and lack of clarity. He said that FIRA should be far more open and much less secretive. Most importantly he implied that Gillespie, the minister in charge, now regarded FIRA as an unfortunate impediment to growth, instead of a valuable step to regaining control of our own economy.

It wasn't long before Gray's warnings about FIRA and Gillespie came true in government policy. Bertram Barrow, FIRA commissioner, said he now viewed his responsibility as *encouraging* foreign investment, not discouraging it. FIRA would, in fact, act as a "service" to foreign investors. Yet, as Gray pointed out, Parliament had already declared that the level of foreign investment in Canada was so high it was a matter of national concern. "If there's any service aspect to the service, it should be serving the people of Canada rather than the investors," he said.

The Wall Street business magazine *Barron's* put things in the proper perspective when it urged its readers not to be overly concerned about FIRA: "The only U.S. corporation that would not be warmly welcomed into Canada would be Murder Inc." Meanwhile, Pierre Trudeau appointed a new industry, trade and commerce minister, Don Jamieson, an arch continentalist.

In October 1975 External Affairs invited me to attend an official state dinner given by the minister, Allan MacEachen, in honour of U.S. Secretary of State Henry Kissinger. A black-tie affair, it was to be held on the ninth floor of the Lester B. Pearson Building on Sussex Drive. Just before I received the invitation, I had thrown away my tuxedo. I rarely wore it, didn't like wearing it, and had no future plans to wear it. After deciding to attend the dinner, I headed down to Milne's tuxedo-rental shop and was fitted into a new outfit; the sleeves were three inches too long and needed shortening. Early the next morning I picked up the tux and headed for the airport.

Unfortunately the plane was delayed. I arrived at my Ottawa hotel with minutes to spare, quickly showered, shaved, and put on my rental tux. But instead of shortening the sleeves three inches, the shop had lengthened them three inches. I spent the entire evening either pulling my sleeves up or with my elbows bent. When I shook hands, my entire hand would disappear.

This was the famous dinner when a microphone was accidentally left open, and during dinner Kissinger made several highly disparaging remarks about Richard Nixon, which were reported around the world the next morning and especially prominently in the *Washington Post*. MacEachen was mortified and phoned Kissinger to apologize. Kissinger replied: "It's done. Forget it. Besides, my relations with Nixon couldn't get any worse."

Well, the CIC won some battles, but we were losing the war. At least we had been effective in the battle for public opinion. By late 1975 a national public-opinion poll showed seventy-one percent of Canadians were opposed to more foreign investment, while only sixteen percent wanted more. Some six years earlier a majority had supported more foreign investment.

The 1976 annual CIC meeting was held in Lunenburg, Nova Scotia, in September. At the convention in 1974 I had met an outstanding gentleman, Bruce Willson, president of Union Gas Limited, based in Chatham, Ontario. Bruce and I quickly became close friends and, later, golfing companions. At the Nova Scotia conference, he became the new CIC chairman. Soon after, he published an insightful article in the *Globe and Mail* attacking the corporate behaviour of Imperial Oil, Sun Oil, Union Carbide, Gulf, Texaco, Mobil Oil, Shell, and other foreign-controlled energy companies. The industry reacted with concerted attacks on the CIC and with bitter personal attacks on Willson. At Bruce's invitation, Walter Gordon, Peter Newman, and I met with him at the National Club in Toronto to talk about the CIC and the Trudeau government. Walter still seemed to feel that the CIC had gone beyond the point of being useful. Bruce and I disagreed, but since I was no longer in a position of being able to be very active in the committee, I again pointed out that decisions about the future of the organization should only be made by its elected executives and members.

I spoke at Simon Fraser University in Vancouver soon after and had dinner with Pauline Jewett at her university president's home atop Burnaby Mountain. After dinner we sat outside, drinking scotch and watching the sun sink in the Pacific. We talked about politics and old friends, about the state of the country, and about our personal lives.

A few days earlier I had attacked U.S. Ambassador Thomas Enders for not telling the truth about the extent of U.S. investment in Canada. There was a big fuss. The *Ottawa Citizen* lead editorial was titled "Mortgaging Our Future." It read in part:

> The truthfulness of the American ambassador to Canada, which Mel Hurtig of the Committee for an Independent Canada says is open to question, is not as important as the federal government's response to the continuing problem of foreign investment.
>
> The Trudeau government has not come to realize what a threat the continued influx of such capital (mostly from the U.S.) is to the country. In fact, the government is a willing participant in the process of mortgaging Canada's future. It has been a fundamental tenet of Liberal policy since the days of C.D. Howe that Canada's road to prosperity lay in opening the country to unlimited foreign investment. Canadians sold to willing buyers. It's not the Americans who are to blame, but the Liberal governments and Canadian businessmen.
>
> The decisions of United States' multinational corporations could now bankrupt Canada. A renewal of economic difficulties in the U.S. could force plant closings here. Canadian markets could dry up. The house of cards could crash.

In 1976 Graydon Carter, now editor of *Vanity Fair*, agreed to edit an issue of our periodical *The Independencer* and to supervise the editing of future editions. He did a superb job. Mordecai Richler, true to form, ridiculed *The Independencer* as chauvinistic.

By the end of 1976, FIRA had approved eighty-six percent of all foreign-takeover applications and ninety-three percent of all new foreign-business applications.

THAT YEAR WAS A VERY difficult one for me personally. My marriage to Eileen broke down and we divorced in September. To a large extent, but not entirely, the fault was my own. It would be easy to blame all my travels and the demands of a growing business, but there was more to it than that. In some important ways we had grown in different directions.

The most difficult thing I have ever had to do was to sit in the living room of my home and tell my daughters that I was leaving home. They had no idea it was coming; it was brutal for us all. When

I left home in 1976, I moved into an empty high-rise apartment, with no furniture, no dishes, no pictures, not even a radio. I missed my home, my children, and my huge library. I was determined to become self-sufficient, but not only could I not cook, I am a mechanical incompetent. The afternoon of my first night as a "bachelor" I bought a bottle of gin, a bottle of dry vermouth, some olives, an electric can opener, and several cans of soup, plus crackers and cheese. It was a start. That evening after work I sat on the floor of the apartment, leaning up against some unpacked boxes, sipped a martini and read the paper. I then headed for the kitchen, unpacked the can opener, plugged it in, then spent the next half hour trying to open a can of soup. Something was wrong. I tried everything I could think of and read the instructions four times; nothing worked. With sweat accumulating on my brow, I poured myself another martini. It took me over two hours to figure out that General Electric had somehow failed to put a cutting blade in my new can opener. I went to bed hungry, lonely, and discouraged.

Two months later I headed to Gatwick and Lahr, Germany, in an old air force Boeing. The Canadian Club had invited me to speak to Canada's armed forces in Lahr and Baden. It was my first trip to Europe in fourteen years, and I very much looked forward to it. I had a pleasant suite in the officers' quarters in Lahr, a car and a driver, and received superb hospitality. There were guided tours to the Black Forest and Alsace, but the trip's highlight was undoubtedly flying around Europe in the bubble of an air force helicopter with the commander of Canada's Tactical Helicopter Squadron, up the Rhine, down the Danube, over nudist colonies, around ancient castles, skimming the mountain peaks, circling villages — it was a marvellous experience. After speaking in Lahr and Baden, I flew to Oslo and was driven late at night to Drammen, south and west of Oslo. In the morning I opened the drapes of my second-floor hotel room to face a huge sign, yellow letters on a black background, with only one word on it: HURTIG. (My last name is somewhat unusual. There were very few Hurtigs in all of North America at the time, none, for example, in Toronto). At first I thought some friends were providing me with a very warm ostentatious welcome. But then I learned that in Scandinavia and Germany "Hurtig" means quick, swift, agile, nimble, alert, eager, zealous, or efficient (according to Toronto lawyer Fred Catzman). On almost every dry-cleaning store in Norway there was a big sign saying HURTIG.

After several days of hiking and skiing in northwest Norway, I flew to Stockholm, where friends showed me the city, and then to London. Back in Lahr, one evening as I headed to dinner, just as I was closing my door, I heard a door slam at the far end of the dark corridor. A moment later a man yelled "Mel!" As he came towards me, I could see lots of gold on his officer's hat, his shoulders, gold stripes on his sleeves, and many ribbons. It was Major-General Richard Rohmer, lawyer, author, and commanding officer of Canada's reserves. Richard and I had a drink together, and he asked about my itinerary. When he heard I was headed for London, he proposed dinner since he would be there at the same time. Now, a friend in London had arranged for my first blind date in twenty-five years. It was with a woman named Judy, a good friend of Diana Rigg's. "Richard," I said, "you can come for a drink before dinner, but if she's attractive I want you to disappear." Agreed. We all met in the lobby of the Churchill Hotel. She was beautiful, lively, and intelligent. Richard stayed for a drink, for soup, for dinner, for dessert, for two coffees, and for two brandies. I had to catch a plane back to Lahr at five in the morning. I said good night to Judy, but not to Richard.

ON FEBRUARY 12, 1977, we had a packed house of more than seven hundred people for a forum in Toronto celebrating the seventh anniversary of the CIC, but by June of 1977, the CIC was broke again, and the board of directors and executive held numerous meetings to discuss the future of the committee, which had recently lost its executive director, Daryl Logan. In the end the consensus was that "it was absolutely necessary for the CIC to continue."

The 1977 annual convention was held in Toronto in October. Nydia McCool had become executive director. Yet again another "special" fundraising letter was sent to members across the country. The convention was wonderful. Panellists included: Alberta NDP leader Grant Notley; Liberal MPs Paul McRae and Mark MacGuigan; John Robert Colombo; *Canadian Forum* editor Denis Smith; Senator Eugene Forsey; Laurier LaPierre; Bernie Hodgetts, the chairman of the Canadian Studies Foundation; Thomas Symons, the head of the Commission on Canadian Studies; sociologist Wallace Clement; Mel Watkins; and many others concerned with matters relating to Canadian independence. Eric Kierans was the banquet speaker. By the time of the convention the CIC was solvent again, the fundraising letter having proved very successful. The highly respected Toronto lawyer Hugh Morris was elected chairman to succeed Bruce Willson.

Bruce was a kind, gentle, extremely intelligent man who loved his country dearly. At one time he was head of Canadian Bechtel, but resigned as a matter of principle when he disagreed with some of Bechtel's activities. Steve Bechtel offered Bruce a very substantial sum to stay on, but he refused. Bruce's passion for Canada and CIC chairmanship cost him friends and sometimes resulted in bitter attacks from his former colleagues in the petroleum industry. But he was a brave man of strong convictions. I once watched him in action before an energy hearing in Calgary. He made all the petroleum industry's high-price lawyers look like inept newcomers to the oil-and-gas scene. It was a remarkable and courageous performance.

Alas, Bruce became ill in 1991 with a form of leukaemia. I visited him in hospital; he was very weak, but he sat up and we talked for almost an hour. We got around to one of our favourite topics, golf, and I asked Bruce what was the best game he'd ever played. His eyes lit up and he told me hole by hole about a sixty-nine he shot at the Calgary Golf and Country Club, including a closing birdie on the eighteenth hole.

Bruce died the next day. If I had to describe him in only a few words, it would be this: he was a noble patriot and a wonderful man.

By the end of 1977, Hugh Morris was able to report optimistically to the CIC's membership. The great success of the recent conference had produced new momentum and much new vigour, and there was even a small financial surplus, instead of a large deficit.

By 1978, FIRA was actively engaged in *promoting* foreign investment in Canada. While a study by the Department of Industry, Trade and Commerce indicated that current levels of foreign ownership would prove to be "a significant impediment" to developing economic strategies to improve industrial performance, takeovers by foreign corporations soared. Instead of a watchdog agency, FIRA had become a lapdog. Even Herb Gray wondered if the agency had become little more than a "foreign-takeover facilitation service." But according to industry minister Jean Chrétien, in a speech to a Chicago audience, "A continuing flow of direct investment from abroad is an essential condition of continuing economic progress in Canada."

In April 1978 the *Globe and Mail* attacked the Committee for an Independent Canada, this time in a harsh, distorted diatribe by *Globe* publisher R.S. Malone. The article attributed a multitude of fictitious sins to Canadian nationalists, attacking Walter Gordon and painting the CIC with false colours.

I was no longer able to be very active in the committee, although I continued to accept speaking invitations. My publishing business was growing rapidly and taking more and more of my time. Gradually the CIC lost momentum. By October of 1978 the executive were again discussing whether or not the committee should be wound up. But once again a "special appeal" had brought in a reasonable cash flow, and the consensus was that the CIC still had work to do.

The eighth national convention was held in Ottawa in May 1979. By this time membership was down considerably. Moreover, the attendance at the convention was almost all from Ontario. Clearly the organization was in decline. Meanwhile, Walter Gordon had organized the Canadian Institute for Economic Policy, which became his and Abe Rotstein's top priority. Max Saltsman, the retiring NDP veteran MP for Cambridge, Ontario, took Hugh Morris's place as chairman at the convention.

In 1978 I did something I had been trying to do for ten years. I quit smoking. One day I was playing racquetball against a man who was eight years older than I was. Halfway through the game he was standing in the middle of the court, raring to go, and I was leaning up against a wall, puffing, calling time-out. That was it! On New Year's Eve I went to a dinner party and intentionally chainsmoked all evening. I woke up in the morning coughing and feeling terrible. I haven't had a single cigarette since, and now I can't imagine how I could play tennis, hike in the mountains, or have anywhere near the energy I have, had I continued smoking.

In June 1979 Joe Clark became prime minister, and all signs indicated his government would be even weaker on Canadian sovereignty than Trudeau's. Flora MacDonald was the new secretary of state for external affairs. I wrote to her expressing my concerns. She replied: "Without breaking any Cabinet confidences, I can assure you that there are many members of this government who share our views on questions of foreign investment and economic nationalism. We've all worked too long and hard while in Opposition to forget why we got involved in the CIC." But of course Flora wasn't a cabinet minister very long, the Clark government going down to defeat in the House of Commons in December and subsequently in the February 1980 federal election.

By the time of the election, the committee's annual budget was down to a paltry $35,000. Max Saltsman was doing a good job spreading the gospel in Ottawa but with few tangible results. Across the country activity was limited.

In early 1981 a task force was set up to make recommendations on the CIC's future. John Trent reported in March that the task force was still undecided and was requesting more input from members. The same month, Hugh Morris wrote to Trent suggesting it was time to close the organization down. In April the announcement was finally made by Morris: "The CIC has done its job. Its time has come . . . it has been a roaring success in its goal of prodding the federal government into action on U.S. domination of the Canadian economy."

I was less sanguine, saying the committee had had limited effectiveness in influencing legislation, although it had great success in influencing public opinion. I said that I hoped some new organization would take the committee's place, since there was a great need for continued vigilance in matters relating to Canadian sovereignty.

As the CIC was preparing to close down, Walter Stewart wrote about the lack of concern in Canada about foreign ownership and foreign control: "The debate has been going on so long that it has become tedious. It's not like a war, earthquake or forest fire, something that arrives with primal force and produces a short, fervent burst of reaction; this is a matter of charts and tables and long-winded speeches. To carry on the battle requires the fervour of a fanatic, the patience of a saint, the concentration of an accountant, and the endurance of a mule. There are not many takers."

In June 1981 the CIC closed its office in Ottawa and by the end of August it no longer existed.

In July widely respected Southam journalist Christopher Young wrote:

> The Committee for an Independent Canada can die happy. . . . When Hugh Morris announced its death this week, I felt a pang of regret and a recognition that as a consciousness-raising exercise, the CIC had been a success.
>
> Undoubtedly, the most effective of the CIC's leaders and spokesmen was Edmonton publisher Mel Hurtig.
>
> Rest in peace, CIC. Perhaps, in the mood of elegy, it would not be out of place to quote the eloquent words of the historian Thomas Carlyle, writing about Sir Walter Scott:
>
> Nothing that was worthy in the past departs; no truth or

goodness realized by man ever died, or can die; but is all still here and, recognized or not, lives and works through endless changes.

In the end there were two major reasons the CIC closed its doors in 1981. First, the born-again Liberal government that was elected in 1980 came out swinging with a highly nationalist policy. Who knew at the time that the Liberals would so quickly return to their continentalist past? Second, and this is most important, during the CIC's eleven years Canada's capital markets matured, Canadian savings increased, and more Bob Blairs were hard at work expanding Canadian ownership. When the CIC began operations in 1971, foreigners owned thirty-seven percent of all nonfinancial industry corporate assets in Canada. When the CIC closed a decade later, this figure was down to twenty-six percent, still very high by international standards, but a huge improvement over the previous relentless upward trend.

John George Diefenbaker

ONE OF THE MOST remarkable, eccentric, possessed, and determined men I've ever met was John Diefenbaker. He served as Canadian prime minister from June 1957 to April 1963. In the 1958 federal election he brought with him to Parliament the largest majority of any government in the history of Canada to that day.

The antiestablishment populist lawyer from the Prairies had almost a biblical presence on stage, a powerful straight-in-the-eye speaking style that hypnotized his audiences. He ran for public office and lost six times. In 1938, when he led the provincial Conservatives in Saskatchewan, they won no seats. His fortunes finally turned when he was elected to the House of Commons in 1940. Diefenbaker was reelected in 1945, 1949, and 1953, and in 1956 after two previous attempts, he was elected leader of the federal Conservatives.

After his great victory in 1958, in 1962 Diefenbaker and the Tories were reduced to a minority government. A key feature of the campaign was deliberate American intervention from Washington and Liberal accusations that the prime minister was anti-American. The following year the Liberals narrowly won power, but not before

Diefenbaker waged what *The Canadian Encyclopedia* calls "possibly the most spectacular one-man political campaign in Canadian history."

A terrible, acrimonious split developed in the Conservative party. In a 1967 leadership convention, Robert Stanfield defeated Diefenbaker and became the new Tory leader.

The final report of Walter Gordon's Royal Commission on Canada's Economic Prospects was released about the same time as John Diefenbaker became prime minister. Diefenbaker completely ignored the report. He didn't like Walter Gordon and viewed him as simply another big-business Bay Street Liberal. Diefenbaker had only a modest interest in the question of the American domination of the Canadian economy and, when he cancelled the development of the Avro Arrow aircraft, allowed Canada to become even more dependent on and integrated with the United States.

Except in passing on the steps of the Bessborough Hotel in Saskatoon, I had never met the former prime minister. But in September of 1974 he wrote to me after I had taken his place as a convention speaker when he became ill: "I am in agreement with your concern for the future of our country. When you are in Ottawa, I wish you would call on me so that we could have lunch together, and I could have your views at first hand."

We arranged to have lunch in the parliamentary restaurant in November, but again his illness intervened. In April 1975 he wrote to me about a survey I had conducted revealing the slim knowledge Canadian high school students had of Canada. In his letter Diefenbaker said:

> From time to time I speak to Public and High School students on Canada and what it means. I deal with its history, the drama of its pioneers, missionaries and explorers, its constitutional development and the sacrifices made by more than 100,000 Canadians who gave their all in two World Wars. The reception is the same everywhere. They listen with rapt attention and always, following my remarks, many of them come to me and state that they had no idea that Canadian history was so interesting.
>
> The survey you made recently received the widest publicity. I congratulate you on a contribution which I feel sure will bring about a good deal of action. Canadians, I fear, are losing a realization of the greatness of our heritage. In large measure this is due to the bombardment of all Canadians

from our friends to the south of us on radio and television, and this is accentuated by the failure of our educational system to emphasize a knowledge of Canadian history. Without that knowledge and the inspiration that it gives, no one can give to our country the best in citizenship. . . .

I wish you would get in touch with me when you are in Ottawa. I am most anxious to meet you and discuss a most serious problem facing Canadians, mainly the preservation of the independence of this nation.

Of course I was delighted to receive the letter, especially with its last paragraph. I arranged to see Mr. Diefenbaker on my next trip to Ottawa. His secretary, Betty Eligh, called and apologized; unfortunately I had picked a very busy day and Mr. Diefenbaker would likely only be able to see me for a short time in his office just after one o'clock. I then scheduled a full afternoon of appointments on the Hill.

I arrived at Mr. Diefenbaker's office a few minutes before one, anticipating a brief meeting. I left his office at ten minutes after five. We talked for more than four hours, about politics and people, about Canadian independence, about the Liberals and the economy, about my family and his. The Chief wanted to talk, and I sat there mesmerized. He mimicked Lester Pearson's lisp and John Kennedy's accent. He made fun of Dalton Camp and Peter Newman. He praised my efforts as the work of a true patriot. He dedicated photos of himself to me and one for each of my four daughters. He told me hilarious story after story, smiling and laughing frequently, often with a wicked, mischievous look in his eye. Parkinson's disease may have slowed him down physically, but he was as alert and full of spunk as ever.

As I went through the door, the last thing he said to me was: "How is it possible for someone as smart as you to have run for those Liberals?" In May 1979 John Diefenbaker was elected to the House of Commons for the thirteenth and last time. He died three months later.

One person who had come to dislike him was John Kennedy. When Diefenbaker was defeated by Lester Pearson, an elated McGeorge Bundy, who was national security adviser to Kennedy and later to Lyndon Johnson, wrote in a memo: "I might add that I myself have been sensitive to the need for being extra polite to Canadians ever since George Ball and I knocked over the Diefenbaker government by one incautious press release."

So George Ball did what he could to fulfil his own prophecy. And

U.S. national security helped get rid of that great threat, John Diefenbaker. I have always blamed Canadians, not Americans, for Canada's descent into colonial status, but anyone who believes that the Americans do not overtly and covertly directly intervene in Canadian politics is hopelessly naïve.

Walter Lockhart Gordon: The Gentle Patriot

WALTER GORDON WAS A partner in the accounting firm of Clarkson, Gordon and Co., in the management-consultant firm of Woods, Gordon, and president and chairman of his own very successful Toronto firm, Canadian Corporate Management Company Limited. He assisted in the organization of the Foreign Exchange Control Board in 1939, was a special assistant to the deputy minister of finance from 1940 to 1942, and chairman of two royal commissions, one on administrative classifications in the public service and, more importantly, in 1955, the Royal Commission on Canada's Economic Prospects. He was elected to the House of Commons as a Liberal member of Parliament for Toronto-Davenport in 1962 and reelected in 1963 and 1965.

Walter Gordon and Lester Pearson was very close friends for more than twenty years. Not only was Gordon instrumental in Pearson's 1958 election as leader of the Liberal party, he also was a key organizer of the rejuvenating Kingston "thinkers' conference," the party's first policy conference in almost seventy years! As Keith Davey writes in his memoir, *The Rainmaker,* "Quite simply, without Walter Gordon, Mike Pearson would never have become Prime Minister of Canada. . . ."

In May 1963 Gordon became minister of finance in the Pearson government. For him, the problem of the rapidly growing foreign ownership and control of the Canadian economy could be solved largely through one bold, long-overdue stroke — a thirty percent takeover tax, which he included in his 1963 budget. The resulting Bay Street, Wall Street, and financial-press furore forced Gordon to withdraw the proposal within days. Gordon had known full well what he was doing and the reaction he could expect from big business. What he didn't expect, and what dismayed him enormously, was Lester Pearson's failure to stand by him when the budget crisis erupted.

In 1965 Gordon urged Pearson to call an election so that the Liberals could escape their minority-government shackles. Pearson agreed and an election was called for November. Even though the Liberals won with thirty-four more seats than the Conservatives, they fell two short of a majority. As a matter of principle, Gordon resigned, much to the regret of his growing number of supporters in Ottawa and across the country.

But by the time Gordon resigned as minister of finance in the fall of 1965, unemployment had been reduced by almost fifty percent and stood at only 3.9 percent. The current-account deficit had been reduced to less than a third of its figure of six years earlier, the GDP had increased in 1963 and 1964 by a total of nine percent, and the federal government's deficits had been reduced from $692-million to two consecutive deficits of only $39-million.

After Gordon resigned from the cabinet, he stayed in the caucus, but did not attend Parliament often. In 1966, thanks largely to Keith Davey's role as an intermediary, Gordon returned to the cabinet to oversee the task force on Foreign Ownership and the Structure of Canadian Investment, headed by Mel Watkins. Back in Ottawa, Gordon found himself more isolated and unhappy. Then Pearson resigned just before Christmas; the following February Gordon tabled the Watkins report and a month later resigned from both the cabinet and the caucus.

The first time I met Walter Gordon was shortly after he had resigned from the cabinet in 1965. I had been warned that he would likely ask if I had a list of things I wanted to discuss, so I prepared a short list. I was quite in awe at the prospect of meeting the man, and quite nervous. His secretary showed me into his Toronto office, and I sat down opposite him as he peered at me across his big desk. His first words were, "Well, Mr. Hurtig, would you like to start with your list or mine?"

We got along famously almost immediately. We had many common areas of interest and many common concerns. By the time I left, it was "Walter" and "Mel." I always called him Walter thereafter, although I was surprised to note that even Beland Honderich *always* called him Mr. Gordon.

The first time I went to lunch with Walter, we went to the York

Club on Bloor Street in Toronto. It gives me no pleasure to remember the lunch. As we followed the maître d' winding our way through the luncheon area towards our table, I could see bald, fat men in three-piece suits glaring at Gordon with squinty-eyed animosity. It was the first time it ever occurred to me what a courageous man he was, courageous in that he, like Bruce Willson, had on matters of principle bravely stood up to the anti-Canadian policies of his own peer group.

In his book, *A Choice for Canada — Independence or Colonial Status* (1966), Walter wrote that in his years in Ottawa "the influence that financial and business interests in the United States had on Canadian policy and opinion was continually brought home to me." But it wasn't only the White House, the U.S. State Department, and other parts of the Washington administration. "This influence . . . was pressed by those who direct American business in Canada, by their professional advisors, by Canadian financiers whose interests were identified directly or indirectly with American investment in Canada, by influential members of the Canadian civil service, by some representatives of the university community, and by sections of the press."

A formidable phalanx indeed: the compradors and their colleagues. As foreign investment, foreign ownership, and foreign control grew, the organized well-financed public and covert opposition to pro-Canadian policies grew.

When Gordon was in the cabinet, time after time Mitchell Sharp had rallied the right-wing and continentalist forces in the Liberal party. When Sharp proclaimed in cabinet that Canada could not afford medicare, Gordon and all the Quebec ministers threatened to resign and won the day. After Trudeau was elected leader, Gordon became optimistic. As we have seen, the optimism was shortlived. When the Committee for an Independent Canada held its annual convention in Edmonton in 1972, a frustrated Walter Gordon went further than ever before. "Neither the Liberals or the Conservatives are worth voting for," he said.

In the spring of 1972 as the country headed for an election, Walter wrote to me: "I expect I shall decide to come out against the Trudeau government . . . someone wrote to me the other day suggesting I think about the results of the 1911 election and take some encouragement from it. It would be ironical if another distinguished French-Canadian Prime Minister were to be defeated by another Nova Scotian who had made no impact on the public up to that time." Of course Walter was referring to the defeat of Wilfrid Laurier and his reciprocity proposal by Conservative Robert Borden, and to Robert Stanfield.

When Pearson was dying in 1972, there was great pressure from a number of sources for Walter to go to Ottawa to visit his former friend on his deathbed. In *Gentle Patriot* Denis Smith writes about the deterioration of the relationship:

> The end came, for Walter Gordon, as the cumulative result of a series of acts and omissions by Mike Pearson. There was Pearson's failure to support Gordon in the controversy over the 1963 budget. There was the Prime Minister's breathtaking abandonment of Guy Favreau to his hostile critics in the autumn of 1964. There was Pearson's encouragement of Gordon to lead the 1965 campaign and to remain as Minister of Finance, followed by his private assurances to businessmen that Gordon would leave Finance after the election. There was the worthless undertakings made on Gordon's return to the Cabinet. And finally, there was Pearson's bitter castigation of Gordon in caucus and to the press over the Vietnam speech in May 1967, after his much milder comments in Cabinet where Gordon could defend himself. Gordon never again trusted Pearson, and when he left the Cabinet in February 1968, the long association ended. None of the friendships and accomplishments of Gordon's years in politics compensated him for the rupture of this close friendship with a man he had trusted and aided so loyally.

I was concerned about how Walter would react to my resignation from the Liberal party. He wrote to me: "Many thanks for your letter of August 22nd. I quite understand your decision even though it is different from my own. In fairness, however, I must admit that I would be tempted to do what you are doing if (a) I had not worked so hard in helping the Liberal Party to make its comeback in 1962 and 1963 and (b) if I were younger and felt there was still time for me to influence the policies of another party."

In his books and speeches Walter alerted a generation of Canadians to the dangers of excessive foreign ownership and control of Canada. Over the years in my own speeches, his one sentence I quoted most often was this warning: "Canada, during some period of crisis, will be absorbed by the United States, perhaps without most Canadians fully realizing what has happened."

Gordon was a prophet, but not without honour and friends. On January 27, 1976, we gathered in the Canadian Room of the Royal York Hotel in Toronto to celebrate his seventieth birthday. Walter took the subway to the party. Some eight hundred friends sang "Happy birthday, Walter Gordon, we love you!" Among those who organized the event were Beland Honderich, Duncan Gordon, Pauline Jewett, William Kilbourn, Peter Newman, Senator Hartland Molson, Eddie Goodman, Abe Rotstein, and Alex MacIntosh. Robertson Davies said grace, and Keith Davey was the master of ceremonies. Don Harron, Dave Broadfoot, Maureen Forrester, Frank Augustyn, and Karen Kain were among the entertainers. And with all the other lights in the giant room turned out, a bright spotlight focused on a beautiful Catherine McKinnon as she sang a memorable rendition of "Farewell to Nova Scotia." Telegrams of praise were read from around the world, from Pierre Trudeau in Cuba with Margaret, from John Kenneth Galbraith, and from others, all of whom spoke of Walter's leadership, his dedication, and his courage. Peter Newman called him "the conscience of his country."

When it was Walter's turn to speak, he ended by saying: "If I could cry I would cry."

In 1982 Walter and Liz Gordon held a luncheon for my new wife, Kay, and me at Winston's in Toronto. Walter and I had become very close over the years, talking at least once a week on the telephone. At the luncheon he raised a glass of wine and asked everyone to drink to Mel Hurtig becoming prime minister. He knew, and I knew, this would never happen, but it was a nice gesture from a man I had grown to love.

On April 18, 1983, Walter wrote to me. It was one of the few dispirited letters I had ever received from him. It read in part:

Thank you for sending me a copy of your "Continentalism and Nationalism/the Canadian Schizophrenia." It cheered me up after reading the *Toronto Star* over lunch which reported a Gallup poll showing that a high majority of Canadians would like to see Petrocan sold to private interests (presumably, foreign private interests?). It is too bad that so many Canadians do not give a damn about Canada.

I am off to Europe tomorrow and will be away for a

month. When I get back, I am to make a speech on the nuclear threat and will come out in favour of declaring ourselves to be a nuclear-free country. I doubt if anyone will listen.

On the contrary, many listened. Gordon became a key, sought after figure in the peace, disarmament, and anti-nuclear movement in Canada.

Walter Gordon died in a Toronto hospital in March 1987 at the age of eighty-one. I had no idea Walter had been in hospital. Just before dinner I was standing in my living room watching the sun set in the horizon above the North Saskatchewan River Valley. We get wonderful sunsets in Edmonton for much of the year, but I had never seen anything quite so spectacular as the huge blazing red ball of fire that slowly sank in the west. I called Kay to come and watch, and we stood there for some ten minutes as the sky glowed redder and redder and then gradually dimmed as the brilliant disc disappeared.

About an hour later I tried to get Walter on the phone, but there was no answer there or at his country home. I called his daughter, Jane Glassco. She told me that Walter had died an hour earlier. My eyes filled with tears.

Walter Gordon had great compassion for the poor, a strong desire for and a keen insight into the need for social change, and he was very brave indeed, in fact, undaunted in the face of relentless criticism and opposition from the financial establishment. I never knew him to be other than even-handed, never saw him cross with another man or woman in public. His love of Canada inspired us and influenced our behaviour. He was a mentor to countless men and women, who looked to him for guidance. He was a man of honour and a private man who did not always go comfortably into public. I think perhaps I was proudest of him when he spoke out strongly against the Vietnam War in 1967, knowing full well that he would pay the price for angering and embarrassing Lester Pearson.

The evening Walter died I stood at my window for a long time in the twilight. I couldn't help thinking that we were in the twilight of the country, as well.

IV

THE PERILS OF PUBLISHING

GO, Geishas, Martinis, and Mount Fuji

IT IS NO EXAGGERATION to say that the Japanese game of GO and martinis helped to launch my publishing career. Soon after I became a bookseller, I was attracted to the fascinating and beautiful Orientalia published by Charles Tuttle, a firm based in Rutland, Vermont, and Tokyo. Tuttle books on Japanese and Chinese art, haiku, martial arts, Oriental cooking, and origami soon became staples in my bookstore.

There were also several books about the Japanese board game GO, and after reading one I resolved to learn how to play. I discovered a fascinating game whose fundamentals are relatively easy to learn, but whose intricacies make it much more complicated than chess. Aside from golf, it is the only sport or game I know of that has an excellent handicap system, allowing a player of modest ability to play an expert and still have a good contest. Moreover, the game itself is beautiful and played with some ceremony. Two players sit cross-legged on the floor, the nine-inch-thick, sixteen-by-eighteen-inch lined wooden board sitting between them on four thick carved legs. The pieces are identical in size and shape: round black and white glass, slate, or shell stones. Once played, the pieces are never moved unless captured, at which time they are removed from the board. A single game can take anywhere from one hour to the two nine-hour marathon sessions devoted to a single Meijen tournament game.

I found the game great fun and a challenge. Soon my friends Sandy Mactaggart and Ralph MacMillan were playing. Sandy, a bachelor at the time, would often arrive after dinner dressed in flowing purple

Japanese robes, a bottle of sake in his hand, and depart at two or three in the morning after we had completed "one last game."

In the summer of 1962 Ralph and I headed for Japan. We had four goals: to see the country, to play GO, to climb Mount Fuji, and to learn as much as we could about Japanese culture. I had a fifth goal: I wanted to acquire the Canadian rights for Tuttle books since there was no Canadian agent for the line and I was convinced I could sell great quantities to my fellow booksellers and to libraries across the country.

We arrived at the Frank Lloyd Wright Imperial Hotel in Tokyo, unpacked, and went for dinner at a sushi bar with Charles Tuttle and his beautiful and talented Japanese wife, Reiko. Now, Charles and I, aside from our love of books, also liked gin martinis. The four of us sat perched on stools at the bar for two hours, with Ralph thoroughly taken with Reiko, and me trying to get Charles to give me Canadian rights to his books. Alas, just two weeks before, Tuttle had signed a contract for exclusive Canadian distribution rights with the firm of Abelard-Schuman. I was just a bit too late. However, as the evening progressed and the gin flowed, we became — how shall I say? — relaxed and quite good buddies. By the time we headed back to the hotel, I had the Canadian rights for Tuttle books.

Over the next six weeks Ralph and I toured Tokyo and Japan with our little Japanese-English dictionaries in hand. At the time there were still relatively few westerners in the country; for the most part we were alone among crowds of men, women, and children who knew no English. It was a great adventure and a marvellous education. We went from palaces to shrines, from amusement centres to bar-girl clubs, from shopping districts to the Kabuki theatre, from gorgeous gardens to spectacular pavilions, from temples to bookstores, from pagodas to carved golden arches, from giant Buddhas to spectacular waterfalls, from festivals to country bath houses, from hotels to ancient inns, from tea ceremonies to express trains.

In Tokyo we visited art galleries and the Kanda district, with its 250 bookstores. At night we went to restaurants and clubs in the Akasaka district. We shopped on the Ginza and headed north to the ancient buildings of Nikko and to the nearby Kegon waterfalls. Then we headed south to Kamakura, Yokohama, and the magnificent Kyoto, with its famous Ryoanji stone garden, Golden Pavilion Temple, and Katsura Imperial Villa. We sat on the shaded platform verandahs gazing out at extraordinary gardens of camellias, chrysanthemums, azaleas, sculptured cypress trees, ponds, streams, lanterns, and waterfalls.

One night in the pitch-blackness we went cormorant fishing. We sat in long narrow boats, the cormorants perched on the boat's gunwales, as a bright lantern attracted the fish. Suddenly the big bird would dive into the water and almost immediately surface with a fish held in its beak, unable to swallow it because of a cord around its neck.

We had many other adventures, but our two most memorable experiences were climbing Mount Fuji and playing GO. The Japanese had not encountered a great many westerners who knew the game. For the most part they seemed astonished as they watched Ralph and me play. We had a small portable magnetic GO set that we carried with us when we travelled about the country. When we played on the express trains, men would leave their seats and gather around us to watch.

One Japanese businessman was so impressed he invited us to his villa for dinner and a game of GO. When we arrived, we soon found geishas seated to our left and right who taught us games and tricks played with tissue paper, coins, and cigarettes. Lest you get the wrong idea, the most intimate game was one in which we passed a straw back and forth using our noses and upper lips to make the exchange. Then we dined on massaged beer-fed Kobe beef, played GO, and all in all had a fine evening.

One night in Kyoto we wound our way up a dark alley, then through a back door, up two narrow dilapidated flights of stairs, down a long hall lit by a single bare lightbulb, and then, with some hesitation, entered through swinging doors into a smoke-filled GO parlour. About eighty Japanese seated over some forty GO tables looked up at us in great surprise, quickly looked away, and returned to their games. In a few minutes, though, a middle-aged man rose, approached us, bowed, pointed at his spot at a GO table and said, "*Dozo*" — please. Soon we were both playing Japanese opponents. Despite the fact that we were given the maximum nine-stone handicap advantage, we lost every single game. But we learned an enormous amount about the game.

Mount Robson, the highest mountain in the Canadian Rockies, is 3,954 metres high. Fuji is not far behind at 3,778 metres. It is a beautiful mountain that should only be climbed in July and August. Many people have been killed when trapped by snowstorms as they tried to reach the peak too early or too late in the year.

Just before we left Tokyo for Fuji, we learned that the day before, a typhoon had left more than a thousand people stranded on the mountain, with high winds and zero visibility. Nevertheless, we drove to the Fuji-Hakone National Park, visited Lake Kawaguchi, and sat down to dinner at four in the afternoon. The best idea, we were told, was to climb all night and get to the top before the sun rises out of the Pacific around four-thirty in the morning. Ralph and I each had a martini, a Kobe steak, and started up the mountain just before six.

We had each acquired a traditional metre-and-a-quarter long, eight-sided climbing pole. On the way up the mountain there would be ten "stations," mostly set in tiny caves, where one or two Japanese men sat cross-legged in front of charcoal fires with branding irons. As one advanced up the mountain, you stopped at each station and had your climbing pole branded to prove you had indeed climbed that far.

We headed up the mountain via the Kawaguchiko route by ourselves. In just a little more than ten hours later, we were at the summit shrine, the only westerners among some three thousand Japanese. Along the way, the caves offered rest stops, but the sleeping mats were so crowded we had to squat in a tiny space for a few moments' rest and shelter. The higher we got, the more crowded it became. Now we were climbing with burning torches in a long single file. After the eighth stage, the air became thin and cold. It was mid-August and we had started off in hiking shorts and T-shirts. But now we had to don long pants, warm jackets, and gloves. Aside from stops for branding, tea, and a pee, we climbed steadily through the night.

When we arrived at the summit, it was a cold clear morning. At four-twenty-seven the sun began to rise from the eastern Pacific horizon. Soon the sunlight reflected off the golden bars of the Sengen shrine near the summit's volcano crater. Off in every direction we could see a spectacular view of ocean, sea, mountains, lakes, and countryside.

We visited the shrine, then the crater where many young lovers and others took their lives every year. Then we headed back down the mountain in a different direction, via the Gotemba route. Unfortunately a problem arose almost immediately. We had both purchased new climbing boots at the base of the mountain. We weren't five minutes on the way down before I realized that my boots were slightly too small. Every step down produced pain in my big toes and soon I was in agony. The top of the mountain is almost all volcanic ash, and woven reed thongs attached to your boots allow you to slide down much of the upper part of the mountain at a great pace. I tried this, but the pain was unbearable. Some twelve hours later, when I got to the bottom — summit to base is about twenty miles — the boots had to be cut off my badly swollen feet.

We had been up for forty-eight hours before we arrived at the Kiuunkaku Inn in Atami, on Sagami Bay east of Fuji. We headed straight for a steaming hot pool and a massage. I slept for fourteen hours.

There is an old saying in Japan that goes something like this: "If you haven't climbed Mount Fuji once, you haven't lived. If you climb Mount Fuji twice, you're a fool."

I must tell you about a sign listing THE RULES FOR SWIM-MING which we discovered at the swimming pool in Kyoto's Mi-yako Hotel. Rule number one: "Be sure as nails to always wear swim suit."

Although there were no numbers on the streets, homes, or office buildings, we only got lost once; the Japanese people were very helpful, hospitable, and kind to us. It was a wonderful trip and I returned home to Edmonton with many fine memories and my first publishing agency.

From Politics to Publishing

WHEN ALFRED KNOPF, the distinguished, successful, and widely respected American publisher, visited Canada in 1955, he said he came to "see if I can uncover some Canadian writing talent — which I don't expect to do. The country seems to be peopled with involuted and convoluted Englishmen who don't have much to say."

Remarkably, Knopf's words hardly stirred a fuss.

In a speech the following year, the young Toronto publisher Jack McClelland spelled out the problems the publishing industry in Canada faced, starting with a relatively small English-language population and far too few stores that sold books. As well, he said that "overhead costs for sales and distribution are fantastically high. And, paradoxically enough, nowhere else are so many different book titles offered for sale. . . . As a consequence the publisher interested in publishing Canadian books has had first to involve himself in the importation of foreign works. As more foreign works are imported, more Canadian books can be published, but because of the increased competition, relatively fewer Canadian books will be read."

The same year, John Gray, the publisher of Macmillan of Canada, went on record saying in the book *Writing in Canada*: "I doubt that any Canadian publisher derives any important part of his revenue (or any net profit) from Canadian general publishing; his commercial welfare is therefore not identical with that of Canadian writers. Similarly, those Canadian writers who derive any important part of their income from their books (apart of course from textbooks) do not earn it in Canada and are not dependent on a Canadian publisher." A pretty sad situation, but unfortunately more accurate than not.

Six years later, in the 1962 book *Mass Media in Canada*, editor and broadcaster Robert Weaver wrote:

> Some estimates put it that there are fewer than twenty adequate bookstores in the whole of Canada. . . . The publishing of trade books . . . has always been a nervy business with a small profit margin . . . if there are only a handful of good bookstores in Canada, a minority of book readers, and no real profits to be earned by Canadian publishers from Canadian books, how and why do Canadian publishers continue to exist? One answer is that there are some publishers who love their work, and who have a sense of responsibility for the intellectual life of the nation. Another more mundane answer is to be found in the agency system — in my opinion, the most pervasive, the most essential, and in some respects the most destructive force in Canadian publishing.

Weaver went on to point out that while there were more than forty "publishers" listed in the Toronto phone book, only half a dozen had a significant editorial staff and "most of the men who call themselves publishers might as well be selling soap." Moreover, "the agency need not trouble itself with writers (those thorny souls) nor with editors (who can be almost equally thorny) nor with the serious risk and painful guesswork that are the hallmark of original publishing. The agent buys, and he sells, and he goes home at night with a briefcase in which there are no manuscripts to disturb his sleep."

Jim Douglas was a well-liked salesman for McClelland and Stewart in the late 1950s and 1960s. According to Jim, "For many people in the industry only British and American books counted. The big publisher catalogues were Knopf, Little Brown, Lippincott, Atheneum, etc. The catalogue of Canadian books was always the last to be presented. One librarian in Burnaby told me that he doesn't buy Canadian books, period."

Naturally, having learned all this, I decided to become a Canadian book publisher. With the exclusive agency for Tuttle books in place, I began planning a publishing division separate from my retail-store operation. Almost immediately I was amazed and delighted by how very receptive my fellow booksellers were to the Tuttle books. A modest, but good start.

One day back in 1956 a big, long, shiny black limousine had pulled up in front of our first tiny bookstore. A tall, well-dressed, impressive looking gentleman came into the store, bought several books, chatted for a few minutes, then departed, leaving me his card: The Rt. Hon. Viscount Boyd, C.H., Park Royal Brewery, London. Little did I know at the time that Alan Boyd, Anthony Eden's former minister of colonial affairs, would come to play an important role in my life.

Lord Boyd was chairman of the Guinness Corporation, which not only produced the famous brew, but had extensive land and other real-estate holdings around the world, including Alberta and especially British Columbia, where Guinness owned and developed British Properties in Vancouver and built the Lions Gate Bridge.

Boyd would visit Edmonton once or twice a year, and he always came into the bookstore. Soon we were regularly going to lunch or dinner, often together with our wives. Guinness had produced a little booklet as a promotional device designed to settle arguments in pubs. The little booklet had quickly grown into *The Guinness Book of Records*, a hardcover book that was sold around the world in a dozen different languages.

In 1966, over a brandy at my home, Alan Boyd asked me if I would like to have the Canadian rights to the Guinness book. I was surprised and pleased and quickly accepted the offer.

"Fine," he said. "How many would you like to order of next year's edition?"

"How many did your Canadian agent buy last year?"

"Burns and McEachern have ordered one thousand copies each year for the past three years."

"Okay, I'll take two thousand."

He was pleased and I was delighted. At the time we were just gearing up to launch our own Canadian publishing program.

The 2,000 copies we ordered for 1967 disappeared quickly. The following year we ordered 5,000 copies, and the year after that 7,500. Even though the book was an annual, we allowed the retail trade full protection, meaning each and every copy was fully returnable. Moreover, we sold the book in Canada just blow the U.S. retail price, accepting a lower profit margin to boost sales. The booksellers responded accordingly, with excellent orders each year. There were rarely any returns. We worked hard at advertising and promoting the book through television, radio, newspaper and magazine ads, contests, and free promotion copies.

According to Toronto author, editor, and former publisher Jim Bacque, "A Canadian publishing firm must be managed by a genius and financed by an angel." I was no genius and I had no angel, but difficult as the publishing industry was, I had great good fortune to begin with. I always used to laugh when I heard the big tough guys in the major petroleum firms tell the press and government, and anyone else who would listen, just what a difficult, high-risk, free-enterprise business they were in. Compared to publishing Canadian books, oil and gas was a risk-free piece of cake. In 1968 publishing enterprises paid out forty-one percent of their profits in taxes, while oil and gas, mostly foreign-owned companies, paid only twelve percent.

Early on in my bookseller years I had developed a great interest in rare Canadiana, sparked by seeing bookseller Louis Melzack's superb collection in Montreal. I was soon spending a great deal of time in antiquarian bookstores on my travels across the country.

One day Charles Tuttle and I were talking across the Pacific Ocean, and between us we came up with what we thought would be a great idea. Together, Tuttle for the U.S. market and Hurtig for Canada, we would produce *The Canadiana Reprint Series*, rare books reprinted in perfect facsimile, with new introductions by experts in the field, handsomely packaged in new jackets or slipcases. Since the books would almost all be out-of-print titles in the public domain, and inexpensive to reprint, we would retail them at low prices. Charles would do the production work using some newly developed, exclusive technology that faithfully reproduced the books — maps, illustrations, and all — in black and white or full colour. I would locate the rare first editions, select the Canadian scholar to write the introduction, and choose the jacket art.

Canadian librarians, authors, and book collectors loved the idea. Even back in the late 1960s a fine first edition of Franklin's *Narrative of a Journey to the Shores of the Polar Sea* (1823) or *Mackenzie's Voyages from Montreal through the Continent of North America* (1801) sold for well over a thousand dollars. Our facsimiles were much welcomed because the average person could not afford the original editions, and even library budgets rarely had room for such expensive acquisitions.

The first reprint we published in 1967 was a more contemporary work and a quite modest undertaking, but I wanted it to be our first since it was largely based in Alberta: *Johnny Chinook: Tall Tales and True from the Canadian West*, by Robert Gard, illustrated by none other than Walter Phillips. As a bookseller, I knew there would be a demand for the book, since people kept coming into the store asking for it. Grant MacEwan kindly agreed to do a new introduction. The book of folk tales, originally published in 1940, had been out of print for many years. We kept our print run small — 1,500 copies — and were sold out within a year.

The second book we published, our first original title, was Eli Mandel's exceptional *An Idiot Joy*. It promptly won the 1968 Governor General's Award for poetry. Not a bad start.

But it was our third book, *Alberta: A Natural History*, edited by W.G. Hardy, that really put us into publishing in a big way. We sold a phenomenal 73,000 copies, a figure almost unheard of in those days.

We had been running the publishing operation out of the back of the Jasper Avenue bookstore, but soon we needed more space. Fortunately there was a vacant, 1,400-square-foot warehouse just a couple of doors down the back alley. We fixed it up with some badly needed paint, secondhand furniture, and a new window, and it became Hurtig Publishers for the next five years. Soon three women were handling the office work, and two young men were handling shipping and receiving. It was a going concern, with only two problems. First, the electrical system in the building was so bad that our manager, Agnes Primrose, had to stop typing whenever anyone wanted to use the photocopier. Second, a middle-aged flasher, noting the steady traffic of young women down the back lane between the bookstore and the publishing warehouse, visited periodically and practised his art.

I was very lucky in the quality of people who came to work for us. Dianne Woodman, now well known across Canada for her excellent and diverse career in books, sold our titles in Alberta and Saskatchewan, and later such superb book people as Scott McIntyre, Jim Douglas, Mark Stanton, Allan MacDougall, Nick Hunt, Ian Cameron, and Mike Reynolds represented our titles in B.C. and across the Prairies.

What Does a Publisher Do?

M Y EARLY SUCCESS AS a publisher wasn't entirely blind luck. Many years as a bookseller had taught me about editing, pricing, format, jacket covers, advertising, and promotion. Most importantly, they taught me about reading habits and trends, and about the terrible paucity of Canadian titles in many areas. As well, all my years of working with people had taught me to be a pretty good judge of character. This helped enormously when it came to hiring staff for the publishing company. Over the years, whatever business success I had was, to a large extent, accounted for by the talented enthusiastic people we hired to work for Hurtig Publishers.

Not too many people know what a book publisher does. Many think a publisher is someone who prints books. And those who know a bit more think a publisher is someone who sits back in an office sorting through piles of manuscripts saying no, no, no, maybe, no, no, yes, no, no. A surprising number of people think a publisher gets paid for publishing someone's book.

Very few publishers, really only a handful, print and bind their own books, and most of these are university presses with relatively small print runs. It isn't unusual for a book to be paged by one company, printed by another, with the colour work done by yet another firm. After a book has been accepted for publication, two early and key decisions are, what is the book going to look like and how many copies will the first printing be? Then detailed specifications are drawn up, and the production is put out to tender. Over the years, we had more than ninety-nine percent of our books produced in British Columbia, Alberta, Manitoba, Ontario, and Quebec.

Determining the right size of the first print run is an important key to successful book publishing, but it's also damn difficult. If you don't print enough copies, the authors and booksellers will be quite unhappy, especially if you have a bestselling title and run out during the Christmas season. Also, a small printing means a high retail price and a low potential profit margin. The larger the printing, the lower the retail price; the lower the retail price, the better the book will usually sell. On the other hand, if you print too many copies, you end up with unsold inventory and likely lose money.

Our strategy was to try for large first printings to get the price down, and to use the good potential profit margin for lots of advertising and promotion. Of course you couldn't do this with all your titles, because some of them, no matter how much you advertised, would have limited sales.

It takes a certain degree of chutzpah to be a good publisher. But sometimes caution succeeds. An American book, *The Lonely Crowd*, by David Reisman, comes to mind. The first printing was 1,500 copies. It sold over a million.

Of course, if you set your print run based on an estimate of how many copies you hope to sell in a year, which is what we did, your overall inventory is going to constantly grow, since each year you produce both a spring and fall list. Each month we were signing contracts for new books to be published one, two, or three years in the future. And these contracts required author advances, sometimes *large* ones.

While we started off doing very well indeed, we were still regularly increasing (when possible) the size of our bank loan and were still having to turn down on average at least one book a month we would like to have published. In one year, two of the titles we'd had to reject were published by other houses and became bestsellers.

The bookseller is faced with choosing from some sixty or seventy thousand new English-language titles each year, not counting reprints, paperbacks, and new editions. The look of the book — the jacket, the format, the packaging — is vitally important. An attractive-looking book will stand out in a bookseller's display of titles. We spent a lot of time and a lot of money on our jackets, and it paid off. For many years after the Second World War, U.K. publishers lost much of their market share in North America because the appearance of their books was so very dull.

Publishing is a detailed, hands-on business. Even though I was away a great deal on behalf of the CIC, I was able to oversee most of what was happening in my company. For every book, I drew up a detailed, three-page, 120-line budget of costs and anticipated revenue; this helped us make such key decisions as format, size of first printing, retail price, and advertising and promotion budget.

As well as a detailed budget, we had a sixty-item checklist as a reminder of things that had to be attended to with each book, matters relating to contracts, manuscripts, design, printers, indexes and bibliographies, illustrations, jackets, galleys, page proofs, dummies, production schedules, corner clips, legal questions, captions, maps, posters and bookmarks, advertising copy, complimentary and review copies, subsidiary rights, promotion tours, shipping instructions.

Not too long after we started publishing Canadian books, our book prices had become highly competitive with the American books that dominated so much of the Canadian market, despite the fact that the U.S. publishers had comparatively huge print runs. Of course if Doubleday prints 200,000 copies of a book for the U.S. market, by the time they tack on 20,000 copies for Canada, their unit cost is tiny and their profit margin is enormous (though most of the profits of foreign publishers show up outside Canada and not with their branch-plant operation).

Woe to the publisher who fails to pay adequate attention to receivables and inventory. Pretty soon there's no more money left to finance the next list. And true to form, Canadian banks, which have always been eager to lend a hand to finance takeovers of businesses in Canada by well-heeled American corporations, have consistently been ultraconservative in their dealings with Canadian-owned publishing houses.

Except for vanity publishers, the publisher doesn't get paid for publishing books; in fact, it's the other way around. Most trade publishers pay royalties to the author based on the book's retail price, usually beginning at ten percent and increasing to fifteen percent as the quantity sold increases. Alas, many fine authors can work for years on a book and end up with a very modest return for their efforts. On the other hand, though it's rare in Canada, some authors end up making millions of dollars on a single title.

Rather than sitting back in an office going through piles of unsolicited manuscripts, the successful book publisher is one who originates many books, finds the right author for a project, perhaps pairs the author with the right illustrator, finds the right editor to act as the catalyst, and so on. In our company, more than half the books we published started with an in-house idea.

A good publisher must be a prodigious reader of books, journals, magazines, newspapers, and documents. When I was a publisher, I read five or six newspapers a day and averaged at least forty to fifty books a year, aside from the many manuscripts I took home with me.

Certainly you don't have to play poker, go to Las Vegas, or the track if you're a book publisher; every week you get all the gambling you need simply by sitting at your desk.

From The New Romans On

I N 1967 THE POET Al Purdy and I went to a party in Edmonton and three hours later had agreed to work on a book of "candid" Canadian opinions of the U.S. Purdy would solicit and organize and edit the book of essays and poetry by such well-known Canadian writers as Farley Mowat, Margaret Atwood, Mordecai Richler, Margaret Laurence, George Grant, Robert Fulford, George Woodcock, Earle Birney, and Michael Ondaatje, and write an introduction. Shortly after the party, we settled on *The New Romans* as our title.

In 1968 I hired our first full-time editor-in-chief, twenty-two-year-old Calgarian Susan Kent, a great consumer of coffee, who applied for the job after reading an article in *Time* magazine "that made such a big deal of the coffee machine in your bookstore." Susan's first job was to write ad copy for *The New Romans*. Without question it was going to be one of the most controversial books ever published in Canada. By the time of publication that same year, we had an advance sale of more than twenty thousand copies and had sold excerpts to *Saturday Night* and *Maclean's* and U.S. rights to St. Martin's Press in New York.

The reviews were as expected. People either loved the book or hated it. According to the *Brandon Sun*, "Every Canadian who takes his citizenship seriously should read it." The Montreal *Gazette* had little doubt: "You pick it up and groan and after 30 minutes (if you last that long) you put it down with a groan.... In a word, tiresome." In the U.S. reviews ranged from the influential *Publishers Weekly* ("... there is too much truth in its pages to discuss ...") to the *Peoria Journal-Star* ("... sophomoric effusions of exotic abuse"). The *Sarnia Observer* wrote: "We sincerely hope and believe this book won't sell." Many of the U.S. reviews were of shocked outrage that Canadians dared to criticize the U.S.

University of Toronto President Claude Bissell reviewed *The New Romans* in the *Globe and Mail*. Bissell "relished" even "the emotional and biased pieces — Farley Mowat's cadenza of hate; Margaret Laurence's letter of a mother to an American Negress whose 12-year-old son had been cruelly killed by police; Irving Layton's two catalogues — one of America as a brassy heaven, the other of America as the ultimate hell."

In September Margaret Laurence wrote to me from England:

"CONGRATULATIONS on THE NEW ROMANS! Have just finished reading it and I think it is splendid. . . . You and Al are to be congratulated. . . . Reading the book makes me want to go home — mainly because it reminds me how many people there are whom I like and value there."

The New Romans ended up selling some 35,000 copies, big numbers even now, but very big numbers in those days. It was our first number-one national bestseller.

Book reviews are funny things; sometimes they make a book, sometimes they kill a book, and other times they make no difference at all. Over the years I've seen awful books trashed by reviewers, yet still make the bestseller lists. I've also seen excellent books praised by reviewers end up going nowhere. Sometimes, and not infrequently, a reviewer assigned by a newspaper or magazine to review a new title has an axe to grind, a slight to repay, or critical erudition to display. Sometimes a publication assigns a reviewer to a book with the full knowledge that the reviewer will dump on the book. One example immediately springs to mind: the *Globe* assigned Imperial Oil CEO W.O. Twaits to review a new book on energy by Jim Laxer. The results were entirely predictable.

The success of *The New Romans* brought us much attention and the beginnings of an avalanche of manuscripts from across the country. People in the publishing world in Toronto sat up and took notice when we began to take out full-page ads on pages three and five of *Quill & Quire*, the Canadian book trade's journal, reserving the space a year in advance.

Another success in 1968 was *Toasts to the Bride*. When I was a bookseller, many Saturdays a man with a rose or carnation in his lapel would come rushing into the store asking if we had a book of toasts to the bride. Unfortunately there was no such book. I commissioned Merv Huston to write one, and the book has remained in print for twenty-eight years.

Strangely enough, our being located in Edmonton was as much help as a hindrance. What the heck was a book-publishing firm doing operating, in of all places, Edmonton? And, in the case of *The New Romans*, with a number-one bestseller in competition with all the American, British, and Canadian books? Soon the book-page editors knew they couldn't ignore our titles. If anything, we probably received more than our share of attention because we were considered such an anomaly.

Late in 1968 I had been giving a talk in Kingston, and afterwards Al Purdy and I went to a crowded pub for a drink, and then a second drink. By the time we were contemplating a third, Al was looking around the room, which was filled with young people.

"Mel, you know, no one in this whole damn room knows who the hell we are!"

"You're probably right."

"Let's have another damn drink."

Just then our waitress came over. She was young, beautiful, and buxom, this last made all the more obvious by her low neckline. As she leaned over the table to take our order, we were both impressed. I asked her about Kingston, about her job; was she going to school, too?

"Yes, I'm going to Queen's."

I thought maybe she would recognize the name Al Purdy from her English classes.

"What are you taking?"

"Engineering."

Oh well, I'll ask her anyway, I thought. "Have you ever heard of Al Purdy?"

Her eyes immediately lit up and she gave us a big smile.

"*Cariboo Horses*! It's one of my favourite books. I love it!"

Al just about rose off the floor and floated around the room. He was one very happy guy.

The Unjust Society

B Y 1969, DESPITE OUR success and with many new projects in the works, the publishing company was running short of money. But the Canadian Imperial Bank of Commerce turned down our request for a bigger line of credit. Fortunately the Industrial Development Bank came to the rescue with an urgently needed $45,000 loan.

Harold Cardinal was a twenty-four-year-old Alberta Cree who, despite his age, was already president of the Alberta Indian Association. He was a powerful speaker about the many injustices his people suffered. I was convinced that a book by Cardinal would attract many readers, but Harold wasn't interested. Week after week I pursued and nagged him, and finally he weakened; an attractive contract and advance against royalties helped. However, it wasn't long before a problem arose. When Harold didn't feel like it, which was often, or when he felt guilty about his lack of progress on his manuscript, which also was often, he didn't answer either his telephone or his door. Eventually, as the deadline to get the manuscript to the printers approached, we had to virtually lock Cardinal and writer Ed Ogle in a hotel to get a completed manuscript.

Just before Cardinal's book was to be published late in 1969, someone from Indian Affairs managed to obtain a set of galley proofs from a book reviewer and sent a copy by courier to Ottawa, where numerous photocopies were made for distribution in the department. Harold was furious, but I was not too concerned. Obviously Ottawa was very nervous about the book. We made sure that the news of the illicit copying was quickly spread through the media.

The Unjust Society, a harsh, articulate attack on the "faceless people in Ottawa . . . mandarins who would probably not even recognize an Indian if they met one," became an immediate bestseller. Newspapers across the country serialized the book and reproduced Roy Peterson's excellent cover illustration. Our first printing of 25,000 copies sold out in days. The first review came in from the *Victoria Times*, which described the book as "controlled rage." The following week the *Toronto Star* published three excerpts from the book, and sales exploded. There had been eight different ministers of Indian Affairs during the previous eight years, but Anthony Westell's review zeroed in on one of them: "Cardinal accuses Indian Affairs Minister Jean Chrétien of arrogance and deceit, and jeers at him as a pawn of the bureaucrats." And there were numerous other similar comments. If Pierre Trudeau was unhappy, Jean Chrétien was livid.

We sent Cardinal on a cross-country promotional tour; he was poised, self-confident, proud, angry, and articulate. I was delighted with the response to Harold's book, for him, for the publishing company, and not the least for the discomfort it caused in Trudeau's office after he had ignored my own paper that had harshly criticized Indian Affairs. But more particularly, I saw *The Unjust Society* as a possible turning point in the treatment of Canada's aboriginal people. Its influence could be measured by the fact that it went on to sell almost 80,000 copies. In 1969 only five percent of all books sold in Canada were produced by Canadian-owned companies. But Hurtig Publishers, for the second year in a row, had the number-one bestseller.

The Canadian Rockies: Early Travels and Explorations, by Esther Fraser, was the first unsolicited manuscript we published. "I laughed and cried and did all sorts of foolish things when it was accepted for publication," Esther said in an interview. Here was an excellent example of what good publishing is supposed to be all about. Esther had brought a half-finished manuscript to me in 1966, a year before we published our first book. It had taken her ten years of research. I could see it needed a great deal of work, but I encouraged her to finish the manuscript. Unfortunately the completed book needed to be reorganized and almost completely rewritten. With Susan Kent's help, the third draft was finally ready for publication. The book eventually sold 32,000 copies.

Another great success in 1969 was the facsimile edition of Franklin's *Narrative* for which Louis Melzack wrote the introduction. According to Regina *Leader Post* reviewer Max Laidlaw, "No more beautiful book can have been published in 1969 than this." At $20, the illustrated, three-inch-thick book was an exceptional bargain. The same year we published six more titles in *The Canadiana Reprint Series*, for which we soon received our first award. Ironically it came from the American Association for State and Local History for "an outstanding contribution to the study of regional history and the better understanding of national heritage . . ." The award was announced from the association's headquarters in Nashville, Tennessee.

Incredibly we made money on every one of the first fifteen books we published. Soon after we began publishing, our annual profit was twice as much as it was in any of our sixteen retail bookselling years. What an easy business! Or so it seemed.

We had become the first national book-publishing company to be located outside Toronto. There were other regional publishers, but none that successfully produced and sold books of Canadian interest across the country. After, in the face of much scepticism, we showed it could be done, other publishers from St. John's to Vancouver followed.

IN THE EARLY 1970S VERY few Canadian books sold as many as 10,000 copies, and the vast majority sold fewer than 3,000. There were very few bookstores, and the Canadian collections in most public libraries ranged from inadequate to pitiful. Only seven percent of Toronto Public Library acquisition funds were used to buy Canadian books.

While Canadian agents/wholesalers/publishers could profitably sell a hundred copies of an imported book, which required no up-front financial commitment, Canadian publishers were fortunate to break even on the sale of 3,000 copies of a title after editorial, design, typesetting, printing and binding, and other publication costs were considered.

At the same time, there were well over thirty million mass-market paperbacks sold every year across the country. Fewer than two percent were by Canadian authors. As well, American magazines dominated the newsstands. Only a handful ever published a review of a Canadian book.

In 1970 there were just thirty-two Canadian book publishers with fifty or more titles in print. Canadian-owned publishers had only a little over twelve percent of the book market for their Canadian *and* imported books, yet these publishers produced eighty-five percent of all titles with Canadian topics or settings, and ninety-seven percent of all new books of Canadian literature (fiction, humour, drama, poetry, young-adult, criticism).

Also in 1970 the big U.S. publisher McGraw-Hill purchased the 143-year-old Ryerson Press from the United Church Publishing House. About the same time, the important textbook publisher W.J. Gage Ltd. was taken over by a large American publisher. There was a great storm of controversy across the country. The Trudeau government was largely indifferent.

Even before the Gage and Ryerson takeovers, some ninety-two percent of university bookstore purchases in Canada were books published outside the country. There was no other developed nation in the world with such a dismal record.

Donald Campbell, president of Maclean-Hunter, and Christopher Ondaatje, president of Pagurian, had made offers for Ryerson to the United Church. Both offers, and a third from an unnamed Canadian publisher, were rejected. The McGraw-Hill offer of a reported $2-million was just too much for the church to refuse.

In August 1970 the cover of the *Globe Magazine* featured Val Clery's article "The Perils of Publishing." Clery wrote about Jack Cole of Coles Book Stores, who had begun opening a new store a month across Canada. Clery described Cole as "a compact restless man who . . . talks bluntly." He went on:

> I think we compliment the industry when we call it the publishing industry . . . in fact, if the handling of books was analyzed and many of the so-called Canadian publishers

checked into, it would be found that people who were being referred to as Canadian publishers are nothing more than handlers of American and British books. The fact of the matter is that the industry is old, lethargic, conservative . . . and fat!

Mel Hurtig seems another man with the same basic tight-strung vitality as Jack Cole. Urbane, acute and hospitable (his home in Edmonton is an obligatory halt for any bookish way-farer across Canada), he has applied to publishing the same committed pleasure that had helped him succeed in book-selling. He talks with convincing fluency: "The fact is that people in the country are becoming conscious of the fact that we're not the United States, we're not Great Britain, we are Canada, we do have an identity. And, they're ready to read more and more about our history and more and more about contemporary problems."

On the last day of November 1970 Ontario Premier John Robarts announced a royal commission to examine the state of the book-publishing industry. Meanwhile, Education Minister William Davis said he was considering a number of interim measures to assist Canadian book publishers in Ontario.

In his 1970 introduction to our new edition of his *Cross-Country*, Hugh MacLennan wrote: "When Mel Hurtig said he wished to reprint my first book of incidental nonfiction, I would have thought him crazy if I hadn't known that he wasn't." *Cross-Country*, originally published in 1949 and long since out of print, had won the Governor General's Award. According to MacLennan, he received the award

in the days when the G.G. medal came to you without a cheque attached. . . . You were presented with your medal after an hour or two of oratory succeeding the dinner that climaxed the annual convention of the Canadian Authors Association, which was held in a different city every year. When *Cross-Country* was decorated I was too broke . . . to pay for the round trip to Winnipeg, let alone my food and room when I got there, so a more solvent friend volunteered to accept the medal in my name. . . .

Early in 1971 Frank Walker, editor-in-chief of the *Montreal Star*, wrote a glowing review of *The Canadiana Reprint Series*, under the title "One man's madness." We had been adding new titles to the series every year, and praise of this kind helped sales enormously. Reprints of George Back, Marius Barbeau, William Francis Butler, Charles Francis Hall, George M. Grant, Walter B. Cheadle, George Heriot, Samuel Hearne, Alexander Henry, and many others had steady sales, although rarely more than 5,000 copies a title.

Some of our reprint-series titles now sell for up to $200 a copy. Mordecai Richler, Pierre Berton, and Rudy Wiebe are just a few of the authors who have used the series extensively in their writing and research. However, with some reluctance, I decided to discontinue the series. I had been watching with dismay as more and more my fellow Canadian publishers were having their books printed and bound abroad. While it was true that more than ninety-five percent of our titles already were being printed and bound here in Canada, I resolved that henceforth all Hurtig books would be produced in this country. No doubt such a decision was open to criticism; nevertheless, I felt it was consistent with my nationalism. If we were ever going to develop an efficient and profitable book-publishing industry in Canada, we should support Canadian printers, binders, and colour separators.

By the spring of 1971, it appeared as though McClelland and Stewart was in serious trouble and perhaps on the verge of being sold to an American publisher. Many of us called for emergency government legislation banning any further sale of Canadian book publishers to non-Canadians. Within the industry itself, there was fierce debate. At a federal government-sponsored conference on book publishing in Peterborough, the publishers voted sixteen to ten in favour of such a proposal, with seven abstentions. Most of the firms that opposed the suggested legislation were British and American houses.

For virtually all Canadian book publishers, an adequate bank line of bank credit was a serious, often insurmountable problem. Jack McClelland and I agreed completely on what I said to the Canadian Press in Hamilton a few days later: "We don't want forgivable loans; we don't want grants; all we need is a reasonable line of credit."

It seemed to me that Jack McClelland was doing a wonderful, completely unequalled job for Canadian authors, booksellers, and readers. Yet year after year, although he produced a steady stream of bestsellers and other fine books, his firm seemed to totter on the brink of bankruptcy. Finally McClelland, who had refused to rule out the sale of his firm to an American company, received a $1-million loan from the Ontario government to allow him to stay in business. As a result of the recommendations of the Ontario royal commission, the new Bill Davis government promptly took a number of other steps to help book publishers in that province.

But in Ottawa nothing had happened since the sale of Ryerson and Gage. In Ottawa book-publishing policy for years had been determined by the Wood Products division of Trade and Commerce! The government emphasis was on the export of books from Canada, not on the sale and distribution of Canadian books in Canada. As a result, millions of dollars in federal government assistance were either completely wasted or accomplished next to nothing, a perfect example of bureaucrats not knowing what the hell they were doing.

In June of 1971 at the Canadian Booksellers Association annual convention in Halifax, I was named Publisher of the Year, a huge honour, considering I had published our first book less than four years earlier and was still active as a bookseller. The booksellers laughed when I said in my acceptance speech that publishing was a piece of cake compared to bookselling.

At the same convention, Merwyn "Binky" Marks, then managing Bill Duthie's Robson Street Paperback Cellar in Vancouver, a man widely respected for his extensive knowledge of books, received an award in recognition of his long bookselling career. The next morning Binky was found in his hotel room, dead of a heart attack. I don't know if Binky had a smile on his face or not. Xavier Hollander, of *The Happy Hooker* fame, had been a speaker at the convention, and the last time Binky was seen he was leaving the banquet hall with the noted "author."

Jack Stoddart, Sr., spoke at a University of Alberta conference in the summer of 1971. Jack, president of General Publishing Company Limited (and father of the head of the firm that has published this book), spelled out the industry's problems nicely:

> Publishing is a capital-intensive business. The more successful a company is, the more books it has on its list, and the larger the sums of money owing from bookstores and libraries, who often take a long time to pay their accounts. Ever larger quantities of books have to be warehoused, packed, invoiced, and dispatched. The large inventory means money locked up,

but printing and binding bills, salaries, and general overheads
must be paid from cash in hand. Yet banks will not lend publishers the necessary money. This is essentially what happened
to McClelland and Stewart.

And to many others. I thought of Mr. McDiarmid, the prophetic
bank manager, as I heard Jack Stoddart's words. In my own speech I
pointed out that:

> Imperial Oil Limited, the largely foreign-owned and
> -controlled subsidiary of Standard Oil, recently moved a
> fertilizer plant fence so as to qualify for a $10-million federal
> grant under the DREE [Department of Regional Economic
> Expansion] program. Meanwhile, several miles down the
> road, a Canadian-owned fertilizer plant was laying off
> employees.
>   Ten million dollars in loans (*not* grants) to the book-
> publishing industry in Canada would solve almost all of its
> problems.
>   This year our federal government will spend almost
> $2-billion on defence. One percent of that amount in repayable
> loans would completely alter book publishing in Canada. . . .
>   I believe that Canadian publishers would not only survive
> but thrive, given a normal commercial domestic milieu. It is
> this essential point, that is, the absence of a normal market
> environment, that has eluded both federal and provincial
> politicians and bureaucrats. A normal Canadian book market
> will never be achieved so long as foreign publishers' branch
> plants dominate the industry.

Late in 1970 I had a very lucky break. I received a call from
Toronto from a man named Gordon Garner, who had worked for
Ryerson Press as one of their top salesmen. When Ryerson was taken
over by McGraw-Hill, he quit the company, appalled at the sale of
the venerable old Canadian publishing house to Americans. His
phone call came just about the time we had begun to realize we
needed a full-time salesperson in central Canada. Garner loved books
and he loved people: a perfect combination. When someone started
up a new store, Garner attended to it and the owners as though it
was his own family starting out in business. Garner said he had been

"watching" me, and he very much liked what he saw. He and his charming, energetic, eternally optimistic wife, Georgina, opened their own sales agency in Toronto and soon were representing Hurtig Publishers. It was perfect timing for both of us. Our list was expanding quickly, and our number-one province for sales was Ontario. I often asked Gordon's advice before signing a book contract or before making final decisions about formats or print runs. He was a wonderful man in every way, and his great love of books and warm enthusiasm made him a pleasure to work with.

We soon had sales reps across almost all of Canada. As well, we had good freelance editors helping out our authors in five different provinces.

If we were lucky with the talented Gordon Garner, we were equally fortunate with the exceptional young designer, David Shaw, who approached us fresh out of the Ontario College of Art because friends of his were impressed with our growing list and with Gordon Garner, as well. David, who first worked for McClelland and Stewart, proved to be one of the best things that ever happened to Hurtig Publishers.

His first job for us was the cover design for a book by Duncan Pryde called *Nunaga: My Land, My Country*. Pryde was a rascal, but he had quite a story to tell. He had arrived in the Canadian Arctic as an eighteen-year-old apprentice to the Hudson's Bay Co. and soon after managed the isolated Parry Island fur-trading post. In 1970 he was elected to the Northwest Territories Council and reputedly campaigned with such slogans as "Vote for Daddy" and "Everyone should have a little Pryde in the Arctic." To say Pryde was promiscuous and liked women was like saying it snowed in the Arctic in the winter.

Kildare Dobbs, writing in the *Toronto Star*, called the book "a triumph of one man imagining his way into the consciousness of a race of hunters still not far removed from the stone age. . . . Pryde is in many ways a re-incarnation of the great Arctic travellers of the past. And as good a story-teller as any of them." Novelist Hugh Garner reviewed the book in the *Globe and Mail*, concluding: "Don't ask me to lend you my copy; I'm keeping it as a reference book."

Nunaga was a breakthrough for us. Not only did we have another number-one bestseller, but we sold foreign rights to publishers in the U.S., England, Japan, and several other countries.

In 1971 my ten-year-old daughter, Gillian, was attending Glenora school. The teacher handed out thirty-five maps of the state of

Kentucky for the children to study. A fine way for Canadians to learn map reading for the first time. In the high school closest to my home six hundred copies of every issue of *Scholastic Magazine* were distributed. The kids could read all about "our troops in Vietnam" and "our Congress."

Some ninety-eight percent of all mass-market titles sold in drugstores, department stores, newsstands, supermarkets, air and bus terminals, and railroad stations across the country were foreign titles, almost all of them American. In 1971 Canada ranked behind such countries as Austria, Bulgaria, Czechoslovakia, Egypt, Finland, Greece, Hungary, Iceland, Israel, Malaysia, Norway, Poland, South Africa, Spain, and Yugoslavia in a list of comparative book-production figures.

And in 1971, of the forty-three members of the Canadian Book Publishers' Council, twenty-six were foreign-owned, and of the remaining seventeen, only ten published Canadian books, the other seven being simply agents for British and American publishers. In 1971 the president, vice president, second vice president, and treasurer of the Canadian Book Publishers' Council all worked for American publishers. Is it any wonder, then, that the council consistently failed to back proposals that would deal with the foreign domination of the industry? Of course, in this respect it was little different from the (the quotation marks are mine) "Canadian" Petroleum Association, the "Canadian" Manufacturers' Association, or scores of similar foreign-dominated powerful industry lobby groups.

In December 1971 we published *The Real Poverty Report* to more headlines across the country. The disappointing official Senate committee report on poverty had been released a month earlier. Our authors, Ian Adams, William Cameron, Brian Hill, and Peter Penz, had all resigned from the staff of the committee saying that the official report was censored. They produced an 80,000-word document that was a harsh, detailed attack on the Canadian establishment, monopolies, the tax system, and politicians and bureaucrats, which all combine to create and sustain poverty in Canada. An angry indictment of the status quo, the book caused an immediate storm of controversy across the country. It soon vied with *Nunaga* for top spot on the nonfiction bestseller lists.

One bitterly cold winter night I stood on the windswept corner of 103rd Street and Jasper Avenue saying goodbye to the splendid gentleman publisher from Macmillan, John Gray. We'd had a long talk in the Carousel over coffee, and now John was headed to the vendor's for a bottle of scotch, then back to his hotel. His parting words to me were remarkably similar to those I had heard when I had thought about becoming a bookseller. I had told John I was going to sell the bookstores and concentrate on publishing. He said, "Don't do it. It would be a bad mistake. All the best editors, printers, designers, the chain- and department-store buyers are in Toronto. It would be impossible to successfully develop a national house in Edmonton."

Jack McClelland also was very negative. Nevertheless, late in 1971 I made the decision to sell the bookstores. It wasn't easy, but the fact that the budget for our fall 1971 publishing program meant an investment of an additional $180,000 made selling the three bookstores the logical if not the inevitable way to raise the money.

One casualty of my publishing and political career was my reading. I read and worked on manuscripts most evenings at home or on the road. Now I had to abandon reading fiction almost entirely. When I wasn't reading manuscripts, I was immersed in Statistics Canada and OECD (Organization for Economic Co-operation and Development) publications, academic studies, conference reports, journals, and the like. Boring? Not at all! I found them fascinating.

In February 1972, after the sale of the bookstores, my editor, secretary, and I moved into tiny third-floor walkup offices in Ralph MacMillan's Birks building across Jasper Avenue from my main bookstore. *Nunaga* continued as the top Canadian bestseller, and now we added subsidiary sales of the book to publishers in Sweden, Italy, France, and the Netherlands. As well, several book clubs and paperback houses were bidding for rights.

Some of our plans for large "coffee table" full-colour books meant sinking as much as a quarter of a million dollars into one title before any revenue could be anticipated. I knew I had a team of first-class writers, editors, photographers, artists, and designers to produce such books, but finding the money to do them remained a problem. By the summer of 1972, I was beginning to despise bankers. One bank vice president asked me why would we need Canadian publishers anyway, since he could always get any book he wanted from Brentano's in New York.

When I opened my first bookstore back in 1956, about one in every ten books we sold was a Canadian book. When I sold my stores to Buddy Smith in 1972, about one in every four books we sold was Canadian. More and more book buyers were interested in Canadian topics. And more and more I felt there was an excellent future for book publishing in Canada if, somehow, normal market conditions prevailed.

I borrowed money for the publishing company wherever I could. After the loan from the Industrial Development Bank, I went to the Alberta Opportunity Company, who gave us a crucial stopgap loan. Before I knew it I was doing flowcharts for bankers in my sleep.

And we soon needed more space. It didn't take long to locate a dilapidated building tucked away under the north end of the 105th Street overpass, "on the other side of the tracks" from downtown, but only five minutes away from the city centre and five minutes away from my home. The building was a mess, with a pasted-on false stone front, a leaking roof, few windows, and inadequate wiring and heating. But the rent was right. We fixed it up, offices in front, warehouse in back, painting everything in sight and hoisting a big new Canadian flag on the roof.

Agnes Primrose became our office manager, staff supervisor, and liaison with our sales reps. Her jovial personality, efficiency, and excellent people skills were all instrumental in the company's growth and success.

In 1973 I tried to lure Andy Russell into our camp. Andy had been published by Knopf in New York. We made him an attractive offer to work with us on a book about the Canadian Rockies. He replied: "So far I have been pretty happy with my publisher, but your offer is certainly not something I take lightly." We increased the offer, and Andy obtained a release from Knopf.

Another author and I became good friends. In April 1973 Margaret Laurence wrote to me from England. "Am selling my house here this summer," she said, "and moving back to Canada the end of July, for keeps. Have just submitted my new novel, THE DIVINERS, to all 3 publishers, and am in a state of terrible nerves. It is long, Mel, *long*. About 578 pp typescript, and I dunno that I can cut it that much, as all seems to link into everything else. Well. Trouble is, I'm so goddam bound up still with this novel that I find it hard to think of anything else." Margaret didn't offer the book to me because early on I had decided to concentrate on nonfiction, a not uncommon publishing-house decision.

In November 1973 we published another book in my favourite genre. It was *Sellout: The Giveaway of Canada's Energy Resources*, by Phil Sykes, editor of the Sunday edition of the *Toronto Sun*, with a hilarious and controversial (for the time) cover by the brilliant Montreal cartoonist, Terry Mosher (Aislin). The first printing of 10,000 copies sold out in a month. Sadly Phil Sykes entered hospital with a malignant tumour the same week the book was published, and died the following July at the age of forty-five.

With *Sellout* we encountered another lovely little problem book publishers in Canada faced. Increasingly Canadian book paper was being shipped by the mills to the United States. Here we had a best-seller on our hands, booksellers demanding more copies by phone and telegram and through our sales reps, yet we couldn't get the paper to reprint until March!

The reviewer of *Sellout* in the *Edmonton Journal* dismissed the book as biased and questioned the author's ability to discuss energy matters objectively. The *Journal* had asked the public-relations officer of Syncrude, who also happened to have been a senior official in the Social Credit government, to review the book!

In 1973 an Ontario school board caused an uproar when it chartered a flight to New Jersey so that teachers and administrators could fly to the United States to spend their library funds on American books. Every year, more and more Canadian libraries and schools were ordering their books directly from U.S. wholesalers (even Canadian books) much to the dismay of the Toronto publishers and agents. Canadian authors suffered, as well, since usually they were paid sharply reduced royalties on export sales. Moreover, a loophole in the Canadian copyright act was allowing American editions of books by Farley Mowat and Pierre Berton, among others, to be dumped in Canada.

But things were looking rosy for Hurtig Publishers. In our first year of publishing, our sales had been $19,000. In 1973 they were over half a million dollars and headed up.

Looking for the Pot of Gold

ONE DAY I HAPPENED to phone Toronto author John Robert Colombo. The day before he had come to an impasse in his discussions about a book of Canadian quotations that had been scheduled to be published by Fitzhenry and Whiteside of Toronto. John wanted his name in the title, but Robert Fitzhenry said no. I asked John to courier me the manuscript. When it arrived I was astounded by its enormous size. But within five days I called John and told him a contract for *Colombo's Canadian Quotations* was in the mail.

We offered John Robert the largest royalty advance we had ever made on a book — $10,000. But the book was substantial, in the end 735 pages long. It was a huge project for us, not only in terms of the size of the book, but in the editorial work involved. By the time our printing of 20,000 copies was ready, we had invested $125,000 in the book. It didn't take much imagination to anticipate what the results would have been if the book had flopped; at the time our line of credit was only $150,000.

But the book didn't flop; it was a big success. By Christmas we had sold three-quarters of the print run. (By the way, John dedicated the book to a man he greatly admired, Walter Gordon, quoting Denis Smith's line that "no one has done more than Walter Gordon to reveal to Canadians that there is such a thing as the national interest, and that its defence is a normal act of national self-respect.") Over the years we went on to publish many Colombo books; it was a relationship I enjoyed greatly.

Unfortunately the Bill Davis Ontario government took no action relating to some of its royal commission's most important and strongest recommendations regarding the foreign domination of the publishing industry. And while Secretary of State Hugh Faulkner announced his support for the principle of majority Canadian control of the industry, the federal government announced no new policy proposals. Some support.

There was considerable gloom at the annual meeting of the all-Canadian Independent Publishers Association in February 1974. A new study showed that between 1966 and 1973 the sale of Canadian-authored books as a percentage of all publishers' sales had declined by more than fifty percent. In 1973, of total sales of some $291-million, books written by Canadian authors and published by Canadian publishers totalled a pitiful $15-million. Although total book sales in Canada had more than doubled during the period 1966 to 1973, sales of Canadian-authored books published by Canadian or foreign firms had fallen. Canadian content in the foreign-dominated book clubs was a paltry three percent and was even lower as a percentage of the $87-million in books purchased by schools in Canada.

In 1972 I sat in the popular rooftop bar of the Park Plaza Hotel in

Toronto with a reluctant author. "There's no bloody way in the world you can turn a radio show into a book," he kept saying. It took me weeks to convince him. Upon publication two years later in the fall of 1974, the author's own words were:

> Whoosh! To the surprise of everyone except perhaps Mel Hurtig . . . my cross-country promotion tour was like a royal procession. Everywhere I went I was welcomed on the interview shows. In Edmonton, a lady whose husband had spent $250 at an auction to buy her a date with me turned out to be much nicer than I expected. And at the bookstores, the lines were long and the demand for my signature was flattering. We sold nearly 40,000 copies of that book. It was a heady experience and my only regret is I haven't been able to repeat it.

The book was Peter Gzowski's *This Country in the Morning*. What fun it was to watch Peter's book quickly jump to number one on the bestseller lists only two weeks after publication, leaping ahead of Cornelius Ryan's *A Bridge Too Far*, Hans Selye's *Stress Without Distress*, the new Charlie Farquharson, Carl Bernstein and Bob Woodward's *All the President's Men*, and other popular titles. David Shaw's brilliant design of the book won him a prestigious award and $1,000.

By May of 1974, our publishing house was so swamped with unsolicited manuscripts that we had to stop accepting them for six months. Meanwhile, Jack McClelland said his editors were going through four to five thousand unsolicited manuscripts each year at a six-figure cost to the company. According to McClelland, "You publish maybe three out of every thousand submitted. And if you publish twelve, you lose money on half of them, you break even on three and you make money on the other three. But your profit is offset by losses on the others. Publishing is like looking for the gold pot at the end of the rainbow."

In our case, our expanding list continued to leave us chronically short of money. We had a big sales increase in 1973 and were expecting an even larger one in 1974. But as always receivables were slow to come in, and we were pouring large sums into books that wouldn't be on the shelves for years and paying editorial, design, illustration, cartography, and other costs that would not be recovered for a long, long time.

While it is true that my extensive travels kept me away from my business, they also helped. In the spring of 1974 I came back from the trip to Baffin Island with three excellent book ideas about the North. Alas, when I returned from the trip, there was a letter on my desk from the Oblate father Maurice Metayer, who had put together our immensely successful *Tales from the Igloo*, saying he was seriously ill and did not have long to live.

By 1974, some ninety-five percent of all elementary and high school textbooks were published by foreign-controlled publishers. Among all developed countries, Canada now had by far the lowest per-capita number of book titles published. On a list of one hundred nations, Canada ranked ninety-fifth in titles produced! Few developed countries would have tolerated such a dismal situation. But in branch-plant Canada, which had gone from colony to nation and was now in transition back to a colony, there were many more who accepted the situation as being normal than those who viewed it as an aberration.

Bear in mind that all this was during the period of so-called "new nationalism" in Canada. While it was true that after the Centennial and Expo Canadians were more and more interested in their own history, biographies, and accomplishments, the foreign-dominated book-publishing industry did not reflect this new interest. In the fall of 1974 Canadian-owned publishing houses produced around six hundred new Canadian books, but the big foreign publishers that dominated the Canadian market managed the grand total of eighty.

Allan Fotheringham gave us a big boost just before Christmas, with a great column about the Colombo and Gzowski books:

> For a year or so now, Mel Hurtig, the cunning Edmonton publisher, has been telling me about this smash book he had coming, a book of Canadian quotations. And I kept telling him I had never heard of a more petty, chauvinistic, provincial idea. Who would be interested? I reasoned.
>
> Which is the reason, of course, why Hurtig is a successful publisher and your struggling scribe is down here covering park board meetings. The book, *Colombo's Canadian Quotations*, a great fat red $15 book, is merely one of the zinging successes of the Christmas book season. It's on the bestseller list (another Hurtig book, Peter Gzowski's *This Country in the Morning*, is the top seller in Canada) and both Hurtig and Colombo are laughing. Above all, it's a fascinating book, more addictive than eating salted peanuts.

The book is almost worth it for the section on C.D. Howe alone. If any younger Canadian has difficulty understanding why this country turned to John Diefenbaker in 1957, all the beautiful arrogance of the Liberal government of that era is here in Howe telling the Commons, "If we have overstepped our powers, I make no apologies for it."

Or, "Are we having a debate? . . . I do not think this should be allowed to degenerate into a debate."

Or, "If there is some uneasiness in this country about the extent and nature of United States investment in Canada, this is the wrong place to focus it" — this place being the House of Commons.

The year 1974 was very successful for us. During the vitally important Christmas season we had three of the top-ten nonfiction bestsellers and a huge sales increase. Not bad for someone who had been a "full-time" publisher for only two years, while zooming around the country on behalf of the Committee for an Independent Canada. Thank goodness for my great staff!

"Unsavoury, Uninteresting, Not Readable"

B UT WHAT ABOUT THE whole business of editing books, and about editors, the people who are absolutely key to publishing? Editing can make or break a book, and a publishing company, as well.

As I have already pointed out, each year thousands of unsolicited manuscripts pour into the publishing houses — the ones who still allow it, that is. Unfortunately only a small number ever get published. But a good publishing house can pick out of the pile manuscripts with potential, identify a talented author who may become a success in the future, spot a manuscript that needs a lot of work but still has much merit. A good editor may also look at an author's work, reject it, but make helpful proposals about an alternative theme or approach the author might wish to consider.

Of course, many very successful books and authors were initially turned down by publishers. When D.H. Lawrence submitted *Lady Chatterley's Lover* to a publisher, he was told: "For your own good, do not publish this book." The first Tarzan adventure story was rejected by seventeen publishers. Patrick Dennis's *Auntie Mame* was turned down by twenty publishers over a period of five years. Pearl Buck's *The Good Earth*, which helped her become the first American woman to earn the Nobel Prize in literature, was met with the following note from a New York publisher: "Regret the American public is not interested in anything on China." Rudyard Kipling was told he could not be published because he didn't know how to use the English language. And many ultimately bestselling authors have tales of having received their manuscripts back from publishers unopened.

Perhaps the most famous Canadian example of a good bet missed was Sheila Burnford's *The Incredible Journey*. It was rejected by several Canadian publishers, including McClelland and Stewart. One splendid summer afternoon I sat in a lovely English country garden talking to the wife of the publisher at the London firm of Hodder and Stoughton. She told me she occasionally read manuscripts for her husband. One day he returned home from work and she said straight out: "Dear, print 30,000 of this!" She had never been anywhere nearly as enthusiastic about any book before. *The Incredible Journey* went on to become the number-one bestseller in many countries around the world, including Canada, and was made into a Walt Disney movie.

Brian Moore's first literary novel, *Judith Hearne*, was turned down by sixteen American publishers. Fellow Montreal author Mordecai Richler arranged for the manuscript to be sent to André Deutsch in London. The reader's report said, "This is a terrible book. You must publish it." And Deutsch did, to wonderful reviews and excellent sales. Soon American publishers were contacting Moore, including several who had already rejected the book. When the U.S. edition was published, it became *The Lonely Passion of Judith Hearne*, a title that was not the author's choice.

Robert Fulford, author and critic, reminded me of the first Jalna book by Mazo de la Roche. The *Atlantic Monthly* had sponsored a fiction contest for unpublished writers with a large cash first prize. The magazine was inundated with manuscripts. A huge room was piled high with rejected and yet-to-be-read manuscripts, with a dozen readers hard at work going through bundles of all shapes and sizes. *Atlantic Monthly* editor Edward Weeks entered the room and casually picked up the de la Roche book from a reject pile. A reader had pen-cilled, "Unsavoury, uninteresting, not readable." Weeks idly glanced through the first few pages. Three hours later he was still reading the manuscript. One can only wonder what would have happened had Weeks not come by. As it turned out, Mazo de la Roche went on to write sixteen bestselling books about the Whiteoak family, books that were translated and sold around the world.

Bennett Cerf, co-owner of Random House, rejected Vladimir Nabokov's *Lolita*, which was also turned down by Max Schuster of Simon and Schuster. Dial Press returned *Animal Farm* to George Orwell, advising that "it is impossible to sell animal stories in the U.S.A." But Dial was not alone. Victor Gollancz also rejected the book and so did T.S. Eliot, on behalf of Faber and Faber. At least a dozen publishers rejected Ayn Rand's *The Fountainhead* before Bobbs-Merrill published it in 1943.

All publishers have their own priorities and idiosyncrasies. Many books we turned down were published by other publishers. And, of course, we published books that had been turned down elsewhere.

Sometimes, but very rarely, work on a manuscript meant only copy editing, that is, primarily fixing spelling, grammar, syntax. A few writers, a *very* few (Denis Smith is an example) produce well-organized immaculate manuscripts. But many require substantive editing, that is, months of hard-slogging reorganization, rewrites, painstaking fact-checking. Usually the author and editor get along famously, but occasionally they are at each other's throats almost from the very beginning. In those rare cases we would either change editors or dump the project. For the most part, though, an author is eternally grateful to a good editor for improving a manuscript, for picking out errors, and for basic structural advice. I don't care who the author is, certainly including me, I have never seen an author who didn't get so close to a book that they lose at least a certain degree of objectivity.

While the author always got the final say about content, I always got the final say about format, design, and cover art. I also chose many titles, but here, of course, the author had a one hundred percent veto. If I didn't like a working title, I would list possible alternatives as I went through the manuscript. Often the author would be delighted. "I think your suggestion of *Bleeding Hearts, Bleeding Country* is brilliant and right. It fits perfectly," wrote Denis Smith about my suggested title for his 1971 book on the Quebec crisis, the title being a play on the words of Pierre Trudeau. My favourite story about book titles is Colombo's tale about everyone at McClelland and Stewart trying to pressure an author into changing the title of his book because they thought it was weak. The author was George Grant; the title, *Lament for a Nation*.

In my early years as a publisher I used to go through every page of a completed contracted manuscript, marking it up and dictating suggestions for the editor and author to consider. After that I would never see the book again until it was published.

We quickly developed our own in-house *Editorial Style Manual*, which we expanded, updated, and revised regularly. I was very concerned that our books be first-class; over the years we were rarely admonished for our editorial work. As we developed our own house style and refined our editorial rules, it became easier to train the free-lance editors we worked with across the country. A good style manual must cover how to handle a long list of topics: front matter, jacket copy, indexes, bibliographies, back matter, captions, footnotes, tables, galley proofs, page proofs, Vandykes, punctuation, spelling, hyphen-ation, capitalization, indentation, spacing, numbers, names, permissions, italics, heads and subheads, foreign languages, extracts, abbreviations, editorial and design markup, trademarks. It is Wilfred Grenfell, but Wilfrid Laurier. It is the King's Printer to 1953, then the Queen's Printer. It is the *Times* of London, but the *New York Times*. Every manuscript invariably brought new editorial problems to be solved. As one style manual put it, "The publishing industry is notoriously incestuous. Editors travel from company to company carrying with them their blue pencils, boxes of reference books, and deeply ingrained, almost fanatical feelings about the *correct* way to spell percent."

Then there was the thorny problem of authors rewriting galleys, page proofs, and, heaven forbid, Vandykes (proofs of the film used in printing, the final look at the book). We had very strict rules in this respect. The author is supposed to make final changes in the *manuscript*, not to the typeset book, and especially not in the final Vandyke stage, when changes are expensive.

We originated a growing percentage of the books we published. There was no biography of Gabriel Dumont, so I prevailed upon George Woodcock to write one. The only brief history of Canada was out-of-date, so we had Desmond Morton do *A Short History of Canada*, which is now in its sixth printing. Andy Russell's *The Rockies* was a huge critical and commercial success. Sometimes we put an author and illustrator together with great results. We had received an unsolicited humorous book about hockey. One small problem: the drawings were hilarious, but the text wasn't funny at all. It was a clear reject, but I kept thinking that a satirical book about hockey was a great idea. So we married Vancouver humorist Eric Nicol to artist Dave More of Red Deer for a very funny and very successful *The Joy of Hockey*. Eric wrote to me just before publication. "Great," he said. "Just great. I couldn't be more delighted. If this one doesn't move the masses, I'll eat the puck. Au jus. Thank you, Sir, for another treatment royal. . . ." It was signed: "Euphorically, Eric."

The authors went on to do books about golf, football, and tennis. Figure it out: the hockey and golf books sold like mad; the football and tennis books died.

Not only can a good editor turn a book around completely and help make it a great success, but he or she is also charged with avoiding a minefield of potential catastrophes. Once, the excellent University of Toronto Press spelled the author's name wrong on the cover of his book. And Ginn shipped an unusual order of textbooks to California schools with one small problem: the little red schoolhouse on the front cover of the book flew a Canadian flag. The entire shipment went back to Toronto for rebinding. Expensive!

Susan Kent had dropped out of English graduate school at UBC just around the time she saw the article about my entry into publishing. She wrote to me, and the opening line of her letter was "I don't know what a book editor does, but . . ." Susan was one of many people I interviewed for the job as our first editor-in-chief. Of all of them, she was the brightest and most enthusiastic. She lived at our house for several months, working out of the den because we had no place else to put her. Years later she wrote to me: "I learned on the job, page by page and you taught me. When I left to go to England to work for André Deutsch in London, I found I was doing it right; I knew pretty well everything about editing and fit in immediately." Susan, in the words of the *Edmonton Journal*, was "attractive, brown haired, playing literary god to experienced writers much older, to well-known writers who had worked with some of the best editors in Canada, the United States and England. It didn't take long for initial condescension to turn to respect."

According to Susan, "Everyone who came through Edmonton came to see us. We had an amazing, cosmopolitan stream of writers, academics, artists, politicians . . . you name it." When Susan left three years later for adventures in England, a young woman who, at seventeen, had originally come from Ottawa to serve as a clerk in our bookstore, took her place. Jan Walter, now twenty-three, became our new editor-in-chief. When Jan had first arrived in Edmonton, she was shy and inexperienced. She recalls: "I knew zero about books and authors. One day a customer came into the store and asked me if we had Lawrence Durrell's *Alexandria Quartet*. I said, 'Sorry, we don't carry sheet music.' After the customer left, you very gently told me to go down to the fiction section and look under D. You gave me the only copy, told me to take it home and read all four volumes, and then to discuss it with you."

Jan became a marvellous editor, but her first major project, *Colombo's Canadian Quotations*, produced a rough review from the usually even-handed Morris Wolfe, headlined "Quotations Book Needs Good Editor." It was an unfair headline and poor Jan was mortified. That was pretty well the last criticism she ever received. Jan was indispensable to me, but alas, I lost her after she and one of my authors fell in love. Jan moved to Toronto in 1978 and quickly became managing editor at Macmillan ("I was hired because of the excellent training I received at Hurtig's and also because coming from Hurtig's it was expected that I would be able to make a profit. In fact, when I got to Toronto I soon realized that I *was* well trained"). A few years later Jan Walter became director of publishing at McClelland and Stewart and then joined two others in the eminently successful firm of Macfarlane Walter and Ross. Jan is very generous. "You set up the course of my life," she told me. "You gave me a chance and opened up so much for me. I wouldn't be in the book business without you. I loved the books you published. What a great education. You were an ideal employer. You gave us lots of range, gave your response, never talked down. When mistakes were made, you always asked, 'Did you learn anything?'" Her praise was such that I asked her for criticism. She had some: "I thought at the time you should be spending more time with your family. You used to come home, eat dinner, play with the kids, then disappear into the den with a manuscript. But now I understand. When you start a new business . . ."

And what a wonderful new business Jan has developed! As we talked on the telephone while I was writing this book, she was able to tell me that one of her recent titles, Stevie Cameron's *On the Take: Crime, Corruption and Greed in the Mulroney Years*, had sold a phenomenal number of copies — over 100,000.

In the years that followed we had many other fine editors — Sarah Reid, José Druker, and Carlotta Lemieux, to name a few. Carlotta was and is one of the finest editors I have had the pleasure of working with. Her greatest strength was common sense, knowing when to interfere and when not to interfere with a manuscript. She had wide general knowledge, which earned the respect of the authors she worked with. As well, she had an excellent feel for the language. According to Carlotta, a good editor

knows what the author is doing with words. She knows when to leave an ungrammatical sentence severely alone (because it works beautifully) and when to insist on following the rules of grammar.

She recognizes that her role is subsidiary — to aid the author in achieving the results he's aiming for. She should be supportive, searching out his weaknesses (stylistic, factual, or whatever) and helping him to correct them, but she should never try to impose her own style or her views. She should not act like a school mistress marking a composition. While working with the author for the benefit of the book, she should never forget that it is far easier to criticize than to create.

She should establish a good relationship with the author. This isn't always easy, but it is most likely to happen if she starts off right. I think it's very important that one should say something nice about the manuscript when one first contacts the author. Having praised, one can then get down to the nitty-gritty of how the manuscript might be made even better. But the whole thing should be handled very tactfully, bearing in mind that most authors have put their heart into a manuscript. They don't want their dreams trampled on by a tactless editor.

Finally, there is that extra something . . . antennae, empathy . . . I don't know how one would describe it. While an editor has to deal punctiliously with all the minutiae, she should not be a literal-minded, programmed type of person. So much of an editor's work is based on her own personal judgement. Her own character, knowledge, etc., are therefore extremely important factors.

Throughout my years in publishing I was blessed with good staff. In my editors I was doubly blessed.

On Publishing and Perishing

The headline in the *Toronto Star* on New Year's Day 1975 was not an exaggeration: "Publishers face new year with despair." According to *Star* book editor Roy MacSkimming, the situation was bleak. "Just as Canadian authors are selling better than ever in the bookstores, their publishers — some of them — are redoubling their cries of financial despair."

There were renewed threats of foreign takeovers, and two more major U.S. textbook publishers established branch plants in Canada. The same month, Trent University sponsored a two-day conference on "The State of English-Language Publishing in Canada." An impressive list of publishers, booksellers, critics, and authors attended. My talk at the conference was titled "On Publishing and Perishing." I pointed out that, despite Canadians' increased interest in their country, plus more and better writers writing about Canada, despite the expansion of the retail book trade across the country, Canada's book-publishing industry, compared to other developed nations, was pitifully small. We now had the qualified editors, designers, advertising and promotion staff, yet

> just as in the case of so many other industries in this country, book publishing in Canada is massively foreign-dominated and foreign-controlled by people who often have little interest in publishing Canadian books. The foreign publishers maximize their profits by producing run-ons for the Canadian market.
>
> The foreign-dominated Canadian Book Publishers' Council has obviously not served the best interests of Canadian authors, readers, or Canadian-owned publishing houses. Government policies should no longer be based on input from that organization.

I went on to suggest that if there were to be government loans, guarantees, and other assistance, they be made available only to Canadian-owned and Canadian-controlled publishers. And to the surprise of many of my colleagues, I suggested that all duties be removed from books entering Canada. They made little difference to the health of the Canadian publishing industry, but increased the cost of books to the Canadian public.

On January 24 Secrêtary of State Hugh Faulkner announced a program of emergency aid to Canadian book publishers amounting to $1.5-million annually. Exactly one week later Energy Minister Donald Macdonald announced that some $200-million to $500-million would be made available to three foreign-controlled petroleum companies to help with the Syncrude tar-sands project in Alberta. With the Canadian publishing industry in dire peril, Faulkner promptly proceeded to authorize a $1.5-million grant to produce a book as a special gift to commemorate the United States bicentennial. According to the Montreal *Gazette*, this was "the same amount that the secretary of state thought would satisfy the annual needs of the whole Canadian publishing industry."

The next month I spoke in Ottawa at the annual dinner of the Independent Publishers Association. I said that "a normal Canadian book industry will never be achieved unless Canadian publishers could be normal publishers like their colleagues around the world."

Let me explain what I mean by a "normal" book market. For example, when a new novel by Agatha Christie is published by Collins in the U.K., the Collins edition is certainly not sold in the United States. If there is a new Joseph Heller novel, the Simon and Schuster edition is not sold in England. A new Patrick White book is hardly on sale in the Australian edition in New York, any more than a new Alice Munro is exported to the U.S. in the Canadian edition.

If Canada is to ever have a healthy book-publishing industry of its own, then Canadian publishers must have the same ability other publishers have in most of the world. And that means the right to compete for the rights for foreign-authored books, the rights to publish these books in Canada. Not to import the books, but to publish them. Not to merely print them, but to publish them in every sense of the word.

I suppose that some of you will think this is a strange suggestion coming from a "Canadian nationalist." But no one I have ever met has suggested Canadians should read only Canadian books about Canadian topics. But I see absolutely no reason why Canadian publishers should not be able to do what other publishers around the world do, bolster their revenues allowing them to produce more domestic titles by publishing popular foreign authors, instead of our market for these titles being entirely captured by foreign publishers.

I gave several examples where books then on Canadian bestseller lists — ones by Solzhenitsyn, Simone de Beauvoir, Simenon, and Graham Greene — could have been published in Canada, while paying the authors a better royalty rate than they normally received and yet still be sold to the Canadian public at *lower* retail prices. I then went on to blast Hugh Faulkner and the Liberal government for their reliance on foreign publishers for policy input. "One year ago, Mr. Faulkner said, 'The Canadian government believes strongly that the major segment of the publishing industry in Canada should be owned by Canadians.' If that is the government's objective, it is difficult to fathom their failure to take any single step that would at least point the way to achieving their stated goal."

My friends in Ottawa told me that Faulkner was not very happy when he read my speech. However, in April, speaking to the Association of American Publishers in White Sulphur Springs, West Virginia, Faulkner said: "The Canadian government is prepared to intervene to safeguard Canada's cultural industries. . . . If you continue dealing with us as a simple extension of your domestic market, then we are bound to disagree. . . . You will . . . see us in Canada taking measures to ensure the health of our indigenous publishing industry. These measures, I tell you frankly, will include the careful scrutiny of any impending new foreign presence in Canadian book publishing."

Tough words, but we had heard them all before for many years.

Because of my work with the Committee for an Independent Canada, I rarely spoke to the public about the problems of the book industry in Canada. But when I did, I tried to put its problems in perspective. One-tenth of one percent of what the federal government spent on defence would, in repayable loans to Canadian book publishers, completely alter the industry. Or, if book publishers received one percent of the direct grants made to foreign-owned petroleum companies in Canada, our book industry would be among the healthiest, most productive job-creating publishers in the world. And, most important of all, if Canada was a normal book nation along the lines I have described, no government assistance of any kind should be required by book publishers.

Our lead title in 1975 was Andy Russell's *The Rockies*. Jan Walter and I went through some six thousand colour slides before settling on

120 photographs to be included with Andy's text. Day after day, night after night, we sat in dark rooms, sometimes with the photographers, squinting at trays of slides until we were nearly blind. In the end we picked photographs from twenty-four outstanding Canadian photographers, some of whom were quite unknown at the time. Our favourite was young Janis Kraulis, who went on to become one of Canada's greatest nature photographers.

We printed 15,000 copies of *The Rockies*, and by the time the book arrived from the printers, we had sold more than 10,000. Of course the word "sold" is highly misleading. In the world of book publishing "gone today, here tomorrow" is a common saying. Almost all the books publishers sell to the retail trade are returnable for a full refund. We had no such worries with *The Rockies*; a new printing was ordered before Christmas, and the book went on to sell a great many copies every year for more than a decade.

In 1975 we also published George Woodcock's *Gabriel Dumont*. Besides *Dumont*, George wrote and edited a number of books for us, including *A Picture History of British Columbia*, *Faces from History*, *Peoples of the Coast*, and *British Columbia: A Celebration*. Despite our different political beliefs, we always got along well and enjoyed working together. A sad coincidence: this morning I sat writing about George; late this afternoon, as I was heading out to Buena Vista flats to take our dogs for a walk, the announcer on the car radio told me he was dead.

One of my favourite ads in a Canadian library periodical in 1975, was a bold full-page advertisement, featuring an American eagle, with the headline

If You Can Afford Only One Major Acquisition This Year, It Should Be Congressional Hearings on Microfiche, price $15,000 U.S.

Right.

Of Beer and Books:
Guinness Is Bad for You

IN 1975 OUR SALES increased substantially, but we had a drop in profits. Wages, commissions, royalties, printing, and paper costs were all up dramatically. We would have to tighten our belt. But early in 1976 disaster struck.

With almost no notice and with no reasonable explanation, the Guinness people advised that they were taking away the Canadian rights for *The Guinness Book of Records*. After starting out with 2,000 copies in 1967, we were up to 52,000 by 1975. Year after year, the Guinness people in London had constantly expressed amazement and much pleasure at the way we had greatly increased sales for their new edition every year.

When I attempted to reach Alan Boyd, I could get no reply. Over the next few months, I desperately tried to pin Guinness down on their reasons for taking the rights away from our company, but without success. Finally we made an offer that would reduce our margin on the book and increase theirs. In May Guinness rejected our offer and announced that the 1976 edition would be sold in Canada by unnamed others. The only explanation we could think of was that the American publishers, Sterling, who marketed the book in the U.S., seeing our great success, had decided that they wanted the Canadian market, as well. Obviously they had considerable leverage with Guinness, given their 400,000-copy annual sales.

We tried another approach. After much detailed work, we determined we could produce the new Guinness editions here in Canada and still undersell the U.S. retail price by a dollar, add a supplement of interesting Canadian records each year, and yet still provide Guinness with its exact same per-copy royalty. The Canadian printing, paper, and binding industries would profit, creating jobs here in Canada.

Guinness rejected our plan with no explanation, despite the fact that the arrangement we proposed would be pure guaranteed profit for them with no effort or expenditure. Moreover, we offered a $10,000 annual advance against royalties, with the balance payable in full within sixty days of publication. Guinness had already allowed manufacturing rights to publishers in the U.S., Denmark, Norway, Japan, Spain, Italy, Finland, Portugal, Czechoslovakia, France, and other countries. Altogether, the book was produced under licence in eighteen languages.

We received excellent support. The executive director of the Canadian Booksellers Association, Randall Ware, urged the book's co-editor, Norris McWhirter, to reconsider the decision. Several Canadian booksellers wrote to Guinness announcing that they would no longer sell the book. Graydon Carter wrote to tell me that the magazine he edited, *Canadian Review*, would urge readers to "boycott any further editions that presumably will be dumped onto the market. Keep up the splendid work."

There were more than a few letters to newspapers urging Canadians to boycott Guinness products, beer and books together. Moreover, a member of the board of directors of Guinness of Canada Ltd. resigned in protest. The general manager of Guinness Canada wrote to home office warning of political repercussions, and Secretary of State Hugh Faulkner wrote a strong letter to McWhirter. All to no avail. (Late in the year, Norris's twin brother and co-editor, Ross McWhirter, opened the door to his home in London and was gunned down by IRA terrorists.)

My sales reps across the country were at least as angry as I was at the unexpected turn of events. After all, each year they had earned excellent commissions on the sale of the Guinness book. They had worked hard placing it in bookstores, department stores, schools, libraries, and in other outlets across the country. It didn't take them long to communicate their anger to their customers.

We were badly hurt, losing approximately a fifth of our annual sales and a higher percentage of our profits. Moreover, the bank was not impressed with our drop in sales and profit the next year, while we were, as usual, requesting an extended line of credit.

Guinness had been extremely cold-blooded about their action. They refused any explanation and had shown no remorse about ending the eight-year relationship. However, as I told Jamie Portman of Southam news, "It is not inconceivable that the top guns at Guinness are aware of my political activities and have acted accordingly." Not inconceivable at all. After all, isn't that the way a colonial relationship works? I resolved never again to place myself in a position where we were dependent on foreign agencies. At one time we represented eleven foreign publishers in Canada, two from Britain, two from Switzerland, Tuttle from Japan, and the others from the United States. I immediately began plans to end all agency representation and to increase our Canadian publishing lists. Never again would I leave myself in such a position of vulnerability quite beyond my control.

Without question, the agency system had aided in the early development of the publishing industry in Canada. But over the years it became clearer and clearer to me that it had also prevented the customary development of book publishing as it was performed in most developed nations around the world.

IN 1976 WE PUBLISHED OUR first (and one of only two) erotic book. Bill Duthie sent me a copy of *Aphrodite's Cup*, by the late B.C. artist Georges Kuthan, a sensuous portfolio of twenty-five beautiful lino block prints. When we put the book out to tender, three Toronto printers, T.H. Best, John Deyell, and Hunter Rose, all refused to bid. Finally Hignell in Winnipeg produced the book, but not before Jack Hignell had second thoughts and tried to withdraw from the project.

After a great debate with my divided staff, I decided to have each finished copy of the book sealed in cellophane, with a big warning sticker pasted on the front. I felt stupid, but an insider tip that the police department was debating whether or not to raid the warehouse and confiscate the entire inventory hastened the decision. William French gave the book a fine titillating review in the *Globe* and it sold well.

Having been a bookseller who suffered from direct sales by publishers, we most often referred potential bulk sales to booksellers in the area the inquiry or purchase order originated from. Or sometimes, if a rush order had to be filled quickly, we would simply send the local bookstore the money. Al Cummings, now a very successful publisher/packager, wrote from his A Different Drummer Books in Burlington, Ontario: "You're fantastic! Anyone who would send his profit without the bookseller having to sell the book is something else. Please accept our sincere thanks and as the cheque is made out to me I plan to buy a bottle of scotch and will think of you as I ply the inner mysteries of the first glass — after that there is no guarantee *who* I will think of."

In the fall of 1976 we were able to arrange yet another badly needed loan, this time $250,000 from the Alberta Opportunity Company. Ed Clarke, the managing director of the AOC, actually read books! He was the first banker or loan officer I had dealt with who read more than the newspaper's financial pages. By this time, we had a huge sum invested in books that would not be published until 1977 through 1980. Our sales had now passed $1-million, but even though our accounts receivable delinquency rate was relatively low, our major accounts, such as the department and chain stores, rarely paid their bills before ninety days.

By this time, I was in the papers more than ever attacking the sell-out of Canada. Again I received what seemed to be a serious death threat. A few days later a member of my staff phoned me at home just as I was getting out of the shower. When he had arrived at work, he found a very heavy, suspicious-looking, locked black leather bag, with no identification, sitting on the front porch. He immediately gingerly removed the bag and placed it in a snowbank some fifty metres away. He was very apprehensive when he called me, because a strange character had been in the building on a couple of occasions earlier in the week. I told my employee to call the police and I would be right down. By the time I arrived, the police were there, but the bag had vanished, further arousing our suspicions.

About a week later our electrician called me. "Hi Mel, did you get the catalogues?"

"What catalogues?"

"The catalogues I left for you."

"When was that?"

"I left a black bag full of catalogues for you on your front porch last week."

"Oh!"

In 1977 we had an excellent list, and even better lists already contracted for the next three years. Although we dropped all our agencies, our sales increased by almost fifty percent. A confidential federal-government industry study showed we were doing very well. In every key area, receivables turnover, working-capital ratio, return on assets and return on equity, and net profit margin, we were performing much better than the industry average. A little book we published the same year, *The Canadian Metric Conversion Handbook*, sold more than 100,000 copies.

In the fall of 1977 we published a very unusual book, with a rather rude title: *Cover Your Ass! Or, How to Survive in a Government Bureaucracy*, by Bureaucrat X. We sent Bureaucrat X on a tour of the country with a purple velvet bag over his head. In Vancouver he sat, bag on head, next to John Diefenbaker as both waited to appear on Jack Webster's show. The *Ottawa Citizen* had a photographer follow him around until they got a long-distance shot of him taking his hood off in a television station parking lot, which the paper published prominently. The book sold out its first printing of 7,500 copies in a month. It wasn't by any means a great book, but it was a good example of how some imaginative promotion helps.

A Second Mel Hurtig

THE FOLLOWING YEAR a most bizarre thing happened. We had put *The Joy of Hockey* out to tender, and the low bid came from a company we had not previously worked with, the Bryant Press in Toronto. Their president, John Weld, called me to thank me for the order and promised a long, mutually advantageous relationship. Several days later he called back. He had heard I was a golfer; he was headed for the Jasper Park Lodge for a few games, and could we get together in Edmonton for a round before he left for Jasper?

John and I had lunch at my club before our game. Halfway through the meal he said hesitantly: "I've been sitting here thinking about whether or not I should tell you a story about something that happened last week, but I'm not sure . . ."

"Well, John, I guess you *are* going to tell me."

A few nights earlier he had attended a black-tie Big Brothers fundraising dinner at the Hyatt Hotel (now the Four Seasons) on Avenue Road. There were seven other men at his table. After dinner, over brandy and cigars, one of the men next to him leaned over and advised that he was headed downstairs to the S.R.O. bar where a couple of girls would be waiting. Would Weld like to join him? Down they went, and sure enough three young women were awaiting their arrival. They had a drink, lots of laughs, and the three women departed for the powder room. At that point, the conversation went something like this:

"Sorry," Weld said, turning to his companion, "but I missed your name upstairs. I'm John Weld."

"Hi, John! My name is Mel Hurtig."

"Pardon?"

"I'm Mel Hurtig."

At this point, Weld was quite unsure of what was happening. He asked the man: "And what do you do?"

"I'm a book publisher."

"Oh, do you live here in Toronto?"

"Sometimes, but I'm from Edmonton."Now Weld, who had not yet met me, had been talking to me a few days earlier on the telephone, but I hadn't mentioned a trip to Toronto. He was still unsure. "Do you ever produce any of your books in Toronto?" he asked.

"Sure, sometimes."

"Do you by any chance know of a book called *The Joy of Hockey*?"

"Nope. Not one of ours."

The three women were on the way back to the table. Weld turned to the man. "Look buddy," he said, "I don't know what your game is, but I know you're *not* Mel Hurtig."

The man became very flustered, turned red, stammered an apology, and whispered in Weld's ear: "Sorry about that — can't explain it — but for the last couple of years whenever I've been out on the town I've used the name Mel Hurtig."

As John told me this story over lunch, I was at first amused, then incredulous, and finally by the time we had played the front nine, quite angry. I called a friend, Toronto lawyer Aubrey Golden, and told him what had happened. He interviewed Weld upon his return to Toronto and then hired a private detective. It wasn't long before the detective had "Mel Hurtig" under surveillance and had taken several photographs. The next day Weld identified the man in the photograph as the fake Mel Hurtig. The man turned out to be a salesman from a prominent family. We filed a statement of claim in the Supreme Court of Ontario, but discontinued the action (what damages could I prove?) when the man agreed to sign a document promising never to use my identity again.

Years later I was able to give John Weld the largest book-binding contract in Canadian history. And fortunately there were no paternity suits to explain.

In 1978 I asked Morton Shulman to do a book for us on investing, but he wasn't too interested. However, when I mentioned a $20,000 advance (a hefty sum in those days) his interest perked up. In the fall of 1979 we published Shulman's *How to Invest Your Money and Profit from Inflation*. Shulman proved to be the best salesman any publisher could hope to have. The book went straight to the top of the best-seller lists and stayed there for many weeks. We sold some 70,000 copies in Canada, plus U.S. and U.K. paperback rights for a substantial sum. Most subsidiary revenue went to the author, but our share was enough to cover our entire bank-interest costs for the year. Morton's return was well into six figures.

So far I have been telling you about our success stories. But any good publisher will have lots of failures as well. A good idea might not always become a good book. A good book might not always sell. Sometimes the timing is wrong or an author gets bogged down. Sometimes you might work for two or three years on a book, and a few months before your book is scheduled for publication, someone else comes out with a similar title and you're in trouble.

After our great success with his *This Country in the Morning*, Peter Gzowski came back to us four years later with a book idea plus a request for a $25,000 advance. Now, there's nothing a publisher likes better than having the author of a number-one bestseller come up with another great book, especially when the author is someone as popular as Peter Gzowski. Unfortunately I just couldn't get enthusiastic about Peter's idea. He was in love and wanted to do a book about spring. (He was in love with Jan Walter, whom he had met when she'd helped with the final editing of his first book.) Spring? Nice idea, but I couldn't quite see it as a commercially successful book, and definitely not as a candidate for a big advance. Reluctantly, because I valued his friendship and wanted to keep him as an author, I suggested he approach other publishers with his proposal. After a while Peter called me and said he would take a smaller advance, but still wanted us to do the book.

We published 15,000 copies of *Peter Gzowski's Spring Tonic* in the same format as his first book, and again with great design work by David Shaw. We "sold" 13,500 copies, and within six months had 11,000 copies returned to us unsold. Altogether we lost over $35,000 on the book.

In 1978 we agreed to act as consultants for the production of a series of books for the Alberta government, and the consulting fees were very helpful to our bottom line. Both our profit and working-capital positions were our best ever. But now our bank loan was half a million dollars, and we still needed another $150,000 credit line to finance our new publications.

For *The Art of Canadian Nature Photography* we went through 25,000 photographs submitted from across the country. It was a magnificent book, but the sales were only so-so. Another book the same year was a perfect example of a book that *should* have sold well, but didn't. When I was a bookseller, university students would flock to the store to buy copies of an American *Dictionary of Economics*. It contained zero Canadian material. I asked David Crane to do a Canadian economics dictionary, and he produced an excellent book. For reasons I still cannot understand, the book had only modest sales. Well over a year after publication, Canadian libraries had purchased fewer than three hundred copies, and the book had received not one single adoption at any postsecondary institution. On the other hand, we published *Songs from the Front and Rear*, a ribald collection of songs Canadian servicemen sang during the Second World War. It was a smashing success.

Independent booksellers were very worried about the rapid expansion of the three chains, Classics, Coles, and W.H. Smith. In particular, the rest of the trade were concerned about Coles and felt threatened by them because of their frequent forays into price-cutting. I had never met Jack Cole, but in the spring of 1972 he wrote to me: "A continuing disappointment to me is that we are somehow so busy with the book business that we rarely meet the people in it. It would have seemed inevitable that our paths would have crossed long before this — but no such luck! Can we get together either in Toronto or Edmonton and talk about our common interests?"

I was surprised by such a warm letter from a man who had been quoted several times as saying he had never met Jack McClelland. Coles was our biggest customer by far. The next time I was in Toronto Jack Cole and I had a very friendly lunch.

While our publishing program was geared to publishing mostly books of a national interest, we certainly didn't ignore our own province, publishing two histories of Alberta plus a picture history, a history of Edmonton, *Birds of Alberta*, *Wildflowers of Alberta*, *Alberta: A Natural History*, *A Nature Guide to Alberta*, *Parks in Alberta*, *The Best of Alberta*, an anthology of Alberta writing, many books about the mountains, and others by Alberta writers. Our greatest success was *Alberta: A Celebration*, by Rudy Wiebe, Harry Savage, and Tom Radford. It was a big gorgeous coffee table book, published to celebrate Alberta's seventy-fifth anniversary. Aesthetically and financially, for ourselves and for the three authors, it was a lovely success.

Trudeau and the Gorillas

AFTER THE MCCLELLAND and Stewart crisis, the Ontario government demonstrated its concern not only with the large loan to M&S, but also with a comprehensive program of loans, guarantees, and grants to assist Ontario publishers. Ontario assistance to book publishers, measured on a per-capita basis, was over seven times what it was in Alberta, which left us at a competitive disadvantage (not to mention our huge shipping costs), but we were basically unconcerned. By 1980 our sales had passed $2-million, and we continued to show a black bottom line.

And once again we had a number-one bestseller, this time with Henry Zimmer's *New Canadian Tax and Investment Guide*. I tried the patience of my staff by rejecting four proposed jackets for this book. Then David Shaw produced a striking photograph of a roll of hundred dollar bills wrapped in a gold chain; it worked perfectly and the book took off.

From 1975 to 1980 Canadian-controlled publishers managed some seventeen percent of book sales in Canada, but much of that seventeen percent was accounted for by agency books. But by 1980 things were gradually improving: books by Canadian authors made up some thirteen percent of the $930-million book market.

In 1980 two wonderful things happened to me. First, I received an honorary doctor of laws degree from York University. It was my first honorary degree and it meant a great deal to me. Former Ontario premier John Robarts was the York chancellor, and he presented me with my degree and introduced me before I gave the convocation address. In the strangest way, several years later and well after his death, John Robarts would come to my rescue.

My dear mother was not too impressed. Her oldest son, my brother Abe, was a medical doctor; her next son, Henry, was a doctor of toxicology. But her youngest — me — had started off as a truck driver after leaving high school. Mother was in the University Hospital in Edmonton when I returned from Toronto with my elaborate scroll and my new degree. I took the scroll and the chancellor's nice citation up to the hospital. "Mother," I said proudly, "now you have three doctors in the family." She was not moved. "That's not a real degree," she said. I went back to my apartment quite deflated.

However, even my cynical mother was impressed when I was

made an officer in the Order of Canada later in 1980. And what a conundrum I faced. We were allowed to take only one person to the ceremony at Rideau Hall. My father was dead, my mother was too ill to travel, and I was single at the time. How could I possibly choose among my four daughters? I decided to write Ottawa and mention that I had four girls who had never been to Ottawa. If by any chance there were cancellations of any kind, could I please bring my girls?

At the last minute fellow recipients Jean Beliveau and Bob Blair had to cancel. So Barbara, Gillian, Jane, Leslie, and I all headed for Ottawa. It was one of the proudest moments of my life. The ceremony was wonderful, and the party and dance afterwards was great fun, especially with everyone making such a big fuss over my daughters.

The next day I took them to visit the prime minister in his Centre Block office, then to see all the sights in Ottawa, and finally down to Toronto. On the plane on the way back to Edmonton, I asked ten-year-old Leslie what the highlights of her trip had been. She thought for a moment. "Meeting Mr. Trudeau in his office and the gorillas in the Toronto Zoo." Fair enough.

The next year was one of sadness and happiness. My mother died early in the year at the age of eighty-seven. Later in the year some good news: once again Hurtig Publishers was chosen Publisher of the Year by Canadian booksellers, this time "in recognition of the quality of their publishing program and their continued good service to booksellers." Having been a bookseller for so many years, it was important to me to provide the best service we could. This meant turning around orders quickly, providing booksellers with adequate information, and seeing to it that our books arrived in the stores well packed and in good condition. My staff and I had a fine party when I returned from the CBA.

I was delighted that Edmonton's Audrey Whaley (whom I had trained as a bookseller) of Audrey's Books, which had evolved from our main bookstore, won the CBA's Roy Britnell Award the same year, marking the first time the two awards were both presented to firms outside Toronto.

For several years we had been very successfully producing beautiful photography and art books. In 1979 and 1980 I sent Janis Kraulis and his friend Bo Curtis flying across the country in an old Piper Pacer plane for a book to be called *Canada from the Air*. It was a great idea, and as always, Janis's photographs were superb. Some of the pictures in the book were amazing: Niagara Falls, Toronto City Hall, a silver river in the Yukon, the red soil of Prince Edward Island, the beauty of aquamarine mountain lakes, an extraordinary shot of Helmcken Falls in Wells Gray Park. One of the first pictures in the book was taken from a low altitude directly above 24 Sussex Drive. I sent the prime minister a couple of remarkably detailed blowups and a one-word note: "Security?"

Unfortunately, after two years of hard work and a huge investment, *Canada from the Air* was not a success; the colour separators and printers had done a poor job, and the finished product was well below our expectations. I could have cried.

In November 1981 Kay and I were married after being introduced by a mutual friend only a few months earlier. After the wedding we flew to Halifax, where I had a speaking engagement, and then on to Bermuda for our honeymoon.

By 1982 we were receiving about 1,800 unsolicited manuscripts a year and publishing perhaps ten. If this sounds discouraging, consider what a visiting senior editor from New York told me. Her prestigious house received more than 35,000 unsolicited manuscripts in the previous year and had published only thirty-four of them.

Some manuscripts were referred to in the trade as "rubber band manuscripts," ones so obviously inept that the readers needed only to flip through a few page tops before sending it to the reject pile. Quite often very good manuscripts would come in, but the market was already saturated with similar books. We tried hard to refer authors to publishers we thought might be interested in a book that we had narrowly rejected or that was not in our field of publishing. Quite often we were successful, and a number of well-known authors got their start with the publisher we directed them to. Although, I must tell you, one day Jack McClelland phoned and said: "For Christ's sake, Hurtig, would you stop telling your damn authors to send their manuscripts to me!" He was only half kidding.

Despite the often daunting mountain of unsolicited manuscripts, woe to the publisher who ignores them or does not have a staff well trained in spotting the precious stones in the gravel. The good publisher is the one who can recognize potential and offer hope, advice, and encouragement.

In 1982 the recession hurt us and we had our first really bad year. Sales were down by more than $300,000, yet our expenses were the highest in our history. Our working capital declined by almost a quarter of a million dollars, and our receivables were the lowest in many years. But in 1983 we bounced right back with a record-breaking year in sales and profit. In ten years we had grown to become the fourth-largest, Canadian-owned, English-language book-publishing firm in Canada, ahead of such longtime well-established houses as Gage, Macmillan, and Clarke, Irwin. Only McClelland and Stewart, General Publishing, and the University of Toronto Press had higher sales.

In December the governor general and his wife invited us to stay with them at Rideau Hall, which Kay and I both thoroughly enjoyed, although I was rather dismayed when Ed Schreyer somehow managed to edge me on the snooker table. The Schreyers had to leave on a trip, so we had the huge place to ourselves (ourselves and eighty staff, that is) for a couple of days.

In 1983 our bestseller was Charles Lynch's *You Can't Print That*, with sales of almost 45,000 copies. Charles loved to tell the story of throwing an unopened big brown envelope from Hurtig Publishers into the garbage, thinking it was "yet another Mel Hurtig speech" or "more Hurtig advertising junk," then of driving halfway home, suddenly worrying about the envelope's contents, doing a U-turn, and rushing back to the office. He rescued the envelope just as the cleaning lady was reaching for the garbage pail. Inside was a $70,000 royalty cheque from Hurtig Publishers.

The timing of reprints is crucial in book publishing. While Lynch's first book was a number-one bestseller and a runaway success, his second book, *A Funny Way to Run a Country*, had an initial burst of sales and then simply died, but not before we had gone back to press for another 10,000 copies. By the time booksellers' returns came back, we had some 17,000 copies to remainder at forty-nine cents each.

In 1983 we also published one of my favourite books, *Kurelek's Vision of Canada*, with William Kurelek's remarkable paintings and text by Joan Murray. The book contained much of the finest of the artist's fascinating, unique work. Stupid, stupid Mel Hurtig: years earlier art dealer Roger Woltjen had brought Bill Kurelek into my bookstore, but I was too busy to look at the paintings they offered for sale, at a price of between $100 and $500. A Kurelek painting sold at auction for $52,000 in 1995, and major works are expected to go for much higher prices in the near future.

In May 1983 Clarke, Irwin, the respected fifty-five-year-old Canadian publisher of Marian Engel, Robertson Davies, Alden Nowlan, and Timothy Findley, was forced into receivership by its bankers. A few months later the important Toronto printing-and-book-production firm of Hunter Rose was forced to close down, after 123 years in business, and Ken Thomson closed the doors on Fleet Publishers.

While for some Canada's small population was thought to be a problem (only about seventeen million English-speaking Canadians in 1983, compared to some 235 million English-speaking Americans), it was certainly not anywhere near the key problem. Small countries such as Norway, with only four million people, and Sweden, with fewer than seven million, had thriving book-publishing industries. And there were numerous other examples. But in good old colonial branch-plant Canada, imported books continued to dominate the market.

In 1984 McClelland and Stewart was in trouble once again. And once again the Ontario government came to the rescue, this time with some $3-million in loans and grants. While many were critical of this assistance, everything is relative. Just one of several tax concessions made in 1984 to a heavy oil plant would have taken care of all the government support required by Canadian book publishers for fifty or sixty years.

The next year Jack McClelland finally carried out his long-standing threat and sold his company — to Toronto real estate developer Avie Bennett. Jack made an extraordinary contribution to Canadian literature, guiding and developing some of Canada's finest authors, often under difficult circumstances. His flair, his love of books, his panache, and determination all combined to make him a truly wonderful publisher.

The same year Jack sold M&S, I launched the biggest publishing project in the history of Canada.

The Canadian Encyclopedia

ONE DAY, IN 1971 or 1972, I was in Swift Current, Saskatchewan, to speak to a big teachers' convention. I am not one to make much small talk before a speech, not because I am unsociable, but rather because I like to conserve my energy, get a little bit of adrenalin flowing, and concentrate on what I'm going to try to do with my speech. Afterwards I love to socialize with my audience, but beforehand I like to be left alone.

On this occasion we arrived at the large composite school from

Regina about an hour before I was to speak. At my request I was left alone in the library, which was closed because of the convention. For a few minutes I sat looking at my speech notes, and then I began to walk up and down the room examining the contents of the library shelves. There were very few Canadian books. All the reference books and encyclopedias were American. The students could immerse themselves in American history, American heroes, American accomplishments, American politics, American values — you name it. Without question, the U.S. won both world wars single-handedly. Canadian content in the three different American encyclopedias on the shelves was hopelessly inadequate for Canadian school children and often full of egregious errors.

I was disgusted. That day, before I climbed the steps to the auditorium stage, I resolved to publish a Canadian encyclopedia. There was some anger and evidence of *lots* of adrenalin in my speech.

I began to accept more invitations to speak to teachers and students. By August 1975, I had visited more than two hundred schools across the country. I was sickened not only by how few Canadian books were in most school libraries, but also by the appalling lack of Canadian content in the curriculum.

Back in 1957 the American publisher Grolier had published the ten-volume *Encyclopedia Canadiana*. Critic Arnold Edinborough described it as "a brave and financially risky venture." Ivon Owen was the head of Oxford University Press in Canada. He and his colleague Bill Toye and Macmillan of Canada were splendid exceptions to the branch-plant rule; they did a first-class job of producing important Canadian books. Owen reviewed the *Encyclopedia Canadiana* in *The Tamarack Review* in 1959 saying that

> 1958 was also the year of a great national disaster. . . . We refer to the publication of *Encyclopedia Canadiana*. This expensive result of immense labour and some very good writing is hideously ugly in design, abominably produced, and disfigured by pictures badly selected, worse printed, and fatuously captioned. Had we space, we could go on at some length, especially about the stodgy selection and treatment of the biographical articles. . . . But the thing has been done, that's the pity of it; the market will not support a rival.

By the early 1970s, *Canadiana* was "hopelessly out of date," in Bill

French's words. In its pages Pierre Trudeau was still minister of justice, John Diefenbaker was still leader of the Opposition. Moreover, most of the statistical information in the *Canadiana* was badly in need of updating. Modern basic scientific information was close to nonexistent; there were no entries on computers, genetics, electronics, Candu, satellite communication, urban transport, or cable television. There were no references to such subjects as energy policy, language legislation, or Petro-Can. The articles on women, native people, the arts, education, trade, and many others were badly out-of-date. According to *Canadiana*, "The housewife accepts her never-ending work, not for its own sake, but to keep one corner of a hurried world secure and bright and warm."

Despite a considerable lobby, Grolier in the U.S. had refused to give their Canadian subsidiary the money required to produce a new edition. The set soon was out of print and no new editions were planned.

In late 1975 I met in Toronto with Owen, who was now working as a freelance editor, and Morris Wolfe. After further meetings we all agreed that if we could somehow find the money for a new Canadian encyclopedia, Owen would become executive editor and Wolfe the general editor. They were both excellent book men with broad knowledge. As well, I was certain that the three of us could work well together as a team. We began putting together a national advisory board; both historian Ramsay Cook and George Woodcock agreed to join.

The next step was to prepare a detailed submission to the Canada Council, which had already given the University of Toronto Press grants of $660,000 for the *Dictionary of Canadian Biography* (and Ottawa would give them millions more in the future). Early in 1976 we submitted a forty-two-page application to the Canada Council, including detailed specifications and budgets along with numerous letters of support. The encyclopedia would be "the results of the best and most recent scholarship in straightforward, jargon-free language, not without grace [and] the information must be presented in as lively and readable a manner as possible."

We planned to produce one well-bound 1,744-page volume, containing about three million words, with some two hundred black-and-white maps, diagrams, and line drawings. The three million words were approximately the total number to be found in *Canadiana's* ten volumes. The first printing was to be a huge 100,000 copies.

We asked the Canada Council for a total of $750,000 over the five years that would be required to produce the new encyclopedia. This represented twenty-nine percent of the budgeted costs of $2.577-million. Hurtig Publishers would guarantee fifty-three percent of the costs and find the rest. As part of our approach to the council, we offered to provide French-language rights to a Quebec publisher free of any charges.

Soon after we submitted our application, I met with John Evans, president of the University of Toronto. Would the university consider offering us office and library space at no charge, so the venture could be located there? Evans was nothing but enthusiastic and helpful. There was little doubt in his mind that the necessary arrangements could be made.

Several times over the next few months we heard from enthusiastic officers of the Canada Council. This was "the best idea we've ever had . . . the best, most badly needed proposal!" We solicited letters of support for the project, and soon the council was swamped with endorsements from across the country: Alberta Premier Peter Lougheed, Conservative MPs Ged Baldwin and Gordon Fairweather, David Lewis, Knowlton Nash, John Roberts, who was soon to be appointed secretary of state in the Trudeau government, Peter Newman, Robert Fulford, Northrop Frye, author Hugh Hood, editor Douglas Marshall, political scientist John Meisel, Harry Boyle, Donald Chant, Hugh Dempsey, Davidson Dutton, Eddie Goodman, Henry Hicks, Stu Hodgson, John Holmes, Bill Kilbourn, Allan King, Hugh MacLennan, W.L. Morton, Ross Munro, Walter Pitman, George Stanley, Miriam Waddington, Robert Weaver, and many others. Ontario Premier Bill Davis wrote to say: "*The Canadian Encyclopedia* is of major significance to Canada. I wholeheartedly endorse this important project."

The Alberta government offered to contribute $50,000 a year for five years, and Walter Gordon said he would be responsible for raising $500,000 from private companies and foundations if the project proceeded. Assuming that with this base of support we would have no trouble raising the $1.3-million balance through a bank loan, we were very optimistic about the overall financial viability of this mammoth, exciting project.

We waited for news from the Canada Council. Several meetings in Ottawa went by without a word; we were sitting on pins and needles, jumping at every phone call. Finally in June the council wrote us a long detailed letter. The crucial paragraph came on page three:

". . . the Council thus finds itself in a contradictory situation. On the one hand, the desirability of publishing a one-volume encyclopedia has been endorsed by the Explorations committees, by Council members and by our special evaluation committee. You have been requested to modify your project in ways which will necessarily greatly increase its costs. On the other hand, the Council, at this time, may well be unable to provide a substantial proportion of those increased costs."

The Canada Council requested that we set up duplicate French and English editorial and research offices from the outset, and that we guarantee that the French edition would be published at the same time and at the same price as the English-language edition. The costs to make these commitments would be very substantial, but the council simply would not be able to afford their pro-rata share of the increased costs. Catch 22: either we do the encyclopedia their way or we wouldn't get the money, but if we did it their way we wouldn't get the money. I was very disappointed. Not only had we offered French rights to the massive project completely free of charge, but three Quebec publishers had already expressed considerable interest in our proposal.

By the time we abandoned the project, we had spent some $28,000, not a lot of money in publishing today, but a lot of money to us in the mid-seventies. But, more than that, a dream had been squashed.

Happy Anniversary!

OVER TWO YEARS WENT BY. One day I was in Alberta Culture Minister Horst Schmid's office. I talked to him about the encyclopedia, which I still could not get out of my mind. He loved the idea, but it went nowhere. Nor did I really expect it to, since I had become increasingly critical about the heavy foreign ownership in the petroleum industry and had been criticizing the Lougheed government for its energy policies, which I described in a CBC broadcast as "sell whatever we have, sell it as quickly as possible, sell at very low prices to foreign firms in Canada, who in turn sell to their parent companies in the U.S. at very low prices, charge the lowest royalties in the world, and throw in, for good measure, the lowest possible income-tax rates." Not exactly words likely to endear me to the premier, former energy minister Don Getty, or the Conservative cabinet or caucus.

Then in 1979 fate stepped in. Alberta would be celebrating its seventy-fifth anniversary in 1980. The federal government had spent about $36-million celebrating Canada's Centennial in 1967. The government of Saskatchewan was budgeting $6.6-million to celebrate that province's Diamond Jubilee, also in 1980. But the Lougheed government, at the time enjoying burgeoning petroleum revenues, decided to spend $75-million on their celebrations. Why $75-million? Well, it was, after all, the province's seventy-fifth anniversary.

Immediately there was much criticism, both within the province and from other parts of the country. Alberta was accused of flaunting its wealth, of bad judgement, and later, when it became clear that the government was quite uncertain about how it was going to spend so much money, of poor preparation and organization.

I took a chance. I didn't think, given my deteriorating relations with the government, that there would be much likelihood of success, but why not try? On May 29, 1979, I wrote to Peter Lougheed with the idea of a "gift to Canada" as an important part of the province's celebrations. I copied Horst Schmid and the new culture minister, Mary LeMessurier.

There were several interesting aspects to my proposal, not the least being that inflation and other factors had dramatically raised the cost of the project. My hope now was that the Alberta government would agree to contribute $2-million to the development of a new encyclo-pedia, but only if Ottawa would agree to equal the contribution. It seemed to me that if Alberta agreed to put up the $2-million, we would have a much better chance of pressuring the federal government to match the grant. Moreover, from Alberta's point of view, the project would be located right in Edmonton, creating many jobs in the province. The Alberta government, as part of its $2-million "gift to Canada," would purchase copies of the new encyclopedia at cost and give them to every single public and private school, every college, university, and public library in every province and territory in Canada, and to all Canadian government posts abroad.

Unusual things began to happen in the following weeks and months. First I began to receive confidential, surreptitious phone calls from middle-level civil servants — "Look, I didn't make this call, but they're *really* thinking about it" — and later, requests for more information and clarification from assistant deputy ministers. Now I was really getting my hopes up. But then I had another confidential call, this time from a Conservative MLA. Things had gone badly in the caucus; several MLAs and a couple of cabinet ministers hated Mel Hurtig. It didn't look good.

Late one winter afternoon I was sitting at my desk in my office when Bob Dowling, a former Alberta Conservative cabinet minister who was the seventy-fifth anniversary commissioner, called me. He said that he had bad news and good news. He gave me the bad news first: "I'm sorry, but after much careful thought we've decided that there's just no way we can give you the $2-million. We just can't do it. It's really out of the question." My heart sank. Now the dream was gone forever. Dowling continued: "The good news is that we don't want you to go to Ottawa. We don't want any other government involved. We're going to give you all of the $4-million."

I was stunned. I sat there in a daze. Could this be real? We talked on the phone for a few minutes more and scheduled a meeting to begin drawing up the detailed contracts. I will never forget Dowling's last words to me before he hung up: "Well, Mel, thanks a million!"

I sat back in my chair behind my desk quite overwhelmed. How extraordinary, how wonderful, how fantastic! I called the staff into my office and told them the news, then sat alone thinking about the immense task ahead.

On November 15 Mary LeMessurier made the announcement in the legislature. The Alberta government would underwrite the encyclopedia's research-and-development costs to the tune of $3.4 million and purchase $600,000 worth of encyclopedias at net production cost so that the government could give 25,000 copies away to schools, libraries, and postsecondary institutions across the country, as I had proposed. French-language rights would be granted without charge to a Quebec publisher.

Writing in the *Globe and Mail*, columnist Robert Sheppard put it this way: "The Alberta government outdid even Hurtig's chutzpah." And so they had. Peter Lougheed, bucking considerable resistance from his own caucus and cabinet, graciously overlooking years of criticism from me, had made the final decision himself. Peter and I had fought even before he had become premier in 1971. But nevertheless, there was some long-term degree of mutual respect. I admired his energy, his communication skills, his hard work, and hands-on approach to governing the province. Conversely, one Sunday afternoon at a summer party at Pigeon Lake, Peter had given me the ultimate compliment. "Hurtig, you're the one person I know who I'm darn glad didn't get directly involved in Alberta politics."

In the years ahead we would battle more fiercely over free trade, but one thing I can say without reservation: if it hadn't been for Peter Lougheed and his affection for Canada, there would be no *Canadian Encyclopedia* today.

After the announcement, overnight we were deluged with job applications from journalists, authors, academics, editors, researchers, photographers, cartographers, designers, and indexers from across the country, but neither Ivon Owen nor Morris Wolfe was enthusiastic about moving to Edmonton.

One day I had lunch with a friend, William Thorsell, an editor for the *Edmonton Journal*, to talk about whether or not either or both of us were interested in exploring the possibility of his becoming editor-in-chief of the encyclopedia. While Bill and I were friends, we argued fiercely about almost everything. Much to my chagrin, he was the only person I have ever met who could still argue lucidly into the early-morning hours, while becoming half-corked.

At the time, Bill was nowhere near as right wing as he is today, much less certain of his own infallibility, and infinitely more open-minded. Although he was thought to be the logical choice, he had been passed over when the *Journal* appointed a new head editor. During lunch it became clear to both of us that, for a number of reasons, his career in journalism would continue. After lunch, as we stood talking in the parking lot, a beautiful old silver Jaguar caught my eye.

"What a gorgeous car!"

"Would you like to buy it?"

"Don't tell me it's yours!"

"Yep, and I'm getting a *Journal* car next week."

I drove it around the parking lot a few times. It was magnificent. I am not in any way a car nut, far from it, but this old car was something special.

"Is it in good shape?"

"Absolutely! It's in excellent shape."

"How much?"

"For you, $8,500."

"I'll take it."

A week later Thorsell delivered the car and I delivered into his hands a cheque for $8,500. Unfortunately there proved to be a few small problems. Whenever I drove over twenty miles an hour and turned left, even gradually in a traffic circle, water would pour out of the dashboard, soaking my right shoe, sock, and lower pant leg. I often arrived at meetings or parties looking like some large dog had peed on me. But that was the least of the problems. The damn car wouldn't turn off. I would park it on Jasper Avenue, turn the key, get out, lock the door, and head down the sidewalk. The Jag would sit there, chugging away, spitting and coughing. Inevitably whenever an old lady or pregnant woman walked by, the car would backfire loudly, scaring the living daylights out of everyone in the vicinity. I would be hiding in some store doorway.

During the next six months I spent nearly $7,000 in repairs on the car, finally in frustration hiring a student to drive it to Vancouver to a "specialist," paying his airfare back to Edmonton, then back to Vancouver again to pick the car up. When it finally arrived back in Edmonton, I could at last turn the car off and it would actually quit running. One more small problem: it now had a Yellowhead Highway oil leak, which cost $1,500 to repair. Conclusion? Never buy a used Jaguar from . . . Never trust a . . . Buyer beware . . . A fool and his money . . . Don't be stupid!

For years afterwards, whenever my name appeared in the *Globe*, invariably the fact that I drove a Jaguar was mentioned, even long after I ditched it for a car built in Bramalea, Ontario.

Putting the Team Together

WE ADVERTISED THE POSITION of editor-in-chief of the encyclopedia across the country. In December 1979 I interviewed James Marsh, publications editor of the Carleton Library Series in Ottawa. Jim was thirty-six, remarkably underpaid, and had been hard at work editing academic volumes at the Institute of Canadian Studies for almost ten years. I questioned Jim extensively and was impressed, even more so after Morris Wolfe interviewed him and the letters of reference I requested arrived. Jim moved to Edmonton in the summer of 1980 to take command of what would become the largest, most complicated book-publishing project in the history of Canada. We more than doubled his previous salary.

Just before that, I hired a tough, hardworking Scot, Frank McGuire, to become the encyclopedia's managing director. Frank had gone to school in Glasgow and had worked in printing and publishing in Canada for twenty-five years, the last five as executive director of communications for the Alberta government. At one time a Queen's printer in Alberta, he was a meticulous systems man, something we badly needed. He was good at handling crisis after crisis, putting in incredibly long, pressure-packed hours, developing complicated computer systems, working closely with the staff of the University of Alberta, supervising contracts, maintaining liaison with officials in the Department of Culture, and handling hundreds of unexpected scheduling and production problems.

Frank and I got along extremely well, despite the enormous pressure we both faced every month. If we did not meet every day, we talked on the telephone. Unfortunately Frank and Jim did not always get along well, which was a problem, but almost to be expected. They were profoundly different people, with vastly different backgrounds, interests, and skills. Over the years they had many disagreements, yet the job got done. They were, in fact, an excellent team, with the unique talents necessary for an undertaking such as ours. Both the editor-in-chief and the managing director were given contracts with excellent incentives to keep costs under control and to bring the project in on time, which was absolutely critical. If we overspent or were late, the extra costs would likely be difficult or even impossible to cover.

We began hiring additional editorial staff late in the summer of 1980. Ideally we were looking for well-trained generalists with editorial, research, writing, and communications skills — a tall order. There were few experienced Canadian encyclopedia editors, so we hired men and women who would be fast learners and, we hoped, highly productive.

We started off by looking carefully at what other encyclopedia publishers had done: Britannica, Groliers, Columbia, and Random House. I sent Jim to Chicago so he could see Britannica's operation, and then on to New York to Columbia University.

Then we had our first major crisis. We were informed that *Reader's Digest* had decided to beat us to the punch and rush into publication a Canadian encyclopedia of their own. With their resources, they could do it and cut their price so we couldn't possibly compete. In September a number of us met with some of our key consultants in Toronto to discuss the *Reader's Digest* plans. Bob Fulford said that he had already been contacted and been asked advice about editors. He thought this totally unexpected development would be "a disaster" for our project. I agreed. Jim Marsh warned that *Reader's Digest* would have vast amounts of material already published and a storehouse of illustrations to call upon.

We spent the rest of the day talking about what we would want to find in the encyclopedia and who the best authors would be for the various articles: Catholicism, the welfare state, ethnic groups, refugees, nationalism, regionalism, political campaigns, technology, inventions, democracy, graveyards, the beaver, wine, expatriates, satire, radicalism, cities, place names, cartooning, games, watercolour painters . . . you name it.

When I returned from Toronto, I met with Dr. Harry Gunning, president of the University of Alberta. Could we locate our editorial offices at the university, use their computer system and libraries and work with the academic staff when required? In return, we would pay the university an annual fee ranging from $10,000 to $15,000 plus a five percent share of any profits. Harry Gunning was marvellous. He promptly took our proposal to the board of governors, who gave quick approval. We were delighted with the arrangements. And so was the university.

These were still early days in computer typesetting. The University of Alberta mainframe computer was a blessing, but also, at least until we learned how to overcome the problems, produced nightmares for us. Sometimes a power surge wiped out data completely. Sometimes a sentence or a paragraph or a page would disappear. But we could never have done the immense job without the university's computer technology, on-line data entry, computer typesetting and formatting, pagination, indexing, and our own specially developed software programs. Well, perhaps we could have done it, but it would have taken at least ten years, instead of five, and we would have needed far more staff. One additional advantage of the computers was that we would be able to revise and update right up to press time.

We put together an outstanding National Advisory Committee: Dr. Harry Gunning; Dr. Rose Sheinin and Dr. J.M.S. Careless from the University of Toronto; Dr. Davidson Dunton from Carleton; Dr. Eva Kushner from McGill; Dr. Pierre Maranda from Laval; Dr. William

New from U.B.C.; Dr. Tom Symons from Trent; Dr. Catherine Wallace, the chairman of the Atlantic Provinces Education Commission; and Dr. Norman Ward from the University of Saskatchewan.

After the committee's first meeting, Frank McGuire and Harry Gunning flew to Montreal and met with the head of Reader's Digest of Canada, explained our plans, and warned that in our opinion the market would be split with two new encyclopedias; as a result, both would likely fail. Moreover, we were far ahead of them in planning, and our encyclopedia would certainly be much more comprehensive than the one they were planning. They promised to get back to us.

It was still our intention to produce a large one-volume encyclopedia along the lines of *The Columbia Encyclopedia*. However, when a dummy volume was produced, we immediately realized it would be far too big and far too heavy for children and most senior citizens to use. Moreover, the average reader would find the huge book too cumbersome for regular use. After much experimentation, we moved to two volumes and then, as the scope of the project quickly grew and the scheduled contents expanded, we finally settled on three large volumes. The three volumes of *The Canadian Encyclopedia* would contain many more words and illustrations than all ten volumes of the old *Canadiana*. (There was one other rather important reason we decided not to go with the one volume. No bindery in Canada could produce such a big book.)

We made an early decision to have as many articles as possible signed by their authors. The famous 1926 thirteenth edition of *Encyclopedia Britannica*, considered by many to be the finest encyclopedia ever published, had signed articles by Einstein, Freud, George Bernard Shaw, Trotsky, Henry Ford, and many other well-known figures.

Mind you, some famous encyclopedias, although a reflection of their times, were far from objective. In the eleventh edition of *Britannica*, which many people read cover to cover, we are told by a famous anthropologist that Negroes are by nature lazy, intellectually inferior, and preoccupied by sex, but that nonetheless the Negro often exhibits "in the capacity of servant a dog-like fidelity which has stood the supreme test."

The next major step for us was the painstaking construction of the article list. Just who and exactly what should be in the encyclopedia? *Canadiana* had devoted some one hundred thousand words to lieutenant-governors and only eight thousand to artists; our priorities would be different. Our advisers, consultants, and staff all made suggestions for Jim's consideration. Then, once we had our preliminary article list, the next step was to find the right author for each article.

One piece of good news later in the year buoyed us in our preparations: Reader's Digest decided not to proceed with their Canadian encyclopedia.

Throughout 1980 we met regularly with our bank. We would need to borrow millions of dollars to finance the production and marketing. With a $4-million grant from the Alberta government and our proven track record, plus our distinguished National Advisory Committee and our talented staff, I assumed there would be little problem in obtaining the required bank financing. After all, I had been dealing with the same bank for twenty-four years and had never been late one second with one penny of any loan payment. Our firm had been profitable for years and our operations praised across the country. Moreover, wouldn't *any* Canadian bank be proud to be involved in an important Canadian project of such far-reaching benefit to so many different sectors of Canadian life?

Well, actually, no.

WE DID A PAINSTAKINGLY detailed projection that told us we would need a $4-million line of credit to finance the encyclopedia production, advertising, and promotion. Throughout the winter of 1980-81 I discussed the project in detail with our bank and kept them constantly updated with a steady stream of paper. But for reasons I could not understand, they seemed less than enthusiastic, although never actually saying no.

By the spring of 1981, it was clear that the bank was dragging its feet. Our full staff was in place across the country, and thousands of contributors had begun work on their articles. I decided to hold a seminar at the university for several financial institutions, including three banks, the Alberta Treasury Branch, and the Alberta Opportunity Company. All expressed interest, but the Bank of Montreal was most enthusiastic. My own banker, a CIBC vice president, sat through the two-hour presentation with hardly a comment or question until the very end. After all the other bank vice presidents and senior officers had asked a great number of pertinent questions, my banker asked why we needed a Canadian encyclopedia since there already were so many encyclopedias on the market.

Our project's academic consultants came from every university in Canada. As well, we had journalists, physicians, teachers, scientists, environmentalists, archivists, civil servants, curators, museum directors, naturalists, arts correspondents, defence authorities, librarians, trade experts, and many others who advised us on everything from abortion to zoology.

Our authors overwhelmed us with their kindness and generosity: Margaret Atwood, Pierre Berton, John Robert Colombo, Doug Fetherling, Eugene Forsey, Jack Granatstein, Grant MacEwan, Kenneth McNaught, Desmond Morton, Farley Mowat, Peter Newman, Bernard Ostry, Edward Schreyer, Tommy Shoyama, George Swinton, Harold Town, Norman Ward, George Woodcock, to name a very few. David Suzuki, Kenneth Hare, Larkin Kerwin, and J. Tuzo Wilson were among the science, industry, and technology writers. Sports and the social sciences were covered by the best experts available. And Francophone contributors such as Daniel Latouche, Marc Laurendeau, Paul-André Linteau, Fernand Quellet, Guy Sylvestre, Marc-Adélard Tremblay and Pierre Dansereau played an important role. Even Conrad Black accepted Jim's request to write the article on Duplessis.

Unfortunately we could only afford to pay the contributors eight cents a word. But most of those we approached were, in the words of Jim Marsh, "quite thrilled" to be involved in the project. All told, we had only some six or seven complaints about the meager pay. The consultants, depending on their workload, were paid between $250 and $1,000.

We kept the Alberta government informed about our progress through Frank McGuire's regular reports to Alberta Culture's staff. From time to time I would see the minister or premier at some social gathering. Peter Lougheed would always want to know how things were going and good-naturedly jested about my criticism of his government's energy policies, even after *Saturday Night* wrote that "Lougheed's opposition is almost laughably weak: government benches occupy *both* sides of the chamber, with the six opposition members shunted off together. . . . It sometimes seems as though the most vocal opposition consists of one non-elected man — Mel Hurtig, the small-l Liberal maverick publisher. . . ."

By the summer of 1982, twenty-three full-time editors and researchers were hard at work on the encyclopedia in two old houses near the High Level Bridge on the eastern perimeter of the University of Alberta. Some 9,000 articles had been commissioned from over 2,500 experts across Canada, and more were in the works.

Two and a half years into the project we were on time and on budget. Along the way there had been terrible problems with computers, with art and cartographic costs, with the necessity for fact-checking authors whose manuscripts contained errors, with production and scheduling problems that had been quite unanticipated. But Frank McGuire, Jim Marsh, David Shaw, and the cross-Canada editorial team managed to solve the problems and stay on schedule.

Our original plans had been for black-and-white illustrations only, mostly line drawings, similar to those in the *Columbia Encyclopedia*. But when the new one-volume *Random House Encyclopedia* was published, with a great number of full-colour illustrations, we changed our minds. The extra cost would be substantial, but attractive, full-colour illustrations would help sales and appeal to younger readers.

We paid very careful attention to the packaging. After turning down dozens of combinations, we elected for a gold-stamped, midnight-blue linen binding and a light beige, gold-stamped linen slipcase to hold the three volumes. Then each set would be shrinkwrapped and packed in a sturdy oyster-board shipping carton.

By the spring of 1982, it was clear that our long negotiations with the CIBC were going nowhere. But after our seminar, both the Continental Bank and the Bank of Montreal continued to express much interest. In fact, the Continental Bank in Edmonton was very excited about the project. Their head man, Larry Pollock, and his staff were almost as enthusiastic as we were about the encyclopedia. We worked with them for two months, and then they sent head office in Toronto a glowing proposal. Toronto turned it down flat, without asking any questions.

We began detailed discussions with the Bank of Montreal soon after. One summer day the bank's deputy chairman, Bill Bradford from Toronto, and two vice presidents arrived in a limousine at the front door of the office. A few days later, the bank advised that a good offer was in the works, and that they anticipated a long, rosy bank-client relationship.

But by fall, there was still no signed agreement. I was now getting very worried. All the thousands of men and women across the country were producing what was going to be a wonderful encyclopedia, but we had no money to publish it. In September Premier Bill Davis wrote a very complimentary letter, calling our project "of major significance to Canada and to this and succeeding generations of Canadians." We showed the letter to the bank, with a request that they send it to head office. Soon the pace of negotiations accelerated.

Another interesting thing began to happen. As more and more articles about the encyclopedia appeared in Canadian newspapers and magazines, letters containing orders and cheques began to arrive from every part of the country, even though we had not yet set a final price for the set. Three years before publication we had more than a thousand sets sold. That, too, impressed the bank.

An Arm and a Leg and a Trunk and a Torso

BY EARLY 1983, WE had a full-time staff of forty men and women working on the encyclopedia in Edmonton, plus additional editors in Vancouver, Calgary, Toronto, London, and Montreal, as well as our designer, David Shaw, working in Toronto.

By now our computer systems were well ahead of everyone else. Several executives from Encyclopedia Britannica in Chicago and Toronto flew in to see what we were up to. Britannica's editor-in-chief, Tom Goetz, a truly distinguished editor and gentleman, was most impressed with what we were doing and how we were doing it. Three weeks after they left, Britannica offered to buy the entire project from us, guaranteeing us a large profit for our efforts. When we turned them down, they offered to buy 25,000 finished sets, sight unseen, and requested an option, should we allow it, to buy up any unsold sets at cost.

Now, wouldn't you think that the banks, with such an enthusiastic response from Britannica and a firm order for a quarter of our print run, plus a guarantee to buy up unsold sets, would be impressed? Canadian banks? No way. Would they have lent the money to Britannica? Of course.

Even while we continued our discussions with the banks, we knew we would need extra funds to help cover the added costs of the colour work, including hundreds of new full-colour maps. We approached Bob Blair of Nova and Vice President Dianne Hall. Within a month, Nova had approved a donation of $250,000 to help us.

With each passing week, the detailed cash-flow charts and production timetables on my office wall grew longer, from four feet to more than eight. Every week we updated and modified them. Always there were unexpected additional costs and problems to contend with. We knew that the large volumes would have to lie flat when opened; the heavily reinforced special bindings on the book spines would be costly. As an experiment, we shipped dummy sets of the encyclopedia back and forth across the country and some were damaged in transit. We needed sturdier shipping cartons.

Late in the afternoon of Friday, May 13, 1983, I sat at my desk working on production budgets for Hurtig Publishers' fall list. My secretary came in with a registered letter from the CIBC. With much curiosity, I opened the envelope. Inside was a letter calling my entire $700,000 bank loan and giving me two weeks to pay up.

I was incredulous, flattened. With no warning, the bank was quite prepared to wipe us out — not only Hurtig Publishers but *The Canadian Encyclopedia* with it. I phoned the bank, but the manager was gone for the day. I felt a pain in my stomach. I was paralysed with despair. It was the blackest day of my life. Everything I had been working for over the space of twenty-seven years would be lost. We would be unable to pay our bills, we would default on our author and printer contracts; our home and everything else I owned were signed over to the bank on my loan guarantee. We would lose *everything*. The rotten bastards!

I left the office and went home, but said nothing to anyone. Kay made dinner but I hardly ate. We went for a walk and then went to bed early; I didn't sleep for a minute. Saturday I went to the office and sat there all day trying to figure out what I could do. There was no bloody way in the world I was going to sell the entire encyclopedia to Britannica, but even if I did, it wouldn't solve my problems. How was I going to tell my staff? My authors whose royalty cheques wouldn't arrive? My wife and family?

Saturday night I lay in bed tossing and turning. There was no answer, we were going under. Suddenly, at around three in the morning, I sat bolt upright in bed. By God! I jumped out of bed, quickly dressed, and rushed down to the office. Around six in the morning, I found what I was looking for — an early-April Zena Cherry column from the *Globe*. I read it and reread it. My, my.

Sunday night at seven o'clock I slipped into the bedroom at home, closed the door, and called Gordon Lewis, vice president and general manager of the CIBC. Here is how the brief conversation went:

"Mr. Lewis, this is Mel Hurtig from Hurtig Publishers. I apologize for disturbing you at home during the supper hour, but I have something important to discuss with you."

"Can't it wait until tomorrow morning?"

"No, sir, it cannot."

"Okay. What can I do for you?"

"Mr. Lewis, I have here in my hand a clipping about a big luncheon in Toronto, hosted by Russell Edward Harrison, chairman of the Canadian Imperial Bank of Commerce, to kick off the fundraising campaign for the new John Robarts chair of Canadian Studies at York University."

"And?"

"Mr. Lewis, what do you think the reaction will be in Toronto, in Edmonton, and elsewhere across Canada when I announce that the CIBC has just pulled the plug on the largest-ever project in the history of Canadian studies?"

There was a long silence.

"What exactly do you want, Mr. Hurtig?"

"Mr. Lewis, all I want is the time to make new arrangements and to get the hell out of your bloody bank."

There was another even longer silence.

"I will call you at your office tomorrow, Mr. Hurtig."

I slammed down the phone.

Early next morning Lewis called; we could take as long as we wanted to make new arrangements. The bank would withdraw its loan-call immediately.

It took another seven months and many new flowcharts and business plans before the Bank of Montreal's financing offer arrived. We had expected it on August 1, but it finally arrived in December after two long years of negotiations. The terms, conditions, and bank fees were onerous.

I joked afterwards that "if one of our staff had to go to the bathroom once too often, the bank would own the encyclopedia," but it wasn't too far off the mark. If we fell behind schedule, or suffered any number of other woes, the bank would be entitled to cut off further funding.

It was to me to be an absurd situation. Every day across the country more and more people were talking about the encyclopedia and sending in orders, yet still the bank made stringent demands. The bottom line was that unless we could generate a much larger number of sales in advance of having to go to press, the money we needed wouldn't be available. We could still end up with a superb encyclopedia, the product of years of work and the best minds, writers, and artists in the country, but we might not be able to publish it. And, oh yes, we'd have to close our publishing house and declare bankruptcy, and Kay and I would have to move out of our house and lose everything we owned.

But I had no choice, or so it seemed. The documents for me to sign arrived on my desk; they were several inches thick. I sent a set to my lawyer's office for him to review. He would get back to me by the end of the week.

The very next morning, totally out of the blue, I received a phone call from Gerry McLaughlan, president and CEO of the Canadian Commercial Bank. "Mr. Hurtig," he said, "I would like to introduce myself. We're a new bank. I hear you're looking for some money. Can I come over for a talk?"

Within six days the CCB had a contract on my desk. In every respect, it was more attractive and more reasonable than the Bank of Montreal offer: interest rates, life-insurance requirements for my senior staff and me, Hurtig Publishers' operating line of credit, collateral demands, production schedules. It didn't take me long to sit down with my lawyer and accountant. We quickly accepted the CCB's offer.

When I called the Bank of Montreal to inform them that I had received a much better all-around offer, they asked me not to make an immediate decision — to wait at least through the weekend. On Monday morning the Bank of Montreal called me; they were willing to match the CCB's terms, item for item. No way, I thought. I owed the CCB a huge debt of gratitude. Very politely I told this to the Bank of Montreal.

In December the CCB paid the CIBC the $607,000 we still owed them. We bought a million dollars' worth of life insurance for me and three-quarters of a million each for Frank McGuire and Jim Marsh. According to William French, writing in the *Globe and Mail*, "Surely this must be the highest value ever put on the life of a Canadian publisher."

Dic Doyle, then the editor of the *Globe*, said I had obviously made a serious mistake in my attempts to raise funds from Canadian banks. If I had called it *The Mexican Encyclopedia*, I wouldn't have had any problems.

Just as the banks and the Alberta government had negotiated tough contracts with us, we negotiated tough contracts with the twenty-seven different firms involved in producing the encyclopedia. The specifications were very detailed. Penalty clauses were onerous. Schedules were firm. Delivery of finished sets must begin in June 1985 and continue through to early December.

Another crisis occurred when Ted Byfield's *Alberta Report*, as might be expected, ran an article suggesting that the encyclopedia would produce a left-wing view of Canada. One Conservative insider reported to us that members of the provincial cabinet "went berserk" upon reading the article. Mary LeMessurier was instructed to review all completed articles and report back to cabinet. If Hurtig didn't cooperate, funding would be cut off. Great! I could have strangled Byfield. But there was no way I would allow government officials to review, influence, or censor the contents of the encyclopedia. Nevertheless, it was a major problem. After much consternation and debate, we suggested that a highly regarded vice president of the University of Alberta be allowed to see completed articles and report back to the minister. After Peter Meekison's glowing report, we never again had a problem with the Alberta government. In fact, I can say without the slightest reservation that, with the exception of the incident just related, the government was very helpful at all times. Provincial Treasurer Lou Hyndman, Deputy Minister Jack O'Neill, and John Patrick Gillese from Alberta Culture were all very supportive.

Our budgeting was based on producing and selling 100,000 sets. This was a huge number; very few Canadian books had sold 100,000 copies in the entire history of publishing in Canada, never mind a relatively expensive three-volume set. But much to our delight, the orders from the chain and department stores and the independent booksellers came in even better than we had anticipated. The bank's demand that we obtain substantial up-front orders had led us into a marketing strategy that would encourage such orders: there would be a saving of $50 a set on orders placed in advance of the publication date, and one printing and one printing only; those interested in acquiring a set would be wise to order well in advance.

By April 1984, seventeen months before publication, we had orders for $4.9-million worth of encyclopedias, approaching our break-even point of $5.5-million. A month later, our orders passed the 105,000 set mark. We increased the print run to 150,000 sets — in the words of Bill French "an astonishing figure."

While all this was happening, our regular publishing program was booming. At the summer 1984 Canadian Booksellers Association trade fair, everyone was excited about the encyclopedia. We set the final retail price at $175, but the prepublication offer brought it down to $125. At that price it was a remarkable bargain. A few weeks earlier, a black and white *Encyclopedia of Japan*, with fewer words and many fewer illustrations, was published at a price of $700.

Most encyclopedias are not sold in bookstores for a variety of reasons, but the fear of price-cutting is one of the most important. Britannica urged us not to sell the set through the retail trade, but I rejected their proposal. On publication day I wanted Canadians in communities all across the country to be able to go into their book or department store and come away with their set of the encyclopedia. While I recognized the validity of Britannica's warnings, I felt it was a chance worth taking.

How Mothers Began Dying

WHILE WE WERE WORKING away on budgets, production schedules, contracts, sales, advertising, and promotion plans, Jim Marsh was working eighteen-hour days, seven days a week. He was and looked exhausted, haggard, and thin, with big black circles around his eyes. By the spring of 1984, more than a thousand articles were late, some of them over a year late. Many had to be reassigned to new authors. All told, Jim had assembled 375 expert consultants to help solve our editorial challenges. The encyclopedia would include thousands of new topics not previously included in any Canadian encyclopedia, from Land Claims to the Status of Women, from Astrophysics to Pornography, from Genetic Engineering to Greenpeace, from Prostitution to Film Animation, from Ecosystems to Folk Music.

How do you decide what to include? Should a chief justice have precedence over a Stanley Cup winner? Fort Vermilion over a nineteenth-century entrepreneur? Miss Canada over a nuclear physicist? A poet over a broadcaster? Why not all of them? Why not ten volumes or twenty volumes, instead of three? The answer was simple: we wanted to produce a comprehensive, authoritative encyclopedia that average Canadian families could afford to buy for their own homes.

Still, do you give more space to Emily Carr or to Syl Apps? To Alex Colville or the Guess Who? Who should get a longer biography and a big colour photo — Wilfrid Laurier or Wayne Gretzky? Should a lieutenant-governor make way for an award-winning short-story writer? Is it important for Canadians to know that Canada has no indigenous earthworms?

And then, how do you decide who should be asked to write the article on Mackenzie King? On Social Credit? Who can best produce even-handed objective articles about economics? Who will be fair, accurate, and lively about the theatre? How do you choose the best authority, the most reliable, the fairest, the most objective? And can that person write in a clear, understandable manner? We did not want an encyclopedia written by academics for other academics. Nor were we aiming to produce volumes just for children. But we definitely wanted an intelligent high school student to be able to use the encyclopedia without difficulty and *enjoy* using it.

Then, what about that long, long list of subjects that were bound to be controversial, abortion, for example? The abortion article was sent out to fourteen different readers for their comments and suggestions before Jim Marsh finally approved it.

Of course, contributors were not always happy with their articles being shortened or with the changes our editors suggested. Marsh was called both a communist and a fascist on more than one occasion. On controversial topics we tried for "informed opinion." For example, we presented both sides of the debate about nuclear power and worked very hard to provide a balanced perspective wherever controversy was inevitable.

We had to reject a good number of articles, mostly because they simply did not meet our standards. Some of the authors didn't mind, but some were furious. One of Jim's senior editors rejected an article from one of Jim's good friends in Ottawa. The author was very upset. Jim backed his editor and lost a friend. Hundreds of articles were rewritten more than once. Even some of the most brilliant academics had difficulty writing to the level we needed. One article was assigned to thirteen different contributors, the all-time record. Some contributors gave us nightmares. Costly nightmares. Letters, telegrams, faxes, and phone calls would go unanswered; deadlines would pass and new "final" deadlines would be set, to no avail. Finally we hired extra staff who spent their entire days chasing down late contributors by long-distance telephone. One delinquent author of an important article claimed that his brother, his father, and his mother-in-law all died over the twelve-month period in which his article had been due.

An amazing phenomenon occurred during the final year of the editorial process: mothers across the country began dying. One mother died twice.

Probably the most novel excuse came from an author assigned to a very important topic. He had had, he told our female editor, a very bad vasectomy. He was now too depressed to complete the article. Another contributor's house burned down and all his notes for his major article were lost. Several authors had heart attacks and one claimed a complete memory lapse; he didn't remember signing the contract to do the article.

One of my favourite stories concerns the article we commissioned on sheep and goat farming in Canada. It was to be 500 words. Month after month, season after season went by, and still no article. We spent hundreds of dollars in phone calls and telegrams prodding the author. Finally it arrived. It was 9,000 words and entitled "Sheep and Goat Farming in Quebec."

Another article assigned at 300 words came in at over 5,000.

Much to our surprise, as a result of our fact-checking, we discovered several cases of out-and-out plagiarism. As well, we found that some of our authors were not exactly well acquainted with their subject area. We made the decision to fact-check every single article, a monumental task that proved essential.

By the end of April 1984, our computers showed that of 3,120,486 words commissioned from over 2,800 contributors, 2,712,466 had been received and 1,879,889 had been approved by Jim Marsh. Some 8,000 articles had been assigned, 1,600 illustrations had been identified, and 300 new maps — enough for a whole new atlas — had been commissioned. Hundreds of tables, diagrams, and graphs were in the works. And work had begun on a detailed index, cross-references, and suggested further readings for many articles. In the end we had 400,000 words too many and had to chop articles and eliminate some entirely.

By the time the volumes went to press early in 1985, Jim had read each of the 8,000 articles at least twice. I read most of them twice, frequently making suggestions for Jim to consider. Sometimes he accepted my suggestions, sometimes he ignored them. Except in the case of my own biography, which I did not wish included, I never once insisted on any additions, deletions, or changes to editorial content.

Altogether some 3,000 men and women from every area of Canada contributed to the encyclopedia. Without them we could never have proceeded, and the vast majority laboured long and hard and produced first-class entries. Hundreds of very busy, very famous Canadians helped us because they believed in the project. I think there was only one well-known Canadian author who turned us down flat: Mordecai Richler. Even Daniel Latouche, the sovereigntist political scientist with close ties to the Lévesque government, who had helped draft the wording for the 1980 Quebec referendum, was very helpful to Jim Marsh. Of course he recognized the irony of what he was doing.

In the Edmonton area alone, about 350 people were directly involved in editorial, illustration, consulting, indexing, and other work. For five years the encyclopedia made a good contribution to the local economy.

The press run was set at 150,000 sets, which with overruns turned out to be 463,500 volumes, by far the largest book-production job in Canada's history.

The paper for the encyclopedia was manufactured in St. Jérome, Quebec, and shipped to Montreal. Nearly 90,000 yards of cover cloth were produced in Cornwall, Ontario, and the colour separations were done in Vancouver. If all the printed pages coming off the high-speed web offset presses in Montreal had been laid end to end, there would have been more than 54,000 miles of paper, enough to circle the globe twice and then some. Altogether 1,200 tonnes of paper, a record order, were used in the first edition and a million metres of thread. Special new inks had to be developed for use in the web presses. The final packaging of the sets would be done in Oshawa, Ontario.

I sent Frank McGuire to Montreal to supervise the press run for the first volume. Just before the big presses were scheduled to be switched on, McGuire discovered a Borduas painting was upside down.

It took almost a full year to print and bind and collate and package all the sets. A fleet of trucks were needed to bring the millions of pages from the printers in Montreal to the two binderies in Toronto. As part of the contract with Ronald's Printing, we arranged for a transfer of work from Montreal to their Edmonton plant, resulting in the creation of more than a hundred man-years of work in the plant. Peter Lougheed was pleased.

Stabbed in the Bookjacket

B Y THE TIME THE FIRST volume of the encyclopedia went to press, ninety-six percent of the 150,000 sets had been reserved. Of course, that didn't for a moment mean they were actually sold, quite the contrary. Half the sets "sold" to the retail trade were returnable. Conceivably we might not know until well into the following year whether the project had been successful and whether we would be able to pay the bank back the millions of dollars we owed them. It looked promising, but nothing could be taken for granted.

The largest-ever advertising and promotion budget for any previous Hurtig book had been $20,000. Our budget for *The Canadian Encyclopedia* was $700,000! All told, including money that the department stores, chain stores, and independent booksellers spent in cooperative advertising, well over $1-million would be spent on advertising and promoting the encyclopedia.

Then out of nowhere came a rude surprise. Right in the midst of our print run, the Mulroney government decided to produce its own encyclopedia and began putting it out in a magazine format. I couldn't believe it. (Perhaps I shouldn't have been surprised. After all, the culture of the CIBC was reflected, when the bank had earlier called our loan, by the presence of both Mulroney and Conrad Black on its board of directors.)

At first I wasn't worried. It *looked* like a magazine, and the contents were scheduled for publication over a long period. But the Canadian president of Encyclopedia Britannica phoned and, to say the least, he was *very* worried. There was no question in his mind that the federal government's action would severely hurt our sales. His exact words: "This is a disaster. People can only afford one Canadian encyclopedia. The government is spending and will spend a fortune advertising their project. It's going to hurt, and hurt badly."

Now, given our heavy commitments, the advanced state of our work, the heavy print and electronic media publicity across the country, given that the fate of our publishing company hung in the balance, entirely dependent on the encyclopedia's commercial success, why would the Mulroney government decide to do something so rotten? Surely it couldn't have had anything to do with the fact that I had recently formed the Council of Canadians, apprehensive that Mr. Mulroney was about to negotiate a free-trade agreement that many of us feared would massively abandon Canadian sovereignty. Surely not.

Newspapers across the country condemned the government's move. Incredibly Secretary of State Walter McLean claimed that the reason they were proceeding with their government encyclopedia was that they couldn't find a private publisher to do the job!

In the words of Britannica's president, David Durnan, "If private enterprise did something like this, they'd have us in court for misrepresentation." The editorial page of the *Edmonton Journal* gave an angry denouncement: "An encyclopedia it's not. . . . The Canadian publishing industry has enough problems without having its champion stabbed in the bookjacket by his own government."

Well, not exactly *my* own government.

Finally in mid-March after a great deal of negative press, Walter McLean phoned and apologized. He said it had been "gross stupidity" for the government to have called their magazine an encyclopedia. The decision to do so was made "at the last minute" with little thought. They would henceforth not use the word "encyclopedia" and would discontinue their advertising campaign.

On June 28, 1985, I presented Peter Lougheed with a specially bound limited edition of the encyclopedia in a ceremony in the marble rotunda of the Alberta legislature building. I don't know whose smile was bigger, his or mine. I was very proud and Peter was at least as proud of Alberta's gift to the nation. On Canada Day he presented the first numbered set to Brian Mulroney and his family and then the second set to Her Excellency, Governor General Jeanne Sauvé, at a reception in Rideau Hall.

By the date of publication in September, we had orders from forty-three different countries around the world, all fifty American states, and from every part of Canada. Now the bottom line for us was that we could make $2-million or lose $2-million.

On September 6, 1985, we had a party for 1,100 people at the Citadel Theatre in Edmonton to celebrate the official launch of the encyclopedia. When the time came for me to speak to the full auditorium, I was led to a huge dummy set of the encyclopedia sitting on the front of the spotlit stage. Our promotion chief surprised us all when she pulled a cord dangling from the front of the set and suddenly a lectern and microphone popped up at the top. I was led to the back, where stairs were set into the rear of the dummy leading up to the lectern. I mounted the stairs with a somewhat dazed look on my face, and then a very big smile. The whole auditorium cracked up. After my speech Peter Lougheed, Bob Blair, Mary LeMessurier, Harry Gunning, Jim Marsh, and Frank McGuire all spoke briefly, all to great applause. Then Tommy Banks's orchestra struck up and the partying began.

I had forecast that Hurtig Publishers would be sold out by Christmas, but we quickly realized that the estimate had been far too pessimistic. Four days after publication we were completely sold out of all 154,500 sets. By early November we had orders for another 40,000 sets, which we could not fill. Many bookstores across the country had sold out in September or early October. Eaton's had ordered 12,500 sets, were sold out by publication date, and wanted another 10,000. But there was no way we could fill any of these orders; we had promised one printing and one printing only in our advertising, and that would be it. Mind you, there might still be large returns from the retailers, especially if pre-cutting occurred.

In the end some minor cases of price-cutting did occur in Toronto and Montreal. Whenever that happened we immediately offered full refunds to people who complained. No one took us up on the offer.

Looking back, I don't think it's an exaggeration to say we faced crisis after crisis with the encyclopedia and sometimes imminent disaster. There was to be one more test. On Labour Day morning my clock radio had woken me up just before seven. I lay in bed listening to the news. The first item announced that the Canadian Commercial Bank had gone under. Good Lord!

We had about $1-million in cheques out and another $2-million owing printers, binders, packagers, truckers, newspapers, and magazines. The next two nights were almost sleepless. But much to its credit, the Bank of Montreal stepped in and provided us with the money we needed. By this time there was virtually no risk for the bank. We paid the entire loan back in less than two months.

We were also able to pay off our entire Hurtig Publishers operating loan by the end of the year. For the first time since I opened my tiny bookstore twenty-nine years earlier, we were entirely debt free. Debt free! What a relief! What a wonderful feeling!

The total cost of the project was almost exactly $12-million; we had budgeted $11.8-million, so our cost overrun after five years of work was less than two percent. We had scheduled publication for September 1985, and after five years were right on time. I was very proud of Jim Marsh, Frank McGuire, David Shaw, and all our wonderful team.

The reviews exceeded our fondest expectations: "Mel Hurtig and company have captured a nation in a nutshell" was the *Globe and Mail* headline for William French's review. He went on to say: "A reader quickly gets the feeling this is an encyclopedia one can trust. It covers just about every conceivable aspect — and some inconceivable ones — of Canada and Canadians, past and present. The slipcase should carry a warning that those who enter here do so at their own risk; they may disappear for days, and search parties may be required." James Adams, writing in the *Edmonton Journal*, called the project "the literary-reference equivalent of the CPR."

Pierre Berton was full of praise. "I cannot control my enthusiasm for *The Canadian Encyclopedia*, a copy of which I now have thanks to you," he wrote to me. "It's an absolutely first-rate work and the best thing I can tell you about it is that in the first three days that it's been in my office I've used it about a dozen times. I think you ought to be congratulated for your dedication and hard work. I have a nodding idea of how much this must have taken out of you."

By mid-September, letters and telegrams of congratulations began pouring in from across the country. Moreover, less than a week after publication it had become clear that we needn't worry about any returns. Coles sold over 4,000 sets in just a few hours. Across the country, many independent bookstores sold out their entire order within the first week. Most bookstores sold the sets for the prepublication price of $125 the first few days, then upped the price to $175, giving them a bonus profit margin. Bill Ardell, president of Coles, said they were "glowing" because of the unprecedented volume created by "the beautiful marketing." The head buyer for Coles wrote: "Great product, great price, great promotion, great reviews, great sales — everything worked." Pierre Elliott Trudeau wrote to say: "I am all the more delighted because its publication comes at a time when my three boys are ready to gather a wealth of knowledge from it. . . . You may well be proud of this fantastic achievement."

All in all we received thousands of letters after the encyclopedia was published, more than ninety-five percent favourable. But we made sure to pay careful attention to all criticism and all advice. Much of it was valuable. A young girl wrote us a three-page letter explaining passionately why her mother, an opera singer, should have been in the encyclopedia. And she was right. Her mother should have been. We made sure she was, in the second edition.

Betting the Farm Again

NOW I HAD TO THINK carefully about my future. And now logic and emotion were at war within my head. We had more than $2-million sitting in the bank and invested in interest-bearing instruments. Instead of paying the bank a huge amount of interest every month, we were being *paid* interest, something entirely foreign to my experience.

Hurtig Publishers had good lists lined up for 1986 and 1987; honours, awards, medals, and citations were being bestowed on me by universities, societies, and other organizations. I had a chance to play golf, go hiking, work even harder against Brian Mulroney, read books I had piled up in my den, living room and bedroom — in other words, to enjoy an interesting, somewhat hedonistic life. That would have been the *logical* thing to continue to do.

But what about those tens of thousands of Canadians who wanted sets of the encyclopedia for themselves and their families and couldn't get them? And what about keeping the encyclopedia up-to-date? Moreover, we had learned an enormous amount about what to do and what not to do when putting out large reference works; was now the time to let all our skilled staff go? Or should we put it all on the line again, risk everything again, and produce an expanded, updated new edition? Logic said an emphatic *no*. Emotion said *yes*.

I met with Jim, Frank, and Barry Hicks, who was now our chief financial officer and soon to become the vice president of our firm. Barry had worked on the encyclopedia account at both the Bank of Montreal and the CCB. When the CCB went under, he was out of a job. He knew everything about the encyclopedia's financial details and made a valuable new addition to our staff.

In July 1986 I had lunch with Ron Besse in Toronto to explore the possibilities of his firm, Canada Publishing Corporation, buying Hurtig Publishers and committing to keeping the encyclopedia updated. Ron flew out to Edmonton with his right-hand man and soon offered me $3-million for Hurtig Publishers. Anyone with any brains would have accepted. With $2-million already, I could retire, write, paint, hike, golf, and above all devote more time and money to the Council of Canadians.

It was very tempting, but — the heck with it! I turned the offer down and away we went again. We would publish an expanded, updated, four-volume Canadian encyclopedia in 1988. People who wanted to would be able to trade their first edition in on the second. We would keep our key editorial staff, begin work immediately, and donate the trade-in sets to underprivileged families.

The first edition hadn't been perfect (no encyclopedia ever has been). We would correct the errors (not many) and omissions. We had left out Burlington, Ontario; Melville, Saskatchewan; and Dartmouth, Nova Scotia, much to the chagrin of residents of those communities. Perhaps the funniest omission was Sir Frederick Haultain. Why funny? Well, I was nominated to receive the prestigious and valuable Haultain Award. Needless to say, when the judges turned to H in the encyclopedia and found no entry for Haultain, I did not get the award.

Once we made the decision to proceed, we were resolved to make the second edition bigger and better.

In August 1986 we completed a detailed budget. This time, it looked as if we would have to borrow $5-million from the bank, even though we would be reinvesting all our profits from the first edition into the second. Since we had repaid the entire $4-million bank loan for the first edition so far ahead of schedule, we anticipated little problem obtaining an additional million-dollar line of credit.

Like the first, the second edition would be a monstrous job. There would be 1,800 new articles, 673 new illustrations, forty-three new maps, and a total of 750,000 new words. More than sixty percent of the articles in the first edition would be updated or expanded. The new content meant four volumes in the boxed set, instead of three. One valid complaint we had about the first edition was the index. It proved to be quite inadequate. This time, the index would be much longer and much more detailed.

In the spring I had the great pleasure of visiting the president of the University of Alberta, Myer Horowitz, who had succeeded Harry Gunning. I told Myer it would be helpful if he could gather a few of his key people for the meeting, but I didn't tell him what I had planned. When I arrived at his office, there was a good group assembled. I reached into the inside pocket of my suit jacket and pulled out a $50,000 cheque made out to the university, much to the amazement of all present. It was the first instalment on the university's profit-sharing arrangement, with much more to come. Myer gave a thank-you speech saying that in all the years the university had been involved in joint ventures with business, this was the first time it had received any profit back. There were big smiles all around.

In 1987 Les editions Alain Stanké of Montreal published the French version, *L'Encyclopédie du Canada*, with the help of the Canada Council, which paid for the cost of translation and the additional editorial work.

Meanwhile, John Crosbie kept attacking "the peddlers of encyclopedias" in his speeches in the House of Commons and across the country. One day we both got into the same elevator in the Centre Block. Crosbie stared at me, his eyes narrowed, and he said: "So you're the encyclopedia peddler." I said: "And so you're the guy who hasn't read the Free Trade Agreement." End of conversation.

A Big Gamble and a Big Betrayal

I T TOOK THREE YEARS of hard work to produce the second edition. The printing was scheduled for 100,000 four-volume boxed sets, but once again the advance orders caused us to increase the print run, this time to a total of 113,300 sets — 453,200 volumes.

The new edition would have to retail for $225, but again we offered a $50 discount, for a prepublication price of $175. For those who wished to trade in the first edition, the net cost would be $125.

Our total cost of the second edition was $12.4-million. Of this amount, some eight percent came from grants and the balance from cash flow, our own previous profits, and, of course, a big bank loan. Once again we had a million-dollar advertising and promotion campaign planned, beginning with full-page ads in newspapers across the country.

And once again, advance sales were excellent. The book and department stores had all made huge profits on the first edition and had sold every single set they had purchased. By the summer of 1988, we had presold some 80,000 sets (of course, once again on a returnable basis).

In my foreword to the second edition, I said: "For many years there has been discussion and debate about the so-called 'Canadian identity.' There is indeed a clearly definable 'Canadian identity' and it is readily described in the pages of these four volumes."

In September we had a big party at the St. Lawrence Hall in Toronto to launch the new edition. There was lots of good food and drink; the waiters were dressed as Louis Riel, Barbara Ann Scott, John A. Macdonald, and other famous Canadians.

Halfway through the evening Barry Hicks pulled me aside. Nigel Berrisford, of the W.H. Smith bookchain, had challenged him: "Is it true that Coles is going to slash the price of the encyclopedia to $99 beginning tomorrow morning?" As in the past, I had worked closely with the retail trade on both editions and had worked out generous advertising allowances with retailers who made major purchases. I had worked for months with both Smiths and Coles, talking to their key staff every week. It was totally inconceivable to me that Coles would do something of the sort Nigel was suggesting. The trade always had to contend with price-cutting, but slashing the price all the way down to $99 was truly a predatory act. I told Barry to go back to Nigel and tell him there was absolutely no truth to the rumour. It was out of the question that Coles, having made an enormous profit from the first edition, having worked closely with me on the second, would betray me in this way; they would clearly understand the devastating repercussions.

The problem of price-cutting has always plagued publishers whenever a book or project has required a large investment. Jack McClelland had written to me back in 1978 to say: "Our main problem is the price war. We really don't know how to deal with that. With the Newman book and the Berton book we either face a bonanza or we face disaster and we certainly don't know which. Books are pouring out of our warehouse to the discounters. All the indications are that they are going to pour back in January from the non-discounters so we don't really know what to expect."

The morning after the launch party, *The Canadian Encyclopedia* was on sale in Coles stores across the country for $99. Given their in-store signage and their advertising, it was clear the people at Coles had planned the move for quite some time, all the while working with me in a friendly smiling manner.

Smiths had no choice; they immediately matched Coles' price. The department stores, independent booksellers, and wholesalers were furious, and much of their ire was directed at me. As well, many of the individuals who had ordered sets from Hurtig Publishers demanded refunds. By the third week of September, total chaos reigned. It was difficult to guess what the end result would be, but the damage would clearly be substantial. Moreover, Coles' action immediately put a project we had begun to work on, a junior encyclopedia, in jeopardy.

Altogether we ended up writing $865,000 in refund cheques. Independent booksellers returned over 20,000 sets. After the dust had settled we still managed a profit of some $750,000, but never again would we be able to invest heavily in a project and market it through the retail book trade. Of the 113,000 sets we produced, 23,000 remained unsold by year end. The unsold sets represented some $2.3-million in revenue that had been scheduled for the junior encyclopedia.

It was another round of superb reviews that saved our bacon. *The American Review of Canadian Studies* said: "It should be in every possible library in as many countries as possible. . . . The editor and publisher are to be highly praised for this remarkable achievement." *The Canadian Library Journal* used exactly the same words: ". . . a remarkable achievement." And the *Globe* said: "In almost every way, the new edition is superior to its predecessor."

After the storm of complaints over price-cutting, the letters of praise started to pour in. One, from Foam Lake, Saskatchewan, was typical: "I am 15 years old, and very curious about this great country of ours. However, it was difficult for me to find a book or collection of books which contained modern, accurate and interesting information on this subject . . . until your Canadian Encyclopedia came out. They were (and are) just the thing I had wanted."

This time we paid the bank back our $4-million loan in four months, again well ahead of schedule. I could also stop paying the premiums on the $7-million in life insurance the bank had made me buy.

In June 1988 the Canadian Press asked me what was next. My reply: "Almost certainly we are going to be looking at an electronic version. We're talking about the whole encyclopedia on one little compact disc."

Surely you can't be serious! was the common reaction. And why would you want to do it on a disc? was another. The next year we began work on a CD-ROM with a Toronto software company. The fact that the entire manuscript was already in the University of Alberta computer made the job much easier. Late in 1990 we produced the first major CD-ROM reference disc in Canada, with all 2,736 pages from the second edition on one four-and-three-quarter-inch disc.

Some final thoughts on *The Canadian Encyclopedia*. The University of Alberta was splendid; without the help of Harry Gunning, Myer Horowitz, vice president Lorne Leitch, and many members of the university staff, there never would have been a new encyclopedia. All told, we were able to partially reciprocate with $111,000 in profit-sharing payments to the university, $648,000 in payments for various services, and $32,000 worth of complimentary sets.

There were complaints over the years, of course, mostly from my political opponents, about the grants we'd received. But in the end the tax revenue the Alberta and federal governments received from profits, payroll taxes, sales, and other forms of direct and indirect taxes were several millions of dollars more than the total of all government grants received.

Seventeen years after my idea in Swift Current, more than five thousand Canadians had been paid for their work on *The Canadian Encyclopedia* and hundreds of work-years created for men and women across the country. Adding the first and second editions together, some 250,000 sets were sold, far exceeding my wildest dreams. The fact that all these sets were sold was of course vitally important to the success of the project, but more importantly, all the wonderful material about our country is now in homes, schools, libraries, and offices across Canada.

Who ever said life was fair? The wonderful, enthusiastic, athletic Gordon Garner, hardly ever sick a day in his entire life, a runner and ardent tennis player, said goodbye to his wife, Georgina, one morning after breakfast and headed out to his car in the garage. Georgina found him dead in the car a few minutes later. He was only fifty-seven.

A New National Curriculum

THE LETTERS CONTINUED to flow in pleading for a junior version of *The Canadian Encyclopedia*. Once again we had to think carefully about the financial and personal commitments involved. The book-publishing industry is notorious for the poor wages paid to editors and other staff members. Our company was always better than average, but rarely could we afford the wages paid for similar work in government. Still, sometimes we were more than able to make up the difference. In 1988 I was able to give one of our staff a $50,000 bonus, another $25,000, another $16,000, and hand out more than a dozen other large bonuses. But when we finished work on the second edition of *The Canadian Encyclopedia*, was I going to let most of our great editorial staff go? I thought not, but it was an awfully large payroll to sustain, with many more staff than needed to keep the encyclopedia up-to-date.

By the summer of 1988, even before the second edition of the encyclopedia was published, I had made the decision. Most key staff would be retained, and we began working on *The Junior Encyclopedia of Canada*. When the long complicated planning was over, after much discussion, debate, and consultation, this is what we knew. *Junior* must be an entirely new work, not a rewriting of the adult encyclopedia. It must cover all aspects of all the subjects one would expect to find in a comprehensive reference work on Canada, but it must at the same time concentrate on subjects of greatest interest to children. It must present information as clearly as possible, be free of jargon, and wherever possible be written in a pyramid style from the simple to the complex, so that even the most difficult subjects would be understandable. The entries and vocabulary would have to be intensively tested in schools. To a far greater degree than in the adult encyclopedia, the text would have to be enlivened with anecdotes, examples, time lines, illustrations, and sidebars. The overall goal of the finished volumes was to "astonish at the scope, beauty, and diversity of Canada" and "be spectacular, by any measurement."

There was nothing remotely resembling a national school curriculum and no comprehensive source to which young Canadians could turn for information about their country. *Junior* would be the first attempt to provide such a source. Special attention would have to be given to research topics frequently assigned by teachers across the country, such as biography, wildlife, prejudice and discrimination, the environment, the political system, Confederation, multiculturalism, history, and geography. There would have to be extensive coverage of the sciences and social sciences, architecture, painting, applied arts, sculpture, printmaking, design, ballet, theatre, literature, and music. The text would be enlivened with special articles such as "How a book gets published," "How to track a submarine," "The Gretzky Trade," and "What happens to a cheque after you cash it." Again, all controversial articles would be read by experts to ensure objectivity, and all factual material again would be checked by our own staff and by outside experts. Thousands of cross-references at the end of the entries would lead readers to other relevant articles, and more than one hundred careers, from accountant to zoologist, would be described.

Without question *Junior* would be the most extensively and beautifully illustrated reference books in Canadian history. Many of Canada's best-known and most talented photographers would be represented. Specially commissioned new artwork would be painstakingly prepared at great cost with full-page illustrations of, for example, the life of settlers in New France, Huronia, Upper Canada, and the West. Some ninety percent of the subjects to be covered in *Junior* would not be in any other junior encyclopedia. As the planning progressed, we became more and more excited about what we were doing.

Once again, however, we faced the question of how we would finance another immense new project, this one even more expensive than the others. And once again I would bet the farm; every penny of our retained earnings from thirty-four years in the book business would go into the project.

We put together a submission for both the CRB Foundation in Montreal and the Department of Communications in Ottawa. Since Ottawa had not funded any portion of the original *Canadian Encyclopedia* development costs and since the federal government was continuing to pour millions of dollars into *The Dictionary of Canadian Biography* and other large Toronto-based reference projects, we thought it would not be inappropriate to ask the Department of Communications if they would assist with our development costs. After a full year of negotiations, DOC agreed to put up a total of $950,000 over three years if we could find a matching grant from the private sector, a foundation, or another government. Our own investment would be some $3-million; the rest would have to come from the bank.

The CRB Foundation, which was Charles Bronfman's foundation, was very enthusiastic about the idea of a junior encyclopedia. In short order they agreed to put up $900,000, also over three years. Off we headed to the bank again with a commitment for almost $5-million in funding. But this time, we would likely need a loan of at least $7-million.

In all of 1989 Jim Marsh managed one day off — Christmas Day — as we rushed to meet press deadlines. As well as his team in Edmonton, Jim again had full-time editors in Vancouver, Toronto, London, and Montreal working with him. In some cases, teams of researchers were assigned to prepare material for Jim so he himself could write the entries on AIDS, Meech Lake, etc. Jim, a keen hockey fan, wrote most of the many hockey articles himself.

Junior was also intended as a teaching tool. We field-tested some one thousand articles in schools across the country, which was enormously helpful. More than 1,500 students and scores of teachers were asked for their comments on preliminary versions of articles. Were they readable? Interesting? Suitable? What have we missed? How could we improve the illustrations? How could the books be made more useful for the curriculum? The kids and the teachers were direct and to the point in their criticism and advice.

Now, what about the marketing? Was there any way the new encyclopedia could be made available in bookstores? In the November 1988 edition of *Quill and Quire* I wrote:

> What a lesson we've learned — the hard way! The ear-to-ear price-slashing . . . came to us as a *complete* surprise. We weren't so naive as to believe there wouldn't be a certain amount of price competition, but we never for a moment expected the catastrophic destruction of the suggested list price and the inevitable consequences for ourselves and all independent booksellers.
>
> We're looking for solutions. We've asked the Canadian Booksellers Association for advice. We'll be consulting a lot of booksellers in the next few weeks. So far we've had many well-meaning suggestions, but unfortunately, most of them contravene Canada's Competition Act and other laws. . . .

After a great deal of agonizing and discussions with many booksellers, we reluctantly came to the conclusion that it would be impossible to market *Junior* through the retail trade and risk the chance that jugular price-cutting would strike again. After many months of work, we developed a massive direct-sales campaign, although we would also supply bookstores with freestanding floor displays and sample sets at no charge, and provide the retailers with a commission on every order they took. For the bookstores there would be no inventory to finance, no shelf space filled, no shipping costs, and no risk, yet their net profit per set would be the same as they would receive in selling a $50 book with normal trade terms. It was the best thing we could think of, but the booksellers weren't thrilled, especially since the main thrust of our marketing campaign would be direct sales. Nevertheless, we budgeted to pay out over a million dollars in commissions to booksellers across Canada. (We were very careful to make certain that booksellers received proper credit for sales in cases where their customer sent an order directly to us after picking up a brochure in the bookstore. Every brochure was coded so we could trace it. In the end we paid bookstores commissions for twice as many orders as they themselves had recorded.)

In our direct sales test-marketing campaign, we tried out three different prices, different methods of instalment payment, contests and prizes, and we promised to allow anyone unhappy with the set to return it to us collect. While we had spent record-breaking amounts advertising and promoting *The Canadian Encyclopedia*, the marketing budget for *The Junior Encyclopedia* would have to be much higher, some $3-million, because of the heavy costs associated with direct marketing.

Encyclopedia Britannica had few doubts about the product and its likely sales. As soon as they saw some finished pages, they offered to purchase exclusive marketing rights to *Junior* and estimated it would sell *two or three times as many sets* as *The Canadian Encyclopedia*! Such an arrangement would guarantee Hurtig Publishers a good profit, eliminate all our risk, and substantially reduce our workload, allowing us to concentrate on future editorial updates and our continuing trade-book publishing program.

But did we *really* want to give Britannica, a U.S. company, exclusive marketing rights to *The Junior Encyclopedia of Canada*? Again, I thought not.

The Secret Weapon Fails

B Y MARCH OF 1990, publication year, we were getting very concerned. The advance orders from our direct-sales campaign were not coming in nearly as fast as we had expected. The country was entering a deep recession; people were worried about their jobs, the standard of living of families began a sharp decline, and household savings deteriorated. There was some irony in this — I had predicted the recession in two newspaper articles. Unfortunately producing a new encyclopedia is like managing a juggernaut; once the process had begun and huge sums of money are poured into the machine, it becomes impossible to stop.

Appropriately enough, on April Fool's Day 1990 we moved our offices out from under the dark north side of the Fifth Street overpass to the thirteenth (!) floor of the Oxford Tower in downtown Edmonton. Our old building was too small to accommodate the staff we were adding, it was a firetrap, and the area was more and more afflicted with crime and violence; female members of the staff were concerned about going to and from work in the poorly lit streets. The new offices were beautiful, but I was becoming increasingly worried about the advance sales of *Junior*. By the end of the month we had advance sales of only a disappointing 3,000 sets.

In May Arlene Perly Rae's Kid's Books column in the *Toronto Star*'s Saturday Magazine was headlined "Finally, the facts, and all Canadian." It raved about our upcoming publication. Her advance review helped bring in enough orders to let us meet bank requirements.

In the summer of 1990 the first really bad definitive news came in. We had spent hundreds of thousands of dollars on a test-marketing campaign designed for us by a well-regarded Toronto marketing company. Both we and the senior staff of the marketing firm had been very pleased with the attractive mail-out package and special advance-order money-saving offer we had put together. The brochures, envelopes, response cards, quotes from well-known Canadians, and letters from the encyclopedia's editor and the publisher were beautifully designed, the entire package the result of a dozen different preliminary test mailings. But the subsequent test-marketing itself was a failure.

As we headed for our September publication date, I was becoming more and more concerned, but still optimistic that, when the reviews appeared, people would want to own the set.

By September, the project had cost some $12.6-million. Our advance sales were just over 10,000 sets, a *much* lower total than we'd expected, especially since we had again offered the reduced pre-publication price.

On September 10 we launched *Junior* with a big party at Roy Thomson Hall in Toronto. In her speech, Minister of Communications Flora MacDonald talked passionately about growing up in Cape Breton, voraciously reading books, but not being able to find out anything about Canada. "Mel," she said, "has launched a secret weapon which really is a national curriculum . . . something to weld the country together."

We prayed for good reviews. We were certain that when the reviewers saw the set, they would be impressed. And that's exactly what happened; the reviews were even better than we had hoped. *Calgary Sun* editor Chris Nelson predicted we would sell 100,000 copies before Christmas. Oh, if only!

One review we particularly cherished came from *Canadian Materials*, published by the Canadian Library Association:

> Generally, in the past, when a Canadian reference work was published for the first time, the reaction was "It's about time!" With the publication of *The Junior Encyclopedia of Canada* we are no longer catching up; we are now leading the pack. Notwithstanding the media hype that announced its publication, this is an outstanding reference work. . . .

But by the time I reached Halifax on my cross-Canada promotion tour, things were not looking good. Every morning of my trip I phoned our office in Edmonton for the previous day's sales figures. For any book published any year in Canada, the figures were impressive; for *Junior* they spelled trouble. W.H. Smith had sold some 25,000 sets of *The Canadian Encyclopedia* within two months of publication. In contrast, they sold only 1,300 sets of *The Junior Encyclopedia* in the first two months after its publication. Sales for all "high ticket" books were off dramatically in the fall and Christmas 1990 bookselling seasons.

By October, we had already spent $1.5-million on carefully designed advertising and promotion. By November, the disappointing sales left no doubt; we were now in *big* trouble. Bank interest costs alone were running over $47,000 a month.

When I returned to Edmonton, Barry Hicks and I had several urgent, pressure-packed meetings. We both began arriving at the office before six in the morning, searching desperately for a solution to our problem. By early December it became clear that, for the first time in my life, I would soon have a problem meeting bank payments.

In mid-December, in what was certainly one of the worst days of my life, I drove to the encyclopedia's offices and broke the news to the staff. There was no alternative; we would have to close the operation down. To say they were devastated is a terrible understatement. My voice broke often and tears filled my eyes as I related the awful position we were in. The men and women who had worked on the encyclopedia were exceptional people who loved their country and who loved what we had accomplished together. Now, ten days before Christmas, I had no choice but to give them notice; there was no money to pay their wages.

Because we had planned updating yearbooks we had inserted an owner registration card in each set, with a space for comments at the bottom of the card. The comments poured in, many of them written by children: "We love it!" from Toronto; "Absolutely outstanding," from Whitby; "Great investment for our two children. Thank you!" from Victoria; "You have done a great job!" from Kanata; "Our whole family enjoys reading these books," from Fort Saskatchewan. Every new batch of postcards made me feel more and more that, despite the very serious problems we were facing, we had made the right decision in proceeding with *Junior*.

By late December, it was clear we were in real danger of going under.

Gordon Wilson, president of the Ontario Federation of Labour, and Don Aitken, president of the Alberta Federation, both wrote to Ontario Premier Bob Rae stressing the very substantial direct economic benefits to Ontario of the encyclopedias. Could Ontario provide at least some temporary assistance? Unfortunately the answer was no. When we asked the Alberta government for a temporary six-month $750,000 loan guarantee, the answer was also no. In neither case did I think we would have much chance of success, but at this stage we were prepared to try almost anything to save the company. I had been very critical of Don Getty for years, especially during the debate about the Free Trade Agreement, so there was really very little chance of success there. Moreover, Minister of Culture Doug Main had made it clear: "Hurtig, now you're going to pay for your politics."

The Fall of the House of Hurtig

I N THE END WE sold only 35,000 sets of *Junior*. When I say *only* 35,000 sets, two things help put that number in perspective. First, the 35,000 sets were enough to place *Junior* high on any Canadian bestseller list. Second, we needed to sell some 63,000 sets in order to pay the bank back the money we had borrowed. By February 1991, we were under considerable pressure. By the end of the month we were forced to lay off several long-term Hurtig employees and cancel plans for our entire fall list. It was brutal.

What had gone wrong? We all know how easy hindsight is, but a letter from a friend in Toronto helped clarify things. Toy manufacturer and distributor Tom Taylor wrote: "I wanted to make you aware that every children's product priced over the $100 mark was in severe difficulty this past Christmas. As an example, even the once invincible Nintendo's sales were crushed. The recession was everyone's major problem, including yours." The recession and the high interest rates proved a deadly combination. While the future potential for both encyclopedias were unquestionably superb, while we had an excellent backlist of fine titles with steady continuing sales, and a superb list for 1991 and 1992 already in the works, our monthly bank interest payments were too great a burden.

We tried everything we could and then some to save the company. And lots of fine people tried to help. By early March, I had pretty well exhausted all possibilities. Often I was in the office at four in the morning unable to sleep, examining every possible alternative, and on the phone to Toronto, Ottawa, and Montreal at six.

In the middle of our worst difficulties the Spicer Commission announced that "other ideas to promote the unity dialogue are still being considered, including a unity train to make young Canadians aware of different parts of the country." Well, this was precisely one of the chief goals of *Junior* and a goal we had achieved, according to all reviews, with great success. Meanwhile, Jacques Payette, the president of Les Editions Heritage in Montreal, was very anxious to do a French edition of *The Junior Encyclopedia of Canada* in 1992, in time for the nation's 125th birthday. Payette cared deeply about Canada and felt that a French edition of *Junior* would be invaluable in Quebec. We sent Keith Spicer a set of *Junior* and said: "Look, here is the unity train all done, all ready." We suggested to the secretary of state that, as part of the huge multimillion-dollar 125th anniversary budget, they at least help publish the French edition. It was not to be.

When you are in big trouble, it doesn't take long to learn who your real friends are. Several people I thought might step in with offers of assistance didn't. Others were marvellous. Even though we are on quite opposite sides of many issues, Roy Megarry, publisher of the *Globe and Mail*, was superb. He phoned the president of the bank, described me as "a great Canadian," praised *The Junior Encyclopedia*, and without being asked, promised that the paper would provide free advertising to help market it. Keith Davey, Louis Desrochers, and Bob Blair also helped with some timely calls, which bought us more time to try to solve our problems.

By the spring of 1991, the *Toronto Star* was headlining our situation: "Canadian book publishers are facing a sea of red ink." McClelland and Stewart and Key Porter were cutting back their new titles; both

Coles and W.H. Smith were chopping the number of books they bought from Canadian publishers; Jack Stoddart was pessimistic, and both Summerhill Press and Lester and Orpen Dennys were forced out of business. Book sales in the first few months of 1991 were down thirty percent from a year earlier. And a federal-government study showed that several major publishers were "significant financial risks." Established publishers were letting staff go, and more layoffs were anticipated. According to Anna Porter, "Things are looking very, very bad out there." Canadian publishers were continuing to produce more than three-quarters of all new Canadian books, but held only some twenty-five percent of the English-language book market. The protracted recession was battering them. Moreover, the GST, the first national sales tax applied to books in Canada, was hurting bookstore sales. Almost without exception, the publishing industry was depressed; doom and gloom prevailed.

In April I told *Quill and Quire*: "It's very simple. We either have to sell the company, come up with new equity investors, or rob a bank." We had tried everything we could think of. Now "my major concern . . . is to make sure that whatever happens, the encyclopedias . . . which are widely regarded as national treasures, be continued."

Avie Bennett purchased Hurtig Publishers in May 1991. On May 23 we spent hours in the boardroom of an Edmonton law firm signing documents prepared by four different law firms. Five days later, at a press conference in McClelland and Stewart's offices in Toronto, we announced the sale of Hurtig Publishers. It was a very sad moment for me, but also a huge relief. I tried to look cheerful and joked that "it must be a perfect deal because Avie thinks he didn't pay enough and I think he paid too much."

Avie was very gracious. "I have long been an admirer of Mel Hurtig, of his unselfish nationalism, his commitment to Canadian publishing, and the risks he has taken. We are now happy to share the risk that he took in launching the two most ambitious publishing programs in Canadian history.

"I have only one regret and that is, some other publisher got hold of this new author before I did."

On May 30, in a lead editorial titled "Hurtig's gift to Canada," the *Edmonton Journal* published the obituary of Hurtig Publishers:

"Nobody, for a second, should feel sorry for Mel Hurtig," the man himself said on Tuesday as he announced the sale of

Edmonton's best-known publishing firm to McClelland and Stewart of Toronto.

Fine Mel, we won't express sympathy. Pity wouldn't sit well on your shoulders. But permit us to feel sorry for a country, a province and a city that have benefited enormously from the contributions of Hurtig Publishers Ltd. and will miss its independent, creative spirit.

The country is losing one of the few unabashed voices for Canadian nationalism in its corporate sector. It is losing the benefactor that created *The Canadian Encyclopedia* and *The Junior Encyclopedia of Canada*, both invaluable gifts to a nation with an uncertain view of itself. Have we even said thank you for those treasures?

In an interview about my future, I told the *Edmonton Journal*: "My life as a bookseller and publisher has been exciting, interesting, fascinating and enjoyable. Although my net worth has diminished by eighty percent, I honestly do consider myself to be a lucky person. I've got a great wife, a great home, a wonderful family, my health, and I've always wanted to be a writer. If I can be successful in writing some books, what a nice full life that will be."

Did I have regrets about publishing *Junior*? the press asked. In many ways, of course, the answer had to be yes. But as I told *Maclean's*: "If I had the choice of walking away with a million dollars cash and not publishing *Junior*, I would still choose to publish it. I am extremely proud of what we did."

From Bookseller to Publisher to Author

THERE WERE TWO THINGS I had always wanted to do but never had the time for; one was to write books and the other was to paint. Over the years I had written hundreds of articles, reviews, speeches, research papers, and so on, but I had never written a book, although pieces I had written had appeared in a dozen or more Canadian books. And over the years, I had sold millions of books written by others; how marvellous it would be to write one of my own!

Who can ever deny that life is strange? If *The Junior Encyclopedia* had not run into trouble, I would never have had the time to write *The Betrayal of Canada*. Jack Stoddart had come to Edmonton to examine the possibility of buying Hurtig Publishers. Just before he returned to Toronto, I gave him a copy of a long paper on taxation I had just completed; it was a detailed and thorough exposé of just how terribly unjust the Canadian tax system had become, strongly favouring the wealthy and big corporations while penalizing the average Canadian. A few days later Jack called me and asked me to do a book about the tax system for Stoddart. I said no, but I would give him something better, which would include a chapter on taxes.

I began working on the book day and night. Rhonda Bouchard, my sole remaining employee, and Lisa Shaw in Winnipeg helped me with the research. I finished the last chapters in Janis Kraulis's hillside home overlooking Fulford Harbour on Saltspring Island. It was a tough book, highly critical of the Canadian business and political establishment, and it was packed with new research not available elsewhere. I couriered the last chapters to Toronto, and my wife and I set off on our drive back to Edmonton. On the way, I told Kay that after *Betrayal* was published, I would likely never again receive another honorary degree from any university. I also said I would be thrilled if the book were successful enough to appear for at least one week on any bestseller list.

I had hoped that *Betrayal* would produce some of the same sort of response that had greeted George Grant's *Lament for a Nation*. My book was a passionate appeal for the survival of our country, a warning that if important changes were not made soon, it would be too late. While I was writing the book, the *Economist* magazine had an article that concluded: "Sooner or later, Canadians are going to become Americans. Too bad." This was hardly news to me, but the more research I did for my book, the angrier I became. The documentation in *Betrayal* was myth-destroying, the arguments the hardest-hitting indictment of the Canadian business and political elite to be published for many years. Some of the tables and graphs in the book were startling, contradicting taken-for-granted fundamental assumptions.

In chapter after chapter the book went after long-standing myths: that Canadians are overtaxed compared with most industrialized countries; that Canada is an overcentralized country; that foreign investment has brought large benefits to the Canadian economy; that social programs were bankrupting the country; that the FTA was creating jobs in Canada. *Betrayal* strongly attacked those who were selling out Canada. I wrote that "the nation's pimps are their own best cheerleaders. In other countries they would be regarded as contemptible sellouts," and dedicated the book to "four wise and courageous Canadians," Tommy Douglas, Walter Gordon, George Grant, and Eric Kierans.

In his *Memoirs* Pablo Neruda wrote: "My first book! It's a moment that will never come back." How thrilled I was to get my first copy of *Betrayal* from Stoddart. And what a great job Carlotta Lemieux had done editing my cumbersome prose. On the first Saturday in October the *Globe and Mail* carried a well-illustrated, page-and-a-half extract from *The Betrayal of Canada*, beginning on the front page of the Focus section. It was a tremendous boost for the book. Soon after, *Globe* columnists and editorial writers began attacking me and *Betrayal* vigorously. Too late! The damage had already been done. The book soon appeared in number-eight spot on the *Globe* bestseller list. David Olive, editor of *Report on Business* magazine, wrote the review in the *Globe and Mail*. For Olive, *Betrayal* was "dreary, simplistic, hand-wringing . . . a pointless refighting of the lost battle of 1988. . . . Hurtig has produced a volume that rarely rises above the level of urgent sophistry."

The next review was from *Maclean's*, which described the book as "a magnificent tirade." Probably the funniest reaction to *Betrayal* came from *Financial Post* columnist and McGill University economist William Watson, who pompously declared he had no intention of reading the book and then proceeded to write a series of three articles attacking what I had written.

But for every bitter attack on the book, there was a review of the other kind. For instance, in the *Toronto Star* Walter Stewart called *Betrayal*

> a meticulously documented account of how this nation turned itself into an American satellite, a declining, deindus-trialized warehouse economy with little real function in the North American context except to serve as a resource base, and market, for the American corporate machine.
>
> With its charts and tables, it makes, I think, an unanswer-able argument for his thesis that we have been betrayed into surrendering our nationhood, betrayed by both Conservative and Liberal governments.

The Montreal *Gazette* handled the book well, assigning two columnists to write side-by-side reviews because the book was so controversial. One side called the book a "shallow rant . . . sleazy con games . . . [a] tirade . . . [he] throws as much mud as he can at his targets in the hope that some will stick. . . . The publishers of the book, Stoddart, and others who helped should be ashamed of themselves for collaborating with him." The other side said it was a "trenchant analysis and a clear set of choices [that] concentrates on the needs of ordinary Canadians. To the members of the Business Council on National Issues, that may seem like a betrayal. To me, it sounds like very good sense."

Stoddart's first printing of 7,500 copies was gone in days. So were the second and third printings. By mid-October it was number one on the *Financial Post* bestseller list, and soon took the top position on the lists of *Maclean's*, the *Globe and Mail*, the *Toronto Star*, the *Edmonton Journal*, and the *Vancouver Sun*. I was in my hotel room in Toronto when a bottle of fine champagne was delivered to my room. It was from Jack Stoddart. *Betrayal* was number one on every major bestseller list in the country.

It stayed number one all through the Christmas selling season and for months into 1992. The more it was attacked, the more it sold. And the more it sold, the more word of mouth generated even more sales.

While Canada's continentalist economists criticized the book, I was very pleased with a speech that Dr. Douglas Peters, senior vice president and chief economist for the Toronto-Dominion Bank, made to an Economic Outlook Conference a year after *Betrayal* was published. He said:

> I am delighted to be here in Edmonton this morning to talk to you about the Canadian economy and about economic policies. But I do feel that I might be bringing coals to Newcastle in talking about the latter, for recently there has been a good deal of common sense economics coming from Edmonton. Unfortunately, I am not referring to politicians who come from or reside in Alberta, but rather to Edmonton businessman Mel Hurtig and his recently published book. There is probably more Prairie common sense in that publication than in all the Canadian government publications put out in the past five years. I recommend the book to you. If you love this country Canada, you should read Mr. Hurtig's book.

One sidelight. Mexico would not allow the delivery of bulk ship-ments of *The Betrayal of Canada* into the country. Christine Lee, executive director of the Gordon Foundation, attended a NAFTA conference in Wisconsin late in 1991. Most of the Mexican delegates represented the strongly pro-NAFTA Salinas regime. But several Mexicans, representing labour and academia, had grave doubts about the proposed agreement. One of them spotted Lee's copy of *Betrayal* and asked to borrow it overnight. The next morning he requested sixty copies be shipped to a California address from where they would be smuggled across the border. Why? Because "If you ship them to me in Mexico, I will never get them. Never!"

The Betrayal of Canada stayed on the bestseller lists for eight months and sold almost fifty thousand copies, far more than I had ever dreamed possible.

Early in 1992 a very pleasant thing happened. The University of British Columbia wrote to ask if I would accept an honorary Doctor of Laws degree and deliver the address at their May convocation. I gladly accepted; it would be a special honour since my youngest daughter, Leslie, was graduating in Canadian history from UBC.

Betrayal was also special for me not only because it sold so well and influenced so many people, but having been a bookseller and publisher for thirty-five years, it was a thrill to now see my own first book in print. And after the heavy battering I had in late 1990 and early 1991, its great success was a wonderful change.

V

THE GREAT DEBATE

A Fatal Trap and a Falling Sky

I T WAS ALWAYS TEMPTING for me during those absorbing days spent planning and publishing the encyclopedias to back away entirely from politics, but the more I saw of what was happening in the country the more concerned I became. And the more I learned about the growing influence of big business on public policy in Canada, the more determined I became to do whatever I could to head off their continentalist agenda.

In 1982, Pierre Trudeau appointed Donald Macdonald to head a new royal commission to look into Canada's economy and its prospects. By the time the commission's report advocating free trade between Canada and the U.S. was published, Macdonald, once considered a Canadian nationalist, had metamorphosed into yet another continentalist Bay Street lawyer. Was it any wonder that the report turned out as it did when it had so much input from doctrinaire pro-free-trade economists and the Business Council on National Issues, Canada's powerful big-business lobby group?

At the 1983 Conservative leadership convention John Crosbie came out strongly for a Canada–U.S. free-trade agreement. Crosbie's father, Chesley, had bitterly fought Newfoundland's 1949 decision to join Canada; instead, he'd campaigned for formal economic union with the United States. There was little doubt where John Crosbie stood. "I would support a free-trade agreement with the devil if that appeared to be a good thing," he said. No doubt.

In June 1983 fellow Conservative Eddie Goodman wrote an open letter to Crosbie in the *Toronto Star*, describing his pro-free-trade proposals as "a fatal trap" that "would mean the immediate loss of tens of thousands of Canadian jobs" and "the total subjugation of Canadian interests to those of the U.S. I cannot believe you could seriously consider such a proposal let alone advocate it."

When Brian Mulroney narrowly defeated Joe Clark and was elected Conservative leader, the popularity of the Liberal party was headed straight for the bottom of the bay. The Liberals had been in office far too long, were worn-out, bereft of new ideas, and the country was just emerging from a serious recession. Anyone *but* Trudeau was uppermost in the minds of many voters across the country. When Trudeau resigned in February 1984, the contest to replace him as Liberal leader would clearly be between John Turner and Jean Chrétien. I visited the June Ottawa convention, and I was far from impressed by what I saw and heard. After Turner's election, I responded to a journalist's question by saying: "Turner is taking the party to the right — he's a man of continentalism. Liberal and Tory nationalists feel frustrated. There's no place for nonsocialist nationalists to go, so we'll have to find one of our own."

The Conservative party of Brian Mulroney was certainly not the party of the great nationalist John A. Macdonald, of anti-free-trade Robert Borden, of Arthur Meighen, R.B. Bennett, or John Diefenbaker. For Prime Minister Borden, the 1911 reciprocity election meant that Canadian voters were being asked to "determine not a mere question of markets, but the future destiny of Canada." For Brian Mulroney, free trade with the U.S. was Canada's *only* alternative, and opponents of the idea were "a small group of timid souls."

In the September 1984 federal election, without a mention of free trade, Brian Mulroney and the Progressive Conservatives captured fifty-two percent of the votes and a record 211 seats in the House of Commons.

Washington had watched the election carefully; Brian Mulroney was their man. For Mulroney's friend U.S. Ambassador Paul Robinson, the election was a great victory. Robinson understood clearly that, despite Mulroney's anti-free-trade rhetoric in 1983, the new Conservative prime minister was strongly in favour of a comprehensive Canada-U.S. agreement, an agreement that would go well beyond normal trade agreements. Within two months of Mulroney's election, officials from Ottawa and Washington were talking about a precedent-setting, all-inclusive agreement.

Even before his election, Mulroney had been received in Washington in a manner that surprised people in the Canadian Embassy. Ronald Reagan and George Bush greeted him with private meetings and photo opportunities not normally given to visiting Opposition leaders. Time and again Mulroney amazed even the Americans. No matter how hopeful they might have been for a new Canadian prime minister who was sympathetic to an American agenda, Mulroney surpassed their fondest expectations.

In her excellent book *Yankee Doodle Dandy: Brian Mulroney and the American Agenda*, Marci McDonald explained that Mulroney, the son of a taciturn Irishman, Benedict Mulroney, "came of age in a universe whose unquestioned raison d'être was to service the needs of its distant American seigneur who, once a year, swept into his fiefdom, trailing intimations of glory — wealth and grandeur of mythic proportions to a daydreaming north-shore electrician's son." The colonial stories of Colonel McCormick and Baie Comeau need not be repeated here. The young Mulroney's singing of "Dearie" for the colonel was to become highly symbolic. The Iron Ore Company of Canada, which Mulroney ran for Hanna Mining of Cleveland, controlled Canada's largest reserves of ore. Brian Mulroney was an employee who took his orders directly from the U.S.

In the years before the Free Trade Agreement, Canada had better trade-growth rates than any of the world's major trading nations. We had record-breaking merchandise trade surpluses, and domestic investment was also setting new records. In the decade before Mulroney's election unemployment had averaged eight percent. And most importantly, in terms of standard of living as measured by real purchasing parity, Canadians had climbed to a position just behind the U.S. and well above all other nations.

So, contrary to the dreadful scenarios of doom and gloom presented by the proponents of free trade, Canada was doing very well. The sky was not falling. How incredibly ironic, then, that the message from the continentalists was that those opposed to free trade were "fear-mongers."

Moreover, thanks to years of GATT negotiations, culminating in the 1979 Tokyo round, the average tariff on industrial goods entering into the United States was soon to drop to only four percent, making the exchange rate a far more important factor in trade than remaining tariffs.

Philosopher Bertrand Russell once said: "If you lay all the economists head to toe in a line, they would still be pointing in the wrong direction." If you could lay Richard Lipsey, Murray Smith, Wendy Dobson, John Crispo, and friends in a straight line, they would all be pointing to Washington. Canadian economists, rigid adherents to classical economics, somehow oblivious to the fact that all theories of free trade fly out the window when most of the trade is done between parent companies and their subsidiaries, enthusiastically joined the doomsday chorus. The C.D. Howe Institute advertised their pro-free-trade book by Lipsey and Smith with ads warning "Canada's future is at stake!" For Richard Lipsey, there was little doubt about how important a free-trade agreement was: "The debate about free trade is probably the most important thing that's ever happened in our history. And it's certainly the most important thing that's ever happened in our country since the end of the Second World War."

This last statement was quite a departure for him. Earlier, when I had debated him at the Department of External Affairs, Lipsey had said: "We're talking about a modest change . . . we're not talking about something new . . . we've been doing it for thirty years."

As for John Crosbie, at least he was honest. "The Tories would never reveal their real intentions," he said, "because no one would ever vote for them."

The year Brian Mulroney was elected leader of the Conservative party, foreigners were taking almost forty-four percent of all nonfinancial industry profits in Canada. The same year, ninety-three percent of the takeovers of Canadian businesses had been approved by FIRA.

In December 1984, only a few weeks after the Tories were elected, Brian Mulroney spoke to two thousand cheering American executives in New York, announcing that "Canada is open for business." The previous week, his government had announced that FIRA would be replaced by a new agency, Investment Canada. According to Mulroney, Canada had been hostile to foreign capital, but things would now change. With ninety-nine percent of the rubber industry foreign-owned, ninety percent of the chemical industry, ninety-five percent of the tobacco industry, eighty percent of the electrical-apparatus industry, seventy-two percent of the transportation industry, and so on and so on already foreign-owned in a "hostile" Canada, one wondered exactly what a friendlier, more open Canada would look like.

The day after Mulroney's speech, I spoke to the Canadian Club in Ottawa. It was my first speech against free trade, but I returned to the question of foreign control of the Canadian economy, asking again exactly what would we have left if we kept selling off all that we owned? As far as FIRA was concerned, "if you don't have in place proper mechanisms to screen foreign investment, foreign investment will essentially mean foreign ownership; excessive foreign ownership means foreign control of our country." I said that the new agency should be called "Sellout Canada" and that we were now facing an unprecedented wave of continentalism.

After I finished speaking, the president of the Canadian Club warmly thanked me and then presented me with a big American coffee-table book.

The Conspiracy of the Compradors

THE *RANDOM HOUSE Dictionary of the English Language* defines "comprador" as "a native agent or factotum, as of a foreign business house." In *Webster's Third International Dictionary*, a comprador is "one held to be an agent of foreign domination or exploitation." Interestingly, the word does not appear in the *Gage Canadian Dictionary*.

In all the thousands of speeches I have given across Canada during the past thirty years, I don't believe I have ever used the word "conspiracy." I have repeated over and over again that the sellout of Canada should not be blamed on Americans or other non-Canadians, but rather on the Canadian business establishment and our own myopic and inept politicians.

It has taken some time, but it is clearer and clearer now, as the evidence steadily mounts, that the concept of a comprehensive bilateral agreement originated in the United States and that there was a secret, cleverly conceived conspiracy to sell the agreement to Canadians as a Canadian initiative. The conspirators were both Americans and their Canadian compradors, and their chief agent was Brian Mulroney.

At first, Ronald Reagan's "North American Accord" was thought of in the U.S. as essentially a means of giving Americans greater security for supplies of Canadian oil and natural gas. But Canadians had long been apprehensive about any continental energy policy. The people close to Reagan recognized that it might be much easier to sell a comprehensive "trade" deal.

Paul Robinson, a Reagan friend and bagman from Chicago, was appointed U.S. ambassador to Canada in 1981, a patronage award for his abundant fundraising. Robinson was a flamboyant, outspoken, and undiplomatic ambassador who succeeded in offending millions of Canadians. For Robinson, FIRA was not to be tolerated, the metric system was "rubbish," and Canadian energy policy violated the U.S. constitution. Moreover, according to him, the testing of cruise missiles in Canada was not an issue Canadians should be concerned about. At best, Robinson was a loudmouth bully, arrogant, vulgar, and boorish. Ronald Reagan had sent him to Ottawa to help put the socialist Pierre Trudeau in his place. Robinson had another goal: to help make his pal Brian Mulroney prime minister.

Reagan had first talked about his North American accord during his campaign for the U.S. presidency in 1979. For him, and for many powerful people in Washington, the primary goal was greater energy security for the United States. Canada and Mexico had "abundant" oil and gas reserves; in the United States, the fear of OPEC and the Iranian ayatollah were growing. But after Reagan's election victory in 1980, the Trudeau government showed no interest in a continental energy policy. On the contrary, the newly reelected and self-confident Liberals were headed in exactly the opposite direction: FIRA, the National Energy Program, and other nationalistic policies. Soon after Robinson arrived in Ottawa, he met with Mulroney. As both Marci McDonald and Lawrence Martin have reported, Mulroney had been talking about free trade for years with former Joe Clark adviser Duncan Edmonds. Robinson and Mulroney got along extremely well. Why not? According to Ambassador Robinson, Brian Mulroney was "a friend of America."

Tom d'Aquino, of the Business Council on National Issues and a former lobbyist for *Time* magazine, was there to help. Free trade was at the top of his agenda, too, and it wasn't long before he and Robinson were working closely together. But they both realized that the idea would have to look as if it was initiated in Canada, not in the U.S. Nor would the words "free trade" be used. Instead, it would be a "trade-enhancement agreement." Who could object to that?

Tom d'Aquino, W.O. Twaits of Exxon-controlled Imperial Oil, Alf Powis of Noranda, and Rowland Frazee of the Royal Bank met privately with another powerful Reagan supporter, Bill Brock, who agreed that it must appear as though the idea for an agreement had originated in Canada.

In the spring of 1983 U.S. Vice President George Bush met with d'Aquino and other BCNI leaders in Ottawa. Meanwhile, Derek Burney, from his U.S. desk at External Affairs, was talking to both the Reagan administration and the BCNI about free trade. Well before Burney produced a new policy trade paper for the Canadian government, he provided the U.S. government with a draft copy. Marci McDonald didn't mince words: "As officials relate the backstage story of the prelude to free-trade talks, one aspect stands out: the conspiratorial glee with which a tiny band of officials joined efforts to put the issue on the Canadian agenda through a mixture of guile and outright deception."

Burney, a conservative continentalist and one of the chief driving forces for a comprehensive Canada-U.S. agreement, would soon go on to become Brian Mulroney's chief of staff. For d'Aquino, there was little doubt about the objective: much closer commercial union with the United States. For Burney, it was clear that any efforts towards a comprehensive agreement would have to be disguised. And how would one describe d'Aquino's role? In the words of *Economic Reform* publisher William Krehm, "Tom d'Aquino has for a decade flapped his wings over the Canadian scene like a bird of ill omen. As director of the Business Council on National Issues, his job has been to present the greed of transnational corporations as our destiny."

In the United States another friend of Brian Mulroney's, American Express head James Robinson III, played a pivotal role. American Express spearheaded the U.S. business pro-free-trade campaign. After all, there were more American Express cardholders in Canada than in any other country outside the United States. A long list of Fortune 500 companies were involved: IBM, Procter and Gamble, Goodyear, Dupont, Metropolitan Life, and Alcoa, to name a few. Amex alone hired four powerful lobbying-communications companies to assist them.

Meanwhile, U.S. Senator Spark Matsunaga said, in the April 8, 1987, Montreal *Gazette*, that "the concept of [Canadian] culture protection is really a misconcept. . . . I think that the sooner your culture and ours can blend, the better. . . . It's coming, whether you like it or not."

Back in Canada the pro-free-trade business "alliance," representing mostly BCNI members, operated out of David Culver's Alcan offices in Montreal. David Culver was a good friend of James Robinson's and an American Express director.

The confidentially funded C.D. Howe Institute, a long-term right-wing continentalist organization, also played its part. The institute and its Canadian-American Committee (now the North American Committee) have produced a long list of one-sided, highly subjective, selective studies pushing continentalism and laissez-faire. Sadly, with only very rare exceptions, the Canadian press in their editorial pages and columnists across Canada accept these studies as gospel, citing them chapter and verse, rarely if ever bothering to delve into the funding, methodology, and authenticity of the studies or to seek alternative opinions about their conclusions. Who was the Howe Institute's senior policy adviser, for instance? None other than pro-free-trade guru, Richard Lipsey.

The board of the C.D. Howe Institute is self-appointed. According to president and CEO Tom Kierans, "the larger core donors" play the most prominent roles. The amounts donors provide the institute are confidential, even though the federal government gives them a tax number. The institute is a co-sponsor of the North American Committee, along with the U.S. National Planning Association, which has been and continues to be a steady recipient of funds from the U.S. government, directly and probably indirectly as well. It's important to understand that the National Planning Association has worked for the office of the U.S. trade representative, the U.S. Commerce Department, and the State Department.

Many American corporations are active on both sides of the border in both the NPA and the C.D. Howe Institute. The Canadian chairman of the North American Committee is chosen by the board of the C.D. Howe Institute. The chairman, David Beatty, invites people to become members of the committee. The work of the committee — the research, publications, the running of meetings — is done by the Howe Institute. The purpose of the committee is to "promote understanding between the countries and also free trade. We have a commitment to open frontiers." Virtually all of the C.D. Howe Institute's budget comes from big business: the banks, petroleum companies, conglomerates, and transnational corporations. As for their objectivity, according to one very senior former employee, "the institute has become an eastern Fraser Institute . . . dogmatically market-oriented . . . constantly publishing monetary diatribes . . ."

In the United States, Peter Restler is the American co-chairman of the North American Committee. Restler's investment firm, CAI, specializes in "Canadian opportunities." On the board of CAI is none other than the ubiquitous David Culver, who so ferociously promoted the FTA. Oh yes, former C.D. Howe economist Wendy Dobson left to become an assistant deputy minister of finance in Ottawa while the Mulroney government was in power.

Get the picture?

Blindfold into the Dark Quickly

FOR ALLAN GOTLIEB, Canada's ambassador to Washington from 1981 to 1989, our options were almost nonexistent. The choice must be closer integration with the U.S.; the overwhelming might of the U.S. was to be feared; Canadian autonomy would have to be downplayed. Some ambassador!

It's hard to know whether to laugh or cry at statements by Gotlieb and Derek Burney that they had expected, in the face of the integrating free-trade agreement, that the government of Canada would take steps to strengthen Canadian culture. Of course, exactly the opposite has happened. In a confidential memo, U.S. trade negotiator Peter Murphy stated: "The Canadians have agreed to define as narrowly as possible the cultural industries." Moreover, a punitive clause in the agreement makes it virtually impossible for any Canadian government to introduce significant new cultural legislation without the prospect of American retaliation against *any* Canadian industry. And, of course, the Canada Council under Allan Gotlieb, the CBC with, incredibly, John Crispo on the board of directors, and almost all Canadian cultural programs and institutions faced massive cuts in their government support. Laugh or cry? Neither. We should be fiercely angry with men like Gotlieb and Burney.

Myer Rashish, Ronald Reagan's undersecretary of state for Economic Affairs, was directly involved in the conspiracy to make the free-trade plans appear to be a Canadian initiative. So, too, was Clayton Yeutter, former president of the Chicago Mercantile Exchange, who was appointed by Reagan to replace William Brock as U.S. trade representative.

Without question, David Rockefeller's Americas Society played a key role in the plans. Rockefeller, former U.S. intelligence officer, former chairman of the Chase Manhattan Bank, longtime friend of South American military dictators, friend of Paul Desmarais and Maurice Strong, maintained a Canadian Affairs division headed by former *Time* magazine correspondent Lansing Lamont.

In Ottawa early in 1985 the game plan began to leak out: tell Canadians as little as possible, keep them in the dark as long as possible, promise them anything and everything, then make them take a blindfolded leap of faith into the dark quickly. In October 1985 a confidential report leaked from the PMO indicated that "there's a real potential for conflict between our desire for a successful conclusion to the trade negotiations and our pursuit of cultural sovereignty, if the latter includes restrictive policies on ownership, market access and subsidization." According to the memo, the issue of the loss of Canadian sovereignty was "a communications issue." The prime minister and cabinet members henceforth should routinely mention sovereignty in their speeches. A suggestion was made that even the Governor General should be involved in the campaign to downplay the sovereignty issue.

For the Mulroney government, the strategy was to "divide and neutralize" opposition and to "head off the development of a major coalition on the negative side of the issue." What was desired was "a low-profile approach" and the encouragement of "benign neglect" from a majority of Canadians. In other words the government of Canada was now also directly engaged in a dishonest conspiracy to sell Canadians a deal that would profoundly change their country and alter the lives of all Canadians.

The memo went on to say: "It is likely that the higher the profile the issue attains, the lower the degree of public approval will be. The strategy should rely less on educating the general public than on getting across the message that the trade initiative is a good idea. . . . In other words, a selling job."

In his statements throughout 1985 Mulroney constantly referred to "expanded trade" and "enhanced access," not to free trade. As confidential talks began with the provinces, my sources in three provincial capitals made clear that the Mulroney government's strategy was to keep Parliament and the Canadian people in the dark as long as they could.

Two other Canadians deserve special mention here: contintenalist Michael Hart, from External Affairs; and Brian Mulroney's finance minister, the dull pedantic Michael Wilson (who went on to rack up a spectacular record of deficit spending while promising fiscal responsibility).

It now seems evident that the Mulroney government did not really understand what they were getting themselves into. There was never any mention of the costs involved in a free-trade agreement, only the supposed benefits. But wouldn't the Americans have a list of things they wanted? And since the agreement was becoming such a big issue in Canada, wouldn't the Tories find themselves farther and farther out on the plank as the federal election approached?

Some idea of how ill prepared the Canadians were can be found in the October 1986 comments of the *Washington Post* — "Mulroney gives every evidence of having embarked on these talks without having given any great thought to them" — and from Simon Reisman's comments in Vancouver a month later to the effect that "the United States must back away from countervailing duties or there can be no free trade agreement."

Clearly this made no sense at all. William Brock, William Merkin, Peter Murphy, U.S. Ambassador Thomas Niles, and U.S. Trade Representative Clayton Yeutter had all made it very clear that the U.S. would do no such thing. As Jennifer Lewington of the *Globe and Mail* reported from Washington, "On several occasions Washington sources laughed derisively when told of a new twist in the Canadian position."

My own government sources in Washington, Ottawa, Toronto, and Winnipeg constantly advised that there was a huge gap between what the Canadian public was being told and what was actually happening behind closed doors.

By late 1985, the covert conspiracy had succeeded. Canada was not only seen to be the supplicant, but it actually was. As every day went by, Mulroney and his government went farther and farther out on the bilateral and political limb; now there was no turning back, regardless of how tough the American demands became. Derek Burney helped orchestrate the Quebec City "Shamrock Summit" where Mulroney and Reagan agreed to start official free-trade talks, though the talks would be described as discussions to enhance trade and investment. Ambassador Paul Robinson was all smiles as he stood next to Reagan while the opening agreement was signed. Soon after he left Ottawa, mission accomplished.

The Council of Canadians

NOT LONG AFTER Brian Mulroney's election, the calls came flooding in from across the country. "Where is this man taking us?" "*What* are we going to do?" In November and early December of 1984 I had quite a few speaking engagements; wherever I went people wanted to hear what I thought we could do to head off Mulroney's continental agenda. Certainly I was as worried as anyone, but I was also less than a year away from launching *The Canadian Encyclopedia* and had to pay careful attention to my business. I had also been working very hard; in December Kay and I headed off for a golfing vacation. My assistant, Rhonda Bouchard, knew that I was only to be interrupted for what she thought were "important" political calls; they arrived every day, and so did many worried letters, which Rhonda forwarded.

When I returned to Edmonton, I called a small group together for a meeting in my office. On January 11, 1985, eleven of us talked for a couple of hours. Did we need to revive the Committee for an Independent Canada? Should we try to start a new organization? Were there other alternatives? I must admit I had an ominous sense of déjà vu. Did I want to go through the whole CIC experience again? Would I have the time? Could we be effective? The other ten men and women at the meeting had no doubt: we must start a new, broadly based, nonpartisan organization, and we must do it quickly. Easy to say.

I called a meeting in Toronto for February 9. Grace Hartman, former Canadian Union of Public Employees president, was helpful in setting it up. The meeting of some eighty men and women was intended to be exploratory. Again, should we try to form a new national organization? Was it really necessary to do so? Where would the money come from given the fact that we would almost certainly not be granted the charitable tax status that would make fundraising easier? We would make no firm decisions at the meeting, but decided to hold similar gatherings in Ottawa, Montreal, and Vancouver to see if there was a consensus. What, then, if the response was positive? Where would national headquarters be located? What kind of democratic structure would be best? What commitment could those in attendance make?

Among those I invited to the Toronto meeting were Marion Dewar, Walter Gordon, Bob White, David Suzuki, George Ignatieff, Herb Gray, Pierre Berton, Maude Barlow, John Trent, John Fryer, Mel Watkins, Bob Page, Robin Mathews, Sheila Copps, Jim Lorimer, Aubrey Golden, Jeff Logan, Gerry Caplan, Doris Anderson, Heather Robertson, Stephen Clarkson, Peter Herrndorf, and many other well-known and not so well-known Canadians.

Several Conservatives were invited. None came. That no prominent Tories chose to join the Council of Canadians after so many had been active in the CIC was certainly worth pondering. New to power, with all the privileges of office and the patronage plums awaiting, why would they risk the boss's anger by becoming involved with a new nationalist organization that was critical of the government's policies? Flora MacDonald and Eddie Goodman, with whom I had worked so closely in the past, didn't return my phone calls.

We had very little money to begin with. I made it clear that if there was no public support, if we formed an organization it would be unlikely to last more than a few months. For us to succeed this time, it would have to be through our membership fees and small donations, not because of large amounts from a few generous donors.

In gathering the people together for the Toronto meeting, I had particularly reached out to the NDP, to labour, and to a good number of people not associated with any political party. My hope was that any new organization would be seen to be politically nonpartisan and that it *would* be nonpartisan, though all must be steadfastly committed to Canadian sovereignty.

Only one person showed up at the meeting who hadn't been invited. Paul Martin, Jr., called me from Montreal and asked if he could attend. I had an hour-long talk with Paul after which I politely told him I didn't think the new organization was really for him. I liked him a great deal, but it seemed to me that we were miles apart in our thinking about Canadian independence.

A frail seventy-nine-year-old Walter Gordon gave a short, passionate speech at the beginning of the meeting. There were many other eloquent and very concerned speakers. Three hours later, there was a unanimous vote in favour of a new national organization dedicated to preserving Canadian sovereignty. Ronald Reagan was coming to Canada in mid-March; could we announce the formation of the new group at that time? Yes, we decided. Our subsequent meetings in Vancouver, Ottawa, and Montreal reached a similar conclusion.

We held our press conference at the National Press Building a few days before Reagan's arrival. Before that, we had polled those who had attended the earlier meetings and had chosen the name Council of Canadians. Two days later Dalton Camp, writing in the *Toronto Star*, had no doubt whatsoever: perhaps the COC might last ten weeks or until Mel Hurtig's first cross-Canada speaking tour, but not beyond. "And, we shall never see its — or Mel's like again." Peter Lougheed was just as certain: the COC would never manage to enlist one hundred members.

In a letter to the *Toronto Star* I wrote that "my challenge for Dalton Camp is simple and straightforward. He says the COC will not survive 10 weeks. I am willing to bet a case of good Canadian rye whisky (or if he prefers, American bourbon) that he is dead wrong. I say let's make it a full year, 52 weeks. Next March 11th, the editor of the *Star* can judge who has won the bet. Anyone else wishing to place side bets or to attend a COC meeting is welcome to call me toll free."

We got a bunch of new members from the letter, but Dalton Camp never did pay his bet.

In our Ottawa press release, I said that "the new organization is very concerned about the dangers of a possible comprehensive bilateral trade agreement with the U.S. and the potential harmful effects to the Canadian economy of such an agreement. The COC will devote much effort towards studying the economic and political ramifications of the soon-to-be released Macdonald Royal Commission, which is widely thought to be on the verge of recommending a free trade agreement with the U.S." The release emphasized that "the COC does not support anti-Americanism or chauvinistic nationalism. Rather . . . the new organization will advocate positive policies in the national interest, similar to policies other nations around the world adopt in the best interests of their citizens."

Some of the members of the COC listed in the opening press release, aside from those already mentioned, were Margaret Atwood, Jack Biddell, Rev. Roland de Corneille, Susan Crean, Tommy Douglas, Una Maclean Evans, Dr. Margaret Fulton, Graeme Gibson, Reshard Gool, Bob Hawkesworth, Pauline Jewett, Eric Kierans, Margaret Laurence, Robert Laxer, Paul McRae, Hugh Morris, Farley Mowatt, Peter Newman, Eric Nicol, Lorne Nystrom, John Orr, Nelson Riis, Sydney Sharpe, Lloyd Shaw, Charles Taylor, Joyce Wayne, and Bruce Willson. Paul Martin, Jr., also joined.

When we announced the formation of the Council of Canadians, I said that I believed that the new organization would be much more broadly based, both politically and geographically, than the old Committee for an Independent Canada. The council had as its "fundamental policy goal" the maximization of Canadian economic, political, social, and cultural sovereignty. Aside from the free-trade debate, we advocated support for public broadcasting, for Canadian-content levels in television and radio, for bilingualism, for a strengthened copyright act, for greater Canadian film production and distribution, for more Canadian content in schools and postsecondary institutions, and strengthened support for the arts in Canada.

In areas of economic policy we advocated a multilateral approach to trade; the development of well-thought-out national industrial strategies; more control over monetary policy, the Bank of Canada, and the activities of Canadian banks; reducing foreign ownership; the encouragement of widespread share ownership; increased research and development; much better use of our natural resources; and a host of other detailed economic policies.

In foreign and defence policy the COC advocated that Canada work for a strengthened United Nations, for the deescalation of tension between our superpower neighbours, for steps to ensure Canadian sovereignty in the Arctic, and an activist role in world arms-control discussions.

As for our basic economic position, we said: "While we accept the long-standing Canadian tradition of a mixed economy of private and public enterprise, we believe new economic policies should focus on the predominantly Canadian-owned, small and medium-size businesses which create the majority of new jobs in Canada." To say "majority" was an understatement. The *only* new jobs being created in Canada were by small and medium-size Canadian businesses. We also advocated much more autonomy in the Canadian trade-union movement.

Within four months we had COC chapters up and running in Vancouver, Edmonton, Calgary, Regina, Saskatoon, Winnipeg, Toronto, Ottawa, Montreal, and Halifax.

The night the COC held its first public meeting in Ottawa some 250 attended. The next day we appeared before the parliamentary committee studying the Investment Canada bill. When I opened my testimony, I urged delay of the proposed legislation as it would drastically weaken our foreign ownership and foreign-control safeguards. It would be much better if the government were to finally get the Economic Council of Canada to fulfil its stated mandate and study the economic impact of foreign ownership and control before the government rushed through legislation that could seriously hurt the standard of living of most Canadians.

In June 1985 *Canadian Business* magazine carried a long article I'd written entitled "Giving away the store." It produced scores of supportive letters from small business from all regions of the country and a substantial amount in donations for the COC. In the article I spelled out how the Mulroney government's plans "will inevitably turn us into an economic and political satellite of the U.S., a mendicant colony no longer able to determine its own priorities or its own national interests." Most readers were appalled by the article's figures relating to foreign ownership, by the heavy outflow of funds from Canada directly related to foreign ownership, and by my warnings about Canada's growing foreign debt, "an amount greater than the total debt of Mexico, Brazil, and Argentina combined," and the inevitable high interest rates that had to result from our myopic economic policies. I ended by saying:

> Surely Sir John A. Macdonald must be spinning in his grave. The Conservative party that produced the national policy that nurtured a proud, separate country on the northern half of the North American continent has become the Neo-Continentalist party, ready to sell all to the highest bidder, ready to abandon all but the pretence of independence, ready to forever bid goodbye to Macdonald's dreams of a true north strong and free. What we desperately need now is a *new* national policy. What we're getting instead is a blind leap into economic and political oblivion.

Heading for a Court with No Laws

BY THE SUMMER OF 1985, the COC had built up an excellent mix of Liberals, NDP members, and even two longtime Conservatives, Bob Page and Bruce Pallett, but most of our members had no formal political affiliation at all. And during the summer, as Mulroney's intentions became clearer, the Great Debate began in earnest. On one side we had the prime minister and his cabinet, along with some 180 other Conservative members of Parliament, the powerful Business Council on National Issues, the Canadian Chamber of Commerce, the Canadian Manufacturers' Association, the Conference Board of Canada, the Canadian Petroleum Association, the C.D. Howe Institute, the Fraser Institute, the Economic Council of Canada, the Macdonald Royal Commission, most provincial premiers, many prominent Liberals, including Marc Lalonde and Paul Martin, Jr., the *Globe and Mail*, the *Financial Post*, and virtually all of Bay Street and Wall Street. On the other side were the Council of Canadians, the Canadian Labour Congress, the NDP, and about half the federal Liberal caucus. John Turner's best effort was to describe the idea of free trade as "premature."

While all this was happening, Statistics Canada reported that in 1984 Canada had a record merchandise trade surplus of $21-billion and that 1985 should produce another near-record surplus.

Once again I began travelling across the country, even though the encyclopedia publication was imminent. By summer, we had new COC chapters in Victoria, Windsor, Cambridge, Hamilton, and Kingston. Meanwhile, our treasurer, Ken Wardroper, was constantly reminding us just how short of money we were. Although we were never optimistic about the outcome, we tried very hard to obtain the tax-credit status the Department of National Revenue granted many other public-interest organizations. To no avail. A senior department official said, "Off the record, the government doesn't like your political agenda." When asked how an organization whose major goal was to preserve Canadian independence could be deemed contrary to the public interest, he simply shrugged.

In July I appeared before a special joint committee of the Senate and the House of Commons on Canada's international relations. In my testimony to the committee I pointed out that Canadians were being urged to "take a cold shower" and learn how to "compete eyeball to eyeball" with the Americans. This would mean "rationalization" of Canadian industry and inevitably result in "some dislocation." To compete eyeball to eyeball on a level playing field, surely we would have to have similar tax rates and similar labour laws. How could we possibly fund our more caring, compassionate society and medicare, for example, with the same tax rates as those in the U.S.? And did we really want our environmental, corporate concentration, and other important laws and standards to be set in the U.S. by American politicians and American governments? If so, what was the use of having a separate country? Moreover, did we really want to become even more vulnerable in our trading relationship since it was abundantly clear that the U.S. had no intention of abandoning countervail, antidumping, and other trade weapons. As well, I said: "I am a businessman, and I have been in business for myself for the last thirty years. . . . If tomorrow morning, Mr. Chairman, my sales manager came to me and said that he wanted me to know that we have reached the position where seventy percent of our business is now with Classic Books, well, I would have a small heart attack." Classic could demand from us anything they wanted: larger discounts, more advertising allowances, longer payment terms — you name it — and we would have little choice but to acquiesce. What exactly was our goal? Eighty percent of our exports going to only one country? Or was it ninety percent? In any event,

> by 1987 under the terms of GATT, which we have negotiated already and which the Americans have agreed to, ninety-six percent of our exports to the United States will carry a tariff of less than five percent and if already today seventy-four percent of our exports to the U.S. are tariff-free, how is it that we Canadians now have such dismal economic conditions? We have been doing so much trade with the United States; we have had huge trade surpluses with the United States. How is it then that our economic situation is so bad? How is it that we are locked into 1.3 million to 1.5 million unemployed Canadians and millions of Canadians are living below the poverty line?

Since, I went on, we were already among the world's leading per-capita traders with recent record merchandise trade surpluses, was it not possible we were doing the wrong kind of trade, exporting capital-intensive resources at relatively low prices and importing labour-intensive finished goods? And was it not already abundantly clear that merchandise trade was not the be-all and end-all panacea that the pro-free traders were promising? Moreover, what about the current-account deficits we were incurring with the United States every year and our burgeoning international debt? Surely we should be paying much more attention to these serious problems. How is it that almost no one was even mentioning them, especially since it was clear that U.S. demands relating to investment would certainly exacerbate the situation?

And why was it that "every time some backwoods U.S. congressman stands up and introduces a bill in relation to Canada that does not have a chance in heck of being passed by the U.S. Congress because it violates GATT, and he does it only to impress the voters back home, we Canadians . . . sit bolt upright and then start extending our cap on bended knees, saying *please* do not do this to us."

Canada was and had for a long time been the fastest-growing market for American exports. The U.S. exported more to twenty-five million Canadians than to all the 320 million in the European Community. Millions of Americans worked in industries heavily dependent on their exports to Canada.

> The United States gets enormous two-way economic benefit from its trading relationship with Canada. . . . I think one of the most important things this government should do is make it crystal clear to the United States that they should not shoot themselves in the foot, that one of the worst things that could happen to the United States and to the job level in the United States would be for Canada, as a result of American threats and actions, to start taking steps to become much more self-reliant and concentrate a lot more on producing goods for our own domestic market, instead of being the world's leading per-capita importer of finished products. . . .

Something we should have done long ago. In answer to a question from Lloyd Axworthy, I pointed out that any trade strategy should be directly related to job creation in Canada, and much more attention should be paid to opening up the Canadian market for our own Canadian companies. I concluded that "much more important than tariffs and much more important than nontariff barriers to creating jobs in Canada is the value of the Canadian dollar and the interest rates charged by Canadian banks."

Hardly anyone seemed to be raising these important issues in relation to the free-trade agreement. But the value of the Canadian dollar would have a *much* greater impact on jobs in Canada than the remaining tariffs in our trade with the U.S.

One provision in a prospective agreement would likely be "national treatment." Not one in a thousand Canadians had heard of it, let alone understood its implications. Abe Rotstein described the implications and other consequences of a free-trade agreement this way: "The price for the 'secure access' to the U.S. market on which we are so intent, is the silent American presence at the table for virtually every domestic decision we shall make in the field of industrial policy. . . . Under a free-trade regime it will be difficult to discriminate between those policies that we are required to adopt as part of our treaty obligations, and those policies designed to do something for the other 75 percent of the economy not involved in export trade to the United States."

Although I had never encountered the University of Toronto's John Crispo before, when I did I soon began to think he was consistently helpful to our cause. He was so loud and pompous that he turned many people off. Over and over again I heard people say that Crispo left them cold. He would accuse us of a long list of nonexistent or illogical positions and then, with great vigour and dexterity, shred our "positions." We were, according to Crispo, in favour of the status quo. We were anti-American. We were Luddites. We were isolationists and the rest of the long-familiar list so similar to the attacks made on Walter Gordon twenty years earlier.

For Crispo, the answer to Canada's economic problems was free trade with the United States. "There is only one alternative for us," he told the Senate-Commons Committee. "It is the American market. . . . We are so dependent on them."

Yet, as I wrote in the *Globe and Mail*, "Professor Crispo effectively, firmly and permanently hoisted himself on his own petard in his committee testimony. . . . When asked what his response would be if Americans would not surrender punitive policies such as counter-vailing duties, he unhesitatingly replied: 'I would not sign a free trade agreement that allowed that to take place . . . I would not be party to it.' Contrast this with the recent and repeated statements from *all* the senior U.S. trade officials to the effect that *under no circumstance* will the U.S. surrender countervail."

Well, of course, we knew that from the start. But somehow Mulroney, Wilson, Crosbie, Lougheed, Carney, Lipsey, Crispo, et al. didn't. In August, Richard Lipsey appeared before the committee referring to the proposal for the establishment of a new trade-dispute-settling body. Lipsey said: "Such a mechanism without a formal agreement (to define subsidies) is like a court without laws; if we have not settled by formal agreement such matters as what constitutes acceptable subsidies, there is nothing for a dispute-settlement body to settle."

Precisely. It was one of a very few occasions that I agreed with anything Lipsey had to say. To this day there is no such agreement, nor has the U.S. *ever* been interested in so binding its arsenal of trade weapons.

A Marriage with No Divorce

THE FOUNDING CONVENTION of the COC was held in Ottawa during the 1985 Thanksgiving weekend. Some two hundred men and women from across the country attended. I was elected chairperson, Halifax businessman Lloyd Shaw was elected deputy chairperson for the Maritimes, Montreal executive Céline Hervieux Payette, deputy chairperson for Quebec, and Ottawa Mayor Marion Dewar for Ontario. Former Canadian ambassador Ken Wardroper continued as treasurer and Robert Laxer was appointed head of a special committee that would concentrate on our attempts to defeat the proposed free-trade agreement.

By the time of our convention, we were already facing a $15,000 deficit. Plans to move our temporary office from Edmonton to Ottawa had to be abandoned until the organization's financial picture improved.

In my closing speech at the convention I said that "the very survival of our country is at stake . . . Canada's economic, political and cultural sovereignty are endangered. . . . If we're not successful we will enter into a marriage from which we will never escape . . . a marriage with a tough, aggressive, strong-willed partner . . . a marriage from which there is no divorce."

I concluded by saying: "Ten days ago, a leaked government report warned against letting opposition to free trade crystallize. Well, that opposition has now crystallized."

John Orr, a consultant from Victoria and an ardent Canadian nationalist, produced a fascinating study that showed that even though American ownership and control had increased rapidly during the past fifteen years, employment at U.S. firms in Canada had increased by less than a third of the comparative rate in Canadian-controlled firms. "U.S. firms [in Canada]," Orr said, "are importing more and more from the U.S., acting as warehouse and distribution centres. They're not creating jobs, that's for sure. Under a free trade agreement this trend would only grow. It's suicidal."

While I was in Ottawa, a plain brown envelope was delivered to my hotel. It showed that American lobby groups had threatened that if former communications minister Marcel Masse didn't ease up on his proposed legislation to protect Canadian magazines, they would bring pressure to bear to curtail the import of asbestos from Canada. Masse's riding was very dependent on asbestos production.

In October I sent a special-delivery letter to Beland Honderich, publisher of the *Toronto Star*: "The major problem we face is that the average person walking down Yonge Street or Jasper Avenue or Granville or St. Catharines or anywhere across the country really doesn't understand the ramifications of a 'free trade' deal. For most Canadians the idea of free trade means lower prices for U.S. goods they buy and greater access to the American market. We somehow must find a better vehicle for making the public aware of the enormous consequences of economic integration with the U.S."

The same month, Ronald Reagan, speaking about the "trade" discussions, announced that "we seek to include everyone in the success of the American dream." As I watched him convey that good news on television, I wondered if "everyone" included American blacks, the homeless and poor in the downtown cores of American cities, the elderly, the sick and the disabled who received hopelessly inadequate social-assistance benefits in the U.S.

In November 1985 I pitched in another $5,000, and Ken Wardroper came to Edmonton to make the necessary arrangements to transfer the national office to Ottawa. The same month, Robin Mathews and Jim Hyndman, Canada's former ambassador to Cuba, circulated a detailed constitution for the consideration of our members across the country. As well, we sent our members a draft of economic, cultural, social, foreign, and defence policy suggestions for consideration, plus suggestions about a proposed structural organization for the national body and for local and provincial organizations, put together by John Trent and his colleagues.

I very much liked what was happening. The COC was quickly becoming a democratic grassroots organization. While there was still a significant amount of top-down decision-making, the constitutional and organizational changes we were suggesting for members' consideration would soon change this. My goal was to see the board of directors take their orders from the active members, not the other way around.

Our opponents were fond of saying that the real reason I so strenuously opposed the free-trade agreement was out of concern for my own business interests. This made about as much sense as saying I was constantly insulting my bank manager in the hope of getting a big loan. First, there had been no tariffs on books entering Canada or the United States for many years. Second, throughout the free-trade debate, and for many years before, I had been a strong critic of

Alberta premiers Peter Lougheed and Don Getty and many of their cabinet ministers, as well as a vocal opponent of both Pierre Trudeau and Brian Mulroney and their governments. Such criticism made enemies. If my business was my principal concern, I would hardly be consistently attacking the federal and provincial governments, which dispensed loans, grants, and guarantees to my industry. Moreover, my attackers constantly referred to the book industry as a "protected industry." If the book industry in Canada was "protected," then the passenger pigeon had also been "protected."

It seemed to me more and more, from the leaked documents and surreptitious phone calls I was receiving almost every week, that Ottawa was plunging ahead without really knowing where they were going. Why would we want to open the door further to more American ownership and control of our economy? Newly released foreign-ownership figures showed that nonresidents already controlled, for example, more than half of all manufacturing, and most of the petroleum industry. Just how much is enough? Why would *any* Canadian, in these circumstances, want to make it even easier for foreigners to come in and take control of what was left?

By comparison, at the time Britain had some three percent foreign ownership, France and the United States two percent, and Japan less than one percent. Could anyone imagine any of these countries accepting the levels of foreign ownership and control that existed in Canada?

How much would be enough for Brian Mulroney and the BCNI? In 1983 some eighty-five percent of Canadian petroleum-industry profits went to foreign-controlled firms. What would be enough for the compradors? Ninety percent? Ninety-five percent? Or were they aspiring for one hundred percent? How many Canadian industries were they prepared to abandon to foreign ownership and control?

At the same time, abundant evidence had been accumulating about how harmful foreign domination was for the Canadian economy and our standard of living: continuing low levels of research and development; terribly excessive imports by foreign subsidiaries, some four times the average of Canadian-owned corporations; advertising, architecture, insurance, engineering, computer development, data processing, management, and other jobs imported, mostly from the U.S., instead of being performed in Canada by Canadians.

Already more than 100,000 data-processing jobs had been lost to the U.S. Moreover, Canadians were heading for a purchasing binge in 1986 of some $9-billion worth of computer goods and services, but three-quarters of the one hundred largest electronic companies in Canada were already foreign-owned, and only two of the top ten computer companies in Canada were now owned by Canadians.

In 1985 an average of over $1-million in interest payments, over $300,000 in dividend payments, and over $800,000 in business service payments left Canada *every hour of every day* to pay for foreign investment in Canada, much of which was financed by Canadian financial institutions in the first place. Next year, the haemorrhaging would be worse and the following year much worse still.

What was the solution? For Grant Reuber, president and CEO of the Bank of Montreal, the answer was even more of the same: "Increase the number of foreign investors by making it easier and more profitable for foreigners to invest here."

By the end of 1983, Canada's escalating foreign debt had ballooned to $244-billion, and our international services deficit jumped from $5-billion in 1975 to $20-billion in 1985. Did we really want to continue with the policies that produced these dismal results? Apparently not; we wanted to make them even worse.

Encouraging the inflow of foreign investment meant upward pressure on the Canadian dollar. A higher-valued Canadian dollar meant problems for exporters. Here we were aspiring for a free-trade agreement to increase our exports by wiping out the small remaining tariffs, while at the same time encouraging the inflow of foreign investment, which would inevitably hurt our trade balances far more than any modest benefits received from the abolition of tariffs on goods exported to the United States.

When the Canadian dollar was low, exports surged. Yet the Bank of Canada's tight monetary policy and the Mulroney government's "open for business" policies boosted the dollar higher and higher.

In the House of Commons External Affairs Minister Joe Clark continued to deny that investment was necessarily going to be part of the trade deal, but a leaked internal memo written by Peter Murphy put a lie to this: "Investment is another critical component for any agreement. I have stated that investment must be dealt with if there is to be agreement. This was later highlighted by Vice President Bush, Secretaries Shultz and Baker and Senator Bentsen."

Another report leaked to me in advance of publication showed that in 1981 seventy-six percent of the exports of subsidiaries in Canada went to their parent companies or affiliates, and seventy-eight percent of their imports came from their parents or affiliates. Under these circumstances, how could there possibly be "free" trade as envisioned in any theories of classical economics? Obviously there couldn't be.

As the weeks and months went by, it seemed clearer and clearer that Mulroney was prepared to surrender the nation for "guaranteed access" to the United States market — an unattainable, mythological, phantom, utopian impossibility. And the more I heard, the more it seemed to me that the proponents of free trade, while talking about "an outward-looking strategy," seemed instead to be willing to turn their backs to the world while resolutely facing towards only the U. S.

In November I debated Carl Beigie, the founding director of the C.D. Howe Institute. Beigie argued, as the Canadian Press reported, that "enhanced trade with the United States is the only option that can spur the increased productivity and efficiency needed to make Canada competitive and able to pay for programs such as medicare and unemployment insurance." I argued exactly the opposite, that free trade would lead to a stampede by big business demanding that the government savage Canada's social programs so they could compete on a level playing field by paying lower taxes. In the spring of 1985 the *Globe and Mail* had published a lead editorial suggesting that Canadian tax policies should be the same as in the United States. There was no explanation how, under such an arrangement, medicare and Canada's other social programs could be financed.

At the end of its first year the COC had some three thousand members in eight provinces. We had been very much in the forefront of the national debates about free trade, foreign ownership, social and cultural policies, and Arctic sovereignty. The COC appeared before parliamentary committees, sponsored public debates, and made presentations to provincial premiers and to numerous provincial and other federal bodies.

As we became increasingly vocal and better organized, the continentalist attacks escalated. Amazingly we were attacked for being afraid of our ability to compete in world markets. No one I worked with over the years *ever* matched that description. On the contrary, we were full of confidence that we could compete extremely well, if we were able to control our own industrial and resource decision-making processes.

Also late in the year U.S. Trade Representative Clayton Yeutter was very frank: "Free trade talks with Canada shouldn't be an end in themselves, but should ultimately lead to the creation of a North American common market. Free trade is just the first step in a process leading to the creation of a single North American economy."

Not much ambiguity there. Nor in Robert Bourassa's uncharacteristic December 1985 statement that "free trade will lead to a customs union which will in turn lead to common political institutions." But wasn't that *exactly* what we Canadians had resisted throughout our history? How could we possibly have "common political institutions" and a single economy and still have a country of our own?

But perhaps we opponents were overstating the nature of the free-trade agreement. Was it, after all, really such a big deal? According to Canadian GATT negotiator Mel Clark, "This is much more than a bilateral free trade agreement — it's well beyond what the European Common Market is after 30 years!" And, according to Mitchell Sharp, "This is not an ordinary, conventional trade negotiation of limited application. It raises issues of the most fundamental nature and has already provoked a national debate about . . . our political independence and our cultural institutions."

For Sharp, this was a very bold statement. Unfortunately his disciple, Jean Chrétien, was unable to comprehend its implications.

For many of us, Brian Mulroney's appointment of Simon Reisman as chief free-trade negotiator was devastating. Reports indicated that Reisman believed our negotiating position was so weak that the export of fresh water would have to be put on the table. I said that "appointing Reisman as bilateral trade negotiator was like appointing an arsonist as fire chief."

But Thomas d'Aquino of the BCNI was happy: "I will probably go to bed and sleep more soundly knowing that Simon Reisman is in charge of our negotiating effort." In fact, Reisman, prior to being appointed, was an adviser to a proposed enormous, multibillion dollar scheme to export Canadian water to the United States, known as the GRAND (Great Recycling and Northern Development) Canal. Its supporters included such high-powered Americans as Stephen Bechtel and former U.S. defence secretary James Schlesinger. But, according to Richard Lipsey, not to worry: "Simon Reisman is so much more sophisticated, so much more knowledgeable than the team he's up against. The Canadians have been studying this thing. I've written some papers for him myself. In the words of a well-known Canadian administrator, it's the best-researched policy that's ever happened in Canada."

On the other hand, in the words of Ontario Premier David Peterson, "Simon Reisman was one of the more objectionable guys I've met. . . . He was willing to take anything."

Bombing the Polar Sea

THE AMERICANS HAD long wanted to establish that the passage-
ways through Canada's Arctic islands were international
waterways rather than under Canadian jurisdiction. What
better time to do this than with toady Brian Mulroney in power?

Without requesting permission from the government of Canada, in
the summer of 1985 the U.S. icebreaker *Polar Sea* was sent north, as
a precedent, up through Davis Strait and Baffin Bay and then west into
Lancaster Sound. When the news broke that the Americans intended
to sail the Northwest Passage through Canada's Arctic archipelago
without seeking permission, Canadians were outraged. But from
Ottawa came virtually no reaction. External Affairs Minister Joe
Clark, when confronted by the press, made several wimpy statements,
and that was it as the *Polar Sea* proceeded westward.

I was damn mad, not at the audacity of the Americans, but at the
servile behaviour of the Mulroney government. I decided to "bomb"
the *Polar Sea*. We rented a Twin Otter out of Inuvik and purchased several two-foot-long red cardboard canisters (in case one missed its target),
stuffed them with a few rocks to weigh them down, inserted a message
in each, attached Canadian flags, and prepared to head north to inter-
cept the American icebreaker somewhere in Viscount Melville Sound.
At the last minute I hurt my back and was immobilized. Kay's daughter Louanne and her friend David Achtem, both University of Alberta
students, made the trip to Inuvik for me, where they were joined by
Inuit supporters Eddie Dillon and Roger Gruben and two pilots.

After a harrowing flight the Twin Otter finally located the gigantic
Polar Sea just as it was entering the Prince of Wales Strait. The plane
circled low over the ship several times attempting radio contact, then,
on a final pass, Louanne dropped a cardboard container onto the
ship's deck from some one hundred feet. Inside was a message for
the ship's captain and the U.S. government:

> Canadians consider our Arctic waters, islands and ice to be
> Canadian territory under Canadian jurisdiction. Your failure
> to request advance permission to sail the Northwest Passage
> is insulting and demeaning to our citizens and a threat to our
> sovereignty. It is not the action of a thoughtful, understanding
> neighbour. Canada's history, heritage and identity are closely

tied to our Northern territory. By violating our territorial integrity you have aroused a strong response from Canadians all across the nation. The flags we have set out ahead of you on the ice represent a symbol of our national jurisdiction. The temporary dwelling we have erected is symbolic of the centuries of fishing and hunting by the Inuit on the Arctic ice of the Northwest Passage. We strongly urge you not to further violate our jurisdiction, to stop your vessel and to return to international waters in the eastern Arctic. We request you notify your government that any such violations of Canadian sovereignty in the future will bring strong reaction.

As soon as word got out we were immediately swamped with moral and financial support from across the country; clearly the vast majority of Canadians were on our side. For almost a month we had problems handling the almost nonstop phone calls, and by the end of September, our entire expedition costs of some $11,000 had been covered by donations.

One telegram we received was from singer Nancy White: "Thank you for dropping the Canadian flags on that damned ship. Your only mistake was you should have dropped Farley Mowat on the deck too."

Don Braid, *Edmonton Journal* and *Toronto Star* columnist, called the Mulroney government's performance a "servile, wimpy response, enough to enrage even a lukewarm Canadian nationalist. . . . Never again will I trust these Tories to defend Canada's rights. . . . I find myself wondering if we have a Canadian government at all, or merely a northern branch of the U.S. State Department."

Incredibly, when members of the press had called the Canadian Coast Guard seeking more information about our "bombing" and the ship's progress, the response from the receptionist was that she had been instructed to refer all such calls to — wait for it — the American Embassy in Ottawa!

Right after we dropped the flag and message on the ship, I sent the prime minister a telegram: "Your government's weak actions do not protect our control over our own territory, fail to meet the concerns of Inuit residents, and represent a shocking abdication of your responsibilities to the citizens of Canada." I pointed out that if we acquiesced to the American contention that the waters were part of the international high seas, then Soviet submarines and other military

272

vessels could enter our territory, setting up what would inevitably lead to a serious military confrontation in Canada's North.

> Surely it is in the best interests of all Canadians, as well as Americans, for you to forcefully demonstrate to the Reagan government the obvious advantages for Canadian Arctic waters to be clearly declared internal and under our complete and unchallenged jurisdiction.
>
> Canada would be much better off protecting our northern sovereignty than becoming more involved in European military commitments or ill-advised Star Wars adventures.
>
> In our weakness we are acquiescing to the surrender of a vital part of our history, heritage and identity. Sir, the Council of Canadians urges you to act and to act now lest history remember that it was the government of Brian Mulroney that lost Canadian jurisdiction over the Northwest Passage and perhaps the Arctic islands as well.

The lead headline in the International section of the *Wall Street Journal* read: "Canadian nationalist takes on the U.S., giving country's pride a shot in the arm": "The U.S. Coast Guard has been warned. If its vessels intrude into Canada's Arctic waters again they risk attack from Mel Hurtig's air force."

So, what was Ottawa's response? The pilot, Ross Peden, as well as his copilot, were to be charged with "creating a hazard by dropping an object from an aircraft" and for flying below five hundred feet. I said that the government should be charging the *Polar Sea* for violating Canadian territorial sovereignty: "Instead, they are charging Canadians. It's ironic in the extreme." John Turner defended our actions in the House of Commons, calling the *Polar Sea* voyage "an affront to Canada."

NDP member of Parliament Lynn McDonald said, rather than being prosecuted, the pilot should be given a medal. But Transport Minister Don Mazankowski said that his department was "investigating the actions of Ross Peden." According to Mazankowski's assistant, "The next thing, people will be dropping stuff on the Peace Tower."

By November, public outrage had grown to the point that the Transport Department backed off — there would be no charges laid against either pilot. Ultimately, as a face-saving gesture, Mulroney and

Clark decided to grant the Americans permission for the voyage, permission the Americans had never sought in the first place.

The timing of the incident was most interesting. Brian Mulroney had cuddled up to his friend Ronald Reagan at their Quebec City "Shamrock Summit," promising the Americans closer, friendlier relations, plus new legislation to please the White House, the Congress, and the U.S. business community. Now, in response, the Americans were boldly proclaiming that Canadian sovereignty in the Arctic was nonexistent, an extraordinary embarrassment for the Conservative government.

When most of the fuss was over, I began to receive off-the-record calls from midlevel people at External Affairs thanking me for what I had done. They, too, had been appalled by the performance of Joe Clark and the prime minister. In the end the government promised to do a good number of the things we suggested to protect Arctic sovereignty, except for taking the incident to the International Court of Justice at the Hague for legal resolution of the dispute.

On September 10 Joe Clark rose in the House of Commons to outline measures "being undertaken by the government to enhance and secure our Arctic sovereignty." Two months later Brian Mulroney wrote to me defending the government's position. The final paragraph of the two-page letter bears repeating: "You can be assured, Mr. Hurtig, that no one is more committed to the sovereignty of this great nation than I, and that Canadian sovereignty remains a very high priority of my government." Several of the key promises Joe Clark made in the House, such as the construction of a Polar Class Eight icebreaker, were never carried out.

Goodbye East-West, Hello North-South

I SPENT MUCH OF the next three years speaking out against the Mulroney government's policies, especially the proposed "trade" agreement. As more details of the negotiations were leaked, the more apprehensive I became. Even in my worst fears I could not have imagined some of the aspects of the agreement and the massive abdications of sovereignty the government was planning.

My family: mother Jennie; father Julius; sister Goldy; brother Henry; me; brother Abe.

In our Jasper Avenue book store, at the time (in the early 1960s) and for years after the largest trade book store in Canada. *(Edmonton Journal)*

Getting W. O. Mitchell ready to sign copies of his new novel, *The Kite*, and his earlier bestsellers, *Jake and the Kid* and *Who Has Seen the Wind*.

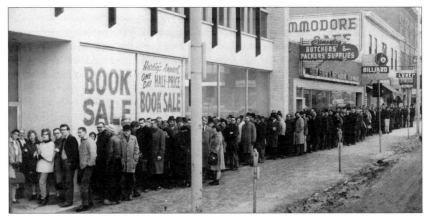

Once a year we rented a large empty store for our one-day, half-price book sale. The crowd would begin lining up hours before we opened.

Trudeaumania, 1968. Pierre Elliott Trudeau being mobbed by fans at City Hall, Edmonton, just before our meeting at the Chateau Lacombe, and some six hours before Robert Kennedy was shot. *(Edmonton Journal)*

Stu Hodgson and me in a Norwegian whalers' graveyard, Baffin Island. Hodgson was Commissioner of the Northwest Territories from 1967 to 1979.

Abe Rotstein, Peter Newman, and Walter Gordon at the King Edward Hotel where the Committee for an Independent Canada was born, over lunch, on February 3, 1970. *(The Canadian Magazine)*

Conservative MP Marcel Lambert and me at the University of Alberta, 1972. Lambert advised the audience that abortion reform wouldn't be needed if women kept their legs together. *(Edmonton Journal)*

Eric Kierans and Pierre Trudeau in Montreal just prior to the 1968 federal election. Less than three years later, Kierans resigned from Parliament in disagreement over the Trudeau government's economic policies. *(Canapress)*

My favourite cartoon on the increasing foreign ownership and control of Canada. (Edd Uluschak, *Edmonton Journal*)

In March 1973, I was elected chairman of the Committee for an Independent Canada, at the CIC's annual general meeting in Ottawa. *(Left to right)*: treasurer Jack Biddell; me; honorary chairman Eddie Goodman; two future CIC chairmen, John Trent and Bob Page. *(Canapress)*

With Margaret Laurence in my back yard, soon after she returned to Canada from England in 1974.

York University President Ian Macdonald gives me an honorary Doctor of Laws degree, 1980, as former Ontario premier and York Chancellor John Robarts looks on. In a strange turn of events, Robarts, after his death, helped save my publishing company.

Governor General Ed Schreyer presenting me with the Order of Canada at Rideau Hall, 1980.

With Walter Gordon at an early meeting of the Council of Canadians, May 1985.

My favourite cartoon on the Free Trade debate. *(Bob Krieger, The Province)*

After we "bombed" the American *Polar Sea* icebreaker in the summer of 1985 for sailing into Canadian waters without permission, cartoonists across the country made fun of Brian Mulroney and Joe Clark's weak performance and their failure to protect Canada's Arctic sovereignty. *(*Yardley Jones, *Edmonton Journal)*

Veteran Canadian diplomat George Ignatieff, star of The True North Strong and Free? conference. His powerful plea for nuclear disarmament electrified the audience. *(Canapress)*

David Suzuki and me at The True North Strong and Free? conference, 1986. Suzuki gave a superb speech and received two standing ovations.

This cartoon appeared soon after the 1994 Chiapas uprising in Mexico. (Bob Krieger, *The Province*)

My daughter Leslie and me hiking the Wiwaxy Gap alpine trail, high above Lake O'Hara, Yoho National Park.

William F. Buckey, Jr., and me on his *Firing Line* television show, McMaster University, 1991. Buckley was brilliant, acerbic, and anxious to pick a fight. I laughed off his provocative, outrageous statements in a good-humoured but spirited debate that pleased both producer and audience.

Kay and me in our home with Victoria and Oliver. *(Edmonton Journal)*

My four daughters *(clockwise from top)*: Gillian, Barbara, Jane, Leslie. *(Jason Stroud)*

Kay on the eighth tee, Jasper Park Lodge golf course.

It was now clear that all our trade eggs would be in one basket. What would happen if a clumsy, uncaring elephant stepped on the basket? My debating opponents kept promising hundreds of thousands of jobs would be created, but when pressed about *where*, they were unable to answer. Even Donald Macdonald admitted that Canadians would have to give ground on our political independence and how we established our social programs. What was becoming clearer and clearer was that the agreement would inevitably result in a comprehensive harmonization of policies; when I asked which Canadian standards the Americans would harmonize to, there were no answers. Moreover, as I said in a 1986 speech:

> What about the supposed huge gains in Canadian productivity from bilateral FT? If we've already had seven consecutive rounds of tariff reductions, if tariffs on Canadian goods entering the U.S. are now mostly either nonexistent or on their way to becoming relatively immaterial, why is our competitive productivity position still about where it was back when we started out with high tariffs? And how come the continentalists predict such *huge* potential gains with the elimination of the tiny remaining duties? Who's kidding whom?
>
> If free trade is the great panacea, how is it the continentalists, who frequently, misleadingly, cite the European Common Market as an example of why Canadians need not worry (though bilateral free trade between Canada and the U.S. is hardly comparative in *any* important way), never mention the double-digit unemployment in the EEC? Ask Mississippi or West Virginia about the benefits of free trade in the U.S. Or ask Newfoundland about free trade within Canada.

By January of 1986, Conservative support in the public-opinion polls had dropped to thirty-seven percent. Fifty percent of voters said their opinion of Brian Mulroney had worsened, while only eight percent said that it had improved. Forty-seven percent felt that a free-trade agreement would weaken Canada's political independence, while twenty-eight percent felt it would be strengthened. But overall sixty-one percent of Canadians supported the idea of free trade, while only thirty-one percent were opposed.

Interesting. In rough terms twice as many Canadians feared a free-trade agreement would harm Canada's independence, while twice as many were nonetheless in support. What could this possibly mean? Actually very little, since the overwhelming majority of Canadians still had little or no idea about what an agreement would actually contain.

Not only did the government begin negotiations with a mendicant mentality, but they had sold Canadians on the idea that we *had* to have an agreement. The Americans, fully aware of the position the Mulroney government had boxed themselves into, adopted a simple strategy: you want access to our market of 242 million people and in exchange you're going to give us access to your market of 25.5 million people? You've got to be kidding. Here's what *else* we want . . .

What Mulroney had succeeded in doing both before and after his election was awakening American manifest destiny. The Americans were now saying, "Look, we're prepared to do this thing, but here is what it's going to cost." Yet no one, not the government, not the big-business Alliance, not the think tanks, not the other business organizations, not the financial press, *no one* talked about the costs to Canada and the consequences of the punitive American demands.

I was becoming increasingly convinced that the agreement being negotiated was less and less about trade and more and more about economic union with the United States. The more pleas I heard about rushing to take advantage of "the window of opportunity" and the urgency of a "binding comprehensive agreement," the more worried I became.

With good reason. By 1986, I was receiving a steady stream of confidential briefings and documents from Ottawa, Toronto, and Winnipeg. A number of concerned senior government employees made certain I knew what was happening behind closed doors. Not only did this substantially raise the level of my concern, but it gave me a great advantage in my debates with the pro-free-trade advocates across the country. Many of them were guessing about the negotiations, whereas I, thanks to my regular briefings, had a good understanding of what was actually happening.

In an article in the *Globe* in February I said that never before in the modern history of Canada had we ever faced such a powerful tide of continentalism generated by big business on both sides of the border, and rarely had the Canadian public been so poorly informed about forthcoming decisions that would so dramatically affect their future. I said that after the agreement was in place for a few years, "can't you hear the assembled voices over brandy around the dining room table at 24 Sussex? Mr. Prime Minister, sir, the position of the Chamber of

Commerce is clear. We just can't afford to pay for medicare and we're going to have to privatize medicare and let the markets work the way they do in the United States." And since countervail and the rest would still surely be in place after an agreement, "why not simply admit U.S. observers into all future cabinet meetings, so they can tell us in advance if policies we're considering would be acceptable? Or, should we pass legislation first and then hustle to Washington every week to see if Congress and the administration are agreeable?"

The same month, Walter Gordon said: "We are flying blind into the most significant economic policy change of the postwar period. . . . The political sovereignty with which we would be left would be little more than a hollow shell."

After my *Globe and Mail* article, as might be expected, the Mulroney government's most vocal free-trade defender, John Crispo, attacked me. I was against trade, in favour of the status quo. Since I was a strong proponent of the multilateral trade-negotiation process, and since few people in Canada had spoken out so long and so forcefully *against* the status quo, I paid little attention to Crispo's diatribes. But I wanted to make one point, which I did in a letter to the paper:

> Canada must surely be the only country in the entire world where, when you enunciate policies that you believe to be in the national interest, when you say we shouldn't sell out our *entire* country to non-Canadians, when you say we have a responsibility to leave *something* to future generations of Canadians, when you say we should work harder and become more self-reliant, some mental midgets inevitably call you "anti-American." These colonial-minded twits must be deaf and blind. Over and over and over again, the so-called Canadian nationalists have made the point that our problem lies with poor, myopic leadership from our own politicians.

I was, of course, accused of being an anti-Conservative Liberal, as well as an anti-American. I found the first criticism amusing, given the "thorn in my flesh" complaint from Pierre Trudeau a decade earlier and my many years of attacks on the Liberal governments he led. As for being anti-American, I told my detractors that if some of the things I'd said about the quality of life in the U.S. were anti-American, then John Kenneth Galbraith and Senator Ted Kennedy were much bigger anti-Americans.

I was also accused of being isolationist and wanting to build a wall around Canada; I said that exactly the reverse was true. The COC wanted Canada to play a much greater leadership role among the world's community of nations, but we couldn't do that as a colony of the United States. Moreover, Canada was already one of the world's foremost trading nations and the most open in the world to foreign investment; it made no sense at all to fall over and lie on our backs.

The public-opinion polls were definitely moving in the COC's direction. We had been receiving excellent media attention and had won most public debates. But clearly we still had a long way to go; the government was moving inexorably towards a comprehensive iron-clad agreement.

In July of 1986 I wrote to the COC board: "I cannot emphasize enough that our financial position is bleak! We have commitments of close to $20,000 and only about $9,000 available. . . . To put it bluntly, we simply don't have the money necessary to do the job. And, obviously, the other side is well organized, well financed and highly visible and articulate." A familiar story. I went on to say that given what was now happening in Ottawa and Washington, "the Council of Canadians *must* be more effective during the next few crucial months. It is Canada itself which is on the table."

In the summer and fall of 1986 we campaigned vigorously against the sale of the West Kootenay Power and Light Company to Utilicorp Corporation of Missouri. The vast majority of the people in the Kootenays and Okanagan were with us. But our efforts were in vain.

A Visit from a Trust Territory

THE COUNCIL OF CANADIANS got another big boost after I was invited to Washington in September 1986 to appear before a congressional committee studying the free-trade agreement. I was instructed by the committee chairman, John Lafalce, to provide 125 copies of my prepared statement to the committee's chief clerk and to appear in room 2220 of the Rayburn House office building at 9:30 a.m. Kay and I arrived in Washington the night before, and checked into the Madison Hotel. The next morning we headed for Capitol Hill; it was hot, humid, and close.

My remarks were titled "Comments about Canadian-American Relations." When Kay and I were led into the hearing chamber, I was surprised by two things. First, the room was packed with spectators and the press, along with television lights and cameras. Second, only three of the twenty-six Representatives on the committee sat gazing down from the long elevated platform upon the sardines below them. By the time Donald Macdonald and John Bulloch had spoken, one of the committee members had left the room, and the other two, including the chairman, Lafalce, wore glazed looks and were yawning frequently.

I woke them up. I prefaced by remarks by saying how very disappointed I was, after a two-thousand-mile trip to Washington and given the importance of the topic being discussed, to find only two members of the committee present. I said no doubt the press would take notice (which they did). Immediately the chairman summoned pages to locate other members of the committee. Several arrived over the next half hour.

I continued by saying how grateful I was for the invitation and then explained the reasons public-opinion polls in Canada were showing increasing doubts about the wisdom of a free-trade agreement. I said there was far too much of a rush, given the importance of the negotiations, and that the U.S. fast-track process should be abandoned. I proceeded to give the committee information about the American ownership of Canada, the growing American current-account surplus with Canada, and an abundance of other information none of them had heard before. I also criticized Senator Bob Packwood, Senator Max Baucus, and several other American politicians for making ignorant, irresponsible threats, for the politically motivated countervailing duties on lumber, for the prevailing American attitude that they could buy up the rest of Canada if they wanted, for the insistence that Canadian cultural industries *must* be on the table. I warned against those elements in the Congress whose hyper-protectionism would inevitably endanger American jobs. I reminded them that, contrary to what Clayton Yeutter had recently said, echoing previous comments by Richard Nixon and Ronald Reagan, Canada, not Japan, was by far the largest market for U.S. goods, as well as the fastest-growing market.

It would be a mistake, I said, for Americans to believe that the federal government's trade policies had been endorsed by Canadians. There had been no mention of a free-trade agreement in the last federal election campaign, and recent polls showed a continuing erosion in the public's support for the concept. I also deplored the fact that so many Americans were so poorly informed about Canada — witness, for example, U.S. Treasury Secretary James Baker's comments that Canada had intentionally depressed the value of the Canadian dollar, when in fact the value of our dollar was rising rapidly.

Finally I reviewed the American wish list in the negotiations: water, oil, and gas; investment concessions; national treatment; unimpeded access to the service sector and cultural industries. I ended by saying:

> In terms of American ownership and control of our country, it was ironic for Canadians to hear and read the words of your own committee member, Representative Marcy Kaptur, that "it seems from these statistics that Canada is really a trust territory of the United States."
>
> Mr. Chairman, Canada is not yet a trust territory and I and my colleagues intend to make certain that does not happen. Canada and the United States can continue to be each other's greatest trading partners with much benefit on both sides of the border, but American demands in the current trade talks are excessive and unacceptable.

Unlike Macdonald and Bulloch, who read their presentations, I never took my eyes off the committee members as I spoke. I saw Chairman Lafalce getting redder and redder in the face. As soon as I was finished, he almost shouted out the first of many questions to come.

"Mr. Hurtig, exactly where do you get your statistics?"

I had anticipated the question, and responded, "Mr. Chairman, all of the numbers I have given you come from either the *Survey of Current Business* published by your Department of Commerce, or the government of Canada's official agency, Statistics Canada. I would be happy to provide your clerk with any specific references, should they be requested."

The subsequent question-and-answer period was confrontational. At all times I was polite and soft-spoken, but Lafalce and some of the other committee members were hostile. Before I left the witness table, the chairman glared at me and said, "It's been a long time since I've had to exercise such self-restraint. For that I'm a better man."

The truth was, he simply hadn't known what to say. He had no facts or figures to counter the material I had gathered in Ottawa and from Washington. Nor had he ever previously encountered a

Canadian who dared to speak in less than reverent tones. So his response was essentially an astonished "How Dare You!" My comments were neither strident nor especially nationalistic. Certainly they were presented in a courteous manner. Yet they were so out of character compared with the obsequious testimony he normally encountered from Canadians that Chairman Lafalce was quite taken aback.

In an interview later Lafalce charged that the opponents of free trade were "torpedoing the talks before they get off the ground. I think we can handle the wavers of the Stars and Stripes. I'm not so sure we can or you can handle the wavers of the Maple Leaf in Canada."

Much to my pleasant surprise, Donald Macdonald came to my defence saying he was "not dismayed at all by the political opposition from Mr. Hurtig's group" and that I deserved another Order of Canada for my efforts. Lafalce replied, "You must have mixed emotions. You don't want Mr. Hurtig to be so effective it would torpedo the negotiations. On the other hand, when he raises objections it will enhance your position at the bargaining table." Donald Macdonald responded: "You took the words right out of my mouth."

Allan Fotheringham's column the next day was headlined "Hurtig rattles U.S. politicians."

By the middle of 1986, as Canadians learned more and more about American demands, there was growing scepticism that a deal could be reached. A survey showed that only nineteen percent of Canadian business economists thought there was a fifty percent chance that Canada and the U.S. could successfully negotiate an agreement.

Brian Mulroney's office received an avalanche of letters from concerned Canadians. In reply, Mulroney signed a form letter that read: "I have noted your concern about the impact trade enhancement may have on Canada's sovereignty. I can assure you that . . . any trade agreement we reach with the United States will strengthen, not erode, Canada's unique identity and social institutions."

At the second national conference of the COC, held in Ottawa in October, we had an outstanding group of panelists and speakers, including Walter Gordon, Stuart Smith, Pierre Berton, Pierre Fournier, Alexa McDonough, Don Braid, Duncan Cameron, and Pamela Wallin. Despite my announced intention to step down as chairman, the board prevailed on me to stay for one more year. Reluctantly I agreed and was subsequently reelected by acclamation.

Both Maude Barlow, as conference chair, and Grace Hartman did a superb job of conducting the three-day conference. The delegates left enervated and more determined than ever to defeat the compradors and continentalists. In my opening remarks to the conference I said that "the last year has been the most arduous year of my life. It's been a terrible schedule." And it had been. Far too many speeches, interviews, conferences, debates, and meetings. Far too much travel. I began to hate airports and planes, hotels and motels. I treasured my time at home, even though when I returned to Edmonton there were long hours to put in at the office.

I told the convention about a conversation I'd had with my daughter Gillian the night before. She was working at the front desk of a large hotel in Vancouver. She said the first question American tourists invariably asked was "Is it safe to walk in the streets at night?" When they left at the end of their trip, they said: "We didn't know there was a city like this anywhere in North America. We're coming back." I then spoke about my trip to Washington. The night before my congressional testimony, Kay and I had dinner with Allan Fotheringham and a writer friend of his at the Jockey Club in the Ritz-Carlton Hotel, one of the fanciest restaurants in the capital. Two tables away from us was John Mitchell, Richard Nixon's disgraced attorney general, and nearby was Jean Kirkpatrick, former U.S. ambassador to the United Nations. And right behind us was Kitty Kelley, who had recently completed her controversial biography of Frank Sinatra. We had a very pleasant dinner, good food, good wine, and good talk. After dinner Kay and I decided to walk the seven blocks back to our hotel. We managed to walk just one block when a police car screeched to a halt next to us.

"Where do you think you're going?"

"We're walking back to our hotel."

"No you're not. It's not safe. Go back and take a cab."

When we had arrived at the airport in Washington, we'd seen a sign saying that Washington is the most important city anywhere in the world. Perhaps this was true. But in "the most important city anywhere in the world," it wasn't safe to walk even seven blocks.

That's one of the reasons we are at this convention today. Free trade . . . is about much more than economics. Those who talk about free trade in the myopic tunnel vision of the Macdonald Royal Commission, and talk about free trade only in economic terms, are surely as wrong as those who talk about free trade only in purely cultural terms. But what the Mulroney government and the BCNI and the C.D. Howe Institute are pushing goes well beyond culture, and even beyond economics.

I spoke about other things in Washington that Kay had never seen before. I took her to see the Lincoln Memorial, the Smithsonian, the National Gallery, and then up to John Kennedy's hillside grave in the Arlington Cemetery, and a few feet away, the simple, modest white cross marking Bobby Kennedy's grave.

I spoke about the visit Kay and I made to the long L-shaped black granite Vietnam Memorial, one of the most impressive and saddest things I have ever seen. As you walk along it, 58,000 names of mostly young Americans killed in Vietnam are arranged chronologically by date of death. Along the ground you see flowers left by grieving friends and relatives, and little American flags stuck into the ground. And you see many men, women, and children crying, sometimes transfixed in front of a name carved in the granite, sometimes asking a guide to help them find the name of their father, their son, their brother, because the names are not arranged in alphabetical order.

It is a heartbreaking sight. Name after name after name, column after column, panel after panel, year after year. You cannot walk along that memorial without thinking how important it is that we Canadians do everything we can to maximize our ability to determine our own future and not get caught up unnecessarily in the grand adventures and aggressions of other nations with other priorities.

When I went to the congressional committee the next day, it was like a Hollywood movie or like the old days of the Senator Joe McCarthy hearings. In the same committee a few days earlier one of the congressmen said: "You know I like Canadians. Canadians are nice people. In fact, some of my best friends are Canadians. But Canadians have been taking advantage of us Americans for the last twenty years, and we're not going to put up with it anymore!"

"Whatever the Legal Arguments Are . . ."

THERE WAS MUCH TALK during the last few months of 1986 that the free-trade negotiations were dead. In my speeches, I said:

> If I know anything at all about the government, they are at least as committed as they ever have been to getting a deal, *any* deal. When you have as your chief negotiator a man who has said that our negotiating position is so weak that we would likely have to put fresh water on the table to get a deal, it gives you some insight into the kind of agreement we're liable to end up with. And when you have a prime minister who has already shown he is prepared to give away anything to get a deal (generic drugs, softwood lumber, film distribution legislation, etc.) you have a pretty good understanding of why the talks will certainly continue and why Canadians should be very worried about the results. Moreover, in the coming months I can promise you that this government will do everything possible to mount a massive campaign to sway public opinion.

Almost every day threats were coming out of the United States. Senator Lloyd Bentsen, the head of the U.S. Senate's finance committee, one of the most powerful men in Washington and a man to whom Ronald Reagan owed many favours, warned that "Canadians should know that the free-trade talks are over for the rest of this decade unless they are prepared to show good faith in negotiations and get rid of their subsidies. Whatever the legal arguments over the legitimacy of these practices on softwood lumber and stumpage fees are, it will be necessary for us to apply countervailing duties."

Run that by me again? *Whatever the legal arguments over the legitimacy of these practices.* Bob Packwood was up for election; Ronald Reagan owes Bob Packwood some political favours. So Clayton Yeutter writes to Senator Pryor: "Dave, don't worry, lumber will be fixed." And so it was, the Canadian government surrendering in an unprecedented abandonment of Canadian sovereignty. Bob Packwood, now disgraced after years of sexually harassing and molesting women and no longer in the Senate, won reelection.

About the government's softwood-lumber collapse, someone said,

"You know, it was like being dragged into an alley and beaten up, and then you say, well, I was only bashed in the head, kicked in the groin, and robbed. It could have been worse."

U.S. trade lawyer Shirley Coffield, who did some work for me, put it this way: "An affirmative finding for the U.S. lumber industry would be a momentous decision and a terrible precedent. We'd be saying, in effect, that the U.S. can determine, for other countries, the value that they establish for their natural resources." Precisely. But there was no need for "an affirmative finding." The cowardly Mulroney government caved in. The message from Washington was simple: forget comparative advantage; if you Canadians take too much of our market, we'll make sure countervailing duties will change the rules.

In the face of such blatant blackmail, what should we have done? We could have, with any backbone at all, told the Americans that we believe in reciprocity, so we will be applying countervailing duties to the $6-billion in electronic-industry and aircraft-industry products shipped from the U.S. to Canada annually. These items were, after all, clearly heavily subsidized by the U.S. Defense Department budget of over $180-billion and other massive subsidies from Washington. Under international law Canada could have legally taken retaliatory action employing embargoes, tariffs, and quantitative restrictions allowed by GATT. Canada was by far the largest importer of American electronics goods in the world, but in addition to the countervailing duties we could have applied, we could immediately have sent trade delegations to Germany and Japan to begin increasing their share of the Canadian market at the expense of IBM, Xerox, General Electric, and other American companies. American electronics producers would have been camped on the White House steps the next morning demanding the removal of softwood duties.

Ronald Reagan, Bob Packwood, and the boys were playing hardball with Canada. In Ottawa, Brian Mulroney, Joe Clark, and Pat Carney were on their knees. The list of Canadian programs and practices the Americans believed "unfair" would fill a small book. But with a timid, obsequious government in power in Ottawa, nothing was safe. Washington alone would decide what constituted an "acceptable" practice.

To me, the free-trade debate was clearly not about nationalism and internationalism. Rather, it was a debate between nationalism and continentalism, and continentalism would be a fatal choice. It was a debate about self-determination, about choosing multilateralism, instead of a growing, narrow overdependence.

I was often asked what I thought the single most objectionable feature of a bilateral agreement was likely to be. There were so many it was a difficult choice. But the "national treatment" provisions would certainly rank high on my list. The necessity of treating American firms exactly as if they were Canadian would rule out a multitude of strategies most countries already employed to improve their competitiveness and their national standard of living. Stuart Smith had given a brilliant industrial-strategy paper at the COC convention. But almost without exception, every one of his proposals for restructuring the Canadian economy would go out the window with national treatment.

Despite all our efforts, the polls continued to show that a slim majority of Canadians supported the idea of free trade. Both the Liberals and NDP had been largely ineffective in the debate. The Liberals seemed confused and divided, and the NDP, for reasons I could not comprehend, were less than forceful in their opposition. It would be up to the COC to do its best to spell out the implications of a free-trade agreement relating to investment, resources, employment, services, marketing boards, culture, agriculture, water, and in a whole host of other areas. As for the press, they were doing a very good job of reporting, but little investigative journalism. At the time, many newspaper editorial writers and columnists had only a vague idea of what "national treatment" meant, never mind its profound implications.

By October 1986, the polls still showed fifty percent of decided Canadians supported a free-trade agreement, but three out of four were now unhappy about the way the government was handling the talks. Clearly, the more Canadians learned about the proposed agreement, the less they liked it. There was still a widespread feeling that the talks would go nowhere. On October 8 Peter Newman, in a letter to me, began a paragraph with "Now that free trade is a dead duck . . ."

The following month Judith Maxwell, chairman of the Economic Council of Canada, said that U.S. protectionism could cost 500,000 jobs in Canada, but the ECC calculated that free trade could produce 320,000 new jobs in this country. Council member Kalmen Kaplansky explained: "The Council was in a hurry. It didn't complete the studies. There were many questionable arguments and no discussion of the downsides or dislocation." So what else was new? The Macdonald Royal Commission had somehow opted for their leap of faith assuming the exclusion of services and culture from a free-trade agreement, and had naïvely assumed there would be *full Canadian control* over resources, energy, foreign investment, and local, regional, and sectoral development strategies.

In December 1986 Brian Mulroney bettered Maxwell: a free-trade agreement would create 500,000 new jobs in Canada! The only way unemployment could "be taken down dramatically in the foreseeable future is by a historic trade initiative."

In 1980 Ronald Reagan had campaigned on a platform of curtailing domestic deficits, reducing trade barriers, and balancing American trade books. By 1986, his government had piled up a deficit greater than all the total deficits recorded by all of his thirty-nine predecessors. An inevitable consequence was heavy reliance on imported capital, which drove the value of the U.S. dollar sky-high, further exacerbating U.S. trade balances and creating the largest trade deficits in U.S. history. The Americans blamed everyone but themselves.

From a personal point of view, 1986 was a great year. I received honorary Doctor of Laws degrees from the University of Alberta and the University of Lethbridge, the Canadian Booksellers Association President's Award, an award from the Association of Canadian Studies, the Alberta Achievement Award, a Royal Society of Canada medal, and the Windsor Press Club's Quill Award. Yet as the year progressed, I felt increasingly that we were in real danger of losing our country.

No Mood to Take Prisoners

B Y JANUARY 1987, more and more information about the likely contents of the deal was piling up. According to Mel Clark, "There's no doubt about it. It's my view that they're prepared to liquidate the country." Big business on both sides of the border was now exerting enormous pressure. According to Hyman Solomon, *Financial Post* Ottawa bureau chief, "In mid-January, a contingent of chief executive officers, all members of the powerful Business Council on National Issues, slipped into Toronto for a quiet, but deadly serious confrontation with Premier David Peterson. . . . If current Ontario uncertainty turns ultimately to hard opposition, Peterson will be facing a corporate enemy that is in no mood to take prisoners."

Soon after, Pat Carney announced that the government would embark on an "information program" to inform Canadians about the advantages of a free-trade agreement. The budget would be in the millions of dollars. Meanwhile, as always, the COC was short of money. Then, without any prior notice, Wallace McCain of McCain Foods sent us a cheque for $25,000. As well, the COC-sponsored True North Strong and Free conference in Edmonton in November 1986 had made enough of a profit to send the COC office in Ottawa a cheque for $5,000. As it turned out, we were slightly outgunned. The "trade communications" unit in Ottawa alone had a modest $12.7-million budget. On both sides of the border, American Express was a big player. For that corporation, the goals were clear:

> At American Express, we are actively supporting and promoting the U.S.-Canada negotiations. . . . Business has a stake — a very high stake — in the outcome of those negotiations. . . . Any trade agreement must address the liberalization of services . . . such as telecommunications, information services, and financial services . . . it is not in the interest of either Canada or the U.S. to shelter its domestic financial institutions . . . [what we need is] a free trade zone in financial services. . . . American Express believes that U.S. firms should have the right to offer their services *either* from within Canada *or* from across the border. . . . The ultimate goal would be a convergence of our two nations' domestic financial regulations.

In March John Turner invited me to give a seminar on free trade in his office in Ottawa. After the meeting, during which Turner, Herb Gray, and others had been very attentive and had asked excellent questions, I wrote Lloyd Axworthy that "John Turner has now had two fine opportunities to show that he is not really a conservative continentalist as so many people have argued for so long. The Liberal performance in the free-trade debate hardly gives those of us who are so concerned about the future of our country much reason to be optimistic."

The next month Turner finally made a strong statement: "The Liberal Party is not in favour of an all-inclusive free trade agreement with the United States because that would put at risk our political, cultural and economic independence and impinge upon our sovereignty as a nation."

The same month, the COC ran a full-page, two-colour ad in the *Globe and Mail* with the bold title "The Future of Canada is on the Table." The ad, the initiative of Wayne Crookes of Vancouver, warned Canadians about the possible, probable, and certain implications of the proposed free-trade agreement, the dangers of increasing foreign ownership, the threat to Canadian sovereignty, and other issues relating to Canadian independence. The response was immediate and remarkable. The ad had cost just under $20,000. Within two months it brought in over $55,000 in new memberships and donations. Even Conservative John Bassett, Baton Broadcasting chairman, sent in a cheque for $50, along with a note: "I believe that there should be freer trade with the United States, but I think the government has gone about it the wrong way and will end up with egg on its face."

On the very next page of the *Globe*, Walter Gordon's obituary appeared. In the words of Hugh Winsor, "In an ironic and unintended twist of timing, the development of Canadian cultural and economic nationalism had come full circle with a single edition of The Globe and Mail."

Early in April I debated Richard Lipsey in Kingston. The debate, sponsored by the *Whig-Standard*, was televised across the country by CTV. All seven hundred tickets to the debate were snapped up within two days. In the debate I spelled out what the American demands were sure to be. The audience and even the panel of journalists were, for the most part, hearing these for the first time: no more nonsense about limiting American ownership of Canada; no more "discriminating" between Canadian and American corporations; complete access to the service sector of the Canadian economy; and as the *New York Times* had bluntly put it, "guaranteed access to Canada's natural resources," including water; and a long list of other demands.

Later in the month I had a talk with Manitoba Premier Howard Pawley to get him to stiffen his opposition to the deal. I asked him to meet with David Peterson in advance of the coming First Ministers Conference in Ottawa and he agreed. That meeting proved helpful to our cause.

When the first national public-opinion poll had been taken about free trade in 1985, eighty-four percent of Canadians were in favour. By March of 1987, that figure had dropped all the way to forty-three percent. Meanwhile, the Mulroney government's support had plunged to only twenty-two percent.

Ronald Reagan was scheduled to visit Ottawa in April for another "Shamrock Summit." Just prior to the president's visit, Brian Mulroney told the *New York Times* that U.S. "trade remedy laws cannot apply to Canada, period." It was an astonishing statement, since most of us fully understood that the U.S. had zero intention of abandoning its protective legislation. Could it be that the prime minister was that poorly briefed, or was Simon Reisman being hornswoggled?

In February I had written to my fellow board members reminding them that in the following October I would be stepping down as chairman of the COC, although I hoped to remain active in the organization. We now had members in almost three hundred communities across the country, and even a few members located outside the country. I had some strong concerns about one located in Virginia, especially when the phone number provided was supposedly "out of service" the day after the membership arrived, and thereafter.

We decided to hold a "Canada Summit" in Ottawa at the same time as Reagan's visit, involving business and labour groups, teachers, farmers, environmentalists, seniors, ethnic groups, cultural organizations, and others. We would focus on the loss of sovereignty Canadians could expect from the "comprehensive bilateral agreement" that was being negotiated.

The Genie Is Out of the Bottle

AMONG THOSE JOINING US on April 4, 1987, for our "Canada Summit" on Parliament Hill were film, television, and radio groups, apparel manufacturers, artists, chicken marketers, the Canadian Conference on the Arts, the Canadian Council on Social Development, the Canadian Federation of Students, the Canadian Labour Congress, the Canadian Nature Federation, the Canadian Teachers' Federation, Inuit representatives, six different Quebec organizations, the National Farmers Union, peace and environmental groups, nurses, anti-poverty organizations, publishers, and many others. It was the beginning of what was to become a formal coalition under the name of the Pro-Canada Network, an alliance of twenty-five organizations opposed to the Mulroney government's plans. We marched to the front door of the Parliament Buildings and tacked up a declaration that ended by saying:

> We the delegates to the Canada Summit, representing organizations whose members form a majority of the Canadian electorate,

Demand that no Agreement of this kind be signed without first having been submitted to the Canadian people for their explicit approval,

Later in the day we were foiled in another plan. We had booked a hot-air balloon and decorated it with signs denouncing the free-trade agreement. We had planned to launch it from a field near Sussex Drive, close to where Reagan's motorcade would pass on the way to Rideau Hall. Everything was ready to go when the RCMP warned that if we launched the balloon we would be arrested. We stood debating whether or not to proceed.

Conspicuous in their presence were several Americans, dressed (are you ready for this?) as cowboys, boots, Stetsons, and all, who were keeping close watch on us. I thought we should launch the balloon, but my colleagues voted me down. As well, the balloon pilot did not seem to relish the idea of being brought down in a hail of bullets.

The next day, Hugh Winsor wrote: "While it lacked the drama at the cathedral at Wittenberg when Martin Luther tacked up his challenge to ecclesiastic authority . . . the government's trade initiative might just have let the nationalist genie out of the bottle and — regardless of the merits of free trade — the genie may prove difficult to stuff back in."

Also in April I confirmed to the Council of Canadians board and chapter chairpersons that I would be stepping down as chairman at the October AGM. By that time I would have devoted almost three years of very hard work to the organization. I felt it was crucial that I pay more attention to my business and my family. So did my banker and my wife. I also felt it would be unwise for me, as founder of the organization, to stay on too long as chairman; there were many talented people who could take my place.

A few days later a confidential Peter Murphy document, obtained by the *Toronto Star*, indicated that exempting Canada from U.S. countervailing measures "could be too much for Congress to accept. . . . [However] it appears some face-saving device may be required to get the Canadians to sign an agreement."

Some face-saving device! Like dispute-settlement panels, for example, but with no definitions of subsidies and with all the U.S. arsenal of legislative trade weapons still firmly in place.

I had written to Ronald Osborne, president and CEO of Maclean Hunter Limited, asking for a donation. After all, *Maclean's* had benefited greatly from nationalist federal government legislation, as had other Maclean Hunter magazines and television stations. Osborne offered us a free full-page ad in *Maclean's*, which we were grateful for. Later we discovered, much to our surprise, that *Maclean's* had sent a $50,000 donation to the Canadian Alliance for Trade and Job Opportunities, and Osborne had notified his employees that "the deal makes sense for Canada." Oh yes, unmentioned was that Maclean-Hunter's greatest profits now came from its cable-TV operations in the U.S.

In May full-page ads, sponsored by the Alliance, appeared in magazines and newspapers all across Canada. Also across Canada, supermarkets were being plied with millions of pro-free-trade brochures courtesy of the Mulroney government. Both the Alliance ads and the government publications were cleverly worded and terribly misleading, and in places blatantly dishonest. The question for us was, how could we possibly counter the many millions of dollars being spent by government and big business given our meager financial resources? Perhaps one way might be the Pro-Canada Network, which held its first formal meeting on May 5 in Ottawa. If an effective national network could be established, it could have a major impact on the debate and help counter the well-financed propaganda we knew had only just begun.

With each passing day it became clearer that a 1988 federal election would decide the issue. A May public-opinion poll showed that only twenty-nine percent of Canadians trusted Brian Mulroney and more than seventy-eight percent said there should be a national referendum and/or a federal election before a free-trade deal was signed.

By midsummer it was clearer still that Mulroney was increasingly committed to making a deal, despite the fact that the Americans would not abandon their countervailing, antidumping, and other laws. Moreover, the reports I was getting every week from my three government sources indicated that American demands relating to investment, energy, agriculture, national treatment, and other areas had escalated since the talks began. As I wrote to my colleagues in July, "my informants say *they can't believe* the extent to which Mulroney seems prepared to give in to get a deal . . . it looks like our worst fears are materializing."

The Business Council on National Issues had been established in 1976 through the initiative of Imperial Oil's W.O. Twaits and Noranda's Alf Powis. By the time the BCNI set up the Canadian Alliance, it represented 150 corporations operating in Canada and controlling assets of some $800-billion. Banks, insurance companies, petroleum and other resource companies, and manufacturers dominated. Major foreign-controlled firms included Bechtel, Xerox, IBM, Honeywell, ITT, Imperial Oil, Shell Oil, Texaco, Ford, and Kodak. In April 1985 they had urged Brian Mulroney to commence formal, comprehensive free-trade discussions with Washington. According to political economist David Langille, "In the course of the last decade, the Business Council on National Issues has become the most powerful and effective interest group in Canada — to the point where it can now exercise hegemony over both the private sector and the state."

The Canadian Alliance for Trade and Job Opportunities was founded in March 1987. Its co-chairmen were Peter Lougheed and Donald Macdonald. David Culver of Alcan was the chairman of the executive committee, and Darcy McKeough, treasurer. In one of its first publications the Alliance stressed:

> The Economic Council of Canada recently completed a major study of Canada-U.S. free trade which concluded that the elimination of tariffs on bilateral trade would result in employment gains of over 375,000 by 1995.
>
> The Macdonald Royal Commission conducted a similar inquiry into the probable economic impact of free trade and concluded that the economic gains would range from 3% to 8% of GNP . . . realized over a period of 5-10 years.
>
> The gradual period of transition would not result in massive disruption to the economy.
>
> . . . a free trade agreement would help enable governments to continue to raise the revenues necessary to support our generous system of social programs.

So much for honesty. By May the Alliance's full-page ads — bold, well designed, and centred by pictures of Lougheed and Macdonald — were appearing across the country. None of the ads mentioned any of the costs to Canada of a free-trade deal.

In June we managed to obtain a copy of the Alliance's interim Fund Raising Report. Of the $1.164-million raised to May 20, ninety-two percent came from BCNI members, and much of that came from U.S. corporations such as Bechtel, Cargill, Dupont, Union Carbide, and 3M. Just as we had suspected, the Alliance was essentially the BCNI under another name.

Over and over again, the Alliance asked and answered their own question: "Won't Canadian business lobby to reduce spending on social and other programs? Won't the agreement gradually force us to align our policies along the lines of the larger and stronger partner?" The answer? "Not at all." Right, and winter probably won't bring cold weather either. What was in it for big business? Eric Kierans summed it up nicely:

> Political, cultural and social values cannot be permitted to set up the basis of society and to dictate the economic policies that will lead to their achievement. So say our corporate masters and, more than anything else, this Agreement proves that it is they who are in charge of Canada. . . .
>
> These negotiations have an object, to smooth the path of Canadian corporate wealth into American markets and citizenship. . . . The government, despite what it says about jobs, jobs, jobs, is faced with the heavy paradox that employment in Canada, sovereignty and political independence are not goals of the Canadian corporate community.

In July 1987 the C.D. Howe Institute, true to form and with perfect timing, released a report warning that Canada would be a big loser if the free-trade talks were not successfully concluded in an agreement. The report was, of course, widely reported by the media in Canada.

For Premier David Peterson, the more he learned about the proposed contents of the agreement, the more he saw it as a sellout. In August he said: "The way it sounds, we are being offered a choice between suicide or being murdered. I'd rather fight."

After an all-day July meeting with Simon Reisman that finally broke up at two-thirty in the morning, provincial trade negotiators called me, very concerned about what they had heard. They made it clear that Mulroney was prepared to give the Americans much more than originally envisaged at the beginnings of the negotiations. The Canadian government was prepared to grant the U.S. expanded rights to invest in Canada and were going to offer protection to only a narrowly defined group of cultural industries, such as publishing and broadcasting. Publicly, the government had said that only trade-related investment would be open to U.S. companies. But now they were including service industries and natural resources.

It was no surprise that by the end of the month, there were hundreds of large American corporations actively lobbying the U.S. Congress to support the proposed deal with Canada. As I wrote in a memo to our board of directors, "They're rubbing their hands in anticipation. They really can't believe what Canada is willing to offer in return for giving away relatively little. The Americans know Mulroney is way out on the plank and desperate to get a deal. They're being very tough bargainers because so far Canada has given in on every crucial demand."

When the talks temporarily stalled in September 1987, it was Tom d'Aquino and other business leaders who contacted James Robinson of American Express to urge that the White House be directly involved in restarting the negotiations. Eventually Derek Burney took over discussions for the PMO, along with Pat Carney, Michael Wilson, and Deputy Finance Minister Stanley Hartt. U.S. Treasury Secretary James Baker now headed their American counterparts.

In September one of the provincial trade negotiators phoned me to say that now, for the first time, he no longer trusted the reliability of the briefings the provinces were receiving from Ottawa. Key material would now be supplied only on a "need to know basis," and Reisman's office was attempting to get all provincial negotiators to sign the Official Secrets Act. He indicated a fierce battle was in progress between the Trade Negotiator's office and other government officials about how much the provincial premiers should be told. A whole series of agreements between the U.S. and Canada had already been concluded, but the premiers were not being told. He felt the briefings the provinces were receiving were "faulty and evasive" and "most likely the public will be kept in the dark as long as possible."

In a September 11 press release I appealed to Canadians to demand a federal election before Canada ratified a free-trade agreement:

> If necessary, the Liberals and NDP members of the House of Commons must disrupt the business of the House and force an election, as Conservative leader Robert Borden did before defeating Wilfrid Laurier in the reciprocity election of 1911. Brian Mulroney has no mandate from the people of Canada to take this unprecedented step. When he campaigned for the leadership of the Conservative Party he spoke out strongly *against* free trade. He was not elected to sell out our country . . . few Canadians understand what the government is doing.

This is no free trade agreement, this is a giant step towards union with the U.S. . . . It's a "leap of faith" into oblivion for Canada.

Two weeks later, another head provincial trade negotiator told me "it would be impossible to have an agreement that would be politically palatable in Canada." Reality had confronted Canada, he said, and U.S. demands were so great that Canadian negotiators were shocked, even though "they continued to give and give."

On October 4 a thirty-page outline agreement was signed in Washington.

By the time of the third annual conference of the COC, held at the Chateau Laurier in mid-October, both the Liberals and the NDP were committed to fight the deal. But more and more we were getting reports that big business on both sides of the border wanted Mulroney to do everything possible to ram the deal through before the next federal election, just in case.

At our convention John Trent was elected chairperson and I was elected honorary chairperson. Even though the free-trade debate was beginning its most crucial phase, I felt a huge sense of relief. The COC had become well organized, well established, and highly vocal and visible. There was excellent spirit in the group, and the talented men and women of all ages would hopefully play a major role in the future of our country. I stepped down as chairman, leaving the COC in excellent financial shape even though our $236,000 in expenditures far exceeded the spending in any year of the CIC's existence. We now had a war chest of some $40,000 and more money coming in every day from concerned Canadians.

Late in the year we commissioned and paid the considerable cost of an analysis by Statistics Canada that showed that from 1978 to 1985 Canadian-owned firms produced more than 876,000 new jobs in Canada while employment in foreign-owned firms dropped by almost 13,000 jobs, despite the fact that foreign corporations in Canada were taking over forty percent of all nonfinancial industry profits.

A few days after the convention I was on the afternoon CBC radio show "Cross-Country Checkup." One caller called me a true conservative. Another caller said I was a socialist.

Into the Melting Pot

IN NOVEMBER 1987 I appeared before the House of Commons committee on External Affairs and International Trade studying the Free Trade Agreement. In my introduction I said:

> It is beyond my comprehension how any group of Canadian citizens could have agreed to such a horrendously bad deal. Those of us who were concerned three years ago, when the first leaks surfaced about the government's intentions, were apprehensive. But *never*, in our worst fears, did we imagine that a government of Canada would ever give away so much for so little gain. This agreement is so bad it deserves to be rejected for any one of at least a dozen different reasons. . . .
>
> This "trade agreement" is a massive abandonment of Canadian sovereignty. If implemented it will be irreversible. We will be saying that once and for all we are giving up on the idea of Canada.

Unlike previous occasions when Walter Gordon and I had been rudely treated by Conservative MPs, the committee members were courteous, thoughtful, and inquisitive. Senator Dic Doyle opened his response to my presentation with: "First, let me say that I for one was much impressed with your presentation, though not in the least by the way in which it was made. . . . We should have expected no less from a man who is as adventurous as you are, as intrepid as you are, who is as given to taking risks as you are. . . ."

That same month we again ran full-page ads showing that since Brian Mulroney had become prime minister, more than 1,600 Canadian companies had been taken over by non-Canadians and that for the past seven years American companies operating in Canada made one-third of all profits, yet created only one-tenth of one percent of all new jobs. We spelled out how the agreement clearly did not provide guaranteed access to the U.S. market, but it did guarantee that the U.S. would share Canada's energy supplies, eventually forcing Canadians to share American shortages.

By then, only seventeen percent of Canadians said they would choose Brian Mulroney as their leader. Fifty-eight percent said they did not trust the prime minister to make a deal they would support, and sixty-seven percent said there should be *tougher* screening of foreign investment, not a weakening of these provisions. The governments of Ontario, Manitoba, and Prince Edward Island were opposed to the agreement.

The more I looked at what the Conservatives were doing, the more it seemed to me that a tunnel-vision government was ignoring the seventy-five percent of GNP related to domestic activity and focusing exclusively on the twenty-five percent related to trade. All recent studies had shown that small Canadian-owned businesses were the only major job creators in Canada and they were for the most part nonexporters. Moreover, I was convinced that much greater gains in jobs and wealth could be achieved by opening up trade *within* our own country. As well, instead of cowering before threats of American protectionism, we should make it crystal clear that we would immediately launch formal GATT proceedings at the first sign that the U.S. was violating the now well-established international trade rules that came from the long years of GATT negotiations; we were nowhere near as vulnerable as the doomsday free traders suggested.

On December 12 Brian Mulroney presented the 218-page text of the agreement in the House of Commons. He received a standing ovation from the Conservative caucus and described the deal as "a major step forward for Canada." Simon Reisman said the deal was a triumph, claiming that Canadian negotiators had outmaneuvered their American counterparts: "You would think that the United States was an underdeveloped country alongside us in terms of the way this negotiation went. . . . Our people were way ahead of them in terms of the analysis, investigation, the facts, the methods, the procedures, the whole business. . . ."

Reisman would later call the Americans "bastards" for the way they were treating Canada under the terms of the agreement the "underdeveloped country" had snookered us into.

When I read the final agreement, it immediately became clear to me that the Mulroney government was once again engaged in a deceptive campaign to mislead the people of Canada. The agreement went well beyond trade; it was indeed a giant step towards economic union with the United States involving an unprecedented abandonment of national powers and massive transfers of decision-making from Canada to the United States. Still, most Canadians were quite unaware of the implications of energy sharing, investment relaxation, national treatment, or other aspects of the agreement.

In the future important government actions would be impossible in many areas. Too much American control? Too little oil to share? Too much U.S. cultural domination? Too expensive drugs? Too bad. Forget it.

Even prominent Conservatives such as Robert Stanfield and former Ontario premier Frank Miller expressed concern about the loss of Canadian sovereignty. Former Liberal finance minister Edgar Benson said: "Under this deal, Canada has given Americans the right to control us on all fronts." Another former Liberal cabinet minister, Jean Luc Pepin, said: "Those who support the agreement must accept that it will put an end to the political structure of Canada as we know it." For John Halstead, Canada's former ambassador to the North Atlantic Treaty Organization (NATO), "What is at stake is the ability of Canada to act as a coherent political entity." On the other side of the border, Harvard political economist Robert Reich (now Bill Clinton's secretary of labour) said: "Canada has been sold a bill of goods. . . ."

Soon after the deal was published, public support crumbled. One government poll leaked to the *Toronto Star* showed sixty-two percent of Canadians thought the U.S. had obtained a better deal than Canada. Moreover, the government's performance in the days leading up to the announcement and thereafter was inept and confused. According to the *Star* reporter John Ferguson, "The Mulroney gang couldn't blow it worse if they were following a script by Mel Hurtig. Free trade opponents would be rolling in the aisles were it not for the fact that hilarity doesn't mix with the solemn duty of saving Canada from the American menace. Pollsters say this government has a credibility problem and that voters wouldn't believe a weather forecast from it let alone something as complicated and controversial as free trade."

Michael Wilson's new agency Investment Canada, which took FIRA's place, was a fraud. Thousands of Canadian companies were taken over, mostly by large American corporations, and not a single application was denied. In the first three years of Investment Canada's operations, 96.2 percent of all new foreign investment consisted of takeovers of businesses operating in Canada, and a paltry 3.8 percent was for new business investment. Most of the money used to expand the foreign ownership and control of Canada, primarily by American corporations, continued to come not from outside Canada, but from Canadian sources.

Friendly Canadian banks and other financial institutions continued to provide Canadian savings to finance the sellout of our country. The outflow of dividend payments and business service payments far exceeded any inflows of new investment capital. In short, Canada was financing its own demise, and under the investment provisions of the free-trade agreement this process was guaranteed to continue. Suicide via the pen. Just before Christmas, the *New York Times* carried an article about me by John Burns. The article again produced scores of letters from the United States (mostly supportive letters from Canadians living in the U.S., but a few virulent anti-Canadian and/or anti-Semitic hate letters as well). Burns ended his story with a final quote from me: "None of this opposition to free trade has anything to do with anti-Americanism. It's not the Americans' fault that they own so much of Canada. It's the fault of our own inept politicians. It's the fault of poor Canadian management of our own affairs."

Rather than a Free Trade Agreement, the final document should have been called the Americanization of Canada Agreement.

At the Crossroads of Our Destiny

I N JANUARY 1988 Brian Mulroney and Ronald Reagan signed the FTA, which was scheduled to go into effect on January 1, 1989. The *Toronto Star*, *Edmonton Journal*, and Montreal *Gazette* (except for the publisher) came out in opposition to the FTA. Most other editorial boards came out in favour.

By early 1988, the COC's annual income had increased to more than $400,000, but the propaganda from government and big business swamped our own campaign. Nevertheless, our active membership had grown to over 10,500, more than the CIC had ever achieved.

The expanding Pro-Canada Network now comprised twenty-nine national organizations, and seventy-five men and women representing all provinces had attended an Ottawa election-strategy meeting. But at the same time, the budget of the pro-free-trade forces was approaching $20-million in funding from the federal government, the Alberta and Saskatchewan Conservative governments, and big business.

In January George Stanley, the man who designed the Canadian flag on the back of a napkin, wrote to me from Sackville, New

Brunswick: "May I add a word of support for the stubborn way in which you campaign for Canada! I am with you all the way in opposing free trade with the U.S. which I see as only a means of surrendering our heritage to the Americans. To me, the whole thing is criminal. At last I can say so now that I am no longer Lieut. Governor of N.B."

Late in January I advised the *Edmonton Journal* that both Ed Broadbent and John Turner had agreed to a debate about free trade in Edmonton, to be sponsored by the paper and televised nationally by the CBC. The publisher of the *Journal* then couriered an invitation to the prime minister, allowing him to set the date for the debate at his convenience and choose the moderator. Brian Mulroney declined.

In February 1988 some 1,400 people attended a meeting in Regina where Bob White, president of the Canadian Auto Workers, Wayne Easter, president of the National Farmers Union, and I spoke. A few days later I released a paper on the energy provisions of the FTA. It had taken many weeks of work to produce the document; the research costs and long-distance phone calls and couriers alone exceeded $6,000. But, over and over again, I heard the same thing from lawyers, government officials, and people in the petroleum industry: "You know, you're the only one asking these questions." When I asked why that was so they would respond, asking not to be quoted, "Because the big multinationals *love* what is happening!" And so they did.

There was little doubt in my mind that once Canadians understood what was actually in the FTA, they would overwhelmingly reject both it and Brian Mulroney. But by early 1988, we were facing a renewed massive barrage of pro-free-trade advertising, speeches, conferences, and much misleading information.

In March Grant MacEwan, long a free-trade supporter, came out strongly against the deal in a *Calgary Herald* column: "I have been slow in declaring my fear that the big trade deal has been drawn without adequate regard for the moral responsibilities that go with resource ownership and guardianship."

We gave the MacEwan column wide circulation. We also continued to circulate copies of Brian Mulroney's unequivocal statement at the 1983 Conservative leadership convention: "Free trade affects Canadian sovereignty and we will have none of it, not during leadership campaigns, or at any other time."

John Crosbie continued to complain about "encyclopedia peddlers." I wrote to Crosbie: "Thank you for all of the publicity and promotion you have provided *The Canadian Encyclopedia*. Our advance sales for the second edition are booming as a result. After the next election, when you are seeking new employment, we hope that you will keep us in mind. We have a couple of door-to-door routes that would be perfect for you."

John Crosbie never read the text of the Free Trade Agreement before it took effect on January 1, 1989. In a 1992 interview with Lawrence Martin, Crosbie admitted he still hadn't read the agreement, moreover "there isn't one person in the whole goddamn government who's read it. I'm the only one who's honest enough to say so."

Throughout 1988 the Citizens Concerned About Free Trade, David Orchard's organization based in Saskatoon, attempted to lure Saskatchewan Premier Grant Devine into a public debate with me on the free-trade issue. Despite a petition signed by hundreds of men and women from across the province, Devine declined. Another reluctant debater was Peter Lougheed. The *Calgary Sun* tried to get Lougheed to agree to a television debate against me, one held at his convenience, but he also declined.

I managed to get my hands on a confidential Bank of Nova Scotia study marked "For Internal Circulation to Senior Officers Only." The study demonstrated that thirty-two major sectors of the Canadian economy, which employed eighty-one percent of all Canadian workers, would receive a negative impact from the trade deal. It wasn't long before we ensured that the study was no longer confidential, much to the embarrassment of the bank, a keen backer of the FTA.

In the spring of 1988 both COC Chairman John Trent and Deputy Chairperson Maude Barlow resigned to allow them to contest nominating meetings leading to the federal election, expected to be held in the fall. Ken Wardroper agreed to serve as chairperson until the next annual meeting and was elected by the board to that position. At great personal sacrifice and expense, he and his wife returned to Ottawa from Victoria.

By May 1988, the now thirty organizations opposed to the FTA that belonged to the Pro-Canada Network had a combined membership of more than ten million Canadians. Representatives of the network had good meetings with John Turner and Ed Broadbent, but Brian Mulroney refused to meet with us.

Late in the month I issued a press release:

The Conservative government is blatantly discriminating

against opponents of the free trade agreement. Revenue Canada has told Hurtig Publishers that $63,000 in donations and expenditures on behalf of the Council of Canadians will be subject to tax.

I wish to stress, as strongly as possible, that I do *not* object to paying taxes on these donations. If that is the policy of Revenue Canada, then so be it. However, such a policy must be applied equally, in a fair and non-discriminatory manner, and must also be applied to donations to and expenditures on behalf of the Canadian Alliance for Trade and Job Opportun-ities, the Business Council on National Issues, the National Citizens Coalition, the Canadian Federation of Independent Business, the Canadian Chamber of Commerce, the Canadian Manufac-turers' Association and the hundreds of large Canadian and foreign corporations which donated to these organizations, or who used corporation funds to support the Conservative government's free trade initiatives. . . . Companies such as the Ford Motor Co., the Royal Bank, Inco Ltd., Noranda and Alcan, to name just a few, fully intend to expense their dona-tions and expenditures as business expenses qualifying for full tax deductions. Some companies such as Shell Oil and the Royal Bank provided at least $250,000 each to support the Alliance.

The press release was very embarrassing for the government. My objective was to make certain that big-business donations would not be regarded as a deductible expense. I had fully expected to pay tax on my own donations. However, the exercise backfired when, obvi-ously under pressure from big business, Revenue Canada reversed their earlier ruling and declared our donations deductible. From now on there would be no doubt that "third party" electoral intervention would be legal, unlimited, and mostly undisclosed.

Just as Marcel Masse tried but failed to do something significant to increase the Canadian presence in the book industry in our own country, Flora MacDonald, Masse's successor as communications min-ister, failed in her attempts to introduce film-distribution legislation. Again, Allan Gotlieb, whom Garth Drabinsky described as very close to U.S. film-industry boss Jack Valenti, was a factor. By the summer of 1988, the legislation that was finally presented was a pale shadow of the original draft bill. It died on the order paper. Flora MacDonald was subsequently defeated in the 1988 election.

Early in June the House of Commons was in an uproar after it was learned that the Mulroney government had thrown another $10-million into promotion of free trade, over and above the $15-million it had already spent. There was, after all, an election on the horizon. The Conservatives' polling showed that the FTA was very likely to be the number-one issue in the campaign. Why not spend even more taxpayers' money selling the agreement? And with good reason; by June, the polls had finally turned in our favour. A Globe-Environics poll showed forty percent opposed and thirty-eight percent in favour, with twenty-two percent strongly opposed and ten percent strongly in favour. Also, by June, despite many previous forecasts by pundits that an election would not be held until 1989, it became clearer every day that the Mulroney government was preparing for a fall election. For us, the key would be the defeat of the Mulroney government or Mulroney's being left with a minority government, in which case the FTA would be dead.

In the House of Commons the brief five-day debate about the FTA was hopelessly inadequate. The inside information was that the government was doing whatever it could to curtail national debate and keep the free-trade issue from dominating the federal election. Incredibly, the Commons External Affairs committee completed its hearings into the agreement *before* the final text was available for scrutiny. Neither commitee members nor nongovernment witnesses were aware of a multitude of key provisions in the agreement. Moreover, the Conservative-dominated committee refused to hold hearings across the country.

Despite all of this, the committee managed to produce one good and strong recommendation for the government: Canada should withdraw from the agreement if Canada was not exempted from the provisions of the forthcoming U.S. congressional trade bill, or if the U.S. violated the standstill agreement. Subsequently Canada was not exempted and the U.S. did indeed violate the agreed-to standstill provisions, but the Mulroney government ignored both the advice of the committee and the American actions.

We now knew that no matter what was revealed about the actual contents of the agreement, no matter what the polls said, there would not be one single change in the agreement, and the government was definitely headed for an election, likely in October.

For the COC, it was a time to redouble our efforts. From July to the election I was on the road almost every week.

After the Tories limited debate on the 120-page agreement (with its 1,150 pages of additional data and schedules), I was reminded of British Prime Minister "Sunny Jim" Callaghan's famous line: "This must be the first time in recorded history that the turkeys have voted for an early Christmas."

Some idea of the mentality that prevailed in the Conservative government during the free-trade debate and before the election call may be found in an August letter from Mississauga MP Don Blenkarn. He was responding to a letter a worried Calgary family had written to the prime minister:

> I have your letter of August 3 to Brian Mulroney.
>
> I do not know what you have been smoking or what you have been reading or what anti-American nonsense has been put together for you but the American economy is bustling like ours is. Indeed optimism has never been greater and Canada and the United States are both growing at frankly phenomenal rates.
>
> What could be better, particularly for Western Canada? I think you ought to take another look at the situation and get aboard with reality.

Over the next five years Canada's "frankly phenomenal" growth rate would be the lowest of any five-year period since the Great Depression.

On October 4 we had a large rally in Edmonton attended by some 2,500 people. Bob White, Pierre Berton, Frank Stronach, and I were among the speakers, as were three prominent Albertans. The next day Alberta premier Don Getty complained to the press about "jokers from the East racing out to the West" to influence public opinion about the FTA. The same day it was revealed that the growth of U.S. ownership and control of corporate assets in Canada had grown by record amounts during the past two years.

The election was called for November 21. Early in the campaign Margaret Atwood and Adrienne Clarkson volunteered to raise $100,000 to help the Pro-Canada Network produce two million copies of the Rick Salutin–Terry Mosher cartoon book *What's the Big Deal?*, which was distributed across the country. Soon after it was sent out, the polls tipped dramatically against the FTA. The Alliance responded with a four-page counterattack in newspapers across the country, but with limited impact.

The twenty-four-page book was brilliant and highly effective.

Mosher (Aislin) donated the superb cartoons and Salutin's easy-to-understand text covered almost all key aspects of the agreement. Without question, free trade was the number-one issue in the election campaign and, in the words of Christopher Waddell of the *Globe*, "the public craves more information about the deal and how it will affect families, jobs, and communities . . . the pamphlet has had a major impact on voter impressions." Not only was the COC instrumental in founding the Pro-Canada Network, it provided the organization with close to $100,000 in financial support, including $40,000 for the cartoon book.

More Money for Daycare!

JUST PRIOR TO the election the Alliance spent another $1.5-million for a four-page supplement that appeared in thirty-five Canadian newspapers. When I again challenged them to reveal their funders, the reply was "We are not releasing this during the election because the situation is so volatile. . . . We are a non-partisan group and the names could be misused." The supplement, *Straight Talk on Free Trade*, tried to answer objections that the COC and others had raised:

> [The FTA] does not affect our sovereignty. It does not harm our social programs. It does not threaten our environment, our fresh water, our energy resources or our farmers.
>
> Getting rid of these tariffs means . . . more and better jobs.
>
> Canada is not and will not become a colony of the United States.
>
> Existing energy and transportation policies are protected and culture is exempted. . . .
>
> Clear trading rules and access to our largest trading partner will encourage employers to invest in Canada with confidence and create new jobs.
>
> Better access to the U.S. market means more opportunity to sell throughout the world and that means more jobs. More jobs, better jobs. More wealth to improve government services such as day-care. You'll find that the average food bill for a family of four will go down by $100 a year.

The U.S. has gained no rights to Canada's resources. . . .
We've retained our dairy and poultry marketing boards.
We can continue subsidies as we wish. . . .

The deceit of the Alliance was not unlike that of Brian Mulroney's. When he contested the leadership of the Conservative party, he promised full disclosure of the contributions to his campaign. Instead, he was the only Conservative leadership candidate who failed to do so. Without question, foreign and foreign-controlled corporations were major donors. In the 1988 "free trade election," Iron Ore alone contributed $100,000 to the Tory coffers.

The Alliance had earlier promised that once the text of the agreement was made public in December of 1987, they would release the complete list of their campaign donors. They repeatedly failed to do so, despite frequent prods and challenges. On November 1, 1988, I issued a press release saying: "Peter Lougheed owes the people of Canada an explanation as to how much of his financial backing comes from the big U.S. multinational corporations and who they are. He should release the full list of donors to the Alliance so the public can see who is really behind this campaign to sell the country."

A major theme of the Alliance was that there would be no big-business pressure to reduce social programs. Those of us who claimed otherwise were called "liars" or "fear-mongers." Yet the Canadian Manufacturers' Association had already made it clear that the FTA would make deep cuts in social spending urgent. Old age security, income supplements, unemployment insurance, family allowance, and other social programs would have to be cut by billions of dollars.

Maude Barlow ran for the Liberal nomination in Ottawa-Centre against thirty-four-year-old alderman Mac Harb. The incumbent was the NDP finance critic, Michael Cassidy, who had won the riding by only fifty-four votes in the previous election. But the polls now showed that the Liberals were well ahead. Maude had already won the Liberal nomination in 1987, but redistribution made another nominating meeting necessary. The nominating meeting ended with bitter accusations and animosity, with Harb the victor.

After she failed to win the nomination, I had a long talk with Maude about her future. She was a consultant in the design and implementation of affirmative-action programs for women and minorities, and had been the director of the Office of Equal Opportunity for Women for the City of Ottawa when I first met her in 1983 and senior adviser on women's issues to Pierre Trudeau. Much to my delight, she agreed to run for the position of chairperson at the upcoming fourth annual general meeting of the COC in October, where she was elected by acclamation.

Maude, as might be expected, came under heavy fire from the business press. She handled criticism gracefully: "I no longer care whether people like me or not. . . . My mother told me that serious people have serious enemies."

Also just prior to the election Duncan Cameron and I wrote in the *Globe* that "the election on November 21 is the most important in our history. If the Conservative Party gains 148 or more seats, the nation will proceed towards integration with the U.S. On the other hand, 147 or fewer Tory seats will mean Canada sets forth on a totally different course, with infinitely greater freedom and opportunity in the future."

Two weeks before the election, support for the FTA had dropped dramatically across the country. Gallup now showed fifty percent opposed and only twenty-six percent in favour. Environics showed twice as many strongly opposed as strongly in favour. In every region of the country those opposed far exceeded those in favour. I had been pushing both Tony Clarke, Pro-Canada chairperson, and Maude to organize a strategic voting campaign, supporting Liberal or NDP anti-free-trade candidates wherever they had a good chance of winning. But on November 8 Tony Clarke issued a memorandum against this approach: "Obviously, the dramatic shifts in the polls . . . have reduced the necessity for such a strategy." He added that the COC did not "intend to proceed with its plans of endorsing candidates in specific ridings. . . ."

It was a mistake. But the reason the Network would not get involved in a strategic voting campaign had much less to do with the polls than the fact that trade unions were major financers of the Network; any idea of urging people to support any Liberal candidates was totally out of the question.

On November 21, 1988, Brian Mulroney and the Progressive Conservatives won forty-three percent of the votes, and 169 of the 295 seats in the House of Commons. Put another way, fifty-seven percent of Canadians voted against Brian Mulroney and the Conservatives, but the Tories won fifty-seven percent of the seats. Anti-free-trade parties took over fifty-five percent of the votes in Ontario, Atlantic Canada, Manitoba, Saskatchewan, British Columbia, and the territories. Only in Alberta and Quebec did the Conservatives win a majority of votes. In more than seventy percent of the constituencies, the combined Liberal and NDP vote exceeded the Conservative vote. But as I've said before, such statistics are for losers.

John Turner had done a superb job in the leaders' television debate, but the Conservative backroom boys had decided to launch a vicious personal attack on the Liberal leader. Much to great consternation from both within and without their party, the NDP had also focused on attacking Turner instead of Mulroney and the Free Trade Agreement. As John Turner told me in a personal interview, "It was the most massive advertising campaign in any two-week period in the history of Canadian politics — or probably any politics: It was negative and it was vicious. It had worked in the U.S. in the Bush-Dukakis campaign and now the strategy was to bomb the bridges, and the main bridge was John Turner. The Chrétien aspect and the so-called 'caucus revolt' didn't help, but the dirty Alliance and Conservative campaign were the main factors." And so, in the last two weeks of the election campaign, the polls turned enough to give Mulroney and the Conservatives another majority government.

My own guess is that the pro-free-trade side spent some $45-million to the anti-free-trade's $4-million. Nevertheless, most public-opinion polls showed support for free trade sharply declining prior to the election. But the only poll that really counted was on election day. According to Brian Mulroney, the Canadian voters "have stated with a clear sense of their identity what they want to be and what they want to do . . . the margin is decisive and the mandate is clear."

There was no such clear mandate. Some 1.25 million more Canadians voted for the Liberals and NDP — both committed to abrogating the FTA — than voted for the Conservatives. Election-day exit polls showed that for those who voted *on the basis of the Free Trade Agreement*, fifty-nine percent had voted for the Liberals and NDP, and only forty percent had voted Conservative. As well, in a national poll conducted by Gallup immediately after the election, sixty percent of those surveyed said there should be a referendum on the agreement before it was implemented, and only thirty-one percent said a referendum was unnecessary. For those pro-free-trade supporters who claimed that the election *was* a referendum on the trade agreement, the voters' intentions cited above mean that if indeed the sole election issue was free trade and the seats were to be calculated accordingly, the Conservatives would have won only ninety seats, and the parties opposed to the FTA would have won 185 seats, with seventeen seats unclear.

There is no doubt that on November 21, 1988, Canada stood at the crossroads of its destiny. Had there been in place a system of proportional representation of the kind that exists in most developed nations, had there been a very well-organized strategic voting campaign, or had there been a referendum on the Free Trade Agreement, it is most likely it would have been rejected. I believe that the two most important days in Canadian history are July 1, 1867, and November 21, 1988.

Just before Christmas I goaded d'Aquino one more time. In a letter to the *Winnipeg Free Press*, he replied: "I look forward to reading a public retraction from Mr. Hurtig when the list of donors is made public early next year." Now, eight years later, we are still waiting for the list.

Brian Understands

I N 1992 THE Mulroney government spent millions of dollars distributing an eight-page "Agenda for Prosperity" brochure across the nation. It was full of remarkably misleading statements, for example, "Canadians have said: cut the deficit. There is now solid progress: the deficit is down." In fact, in 1992 the budgetary deficit was the second highest in Canadian history, and in 1993 it broke all previous records.

When Brian Mulroney became prime minister in 1984, the federal debt was some $170-billion. When he resigned in 1993, it was $466-billion. The year Mulroney was elected, Canada's international investment accumulated deficit was $110-billion. The year he left office, it was over $268-billion. The inability of the Department of Finance to provide proper forecasts for economic planning became a tragic joke.

Not long after the 1988 election, Mulroney's popularity began to decline again. This time it would hit rock bottom. By the spring of 1993 his popularity had plunged to a record low of twelve percent. For the first time in history a prime minister's interest rates were higher than his popularity in the opinion polls.

There can be no doubt about Brian Mulroney's greatest accomplishment during his eight and a half years as prime minister: the Americanization of Canada and the integration of our country with the United States. The relationship between Ronald Reagan and Brian Mulroney was infinitely closer than any previous interaction between an American president and a Canadian prime minister. When his advisers suggested that Reagan take an aggressive position in a dispute with Canada, the president would reply: "Brian understands. I don't have to bring this matter up with him. Brian understands."

Reagan understood, too. Whatever the U.S. really wanted, the U.S. would get. Perhaps some token or cosmetic concessions might be made so that Mulroney could boast of a victory, a "face-saving" dispute-settlement mechanism, for example, but overall the Gipper had no concerns about where Mulroney kneeled. Reagan was a great believer in manifest destiny, which would allow the U.S. "to over-spread the continent." His good friend Brian was eager to cooperate in his idea of "a developing closeness."

If Brian Mulroney was close to Reagan, he was closer still to his successor, George Bush. He was a sycophant to both U.S. presidents. Mulroney had Canada join the Organization of American States, something Canadian prime ministers before him had opposed because of the U.S. domination of the organization. He supported the U.S. invasions of tiny Grenada and Panama while all other OAS nations opposed the U.S. actions. Canada's former ambassador for disarmament to the United Nations, the Conservative Doug Roche, said that "in the security field and defence matters, it was abundantly clear that the influence of the United States was dominant in Canadian decision-making." Because of pressure from the U.S., the Mulroney government tested cruise missiles, softened its call for a nuclear-test ban, and sided with the U.S. in opposition to the United Nations in matters relating to the Gulf War.

While Pierre Trudeau had been aware of and resisted the dangers of excessive decentralization, Brian Mulroney plunged ahead. For Mulroney, Canada's social programs were "a sacred trust" — until, that is, he started to dismantle them. He brought Quebec separatists — notably Lucien Bouchard — into his government and cabinet strictly for reasons of political expediency, and somehow expected them to remain loyal to Canada. Overall, his basic political philosophy was laissez-faire, the belief that left alone, individuals and business working in their own best interests will collectively produce results that will inevitably benefit the nation. But what if all the key decisions, the money, and the real power are held in a relatively few hands and with many of the owners of those hands resident in other countries?

Mulroney managed one other great accomplishment, aside from binding the nation securely into the American net. Almost single-handedly, he turned millions of Canadians against politics and politicians. Yes, there had been many scoundrels before in all the political parties, but Mulroney so debased politics that most Canadians would now choke on John Buchan's statement that "politics is still the greatest and most honourable adventure."

Turner: A Different View

I N THE SEPTEMBER 1984 federal election, the Liberals were wiped out, falling from 146 seats all the way down to forty seats and only twenty-eight percent of the vote. Brian Mulroney had won the biggest election victory in the history of Canada. Soon after, John Turner faced division in his party, internal battles without end, betrayals, and revolt from even within his own caucus. The Liberals were deep in debt, dispirited, and disorganized.

From the time I had first become involved in the Liberal party, I had found myself on the opposite side of John Turner on most key issues. For me, the man who in 1979 had sat on nine corporation boards, represented Bay Street, the right wing, and the continentalist wing of the Liberal party. Moreover, Turner's deputy finance minister during the early Trudeau years had been none other than Simon Reisman, and a close Turner associate was U.S. Secretary of State George Shultz. Turner became prime minister on June 30, 1984, after defeating Jean Chrétien in the contest for the Liberal leadership. An ill-advised federal election call saw the Liberals fall to Mulroney's Conservatives the following September.

In the summer of 1986 I wrote to Turner expressing the concern of the Council of Canadians about what seemed to us to be a weak Liberal position on the proposed free-trade agreement. A few days later Turner replied, taking his strongest position to date:

> I have emphasized our belief that a discussion of trade issues almost exclusively in terms of a bilateral relationship between Canada and the United States is ill-advised.
>
> Like you, we are concerned over the manner in which

Mr. Mulroney is pursuing this initiative. Our dismay over his secretiveness regarding these negotiations has been both public and vocal.

Our immediate but not sole concern is the possible effectson employment and our national sovereignty.

A few days later in a televised address Turner made an even stronger statement about his position and the position of the Liberal party: "Canadians do not know where Mr. Mulroney really stands. Sometimes he talks about free trade; then freer trade; then enhancing trade; and recently in Toronto, trade arrangements, industry by industry. We don't know where he stands, and the country does not know where he stands. Is free trade just another slogan like 'sacred trust'? Has the Prime Minister really thought it through?"

By February 1987, the Liberals were sending out fundraising letters across the country headed "Canada is not for sale!" We began putting even more pressure on John Turner to speak out forcefully and often on the issue of Canadian sovereignty. The Liberal party and the caucus were badly divided on the issues of both free trade and foreign ownership. As for Turner, Jeffrey Simpson described his performance in the *Globe*: "Perhaps inspired by last week's figure-skating championships, Liberal leader John Turner yesterday attempted to explain his party's position on trade with the United States. Mr. Turner skated all over the place, twisting and turning, spinning and jumping and acting for all the world like a man trying to blend two quite different pieces of choreography into a coherent whole."

But by the fall of 1987, after the actual agreement had become public, there was no doubt about Turner's position. Through the balance of the year and throughout the spring and early summer of 1988, Turner attacked the FTA in no uncertain terms. More and more he had become convinced that the "trade deal [would] fundamentally alter Canadian life." In a remarkable gamble, on July 20 he ordered the Liberal-dominated Senate to block the FTA legislation until an election was held. Speaking on July 20, Turner said:

What is at issue is that this agreement fundamentally alters the way we live and the way we are governed in this country. It will decrease our ability as an independent nation to make our own choices in terms of our economic policies, our social and regional development policies, our foreign investment policy, and our ability to pursue an independent foreign policy.

It puts at risk our ability to use our own resources to build our own future. It threatens the future of the family farm and the livelihood of our fishermen. It circumscribes our ability to pursue cultural initiatives.

It eliminates large areas of activity from future policy-making and forces everyone in Ottawa to ask before they make a decision: what will Washington say?

In the late summer of 1988 I distributed a paper showing that, since 1985, ninety-six percent of foreign investment in Canada — mostly American — had been in the form of takeovers of Canadian businesses, and only a paltry four percent had been for new business investment. John Turner was appalled. In a letter to me he wrote: "Yet Mulroney wants to further relax the review process for American takeovers! Clearly, his foreign investment policies stand alongside the trade deal as a second chapter in the Sale of Canada Act!"

What a remarkable transition! Did any of these statements for a moment sound like the words of a big-business, continentalist, right-wing Bay Street lawyer? Hardly!

During the 1988 televised leaders' election debate, there was a memorable moment when Turner pointed to Mulroney and said: "I happen to believe that you've sold us out. Once the economic levers go, the political independence is sure to follow." Immediately after the debate, Turner and the Liberals led the polls, but the lead was shortlived.

Lloyd Axworthy did not hesitate to take credit for John Turner's conversion. "We made a deal — I would go with him on Meech Lake and in exchange he would go with me on free trade," he told me. After I prodded him some more, Axworthy sounded embarrassed, but said it was a very good tradeoff. But Axworthy also told another story. After Turner had returned from a long meeting with senior corporate executives, he was seething with rage. He told Axworthy that "those guys simply don't care any more about Canada . . . they just don't give a damn!"

In a recent telephone conversation with Turner I asked him to define for me *why* he had taken such a strong stand against the FTA. He replied:

I was always for multilateral free trade, for the GATT . . .
tariffs were down anyway, and we always did better in multilateral negotiations. We had a much better chance that way
of playing off the Americans against the Japanese, or the
Europeans. . . . We were in a much better bargaining position.
And I was always suspicious of bilateral deals when the U.S.
is ten times stronger, had ten times the population.

When I was in Finance, we knew that the exchange rate
was a helluva lot more important than the remaining tariffs.
When I saw what Mulroney was negotiating, I said no way!
The U.S. Congress didn't yield any jurisdiction over trade at
all, none. What we got was no free trade agreement.
Congress could still take unilateral action.

Despite all their bragging, it's been the seventy-cent
Canadian dollar that boosted exports.

I asked him about the impact of his stand regarding free trade on him
personally and on his career. "For quite a while it was very costly,"
he replied, "a tough time. Part of my normal legal and business milieu
was not open to me. During the overplayed 'caucus revolt,' the
Conservatives moved in and did everything they could to promote
disunity. Allan Gregg suggested they needed to 'bomb the bridges'
after they fell behind in the polls after the televised debates. Well, the
bridge was John Turner and the bombs were *ad hominum* attacks."

There was one key reason John Turner so vigorously opposed
the FTA: he read it. And he read it with a lawyer's eye, studied its
substantive implications, examined the agreement in a systematic
manner, and found it would put his country's survival in great jeopardy. Turner called his battle against the FTA "the fight of my life."

In May 1989 he announced he would be resigning as Liberal
leader. The day before he left Ottawa, Maude Barlow and I had a
long lunch with him at Stornaway. As usual, he was his old jock self,
joking, swearing, somewhat uptight, clearing his throat often,
friendly, but tough-guy brusque. However, after a glass of wine before
lunch, he became relaxed, casual, and natural; I found him likable,
sincere, emotional in the depth of feeling for his country. He now
minimizes the damage his opposition to the FTA brought to his
career, but it was greater than he will ever admit. Many doors were
no longer open to him; many clients were no longer there. For a man

whose milieu was Bay Street, his actions had been very courageous. He deserves a great deal of respect for standing up for his country and for his principles. If only the man who was to succeed him as Liberal leader had a fraction of his courage and backbone.

A Delicious Moment and a Monstrous Swindle

IN JUNE 1990 the Liberals were to elect a new leader to replace John Turner. The party was still deeply divided on many issues, including free trade. Much to my surprise I was invited to give the keynote address to the first leadership forum leading up to the leadership convention. I had been increasingly critical of the party for years. In one speech I had said: "The truth is that in power, in office, despite all the abundant rhetoric, there now is no real important difference between the Liberal and Conservative parties; they are both the parties of big business and this has meant in the past and will continue to mean the sellout of our country."

So, given the strong criticism of the party I had been dishing out for many years, what did they expect of me? More important, what could I hope to accomplish? I called John Turner and asked for his advice. This is what he had to say: "Be tough. Flush them out. Smoke them out. You know what to do. Tell them that there is a duty, a sacred duty, on the part of all the convention delegates to cross-examine the leadership candidates."

I then called my old friend Keith Davey and asked his advice. I am very fond of Keith; his love of Canada, of politics, his love of people and baseball, and his eternal good humour and optimism make him very good company. However, this time he offered advice I didn't follow: "Whatever you do, don't be too controversial. Don't be too contentious. Don't rock the boat — there's nothing to be gained. Be conservative."

"Pardon?" I said.

When I began my speech I told the large crowd of delegates about the two conversations: "I've brought both speeches today. Which would you like to hear?" There wasn't much doubt. The speech I gave that day at the Royal York Hotel in Toronto was one of the strongest attacks I have ever made on the Liberal establishment and at the same time one of the best received talks I've ever given. I was constantly interrupted by applause from beginning to end, and much to the consternation of the leadership candidates present, there were many shouts of "Hurtig for Prime Minister!"

I said that I believed Mulroney was the worst prime minister in our history. I challenged the Liberal party to elect a strong new leader who would preserve the dreams of the founders of our nation and of millions of Canadians who wanted an independent Canada. I asked how much more foreign ownership they were prepared to accept. "Was it all right to allow nonresidents to take over high-tech companies such as Connaught and Lumonics and Leigh Instruments? Do you think the French and the Japanese and Americans would have allowed *their* vaccine and laser and defence companies to be acquired by foreign owners? Was it all right to sell resource companies such as Consolidated Bathurst and Bow Valley?" I told them they must ask the candidates *where* they would draw the line. And *how* they would draw the line.

Next I asked the delegates to question the leadership candidates about energy policy and in particular the mandatory, unparalleled resource sharing and pricing provisions of the FTA. And to press the candidates on their promises to renegotiate the FTA, and on where they stood on Canada's social programs, on universality, on medicare. What are the candidates' reactions to the growing threat to Canada's social programs?

I told them to ask their candidate what he or she had to say about supply management and marketing boards. About monetary policy and the growing federal debt. About what he or she would do about the badly needed changes in the way democracy functions in Canada: the buying of elections. And about reforming the Liberal party itself. "In the future, full disclosure of *all* contributions. More stringent rules on spending in leadership campaigns. Why not start *now*, by asking the candidates to voluntarily disclose all the sources and amounts of their own campaign funds — *before* the leadership convention in June?" I looked at Jean Chrétien when I said this and he averted his eyes.

I urged the delegates to ask the candidates if they approved of the massive increase in personal income taxes and the decrease in corporate taxes in Canada so that now the net corporate income-tax contribution, after government subsidies, came to only three percent of government expenditures. Did they approve of the escalating levels of corporate concentration in Canada? And what would they do about the oligopolistic, burgeoning banks' continuing to fund the foreign takeover of Canada, while making it increasingly difficult for small and medium-size Canadian business to borrow their working-capital requirements? Did the candidates approve of Canadian savings funding the sellout of our country, while the only real job creators, small Canadian-owned companies, were hard pressed to maintain their financing? And if they didn't approve, exactly what did they plan to do about it?

And what would the candidates do about the growing numbers of Canadian men, women, and children living in poverty?

I had a host of other tough questions. But I ended my speech this way: "Tomorrow morning you begin the public process of choosing a prime minister. I hope you will ask some of the questions I have suggested today and I hope you will not accept vague, disingenuous answers. You have a wonderful opportunity. I hope you will make the most of it."

My speech received a long standing ovation. Many of the delegates crowded around afterwards offering their help in any way I wished.

Jean Chrétien and his wife, Aline, had sat in the front row throughout my talk. He looked unhappy most of the time, but especially when I mentioned the sale of Consolidated Bathurst to the U.S. Chrétien had been on the board of the company at the time, and his father had been a long-term employee there. When I finished my talk, Chrétien immediately left the room.

Soon after, both Chrétien and Paul Martin were cornered by the press. Both promised solemnly that when they were elected prime minister, they would renegotiate the Free Trade Agreement, and if the Americans refused to negotiate, they would abrogate it.

After the speech Pierre Trudeau wrote to me that he had "very much enjoyed reading it . . . very good advice!" For Trudeau, there was little doubt that the FTA was a "monstrous swindle, under which the Canadian government has ceded to the United States of America a large slice of the country's sovereignty over its economy and natural resources in exchange for advantages we already had, or were going to obtain in a few years anyway through the normal operations of the GATT."

The Little Guy from Power Corp.

MANY YEARS AGO Hugh MacLennan wrote to me quoting from Montaigne: "Good does not necessarily follow on the removal of a particular evil. Another evil may ensue upon it and a worse one." Unlike some nationalists, I did not for a moment believe that Jean Chrétien was other than a committed conservative continentalist. He was, after all, Mitchell Sharp's protégé, and Sharp had been Walter Gordon's nemesis. In an interview with *Maclean's* in 1976 Chrétien had no hesitation in saying, "I've never been the greatest nationalist kind of guy." When he became minister of industry, trade and commerce in 1976, he described foreign direct investment as "an essential condition of continued economic progress." The very high level of foreign ownership and control of the Canadian economy represented "no particular concern" to him, despite the fact that the preamble of the Liberals' own Foreign Investment Review Act said that the degree of foreign control of the Canadian economy is "a matter of national concern." But not for the minister in charge of FIRA! In a speech in Saskatoon in 1976 Chrétien told his audience that "foreign investment represents a vote of confidence in Canada" and in his autobiography, *Straight from the Heart*, he describes it as "a good thing."

Chrétien has many political strengths, but his grasp of economics has always left much to be desired. When Trudeau unexpectedly announced a $2-billion cut in government spending, he thought it quite unnecessary to either consult with or even inform his own minister of finance, Chrétien. This says as much about Trudeau as it does about Chrétien, but the stories of Chrétien's lack of skills in economic matters are legion.

In the years Chrétien was minister of finance, the deficit averaged almost five percent of GDP, and the federal net public debt to GDP climbed some three percentage points. Overall, his approach to solving the nation's economic problems was not dissimilar to that of John Crow, the governor of the Bank of Canada during the Mulroney years. An article in *Saturday Night* quotes one of Chrétien's former deputy ministers: "Chrétien was a disaster at Finance because he simply didn't have the disciplined approach that economic policy-making requires, or the patience to plod through piles of information."

In April 1993, attacking the Mulroney government, Chrétien said that the six percent bank prime lending rate was too high: "We lost control of our monetary policy." But when Chrétien stepped down as finance minister in 1979, the prime rate was more than twelve percent. As the debate over free trade began in Canada, Chrétien clearly opposed it. On the very last page of *Straight from the Heart*, he wrote: "Some people say that the only way for Canada to avoid being hurt by American protectionism is to guarantee Canadian access to the U.S. market by free trade. . . . I feel strongly that we did not build our institutions, our traditions, our history, our national pride, in short, this great country Canada, to become the fifty-first state of America. . . . Whatever our problems, I always conclude my speeches with one plain truth: Canada is best!"

In July 1986 I was asked to speak at the Western Canadian Liberals meeting in Calgary about Brian Mulroney's plans for a free-trade agreement. I ripped into Mulroney and the concept of a bilateral agreement. The Alberta Liberals then voted to oppose Mulroney's free-trade plans. According to the Canadian Press, "The impassioned speech ignited the liveliest debate of the conference." And so it had. British Columbia Senator George Van Roggen told delegates that many Liberals wanted a free-trade agreement with the U.S. He called my speech "an emotional appeal to your baser instincts," which it was, baser instincts such as freedom, the desire by people to have a job, the preservation of national sovereignty, and our social programs.

The next day the headlines read: "Liberals rejecting free trade initiatives." The Calgary conference was the last of four regional conferences prior to the national Liberal convention in Ottawa in November, where free trade was expected to be the most controversial issue on the agenda.

The first time I had a long one-on-one talk with Chrétien was in his office in Ottawa in 1985. My daughter Jane, a Carleton University political science student, sat in the back corner of the room while the two of us talked. After the meeting I asked Jane for her impression. "Dad, he doesn't seem to *believe* in anything," she replied. "Everything seems to be a political compromise with no vision." Among the things Chrétien told me was that I needn't worry too much about the free-trade deal because it would never happen.

After the 1984 election Chrétien's performance in the caucus and in the House was listless and indifferent, and he was unfriendly towards those who had supported Turner. Chrétien resigned his seat in the House of Commons in 1986 and returned to private law practice.

In both 1986 and 1987 there was considerable pressure from inside and outside the Liberal party for a much stronger stance against the Mulroney government's free-trade initiatives. At the same time, the conservative Liberal establishment fought any anti-free-trade position. The party was almost evenly divided on the issue. At the national convention a motion supporting free trade was defeated, and John Turner spoke about good neighbours having high fences.

In 1989 Maude Barlow and I met with Chrétien in his law offices in Ottawa. Chrétien shrugged and described the FTA as "an omelette that can never be unscrambled" and he said that cancelling the deal would be "a monster that would create too many babies." What could be clearer than that? We left our meeting with Chrétien very disappointed.

In December Jim Peterson and a number of other Liberal MPs asked me to give them a presentation about the likely long-term economic impact of the FTA. There was a good group of Liberal MPs present, including Paul Martin, Jr., Herb Gray, Sheila Copps, and a number of Liberal senators. It wasn't long before some of those who had been present talked Chrétien into sitting down for a similar session. Early in 1990 several of Chrétien's closest advisers, including David Collenette and Patrick Lavelle, arranged for me to brief their leadership candidate about the economic, social, and political ramifications of the FTA. They rented a large room on the third floor of the Four Seasons Hotel in Toronto, and I gave them exactly the same slide show and talk I had presented in Ottawa. After it was over, Chrétien had only one question: "Mel, tell me how am I going to explain all this to my friends in business?" I said: "Jean, the problem *is* your friends in business."

While continuing to portray himself as the little guy from Shawinigan, Chrétien had become a very successful, well-to-do member of the Canadian power elite. Despite the populist image he so successfully presented, Chrétien was about to become one of the most conservative leaders in Liberal-party history and one of its most continentalist prime ministers. Chrétien is well linked to the business establishment. His only daughter, France, is married to Paul Desmarais's son André. Chrétien has been a senior lawyer in the prominent Lang, Michener law firm, a director of the Toronto-Dominion Bank, an adviser to Gordon Capital, and a member of the board of Consolidated Bathurst and Viceroy Resources. Yet the image he worked very hard at projecting through self-deprecating humour was of the little guy surrounded by "big shots."

John Rae, Power Corporation vice president, ran Chrétien's 1984 and 1990 leadership campaigns, and was later to run his 1993 federal election campaign. When Chrétien won the Liberal leadership, he spent an enormous $2.45-million; most of the money came from large donations. When I asked John Turner if he agreed with me that the Power Corporation and Paul Desmarais had been financing much of Chrétien's campaign, he said: "Of course. I would like to have flushed that out. Not only Chrétien, but Martin and Mulroney too!"

Jean Chrétien was elected leader of the Liberal party on June 23, 1990. In his campaign for the leadership, despite what he had told Maude Barlow and me in private, in public he repeatedly promised to keep "the good parts" of the FTA and to get rid of "the bad parts."

In April of 1991 Tony Clarke and I and a number of others met with the Mexican opposition leader, Cuauhtémoc Cárdenas, who had been "defeated" by Carlos Salinas de Gortari in Mexico's fraudulent 1988 presidential election. Clarke, Cárdenas, and I then met with Chrétien in his Opposition leader's House of Commons office. Cárdenas was at least as concerned as we were about the George Bush, Brian Mulroney, and Carlos Salinas North American Free Trade Agreement agenda, which he felt would severely harm the average Mexican, while even further consolidating wealth and power in the hands of a small number of Mexican economic aristocrats. During our conversation, I mentioned the severe recession in Canada and the large number of job losses in the goods-producing sector of the Canadian economy. Chrétien immediately dismissed my comments, blaming "the recession," not the FTA, for the job losses. Once again, his private words were clearly different from his public ones.

In February of 1992 Chrétien, speaking about the FTA, told students at Johns Hopkins University that "I want to renegotiate, and we also have the option of abrogation." In a meeting the same day with President Bush, Chrétien supposedly told him the FTA was "losing support in Canada rapidly" and should be renegotiated. According to the Canadian Press in Washington, "Chrétien says a Liberal government might abrogate the deal if the Americans won't renegotiate." One of Chrétien's principal complaints and a leading candidate for renegotiation was the onerous energy provisions of the deal.

The charade continued. The same month, in a letter to a concerned retired gentleman in Edmonton, Chrétien wrote: "I believe our first approach should be to pursue the renegotiation of those provisions of the trade agreement that most adversely affect Canadian independence and integrity." And the next month, somewhat more firmly in the House of Commons: "This trade deal . . . is a disaster for Canadians." In an exchange with Mulroney the next day, he described the FTA as "that crazy deal."

In May I wrote to Chrétien and queried his oft-repeated statement that, in a Liberal government renegotiation of the FTA, they would keep "the good parts" and scrap "the bad parts." But I asked, *why* would the U.S. renegotiate? I continued:

> I have yet to meet an informed observer who believes that the FTA can be successfully renegotiated on terms that would be favourable to Canada. Since you would be dealing with the U.S. Congress, and since the U.S. has already in place an agreement very favourable to American corporations, and since U.S. corporate interests would lobby very hard and very effectively against any deterioration in their position, I cannot understand your rationale for "renegotiation."
>
> What troubles me personally most of all is that I believe that you fully understand that renegotiation will *not* be successful and so do most of your caucus (many of them have told me that already). If this is the case, I cannot for the life of me understand why you and your party would adopt this strategy.

Or maybe I could. Was he intentionally misleading Canadians, knowing full well that a federal election was coming and that the polls showed most Canadians opposed the FTA?

A few days later in a letter to a Montreal member of the Council of Canadians, Chrétien wrote: "The Conservative government's record is littered with broken promises. One of their greatest failings has been the Canada–U.S. Trade Agreement. It is simply not working. . . . We have two choices before us — to abrogate the accord, or try to fix it. . . . If it is not possible to achieve an equitable arrangement for Canada, we would be prepared to abrogate the Trade Agreement." The September 11 issue of the *Globe* carried an article by Chrétien headed: "A deal that leaves Canada a sitting duck":

> The problem with last month's North American Free Trade Agreement (NAFTA) is precisely that it fails to provide the free, fair and open trade this country needs.
>
> The three-way trade talks were an opportunity to correct

major flaws in the U.S. Canadian Free Trade Agreement (FTA). Unfortunately, Prime Minister Brian Mulroney's government mishandled that opportunity.

A common subsidy code was supposed to be negotiated by 1996. Those negotiations never got off the ground; NAFTA buries them completely. In their place, Canada has been thrown a crumb — a trilateral committee will "consider" these issues, with no clear mandate or deadline.

When you add it up, NAFTA does not secure market access for a single Canadian product or provide job security for a single Canadian worker. So much for Canada's top priority.

Over and over again through to the 1993 federal election, in the House of Commons, in speeches and interviews across the country, in letters to concerned Canadians, Chrétien pledged to renegotiate the energy, the investment, the subsidy, the agricultural, and other aspects of the FTA, otherwise "abrogation should not be ruled out."

How much difference is there between Brian Mulroney intentionally misleading Canadians about his plans for a free-trade agreement and Jean Chrétien's lies to the people of Canada about his position on the FTA and NAFTA? If Brian Mulroney and his colleagues betrayed Canada, what, then, can we say about Jean Chrétien? At least Mulroney, after 1987, was reasonably up front about his plans to alter Canada. But Chrétien continued to mislead Canadians right up to election day late in 1993. During the election campaign, everywhere he went Chrétien would hold the Liberal Red Book in the air and invite people to "come to see me with this book" after he became prime minister if the Liberals didn't keep their promises. In May of 1993 Chrétien told the *Toronto Star* that a Liberal government would review the Conservatives' extended patent protection on pharmaceutical products. After all, "We have a moral obligation to keep drug costs down." He also promised new legislation to make it more difficult for foreign firms to take over Canadian corporations with assets greater than $150-million. Look through the famous Red Book and you will find many, many broken promises. But Chrétien's blatant deception regarding the FTA is surely a betrayal of profound proportions.

"Moral obligation?" Many of us had hoped that after Mulroney we would at least have a prime minister who told the truth.

Today Chrétien sounds exactly like Mulroney, Michael Wilson, or Tom d'Aquino; after all, he now says, "You can never gain back your virginity." But you *could* stop selling your honour and your dignity and your citizens' home — or whatever is left of it.

Over the years in his "I love Canada" speeches, Chrétien always talked about Canadians wanting a leader "who had a national vision." The *p'tit gars de Shawinigan* appeared warm and genuine and his message was simple. "Trust me" was his plea, even though the lack of substance in his feel-good talks made one wonder what it was we were supposed to trust. What exactly did he stand for? Now, unfortunately, we have a much better idea.

Jean Chrétien's New Conservatives

IT WOULD BE VERY wrong to assume that Jean Chrétien was the only Liberal to mislead Canadians. In an article in the *Globe and Mail*, headlined "Sovereignty being traded for U.S. markets," Roy MacLaren warned, as the FTA was being negotiated, that "free trade with the United States is not really about free trade. It is really about the gradual loss of sovereignty, a loss of independence . . . the agreement that [the Mulroney government] finally negotiated suggests that Ottawa has decided to concede virtually anything. . . . It's not difficult to imagine that a year or two after a 'free trade' agreement came into force there would begin a gradual erosion of Canadian sovereignty, eventually leading to its elimination."

In the House of Commons in May 1992, almost two years after Chrétien was elected leader, Lloyd Axworthy spoke about NAFTA: "We have certain conditions that would have to be met on energy, on investment, on subsidy codes, on agriculture, and if the Americans do not want to talk, we will use our right to abrogate." He later repeated these remarks to American audiences in New York and Washington. Moreover, he said, "one of the reasons it is essential that the Free Trade Agreement be renegotiated . . . would be to expunge articles 408 and 409 from the FTA, in order to regain control over our natural resources."

Paul Martin made similar promises. But as Jeffrey Simpson of the *Globe* put it, "The Liberal Party renegotiation position is nothing more than window dressing to get the party through the next election." In other words, they intentionally misled the people of Canada; they lied to Canadians.

Under pressure from nationalist critics, Axworthy denied, in *Canadian Forum* in the summer of 1992, that there has been a policy change in the Liberal party. "The fact is that for all the NDP huffing and puffing about how Liberals have changed their position or are selling out to the business elite, we are still opposed to the deal. . . . Perhaps the best proof of this claim is to cite the resolution passed at our recent Policy Convention. It clearly states that we will renegotiate the deal to serve the national interest, and if that isn't possible we will abrogate."

By late summer, the Liberals were circulating *Liberal Talking Points on the NAFTA*. Among them: "Once again the Mulroney government failed to defend Canada at the negotiating table, resulting in a deal . . . which Liberal Leader Jean Chrétien says he cannot support." In the face of intense criticism from many of his former supporters, Axworthy wrote that we should not judge him too harshly since he should be allowed to pursue within his party "the most effective tactics. . . . I need to exercise my judgement on NAFTA. And, as you will note, we have come out against it." And in September, again from Axworthy: "NAFTA is not a blueprint for hemispheric prosperity. It is an extension of the continentalist thinking that seeks to entrench in international agreements a laissez-faire economic system. Canada should neither be party to such an agreement, nor promote its expansion."

Of course the Liberals' promise to renegotiate the FTA was blatant deceit. What new concessions could Canada possibly offer as a quid quo pro for changes that Canada wanted? As Ken MacQueen of Southam News put it, "The Liberal policy o' the week is to renegotiate the deal, once the Americans and Mexicans stop rolling on the floor in hysterical laughter."

The well-planned November 1991 Liberal conference in Alymer, Quebec, was a key turning point in the modern history of the party. The conference was a clear indication of what the country could expect from a Liberal government and a decisive move to the right for Liberalism in Canada. The right wing of the party set the agenda and emerged from the conference firmly in control. As Hugh Winsor of the *Globe* put it, "It is not quite a rout, but the Liberal Party of Canada's thinkers conference this past weekend was certainly a shot across the bow for the economic nationalists and other left-leaning Liberals who have until now felt there was a constituency for their ideas in their party." If thirty years earlier the Kingston conference had been a watershed that helped set the stage for the introduction of medicare, the Canada Pension Plan, and other progressive social programs, Aylmer was a huge step back in time, disguised as "an acceptance of globalization." The Liberal party that had pledged to radically alter the Free Trade Agreement or if necessary abrogate it, now became the Liberal party gung-ho for NAFTA, with none other than Roy MacLaren leading the charge.

At the conference the delegates defeated a resolution from the floor that said the FTA was "compromising our right to self-determination and threatening the survival of Canada as a sovereign state." According to the *Toronto Star*, "Winnipeg MP Lloyd Axworthy, known for his strong Canadian nationalist and anti-free trade views, helped turn the tide by throwing his prestige behind the official (Chrétien-supported) wording. 'I urge you to have faith and confidence that Mr. Chrétien will carry out (his pledge to renegotiate) and if he does we will not have the same free trade agreement that we do now,' Axworthy said."

After the conference Liberal MP Mark Assad called me. He said that he couldn't believe Lloyd Axworthy's performance, that obviously Lloyd stood to gain if he didn't disturb Chrétien, that the 1,400 people at the conference were not truly representative of the grassroots of the Liberal party, and that they were mostly well-to-do members who were charged $750 to attend (not to mention their transportation and other costs).

Soon after the conference Assad stood up in caucus and spoke about how concerned he was about the new direction of the Liberal party. To great applause he suggested that Mel Hurtig and Maude Barlow be invited to speak to the caucus later that month. After the caucus meeting, he began gathering signatures from Liberal MPs and senators on a petition to Jean Chrétien to reinforce the invitation. He was interrupted by the party whip and told that the petition was not necessary; the invitation was *fait accompli* and Hurtig and Barlow would be given two hours with the entire caucus on the morning of January 29. On the morning of January 20 the invitation was withdrawn under direct pressure from Chrétien's office.

Many caucus members were outraged by this decision, but the same forces that had organized the Aylmer conference and planned the rout of the nationalist Liberals were now clearly in control. Heavy pressure was brought to bear on the centre-left nationalists not to demonstrate division during the upcoming Liberal policy conference. Controversial issues would be straddled: "We will renegotiate the trade deal" and "We will amend the GST." For the Liberal party only one thing counted: getting elected. Division in the party would not be tolerated.

While some Liberals and some of my colleagues still thought the upcoming national policy conference represented a chance to turn things around, I was very sceptical. Hugh Winsor summed things up on the eve of the conference:

> Convinced that the party and its leader, Jean Chrétien, have lurched towards the right because they are intimidated by the rhetoric about global economic trends and free-market ideology, a group of Liberal MPs encouraged by nationalists such as Maude Barlow, head of the Council of Canadians, and author Mel Hurtig are determined to toughen the party's position on what they see as the major issues facing the country. . . .
>
> As Mr. Hurtig put it in an interview, "If the Liberal party adopts a right-wing continentalist position, it leaves millions of Canadians with only two choices. Either we join or actively support the NDP in the next election, or we start a brand-new political party."

As I had expected, the nationalist Liberals were no force at all at the convention; they were demolished.

During all of 1991 and much of 1992 I was surprised by the political naïveté I found in some of those I had worked with over the years in relation to the Liberal party. They talked about "putting pressure" on Chrétien and the party to change, about how a great many sitting Liberal MPs would inevitably rebel against the dramatic Liberal move to the right, and about how many Liberals would surely remember that they had been elected in 1988 to fight the Free Trade Agreement.

I approached it from quite a different perspective. I said that if they were behaving this way now in opposition, just imagine how they would perform in office with a majority government. I called it the neo-conservative Liberal Party of Canada. I believed that the Liberal party of Jean Chrétien had become a party that perceived that its need for big dollars from big business prevented it from adopting a nationalist, populist, centre-left agenda. The party was in debt. While the Tories, the NDP, and Reform would all be well financed in the next federal election, the Liberals were uncertain about their own funding. The BCNI held the hammer. So big business would call the shots with the Chrétien Liberals, regardless of what a hundred policy conferences might decide, and regardless of what the mood of the electorate might be.

Once again Keith Davey had asked me to run for the Liberals in the election expected in 1993. In May 1992 I wrote him:

> I cannot run for the Liberals in the next election. Not only do I perceive the Liberal party moving to the right, but I also see the party becoming more continentalist. . . .
>
> Show me a political party that is increasingly dependent on big business for its financing, and I'll show you a political party that will never ever be able to bring about the progressive changes that are going to be necessary if Canada is to survive. . . .
>
> Unfortunately, from everything I can see, the Chrétien government will be a conservative government that won't really do things very much different from the present Mulroney regime, which is despised across the country.

In July 1992 Paul Martin was saying that everyone "says the Americans won't renegotiate the trade agreement. That's garbage." Yet, U.S. President George Bush had already made it clear to Chrétien that the U.S. had no intention whatsoever of any renegotiation.

Also in July Martin and Chaviva Hosek, co-chairs of the Liberal party's national platform committee preparing for the federal election, mailed a two-page "Dear Friend" letter to Liberals across the country. The letter spoke about the need for "investing in people . . . maintaining our social programs . . . the need for well-educated people . . . concern for the less privileged and the youth of our country." And then came this sentence: "We must remind people of the greatness of our party; of our traditional values, which include putting people first; and our belief in an . . . independent Canada."

The Liberals' dishonesty relating to the FTA was plain for all to see at the fall 1992 conference of the Council of Canadians, when former British Columbia premier and NDP MP Dave Barrett made Herb Gray look foolish during a debate. For those of us who understood that Gray was fully aware of the disastrous investment provisions in the FTA and that he had been a leading Liberal opponent of the Mulroney trade initiative, his feeble performance in attempting to explain and defend his party's new position was embarrassing.

Carol Goar of the *Toronto Star* had written about Herb Gray earlier. "Even in the unkind world of federal politics," she said, "it is sad to see a crusader climb off his charger and walk slowly to the side of the battlefield. I asked Gray whether the Liberal party was still the bastion of economic nationalism that it had been a decade ago. There was a long pause before he answered. And his reply, when it came, was barely audible: 'I think so.'"

To NAFTA and Beyond

I continued to help the Council of Canadians and the Pro-Canada Network through 1989 and 1990, but by 1991 I was beginning to have doubts about the effectiveness of the two organizations. Beginning in January 1989, the COC was dedicated to monitoring the impact of the FTA and to doing its best to ensure that the next federal election would again be fought on the issue of the agreement. While we had been battered by Mulroney's reelection in 1988, we were determined to do everything possible to defeat him the next time and to continue our fight for Canadian sovereignty. From my perspective, which was shared by many of my colleagues, time was short.

In April 1991 the Pro-Canada Network decided to change its name. The Canadian Labour Congress, anxious to keep the Quebec unions in the CLC yet aware of the increasingly strong separatist leanings of the major Quebec unions, bowed to pressure. After all, how could the separatist unions possibly continue to support and help fund anything that was pro-Canada? They could, however, compromise on the name Action Canada.

I was disgusted by the Network's buckling under. Moreover, it was becoming clearer every week that the trade-union financial support for the Network gave it a dominant position in much of the key decision-making. I have never been anti-union, but my idea of a democratic, broad-based, patriotic coalition did not include one segment dominating the organization. I saw this controlling influence creating the same sort of problems for the Network as it had for the NDP.

We continued our speeches, forums, research, and publications, doing our best to let the public know of the impact of the FTA. By the fall of 1990, a national public-opinion poll showed that seventy-one percent of Canadians felt that the FTA had been a bad deal for Canada.

And Canada had clearly been hoodwinked in relation to Mexico. As late as June 1989 John Crosbie dismissed the idea of a North

American free-trade agreement. After all, Canada had been promised a privileged position; the Mulroney government had sold the FTA to Canadians on that basis. In September of 1990, *Globe* business columnist Terence Corcoran wrote: "Time for the nationalists to wheel out Maude Barlow, fire up Mel Hurtig, and stoke Bob White's engines. If they don't move fast, the free-traders will have expanded the Canada-U.S. free-trade agreement . . . into a continental agreement with Mexico."

Having promised Canadians that in the FTA they were getting an exclusive deal providing unimpeded access to the American market unavailable to others, the Mulroney government now faced the likelihood that the U.S. and Mexico would make a similar deal that would inevitably transfer production away from Canada. The Mulroney government had no choice but to join the negotiations, negotiations in which Canadians had little room for bargaining and little impact.

To soften the blow, Michael Wilson and colleagues spent another $16-million of taxpayers' money in a propaganda campaign to convince Canadians that NAFTA, which would supersede the FTA, was in their best interests.

In my speech to the COC's fifth annual general meeting in October I said it was important that the Liberal party and the NDP clarify their positions on free trade. We were tired of Jean Chrétien's obfuscations and his protracted attempts prior to the election to balance on a policy tightrope designed to please the right wingers and continentalists in the Liberal party and their big-business supporters, while at the same time recognizing the results of public-opinion polls.

Suddenly all across Canada and the United States, the press was full of stories praising Mexican President Carlos Salinas and "the progressive economic and democratic changes he was bringing to Mexico." Only rarely did the true picture emerge: real wages in Mexico had plummeted for nine years in a row; more than thirty percent of the population lived in terrible poverty; wealth was rapidly accumulating in the hands of the already-wealthy few, while the rest of the population was sinking in a corrupt morass controlled by a small elite. Brian Mulroney presented Carlos Salinas to Canadians as a great democratic leader. Mexico was painted as a model for Third World nations. In reality, the Mexican government was a dishonest, violent autocracy, and the country was on the verge of financial catastrophe. In the Mexico of Carlos Salinas, the real minimum wage had declined by more than a third, and the average industrial wage was $1.75 an hour.

In the Maquiladoras, the situation was even worse. Someone sent me a pay stub from Packard Electric (a division of General Motors), a manufacturing plant operating in Juarez, Mexico. The hourly wage for a forty-four-hour workweek was sixty-nine cents.

By the time of the COC's fifth convention, membership had jumped to 16,000. Maude Barlow and her board were doing a good job of criticizing the Mulroney government, alerting Canadians to the impact of the FTA, and of building the organization. Paul Martin, Jr., Lorne Nystrom, Deborah Coyne, Tom Kent, and Tom Axworthy were among the convention speakers.

The title of my speech was "1970-1990. Twenty Years of Canadian Nationalism, Success or Failure?" I said I had never been very happy with the name of the Committee for an Independent Canada. We didn't really want to be independent, but rather, we wanted the country to be able to make our own important economic, social, cultural, defence, and foreign policy decisions, instead of having them made for us in Washington and New York.

We Canadians wanted to go out into the world community as a sovereign nation, prepared to play a larger role as a respected peace-maker and mediator, and as an important economic power, instead of as a satellite of another country — as we were increasingly perceived to be for very good reasons.

I reminded my audience that the Liberals had been in power for seven years when the CIC was formed and, of course, had been in power for most of the years since the end of the Second World War, a period during which the foreign ownership and control of Canada had grown rapidly. I also reminded them that while the Liberals of the early 1970s had become nationalists, then later continentalists, then briefly nationalists again in 1980, by the end of the Trudeau years the party had again swung back to continentalism.

Moreover, many of the Liberals' nationalist policies were poorly conceived and implemented with less than enthusiasm, poorly explained, and weakly defended when attacked. The National Energy Program was very poorly thought out, never once discussed in cabinet before implementation, was highly discriminatory, and had severely alienated Western Canada. In the end the NEP did much more harm than good, producing a huge backlash against nationalism in Canada and becoming an important factor in the 1984 Mulroney sweep.

In my speech I predicted that in the next election we were likely to see the election of thirty to forty Reform MPs and thirty to forty

Bloc Québécois. As for the NDP, would they again disappoint us the way Ed Broadbent had disappointed us in 1988?

I said that the Council of Canadians and the Pro-Canada Network must now focus on the next federal election. Criticizing government policies wasn't enough. Nor was offering well-thought-out policy alternatives. Unless voters had a clear political alternative to allow them to vote for a sovereign Canada, all our efforts would likely once again be in vain. At the very minimum, the COC should immediately begin planning an effective strategic voting campaign, although the difficulties of doing so would be immense. And what if the Liberals and the NDP did not spell out and pledge policies that would save the country? "We will then have no alternative," I said, "but to try to become the alternative ourselves." I ended my hour-long talk by saying that "the idea of Canada is too important to abandon without a fight. As was the case with reciprocity, Laurier was wrong. Let's ensure that it will be the *twenty-first century* that belongs to Canada!"

Alas, almost nothing happened. For the most part for the COC it was business as usual. Very little was done to prepare for the next election for almost two years.

In June 1991 I wrote to Maude Barlow about an issue I have always thought important, an issue I would raise in my forthcoming book *The Betrayal of Canada*. I told her:

> I'm going to be attacking the C.D. Howe Institute and the Fraser Institute and others for not disclosing the source of their financing. Also included will be the National Planning Association and the Canadian-American Committee. Also, in my chapter on election reform, I am going to call for much more stringent rules about political contributions and their sources and full disclosure.
>
> My own feeling is that the COC should . . . change [its] policies so that we do not accept any donations that cannot be disclosed publicly. The more I look at the democratic system, the more I realize how undemocratic it really is. We should be setting an example for the country.

By September of that year, I was becoming increasingly concerned about the failure to begin adequate preparations for the next election. I wrote to Barlow and Tony Clarke:

Yes, Mexico is vitally important. Yes, the Constitution and Quebec are vitally important. But nothing is more important than the next federal election. As I've said many times before, winning all the battles and winning the debates and winning public opinion isn't worth a damn if we lose the big one — the election.

I think we need to decide very early whether we can become involved in strategic voting and if so how. If we can't become involved . . . what are the alternatives? . . .

In sum, we have great people and we have great ideas and we have great energy and we care about our country. We must learn to translate all of this into direct political action. If we don't we'll lose the country.

If there was going to be a strategic voting campaign, we would have to raise a great deal of money to do advance polling and to communicate with the electorate. We would probably have to zero in on forty or fifty key ridings where we likely could be effective. The objective would be a minority government. Such a campaign would be expensive, difficult, and quite impossible to guarantee. But what were the alternatives? There were dozens of reasons why we could fail, but I heard no other suggestions that made much sense.

In December 1991 the Action Canada Network's paper on constitutional development spelled out certain principles adopted at the ACN's November/December general assembly. The paper called for "constitutional change based on the existence of three national entities. . . . A new political relationship needs to be negotiated between these three national entities. . . . The failure to recognize Quebec's status as a nation, not simply a distinct society, merely perpetuates the colonial framework of Confederation in the first place."

But only one page later came this statement: "The proposal to transfer certain social, cultural and environmental programs from federal to provincial jurisdiction poses a threat to national standards for these important policy concerns." In other words, the Action Canada Network was in favour of much greater powers and autonomy for Quebec and Canada's aboriginal people, but not for the other nine provinces. In fact, "Quebec should be recognized as a nation with the right to determine its own political union, either within or outside of Canada." And "plans for a major devolution of powers from federal to provincial jurisdiction [except in terms of Quebec] should be curtailed."

I was appalled. And I was even more appalled when Maude Barlow also came out strongly in favour of a three-nation concept of Canada and began pushing the idea in speeches across the country. Shortly after Barlow announced her support for asymmetrical federalism, a public-opinion poll showed that ninety-two percent of Canadians outside Quebec opposed the idea.

It wasn't long before I began receiving angry phone calls and letters from COC members across the country protesting her "three nations" position. Meanwhile, the COC had somehow adopted a position opposing strengthened economic union and a Canadian common market within Canada, that is, the dismantling of interprovincial trade barriers. U.S. firms could enter Canada virtually without restriction and conduct their commercial activities anywhere in the country, yet hundreds of provincial regulations stood in the way of Canadian firms having the same ability to operate in other provinces. And studies showed that the potential economic benefits of a true Canadian common market outweighed any potential benefits of the Canada-U.S. trade deal. Ken Wardroper was just as unhappy as I was about the council's opposition to the dismantling of interprovincial trade barriers. Once again it was clear that the trade unions' position on the issue had influenced Barlow's thinking. I wrote to her in February 1992:

When I met with you and Tony Clarke in Winnipeg on January 14th, I expressed my grave concerns about your "three nations" position, and your suggestion that Canada should give Quebec whatever it wants. . . . I am convinced, and so are most of the people I have talked to, that your constitutional position is a recipe for disaster, and that the political and economic consequences have not been properly thought out. As one constitutional expert put it: "In short, the three-nation approach is simply an appeasement approach and will promote the disintegration of the country and I very much regret that the Council endorsed it." The Canadian historian Kenneth McNaught, who introduced me on Friday evening in Toronto, said, "I can't understand what's gotten into Maude — her position makes no sense." Pierre Trudeau calls it "a crackpot idea." It seems to me that your position is simply sovereignty-association by another name. . . . It makes absolutely no sense to me whatsoever for a nationalist organization such as the Council of Canadians to adopt such a destructive position. Why give everything away to Quebec nationalists who will *never* be satisfied with anything less than total self-determination and separation?

The Council of Canadians should be in the forefront of the effort to convince the people of Quebec that we will improve the rights of French-Canadians outside of Quebec: that together we can build the greatest country in the world — greatest in the sense of quality of life combined with standard of living. We should be offering Quebec a strong new vision of what *our* kind of new Canada would be like, and why the people of Quebec would be better off and more secure *in* such a strong united nation.

After Jean Chrétien had abruptly cancelled our meetings with the caucus in January 1992, Liberal MPs organized an unofficial meeting for Maude and me. Afterwards we talked about the next election. It became clearer and clearer to me that neither the COC nor the Action Canada Network could ever become involved in a strategic voting campaign; simply put, the unions wouldn't allow it.

The Liberal party had now turned full face to the BCNI. Mark Assad told me on the phone that suddenly there was a mood of "Don't worry about money." And, with the Liberals now ahead in the polls and Brian Mulroney's popularity mired in the basement, the BCNI had turned its attention to the Liberals. If there was any doubt left about the future direction of the party, the appointment of Roy MacLaren (who made John Crosbie look like a nationalist) as trade critic and Paul Martin, Jr., as election policy co-chairman put an end to it.

The Liberals, were they to win a majority government, would not be much different from the Conservatives, and possibly even worse. What, then, should the COC's position be? I wrote to Maude again in mid-May:

> The COC should have a stated policy of campaigning as hard as possible for all candidates pledged to the abrogation of the FTA. The candidates must pledge to campaign in advance of the next federal election and during the next federal election to abrogate the trade agreement. I think it is a mistake to support a single Liberal candidate in the next federal election unless they agree in advance to campaign for abrogation and promise to vote in the House of Commons for abrogation.

In May 1992 Tony Clarke, in a memo to member organizations of the Action Canada Network, advised that "the Action Canada Network and its member organizations have been at the forefront on calling for abrogation of the Canada-U.S. Free Trade Agreement. This will certainly be a major issue in the forthcoming federal election. We must force the political parties to commit explicitly and decisively to cancelling the FTA."

"Force the political parties . . ." In the memo's margin I wrote: "*How* exactly?"

In August an Angus Reid–Southam News poll showed sixty-five percent of Canadians viewed NAFTA as a "more dangerous position," while only twenty-nine percent were supportive. A month later the Mulroney government circulated an eight-page, $1.4-million newspaper supplement claiming that the FTA had been a great success for Canada, and NAFTA would be even better. According to Michael Wilson, "A large part of the blame for the economic difficulties we have experienced rests with a global recession that has affected all major trading nations." What Wilson didn't say was that the recession was longer and deeper in Canada, and that compared to most other industrialized nations, Canada's economy had been badly hurt.

Late in August Tony Clarke advised: "coalitions really spell the new era of social activism in Canada. . . . The new leadership of the CLC is really committed to coalition building and political action [and] they seem to be gathering a greater head of steam." A noble idea, but a political pipedream. How could a CLC-funded coalition do anything but support the NDP? It couldn't, and the well-meaning altruistic people who thought otherwise were as politically naïve as they were noble in their motives.

On October 7, 1992, Brian Mulroney, George Bush, and Carlos Salinas initialled the NAFTA agreement in San Antonio, Texas. Later in October the *Toronto Star* and *Ottawa Citizen* reported that "a broadly based coalition of labour groups and social activists Thursday kicked off a campaign to defeat the North American free-trade agreement." Included in the coalition fighting NAFTA were organizations such as the National Action Committee on the Status of Women, the United Church of Canada, the Ontario Federation of Labour, the Canadian Environmental Law Association, the Ontario Secondary School Teachers' Federation, and the Ontario Coalition for Social Justice. According to a press report, "Jim Turk of the labour federation compared the fledgling coalition to democracy groups in

Eastern Europe before the fall of Communism and predicted they will get the agreement overturned after the next election."

How exactly? I read these words with puzzlement. They were brave, optimistic, and well intentioned. But they seemed to me to be entirely divorced from reality.

For Tony Clarke and the Action Canada Network, something called "coalition politics" was at the top of the agenda. "Welcome to the age of coalition politics!" and, "It is no mystery, we're making history," said the summer 1992 ACN *Dossier*. According to Clarke, "We are talking about the rise of a new kind of vehicle for democratic social change in Canada." Union leader Art Kube spoke about "building a new political culture . . . the creation of social cohesion." And according to National Union of Public and General Employees Secretary-Treasurer Larry Brown, "As Canadians continue moving away from political parties as the principal carriers of political messages, solidarity coalition models have become a critical part of the democratic process overall." Since most of those associated with the "new kind of vehicle for democratic social change" were also supporters of the NDP, and since the NDP seemed to be in a contest with the Conservatives to see who could break their record for their lowest-ever popularity among Canadian voters, I was not optimistic, to say the least.

In the fall I wrote to Maude Barlow about the Charlottetown accord:

> I must emphasize that I cannot possibly be part of an organization that "should support the proposed accord in principle." I can't do that. If the COC did that it would be a foolish mistake.
>
> And, by the way, you are dead wrong about the support for this deal in the West in relation to "more power for the West." A huge increase in "central Canada" seats in the Commons more than negates any modest gains in the Senate.
>
> As I have said to you and Ken previously, why the COC should adopt a position opposed by 92% of Canadians outside Quebec is beyond me.
>
> Rather than being the drum for asymmetric federalism, I think you'd be much better off pushing democratization, democratically-elected constituent assemblies, reform of the whole decision-making process, etc.

In the fall of 1992 the COC held its eighth annual general meeting in Ottawa. My keynote address was also my goodbye to the COC, since the same evening we were to hold the founding meeting of what was to become the National Party of Canada. In accordance with council policy that board members seeking public office must resign, I announced I would step down from my position as honorary chairperson. From the time we had started with our first meeting of eleven people in Edmonton and then eighty in Toronto in 1985, the COC had grown to almost 22,000 members.

The NDP and the Point of No Return

WITH THE EVIDENCE now so clear that a Chrétien Liberal government would be little different from Mulroney's in matters fundamental to Canadian nationalists, what were those of us who saw more of the same as fatal for our country to do? As we examined the alternatives, some suggested we consider joining the NDP.

Just as I have had many good friends who were Liberals and Conservatives, over the years I have had many who were or are NDP members — including Tommy Douglas; on several occasions we shared a stage together. In his prime, he was by far the most dynamic, riveting speaker I ever heard. We kept in touch by phone and mail. In 1979 Tommy wrote to me from his House of Commons office: "I hope you wake up the Canadian people to what is happening in this country. We are becoming an economic satellite with less and less control of our own affairs. The tragedy is that the point of no return is close, and unless we can get some public reaction it may be too late when Canadians find they have become a client state." It was with great pleasure that I published an excellent biography of Tommy in 1987, by Tom and Ian McLeod, although it came a year after his death.

Through the mid-1980s many of us did what we could to pressure the NDP into taking a strong stance against the proposed FTA. In May 1988 Ed Broadbent wrote to me: "I note that you are keeping up the very important battle against the Mulroney-Reagan trade deal. I can assure you that they will have one hell of a time getting it through Parliament."

As previously mentioned, much to our dismay, instead of attacking Mulroney and the trade deal in the 1988 election, the NDP turned their guns on John Turner and the Liberals. At the time few Canadians knew that the NDP had hired an American pollster, for almost a quarter of a million dollars, to give them advice on election strategy. Broadbent's actions during the 1988 campaign turned off many NDP members. Dr. John Ryan, of Winnipeg, wrote to Broadbent shortly after Mulroney's victory:

> I have been a socialist all my life and a longtime member of the NDP. I am terminating my membership in the party, and I want you to know my reasons for deciding to do this.
>
> My alienation from you and the present leadership of the NDP is entirely due to your role and the role of the party during the recent election in which the Tories achieved a majority government and electoral sanction for their economically dangerous and politically disastrous Free Trade Agreement.
>
> Had you or your advisers grasped the full implications of the agreement, it would surely have been evident to you that this proposal represented the most serious threat to the Canadian national interest to present itself since the defeat at the polls of similar proposals in 1891 and 1911. Your loyalty to the political philosophy, history, and traditions of the NDP should have made it inevitable that you conduct an impassioned, personal, all-out campaign against a treaty bound to have such negative effect on the realization of the NDP's historic concerns. You failed to take up this role with the single-minded concentration on basic principles that this clear threat to our sovereignty and independence required. Indeed in a number of crucial ways this role was betrayed altogether.

Of course the NDP was not alone in bringing in Americans for advice about Canadian politics. Both the Liberals and Conservatives, and later the Reform party, brought in U.S. pollsters, fundraisers, and strategists to help in their campaigns. Tory pollster Allan Gregg was fascinated by American political techniques. Dalton Camp and Norman Atkins had hired Richard Nixon's pollster, and even Walter Gordon had employed an American pollster.

On two occasions the federal NDP caucus asked me to brief them on the FTA, and I was happy to do so. Finally in May 1992 the NDP, now led by Audrey McLaughlin, presented a motion in the House of Commons calling for the abrogation of the FTA. Shortly after, Audrey called me requesting a meeting in Edmonton. We had a good friendly talk, but there was no way I would run for the party as she suggested. I found much in the NDP I could not support, not the least of which was the role of the Canadian Labour Congress. In the words of Gerry Scott, a British Columbia NDP member since 1972, "There is one critical fact that requires . . . the party's serious attention: the effective veto exercised by the CLC within the federal NDP in terms of policy and action. To deny that reality is impossible." Many of us were astounded by the NDP's support for the Charlotte-town accord. Bob Rae said that "the night that Charlottetown went down was one of my darkest political hours. I was enormously disappointed — hugely." Not I. I had campaigned very hard for the No side in the referendum. The sight of Bob White of the CLC and Allan Taylor, CEO of the Royal Bank, appearing together on television in support of the accord was a cause of both mirth and dismay among many Canadians. The federal NDP's support for Charlottetown was a tragic, turning-point mistake for the party. Without question, it was pressure from Bob Rae and subsequently the CLC that was the key influence in the caucus's ill-advised decision.

While the trade unions dominated much of the NDP's decision-making and financed much of its activities, only some twenty to thirty-five percent of trade unionists voted for the NDP; most sup-ported the Liberals. Remarkably, in both 1984 and in the crucial 1988 election, more trade-union members voted for Brian Mulroney's Conservatives than for the NDP, just as in 1993 many union members would vote Reform.

I have already mentioned the federal NDPs' poor performance on the question of foreign ownership. Consider the provincial level: Mike Harcourt's terrible acquiescence to an ever-escalating sellout of B.C. and his position on the FTA ("We can't build walls around ourselves," and that the FTA was "yesterday's fight . . . it's old turf") and Bob Rae's weak response to the FTA in Ontario. I find it difficult to understand why any nationalists would have any confidence in supporting the NDP.

The cover of the November 4, 1991, *Maclean's* magazine featured a picture of the three NDP premiers, Michael Harcourt, Roy Romanow, and Bob Rae, under the headline "On a Roll." The federal party stood high in the polls, and most Canadians now lived in provinces governed by NDP. Soon after, the federal party would top the polls with an unprecedented forty-one percent support. But soon after that, the party's support began to plunge.

Many Canadians had long harboured concerns about the NDP's ability to run the economy. What happened in Ontario after the election of the Rae government hurt the party federally as much as it subsequently hurt it provincially. A combination of events in Ontario was fatal to the federal party's chances in the 1993 election: a very serious inherited provincial financial situation, a deep and protracted recession, the FTA and its debilitating deindustrialization of the province, an ill-prepared party thrust unexpectedly into power, and a right-wing press that incessantly and mercilessly pounded Rae and his government.

Why hasn't the NDP been more successful? When Canadians were completely fed up with the incessant wrangling of John Diefenbaker and Lester Pearson, Tommy Douglas was unable to make a major breakthrough for the party. When many Canadians despised Pierre Trudeau and thought Joe Clark was a joke, Ed Broadbent was also unable to lead the party to victory. When Brian Mulroney became the most unpopular prime minister in Canadian history and Jean Chrétien, after a weak performance as leader of the Opposition, was dubbed "yesterday's man," Audrey McLaughlin watched as her party's fortunes were decimated.

I believe there are four reasons for the NDP's inability to be more successful federally. First, for many Canadians the party is perceived to be "too socialist." Second, for others, including me, the party is thought to be "dominated by the unions." Third, there remains the belief that the NDP "doesn't know how to run the economy." Finally, when the NDP joined the Liberals, the Conservatives, big business, and the trade unions in supporting the Charlottetown accord, they completely alienated much of their own traditional constituency. The Rae and Harcourt governments' performances could not fail to hurt the federal party's image. Instead of helping the NDP to the federal victory that so many party supporters projected in 1992, the provincial parties helped cripple their federal colleagues. There is little justice in such an assessment, but justice and politics are infrequent companions in a country where wealth and power are so concentrated and where most of the media are owned and controlled by the wealthy few.

Throughout the latter part of 1992 and continuing into 1993, the federal NDP's support dropped like a brick thrown from the top of the CN Tower. In the 1993 federal election, the party's support would plunge to a meager seven percent. From forty-three seats at dissolution, only nine NDP members would be elected to the House of Commons, the lowest NDP/CCF representation in Parliament in thirty-five years.

Is my criticism of the NDP too harsh? Here are the words of Mel Watkins, veteran NDP member, from *This Magazine* early in 1996:

> Since time immemorial, the federal NDP has been controlled by a group that consists disproportionately of private-sector trade union leaders (particularly the Steelworkers), the brass of the Ontario party, and the Lewis family. It is *their* party and they don't intend to let anyone else take it over. I know, I've been there. Someone who is not one of theirs can take 40 per cent of the vote — as the Waffle did in 1971 or Rosemary Brown did in 1975 — but they won't be allowed to win. No leader other than theirs has been chosen since the NDP was created in 1961. It is a dismal record for a party that claims the name "Democratic."

VI

PATRIOTS, POLITICIANS, AND SCOUNDRELS

The National Party of Canada

D ESPITE AN ABUNDANCE of evidence in this book to the contrary, I was quite intimidated by the idea of starting a new political party. It's true that I had floated the idea a number of times over the years, but the task always seemed daunting, demanding, and fraught with peril. Every time the idea surfaced, I had to consider that a decision to proceed would wipe out most of the great pleasures I received from life. There would be time for politics, for building a new party, and if it was to be successful, time for little else for many years.

There were several reasons that led me to start the National Party of Canada, but one was of overwhelming importance: I was convinced we were losing our country and I could think of no other way I might try to help Canada survive.

For at least two decades I had been giving speeches across the country urging Canadians to get involved in politics. Fewer than five percent of adult Canadians belonged to any political party, and fewer than one percent donated to any political party. The results speak for themselves; the only two parties that have formed majority governments in Canadian history have been dominated by a very small well-to-do economic and political elite where political involvement was often for less than altruistic reasons.

In 1975 I wrote a long article for the *Toronto Star*, which was headlined: "Nationalists must fight for political power." In part it read:

> I used to think that if enough of us worked really hard and travelled to enough church basements, high-school auditoriums, university amphitheaters, service-club luncheons, graduating

banquets, convocations, trade union meetings, national and provincial conventions, community meetings, television and radio studios, parliamentary committee and regulatory board hearings, and if we worked our rear ends off and organized and lobbied and took our message to Canadians across the country, if we did a really good job, then surely the politicians would at last have to react.

I was very wrong.

I was wrong because although we did our job effectively, although we did manage to get the message through, although most Canadians now are with us, we failed for one vital but simple reason.

The nationalists have been defeated because they fought too many minor skirmishes without engaging in by far the most important battle — the battle for political power.

Looking at things as objectively as I am able to, the view must be pessimistic. But, but. All across Canada there are many tens of thousands of Canadians who will never accept the continued pimping of our nation.

It seems to me they have only one last chance: they must quickly learn to mobilize politically. Either they must get together and try to alter one of the existing parties, or they must start a new one.

I personally do not believe the former would work; and every politician and political pundit in the country will laugh at the idea of the latter.

An amalgamation of nationalists and conservationists, anti-pollution and anti-poverty groups and women's rights organizations and political reformers and other progressive activists would have a powerful base to begin with.

Impossible; it can't be done. Most of the columnists and politicians and editorial writers and all the economic elite will tell you so. I too am appalled by the colossal effort that would be involved and the odds against success. If someone has a better idea, I will be the first in line to listen. But, as things stand now, almost everyone reading these words is effectively either an active or emasculated participant in the unique-in-the-world surrender of a nation.

I received some three hundred letters from Ontario supporting the idea of a new party. I also received cautionary letters from two people whose opinion I respected. The first was from Walter Gordon. "As you know," he wrote, "I have grave misgivings about your idea for a new political party. Even supposing it could elect six or eight members including yourself — and I think that would be very optimistic — what could it accomplish? I am still convinced the only practical approach is to work within one of the existing parties. And when one gets down to it, this means the Liberals."

The second was from my former editor-in-chief, Susan Kent. "Have you had the time lately to think your real ambitions over?" she asked. "Wouldn't you rather go on speaking, and create a little extra time for yourself to begin writing? In Ottawa you'll have even less time — you'll spend at least the first two years in senseless and time-consuming in-fighting. I wish you would think about it."

I did think about it. A lot. Reluctantly I came to the conclusion that I just couldn't do it; I didn't have the money, the time, the experience necessary, and I had grave doubts about whether I had the ability to lead such a difficult endeavour. I did nothing, but I continued from time to time to raise the idea for others to think about.

In the fall of 1976 Richard Gwyn wrote a very generous column about me. In part:

> Just for an instant, an event so unusual it is worth recording, Mel Hurtig sounded depressed. Or, if not depressed exactly, then he sounded trapped.
>
> "The nationalist movement is in trouble," Hurtig had said. . . . "Either we (the nationalists) invent a whole new strategy or we have to give up the ball game."
>
> Hurtig's problem is to discover that strategy. He needs to do this for his own sake because, as he admits, Hurtig is "a politician without a home" and for the sake of the organized nationalist movement which is now losing its momentum, "We are going to have to become more political." But how? Join a political party? "We'd just get sucked in. The Liberals, I learned from my six years with them, are the party of big business; the Conservatives are hopeless; the New Democrats are captives of the international unions. Form a new party then? Everyone tells me it can't be done."
>
> In itself, the notion of the nationalist movement, widespread but diffuse, transforming itself an organized political

force seems like one of those bright ideas that get batted around at late-night bull sessions and then get politely folded away in the sober light of the morning after, except that Hurtig has the personality and presence to make the difference. . . .

Hurtig stands out most of all because at a time when almost all our politicians seem played-out and exhausted he comes into the fray imbued with ideas and with passion. He possesses also the courage to reach out for fresh political ideas in a way that almost no-one else is doing these days.

Since Gwyn's column was syndicated, this time the many letters and phone calls came in from several provinces, not just Ontario. Jack McClelland wrote to me in 1979: "We do need a new approach and I am trying to find it. . . . Probably you should start a new party, then I would vote for you, but I'm not interested in the same old ball game. We have lost that one. <u>You don't lose every year for 10 years and pretend you are going to win</u>. So think of a new approach and probably think of a new party." Jack didn't underline the sentence above, I did. I had been thinking exactly the same thing for quite some time.

AFTER *The Betrayal of Canada* was published in 1991, the push for a new party was well beyond my expectations. But in an interview with the *Vancouver Sun* I said, "I would start a new party reluctantly." Later in the year Gillian Steward, former managing editor of the *Calgary Herald* wrote:

> Mel Hurtig sounds exhausted. And after two months on the road promoting his book *The Betrayal of Canada*, it's easy to understand why.
>
> Everywhere he went people turned out by the hundreds. In Vancouver last week 600 people crammed into a space meant for 560, while 250 were left outside.
>
> People have sat through his lengthy presentation of complicated charts and graphs. They have applauded as he assailed the insidious web of foreign ownership, free trade, the tax system and the high dollar for wrecking the economy and the country. And they have bought the book.
>
> People turned out to listen to him despite the fact many

business leaders and politicians pooh-poohed Hurtig and his economic nationalism. They bought the book in the face of overwhelming negative reviews in newspapers and magazines.

Even in conservative Calgary, people crammed into halls to hear him denounce the high levels of foreign ownership in Canada.

At the two speeches Hurtig gave in Calgary, I was struck by the number of young people in the crowd. It would appear that people with dismal job prospects, such as students, identify with Hurtig's view of Canada as a place where government and big business have conspired to benefit themselves at the expense of others.

Pollster Michael Adams's presentation at the Liberals' Aylmer conference in November 1991 had been of much interest. According to Adams, Canadians were so fed up with politicians that only radical changes could save the federal system. Public cynicism had reached unprecedented levels. Jean Chrétien had an approval rating of only twenty-nine percent. Asked whom the polls showed would make the best prime minister, Adams replied that the leader in the polls, at thirty-seven percent, was "none, don't know, and refuse to answer." According to Adams, the polls showed that for the first time in the history of polling in Canada, those polled felt that their children would not have a quality of life as high as their own.

Two months later, according to *Maclean's*, "Many voters are disenchanted with the established parties . . . the electorate [is] deeply disenchanted with traditional politics and political institutions — and . . . eager for radical change to both. Three out of four of the voting-age Canadians polled say there is little to choose among the three mainstream political parties." And, "Only 35 percent of Canadians questioned agreed that Canada needs a new political party." *Only* thirty-five percent? Or should it have read: "Over one-third of all those polled said Canada needs a new political party"? To me, especially since Reform was already in the political mainstream, thirty-five percent was a very high and promising number.

Early in 1992 Maude Barlow, Tony Clarke, and I met a number of Liberal MPs in Ottawa. My major point at the meeting was that we did not need three right-wing parties contesting the next federal election. If the Liberal party continued to move to the right, it would leave millions of Canadians with only two choices. Either we join the

NDP in the next election, or we start a new party. Yes, a new party would split off some of the vote. Yes, it could hurt the Liberals and the NDP. But the mood for true change was very strong, and what was the use of supporting a conservative continentalist Liberal party that would likely simply continue the policies of Brian Mulroney, Michael Wilson, and John Crosbie?

The chances of a new party winning more than a few seats was remote, especially since an election would likely be held the following year. But even a handful of seats in a fractured House of Commons could be very important. And it would be a start.

By early 1992, one poll showed that even Joe Clark was more popular than Brian Mulroney, and the talk among Tories of "finding Brian a job" was increasing. Clearly the party had no hope of being reelected if he continued as leader. At the same time there was continuing cynicism and insecurity across the country. More and more people were afraid they might lose their jobs and their homes. Disdain for politicians and antagonism against pork barrel was growing.

By February, there was a great deal of behind-closed-door Tory talk about finding Mulroney a respectable way out to allow time for a leadership convention before a federal election. Chrétien's performance as leader of the Opposition had continued to be unimpressive. Everywhere I visited, from Newfoundland to British Columbia, I kept hearing the same questions from cabdrivers, waitresses, professionals, students, you name it: "*Who* is there to vote for?"

In March a Gallup poll asked Canadians if they respected political parties. Only nine percent said they had a great deal of respect and confidence in the existing parties. By April, only thirty-two percent of Canadians supported the Free Trade Agreement, while sixty-six percent were opposed, and sixty-four percent also opposed the North American Free Trade Agreement. A tiny six percent saw positive results for Canadians from the FTA, while an overwhelming seventy-three percent believed that Canada had been hurt by the deal.

Despite the polls and the poor state of the Canadian economy, none of the five main parties that would be contesting the next election was making either the FTA or NAFTA an important issue in their pre-election campaigns.

In May I talked to Martin Goldfarb in Toronto. Goldfarb asked me to summarize in writing what a new political party might stand for. I wrote to say that the basic principle would be real democratic reform, in all its aspects. This means:

- much more open government;
- an end to patronage, pork barrel and political cronyism;
- reform of the electoral system to make it much more democratic;
- reform of the House of Commons with many more free votes;
- much more accountability for politicians;
- reform of the tax system to make it much fairer for the average Canadian;
- the elimination of the GST;
- ending the growth of foreign ownership and corporate concentration in Canada;
- abrogating the FTA and working in the GATT for better world trade laws;
- using referenda for key nation-turning issues;
- making more Canadian savings available to small and medium-size Canadian-owned businesses through the banking system;
- shortening the length of time a federal government is elected for, from five to four or even three years;
- new methods to more fairly appoint members to the boards of the CBC, the CRTC, Petro-Canada, Canadian National, parole and immigration boards and other government institutions. . . .

Martin, I cannot emphasize enough that the new party would not accept any money from corporations and would not accept any money from trade unions. That would immediately differentiate us from every other federal political party in Canada except the Bloc. We would not be beholden to big corporate donors or big trade unions.

By the summer of 1992, the Conservatives were down to only seventeen percent in the Gallup poll, while for the seventeenth consecutive month, the Liberals led the polls, this time at forty-four percent, about double the NDP support.

In August Audrey McLaughlin and I held a joint press conference in Calgary to spell out the dangers of the NAFTA agreement.

Soon after, Edmonton lawyer Victor Leginsky and I met with Maude Barlow in Edmonton. I explained to Maude that we were now on the verge of making a decision to proceed with a new party and I would be stepping down as honorary chair of the COC. I told her all the reasons for this decision. Much to my delight, Maude agreed with the decision. She said that she, too, had arrived at the same conclusion: a new party was necessary.

There was little time left. If we were going to fight the next election, we would have to get organized quickly. But I continued to agonize over the decision. The task seemed too formidable and the time remaining far too short.

Yet the prospects of our country now appeared more dismal than ever before. The next election could well be a last chance. And even if we had only one chance in a hundred of success, it would be irresponsible not to take that chance.

I was under a great deal of pressure. What do you do when people phone you and write you and fax you saying we must do something to try to save our country? Sorry, but I'm preoccupied with my business? I need to spend more time with my family? I want to enjoy life more, so try someone else? The letters and phone calls were frequently passionate pleas from men and women who were desperately seeking solutions and increasingly fearful for the future of their country.

From the very beginning I clearly understood we would face a long uphill struggle. Compared with the other parties, we would be badly underfunded. It took the Reform party more than five years to become an important political presence, and they managed to elect exactly one member of Parliament in their first six years. Preston Manning lost his first two attempts to win a seat in Parliament and I would likely fare no better running for a new party. And the media tends to treat new parties with disdain.

I thought and hoped that the 1992 Charlottetown referendum might be a turning point in Canadian history. Despite the fact that the Liberals, Conservatives, and NDP all supported the agreement, as did big business, the premiers, the trade-union leaders, many native leaders, and much of the newspaper editorial elite, despite a major coordinated national campaign to sell the agreement to the people of Canada, despite Brian Mulroney's suggestion that those who opposed the agreement were "enemies of Canada," some fifty-five percent of Canadians, including majorities in six provinces, defeated the proposal in a national referendum.

For me, the victory for the No side in the referendum was a victory for democracy in Canada.

The Founding

THE FOUNDING MEETING of a new, as-yet-unnamed Canadian political party took place in the Canadian Room (formerly the Chateau Grill) of the Chateau Laurier Hotel in Ottawa on November 21, exactly four years to the day after the 1988 free-trade election. Among the forty-five men and women from across Canada who were present were academics, lawyers, business people, farmers, teachers, homemakers, students, accountants, writers, a publisher, a researcher, a nurse, an actor, an executive assistant, a translator, and a journalist — all in all, a very talented and diverse group. Time was of the essence. The question before us was, yes or no, do we form a new party?

I opened the meeting by listing all the pros and cons I could think of. Victor Leginsky explained the Elections Canada rules we would have to consider. Ron Cooper, a former Ontario Liberal candidate, talked about policy formulation. Winnipeg businessman Bill Loewen talked about funding. Bob Campbell, David Estrin, and Julius Grey talked about a new party constitution. How would a first board be structured? The executives? Where would the party's offices be located? Could we nominate fifty or more candidates in time so that the party would be entitled to issue official tax-deductible receipts for donations once an election was called? What would the party be called? Should we try to have a founding national convention before the election or bypass it and concentrate on election preparedness?

By 9:00 p.m. we had made the decision to proceed. Committees were struck, and outline plans and goals spelled out. We would meet again in Winnipeg for two days to begin the detailed planning and to choose a name for the party. Just before we adjourned at midnight, I said that the only people who would attack us would be the Conservatives, the Liberals, the NDP, the Reform party, the Bloc, the Parti Québécois, the Confederations of Regions Party, the BCNI, the banks, the lobbyists, and Canada's business press.

We knew from that moment that the odds would be very much against us and that the announcement of a new political party would be greeted by the press with reactions ranging from aloof amusement to outright hostility. And we were right. But for thousands of Canadians, it was good news.

Four days after our founding meeting in Ottawa, I received a very pleasant surprise in the form of a Dalton Camp column titled: "It's time somebody stood up for Canada."

> It seems to me the general public should welcome the formation of Mel Hurtig's new no-name party. Hurtig has become something of a Canadian artefact, an unapologetic nationalist both economic and cultural, and the news last weekend that he intended to insert himself into the next federal election — along with as many as 50 like-minded candidates — struck me as possibly a good thing.
>
> It may be important that Canadian nationalists now will have — according to the founding leader — a party of their own, one that will be unequivocal about Canadian nationalism in the same way that other parties are about motherhood or debt. . . .
>
> Many Canadians have been disturbed by what they see, the result of the government's limitless enthusiasm for competitiveness, privatization, downsizing, and cost-effectiveness. . . .
>
> Hurtig's mission becomes more clear when we read his book (despite the lurid title), *The Betrayal of Canada*. It is true there are two competing visions of Canada, one of them starkly reflected in Hurtig's book. And even if the reader is a raving continentalist, she will agree Hurtig has some interesting, provocative things to say.
>
> They should be said to a wider public, as a part of the next great debate.

One month after our founding meeting, a Southam–Angus Reid poll produced great news. Presented with this introduction — "The 1993 election will be contested by three newcomers to the political arena — the brand-new National Party spearheaded by Mel Hurtig, the two-year-old Bloc Québécois and Preston Manning's Reform Party in its second appearance" — over half of those polled said that the prospect of these new parties "really appeals" while only forty-three percent said they were satisfied with the mainstream parties.

It wasn't long before the NDP, as expected, began accusing us of splitting the vote. But if splitting the vote was the key determining factor in political action, the CCF/NDP would never have been born in the first place. Nor would the Reform party or the scores of new parties in other western democracies. If after all these years the NDP was all the way down to thirteen percent of the vote, it said a great deal about their failure to sell Canadians their policies. And, at a low thirteen percent, if they were concerned that we would steal away much of their remaining longtime solid-core vote, it could not be very secure to begin with.

As well, our new party would be very different from the NDP and from all other parties. Aside from the fact that we would not accept donations from either corporations or trade unions, we would likely have a higher percentage of businessmen and women in our party than the NDP, but not nearly in the dominant role they and lawyers played in the Liberal and Conservative parties. Our position on the Charlottetown accord would be completely different from all three old-line parties. We would not get involved in provincial politics intentionally, which would also be different from the three parties. And we would be well to the left of the Reform party (which wouldn't be difficult) on the political spectrum. There would be many other basic policy differences that would differentiate us from the other parties, which we would soon outline in a policy book.

Early in 1993 a new poll showed that when asked to choose their favourite leader, Mulroney, Chrétien, Manning, or McLaughlin, a huge thirty percent had responded "none of the above" although no such option was presented as part of the poll.

We met in Winnipeg to commence our detailed planning and to choose the party's name. Not only did the name have to translate properly into French, but the acronym had to work. For example, the National Alliance party was a favourite of several founding members, but the NAP hardly carried the connotation we were looking for. The short list for the party name still had some forty names on it when we finally sent it out for a vote. My own favourite was the Canada party, but we learned that another group had registered that name with Elections Canada the previous summer.

In short order we needed a budget and a staff, an organization plan, a proposal for a constitution, brochures, membership cards, a membership computer system, a campaign manager, fundraising and membership committees, strict internal financial procedures, media and policy committees, research capability, an internal communications system, and a candidate-search committee. It was an awesome task, given that the election would likely be held in less than a year.

In January Stoddart published our outline-policy book, *A New and*

Better Canada, which I had put together with the help of more than a hundred people in three months. The first two printings of 10,000 copies each sold out quickly, and the book soon began appearing on the bestseller lists, reaching number two on the *Globe*'s nonfiction list and number three in the *Financial Post*.

A New and Better Canada spelled out the initial policy principles of the party. In subsequent papers and statements, the platform was expanded and more detailed. In trade policy we would work in the GATT with like-minded nations to encourage the development of a new international trade organization whose policies would reflect the interests of small and medium-sized nations and not just the trade superpowers and their transnational corporations.

In tax policy we would cancel the GST and replace the lost revenue with a long list of long-overdue tax changes; we would close tax-haven loopholes, increase audits on the transfer-pricing activities of foreign corporations, terminate family trust tax loopholes, introducing a more progressive income tax system based on true income and ability to pay, ensure corporate tax changes that would see the corporate tax contribution rise to the average level of the other OECD countries, disallow the deduction of interest costs related to takeovers in areas of the Canadian economy with excessive corporation concentration, stop Canadian corporations that invest abroad from expensing their interest costs in Canada when they fail to pay tax in Canada on the profits of their foreign affiliates, increase to fifteen percent the withholding tax on dividend payments leaving the country, and establish a Royal Commission on Taxation to examine the entire tax structure in Canada and to promptly bring forward recommendations so that we could produce a much fairer tax system for all Canadians.

The reform of democracy in Canada was one of our top priorities. We would end the corporate expensing of lobbying fees; we would take away from MPs and senators the right to set their own salaries; we would strengthen the office of the auditor general to ensure that all government contracts were awarded on the basis of a tendered bidding process, price, quality, and reliability, rather than patronage; we would ensure that all appointments to government boards, agencies, crown corporations, and the like were awarded on the basis of merit, not patronage; we would take away from the prime minister the ability to set the date of the federal election; we would ensure that all nation-turning issues such as the FTA, NAFTA, or constitutional changes were *always* submitted to the people of Canada in binding referenda; we would adopt the many excellent recommendations of the Lortie Royal Commission on Electoral Reform and Party Financing to ensure that future elections were dominated by people, not by money; we would produce the best Access to Information Act of any nation in the world; we would make available to the press, and hence to the public, the results of all government-commissioned public-opinion polls paid for by taxpayers; we would produce the toughest conflict-of-interest legislation for cabinet ministers, MPs, senators, and public servants of any nation in the world.

Soon after the party was announced, we acquired a toll-free number 1-800-565-TNSF (true north, strong, free), which began ringing almost nonstop.

On January 12, despite a severe snowstorm, some seven hundred people squeezed into the 550-seat OISE auditorium on Bloor Street in Toronto for a National party meeting. A few days later in Winnipeg, three hundred showed up at the Fort Garry Hotel, and then the Kerby Centre in Calgary had a packed house. From there, I was off to Medicine Hat, Ottawa, Halifax, back to Saskatoon and Regina, back east to Burlington and Cambridge, and then to Montreal.

Everywhere I went I met all kinds of wonderful men and women I had never known before. After my speech in Winnipeg a senior citizen came up onto the dais and opened his wallet, pressing all his money, more than $100, into my hands with the words "This is the first time I've ever made a donation to any politician. God bless you."

Wherever we went, the crowds were good to excellent. We filled Victoria's five-hundred seat Newcombe Theatre and had to turn two hundred away. The next night in Vancouver we had a crowd of seven hundred. I visited the editorial board of the *Vancouver Sun* and had our best press question-and-answer period yet. In Victoria I had another excellent editorial board meeting, this time at the *Times-Colonist*. A few days later their lead editorial was titled: "National Party a likeable upstart."

On February 24 Brian Mulroney announced his resignation, saying he was leaving both the country and his party in great shape. After all, the Conservative party had an "extremely significant financial surplus." When the press asked me for my reaction, I said we should all enjoy a national holiday: "I think he was one of the worst prime ministers this country has ever had. He decimated the economy. In eight years he ran up a bigger national debt than all the prime ministers in our previous 117 years. He put in process a massive deindustrialization and he's helped integrate Canada into the United States in a manner that would have astounded any of his Conservative predecessors."

But according to Peter Lougheed, quoted in the *Edmonton Journal* at the time, "History will be very positive about Brian Mulroney's leadership . . ."

"A National Vote Is a Rational Vote"

B Y MARCH OF 1993, support for the Reform party had dropped from sixteen percent in 1991 down to seven percent, but the polls showed that the vast majority of Canadians had not even heard of the National party. This was partly rectified in a *Winnipeg Free Press* column by writer and political scientist William Neville, which we circulated widely. Following are the last two paragraphs:

> Anyone who had read typically mind-numbing party plat-forms over the years may well find the National Party's rather appealingly straightforward. That is to say, it is not typically hedged about with all the weasel words and qualifiers that parties have long employed as a means of avoiding firm com-mitments or of wooing one group without offending another.
>
> The Reform Party, whatever its initial possibilities, seems to have become the home for right-wing conservatives who have lost confidence in the Tories. The National Party, on the other hand, seems generally to be pitching itself to middle-of-the-road voters who no longer believe in the mainstream parties' ability to reform our politics or reform themselves. One suspects that there are many such voters out there. The question is whether, in the next few months, the National Party can mobilize them and persuade them that a National vote is a rational vote.

In March Dave Barrett asked for a meeting, and we had a long and for the most part pleasant breakfast. He said he doubted if the National party would get as much as one-half of one percent of the vote in the next election and that if we got one percent it would be "a major breakthrough." He made it clear that he was not concerned about us running candidates where the NDP was the incumbent or might be in a position to win. So much for concerns about "splitting the vote."

The public-opinion polls were clear about where big business stood. Seventy-seven percent of Canadian business leaders wanted the Conservatives to win the next election. This compared with only seventeen percent overall public support for the Conservatives. Never mind that Finance Minister Don Mazankowski had miscalculated his last two budgets by an enormous $17-billion for a colossal $69-billion combined deficit. Never mind the deep, protracted recession and modest "recovery." Never mind that in 1984 Michael Wilson had solemnly promised "an unprecedented response to control rising debt," and never mind that Canada, under Tory rule, had become the largest foreign debtor nation in relation to GDP of any major country in the world. Big business overwhelmingly still supported the Tories. At least they did until it became clear that the Liberals would win the next election.

In March the NDP released their economic plans for how they would turn around the Canadian economy. It was hopelessly weak, so much so that I could not understand what had motivated them to release such an unimpressive document so far in advance of an election not expected until the fall. The document showed corporate profits increasing by almost ninety percent over six years but real personal disposable per-capita income rising by less than half of one percent during the same period. Their federal budgetary deficit reduction and their job-creation projections were both far too modest, and so were their defence-spending cuts. There was nothing in their plans about reducing the levels of either foreign ownership or halting increasing corporate concentration.

On April 3 we had an excellent all-day meeting in Toronto with some of Canada's best economists, tax experts, political scientists, a former federal government deputy minister of finance, plus a senior representative of the Canadian Federation of Independent Business. The list of topics on the agenda was long: the Bank of Canada, Canada's financial institutions, Canadian investment abroad, corporate concentration, domestic debt, foreign debt, exchange-rate policy, interest-rate policy, full-employment strategy, domestic investment, small business, tax policy, trade policy, and transportation policy. It was a fascinating session. Afterwards, one of the economists described it as the best meeting dealing with economics he had been to in many years. Another was overheard to say: "Where else would you ever get a meeting of so many top people to talk about economics and taxes?" The session was very helpful to us in policy matters, and I hoped to have similar sessions at least twice a year in the future.

In April we were able to announce that a well-known former Saskatchewan NDP cabinet minister had joined the National party. In an open letter to "Friends of the New Democratic Party," Ted Bowerman wrote: "The only alternative that challenges my political ideas at present is the National Party of Canada." For Bowerman, supporting the federal NDP was no longer a credible alternative. Their support for the Charlottetown accord had been the last straw. Bowerman had held five ministerial positions in the Saskatchewan government between 1967 and 1982. His father had been a founding member of the CCF and had been elected to the House of Commons in 1945, defeating Prime Minister Mackenzie King in the Prince Albert constituency.

By the spring of 1993, I had more work than I could properly handle and was terribly understaffed. Every hour calls came in from across the country about policy, communications, the party constitution, brochures, nominations, fundraising, and all the normal concerns that develop prior to an election. My staff did a heroic job helping me, but it soon became apparent I would have to step aside from almost all organizational matters and concentrate on one thing — selling the party and its ideas to the public.

Aside from the usual duties a party leader faced, because I had established close working relationships with so many men and women who had come to the party because of *Betrayal* or because of my speeches and articles, it wasn't long before every day's mail brought piles of ideas and documents from new party members from across the country. Could I please read this (135-page) paper on the ozone layer and get back to the author as soon as possible? Could I please incorporate the problems of the engineering profession described in the enclosed (120 pages) in my speeches? Would I read this new book about the grain industry and give my thoughts on the ideas therein?

Obviously the National party had to have a democratic decision-making process. Unfortunately, by late winter I was receiving complaints that this was not the case. At this stage I was almost constantly on the road or in the air or on the platform selling the new party; it was very difficult for me to tell whether the complaints were justified.

However, when Barry Hicks resigned as director of the Leader's Office and when Kathryn Barker, one of our board members, threatened to resign, I knew we had a serious problem.

Barry Hicks lasted only three months in his new job. He left on good terms and remained active in the party, but pointedly warned me about Bill Loewen, who had frequently been rude and bullying to him on the telephone. I had always listened carefully when Barry gave me advice, but his words on his departure from the job seemed unrealistic: "Mel, if I were you, I'd be very careful. Supposing Loewen decides to cut his donations off if he doesn't like what you or the party are doing?" I dismissed the warning.

Victor Leginsky replaced Hicks. It wasn't long before Victor also reported Loewen as rude, abrupt, and bossy. Soon I was getting complaints about the lack of democratic decision-making in the party from our two youngest founding members from Calgary, from our oldest founding member from Edmonton, and from Arlette Sinquin, a board member from Ottawa, who was bright, attractive, and bilingual — and a potential star candidate.

I had begun working with Bill Loewen in 1987 during the free-trade debate. At the time he headed a Winnipeg-based payroll-servicing firm that he later sold to the Canadian Imperial Bank of Commerce for a price said to be in the tens of millions of dollars. Soon after the National party was formed, he announced that he was prepared to put up some $4-million to help launch the party. It was, by any measurement, a colossal sum, but Loewen promised to give the money with no strings attached. I had some reservations at the outset, given my long years of urging reform of the political system, but Loewen underlined that the money was personal, not from a corporation, that he was now out of the corporate world and had nothing to gain personally from the donation, and under no circumstances would he insist on his own policies or a guarantee of powers within the party.

Late in May I received a phone call from Brian Smith, a Vancouver businessman, who had been elected vice president of the National party at the same meeting Loewen had been elected president. Smith minced no words; he himself was also ready to resign. He felt the new party was in imminent danger of collapse because far too many decisions were being made without proper consultation. He ended our conversation with these words: "Mel, the ball is in your court!"

What a mess! Things were going well, membership was increasing every day, donations were coming in, wonderful men and women were becoming active in the party across the country, yet here was a serious problem that at the very least would be awkward to deal with. I called both Brian and Bill and asked them to fly to Edmonton for a meeting on June 9. The atmosphere was tense as Brian and I spelled out the nature of the complaints and the need for more participation in the administrative decision-making. Towards the end of the meeting, Loewen asked if he could still be president; both Brian and I said yes, providing that the appropriate changes were made.

By the summer of 1993, over 1.5 million Canadians were unemployed, almost half that number again were more men and women wanting full-time employment but now working in poorly paid part-time jobs with few or no benefits, and another 200,000 had dropped out of the labour force in despair after looking for work for so long they had simply given up. Millions of Canadians were relying on welfare, and over 1.1 million Canadian children were living in real, debilitating poverty. Across the nation, food banks and soup kitchens proliferated.

The Tories continued to blame "the world recession" for Canada's problems. In my speeches I said I would have been delighted if Canada's unemployment figures had been close to the G-7 or OECD averages of the past few years. In every single important economic category — growth of GDP, gross fixed-capital formation, real domestic demand, growth in employment, and a host of other categories — the G-7 nations and the OECD average had outperformed Canada by an embarrassing margin. Other countries, Japan, Switzerland, Austria, and the Netherlands, for example, had consistently been able to provide their citizens with a high standard of living, low unemployment rates, and low rates of poverty.

For the BCNI and for the rest of the Canadian right-wing establishment, the solution was slash, cut, hack, mutilate, and destroy the social heritage of Canadians. Increasingly there were fewer and fewer differences between the Canadian right and the policies of the wealthy Republicans who had dominated the Reagan and Bush administrations in the United States. Reaganomics was alive and well in Brian Mulroney, Michael Wilson, Kim Campbell, and Preston Manning, and, as we would discover later, in Jean Chrétien and Paul Martin, Jr., and Reaganomics had clearly foreseeable results. The haves got to make more and keep more, and the rest had to simply look after themselves as best they could.

What about the caring, compassionate society that Canada had built up under both Liberal and Conservative governments over so many years? The philosophy of the Canadian establishment could be succinctly summed up in the words of Conrad Black: "Caring and compassion really means socialism, wealth confiscation, and redistribution."

Remarkably the right wing in Canada, the very people who had produced the devastation of the Canadian economy for most of the previous decade and who had enormously increased the debt, now, with the help of their journalist friends at the *Globe and Mail* and *Financial Post*, were managing to focus almost all of the national debate about Canada's economy on the debt and government program spending. Forget the fact that monetary policy, exchange-rate policy, trade policy, tax policy, and other factors had been the principal contributors to the deficits and the accumulating debt. Social programs were "clearly" the villain, and social programs had to be cut drastically.

So, what do you do when you have put people out of work through bad economic management? There were two solutions. First, downsize even more. Second, cut unemployment and welfare benefits. That meant more and more Canadians living in poverty and relying on welfare. Solution? Cut transfer payments to the provinces.

For the previous twenty-five years total social costs for all levels of government in Canada had increased by less than two percent of all government spending, while debt-servicing costs had increased by almost 10.5 percent. The solution? Obvious. Continue record-high real-interest-rate policies, discouraging domestic investment, increasing debt-servicing costs, and ensuring that more and more Canadian dollars pour out of the country every year.

Social programs were never the villain. Gross mismanagement of the Canadian economy was.

Only the National Party of Canada raised the issue of foreign ownership in the 1993 federal election. For the most part the press did not think it was important enough to report. Nor did any other party even mention the heavy and increasing degree of corporate concentration, which I felt was one of the most important reasons the Canadian economy was doing so poorly. When only one percent of the corporations in Canada owned almost ninety percent of all corporate assets, this has nothing whatsoever to do with real free enterprise or true market economics. It does have a great deal to do with the dominance of oligopolies and monopolies. It also has a great deal to do with raw political power. The National Party of Canada pledged to quickly appoint a task force to examine corporate concentration in Canada and examine concentration of ownership in the media.

We felt it very important to create a true common market in our own country. I said that it was high time our parochial provincial politicians looked beyond the lowest step of their legislature building. We needed a new national vision of Canada, not a fractionalized, balkanized country dominated by powerful, greedy provincial potentates.

When Brian Mulroney and Michael Wilson took office in 1984, they promised lower taxes for individuals and higher taxes for corporations. Of course, exactly the opposite happened. Over and over again in my speeches I pointed out that Canadian individuals and families paid higher taxes than in most other developed nations (including countries with more generous social programs), yet corporations in Canada consistently paid lower taxes. Were corporations to pay simply the average contribution to GDP as in other developed countries, individual Canadians could see their taxes reduced by over $2-billion, while another $2-billion could go to reduce the deficit each year.

The National party was the only party that made transfer pricing and more audits of foreign corporations an issue, the only party to present a line-by-line detailed explanation of where the money could come from to replace the unfair and expensive-to-administer GST, the only party promising to legislate against the use of foreign tax havens, the only party promising to take action against tax-avoiding family trusts.

We were also the only party to spell out in detail plans to cut defence spending, to increase federal contributions to postsecondary education, to substantially increase research into breast cancer, and to explain to Canadians in detail how our very different monetary policy would save billions of dollars in debt-financing costs each year.

Moreover, a fundamental economic policy of consistently working towards a full-employment economy would save many billions more in unemployment insurance and welfare payments, as well as help reduce the annual federal and provincial deficits. A healthy economy, with no tax increases for average Canadians and no tax increases for over ninety-five percent of the corporations in Canada, would produce billions of dollars in new revenue needed to finance medicare and other social programs, and to begin to reduce the oppressive federal debt.

The National party strongly supported universal social programs. Universal social programs are much more efficient to administer and hence much cheaper to administer (witness, for example, the huge cost of administrating the grossly inefficient U.S. health system). Universal social programs are less demeaning for the underprivileged, and as long as a truly fair progressive tax system is in place, they are fair to society as a whole. Most importantly they do not produce a two-tiered society, a society of the haves and the have-nots where the haves inevitably decide to reduce the benefits for the have-nots, and where Canadians would progressively move closer and closer to American social standards and values.

I always asked my audiences what they had heard from Jean Chrétien, Kim Campbell, and Preston Manning about these and other important issues the National party was addressing. "Nothing!" and "Not a damn thing!" were the two most common answers shouted back to the stage.

Instead, what Canadians heard was discussion of user fees, privatization, deregulation, downsizing, capital punishment, curtailing abortion, buying expensive helicopters, and virtually nothing about alternate trade and industrial strategies, tax reform, job creation, poverty, and zero about foreign ownership and corporate concentration.

I said that, in no important way, would Jean Chrétien govern Canada differently from Brian Mulroney: "Jean Chrétien is simply another well-to-do conservative from Quebec, with a different party name and a different accent. But they both have Paul Desmarais and the Power Corporation and the Bronfmans as their funders. Is it any wonder that neither Chrétien nor Mulroney would never close down the tax loopholes, do anything about corporate concentration, or seek to genuinely reform democracy in Canada?"

And the Reform party? Aside from their basket of nineteenth-century social policies, a friend phoned Reform party headquarters to inquire as to why in all of their literature there was not any mention of the unemployed. "It's an oversight," came the hesitant reply. Some oversight.

National party policies relating to small and medium-size Canadian-owned businesses were the best thought-out and most detailed presented during the election campaign. Alas, few Canadians ever got to hear of them. Wherever I went across Canada I heard from businessmen and businesswomen about how the banks were putting the screws to them. Time after time, week after week, in province after province, I heard about our Canadian banks cutting off credit unfairly, failing to back innovative new ventures, and treating small business with disdain. The true Canadian entrepreneurs were paying for Canary Wharf and the banks' other huge blunders.

To me, it was very disappointing that while the Constitution so preoccupied the political elite for so many years, the badly needed reform of democracy in Canada was hardly ever mentioned by the old-line parties. Of the almost two hundred countries that belonged to the United Nations, I could only think of three — Canada, Great Britain, and the United States — that still exclusively used the antiquated first-past-the-post electoral system. A modified form of proportional representation would be infinitely more democratic for a country like Canada.

The Lortie Royal Commission on election reform had produced legal opinions that a $1,000 limit for election spending by "third parties" would be upheld by the Supreme Court of Canada as a "reasonable limit" in relation to free speech and election freedoms. But of course there was no chance that the Conservative government would implement any of the important Lortie recommendations. Incredibly some eighty percent of Commons committee meetings on election reform were held behind closed doors, a process agreed to by the Conservatives, the Liberals, and the NDP!

If there was ever a definitive concise statement about what was wrong with Canada, it was in the little-noticed words of Sean Moore from Ottawa, editor of the magazine *Lobby Digest*: "MPs are not lobbied because elected officials play a very minor role in government. Collectively, lobbyists are more influential than MPs." So much for democracy.

All in all our platform, including strong support for culture in Canada and the best-developed environmental policies of any party, was strong for free enterprise in its support for small and medium-size Canadian-controlled businesses and infinitely more progressive in all areas of tax reform. If it was also interventionist, at the same time its heavy emphasis on democratic reform — real power for the people — would put Canada's citizens in charge, not the big corporations. And under the reforms we were advocating, the politicians would have to be much more representative of and responsive to the will of the people.

If there was one fundamental message that found its way into all my speeches, it was this: There are so many great things we Canadians could do as masters in our own house, but very little we can accomplish as frightened tenants who have nothing left with which to pay the rent.

The Woman Who Threw
Herself on the Tracks

MY FONDEST WISH was that the Tories would make the mistake of electing Kim Campbell as their leader. I was not impressed by her, having personally encountered her frenzied, rude, arrogant, and angry debating style during a televised debate about free trade in the CBC's Vancouver studios. After talking to Vancouver friends who had known Campbell when she had finished dead last in a field of twelve candidates running for the B.C. Social Credit Party leadership, I was even less impressed. I was certain she would self-destruct, if not before, then during an election campaign.

And so she did, calling people who didn't belong to political parties "condescending SOBs," claiming to have a vision of Canada with little or no evidence of same, supporting the purchase of tens of billions of dollars worth of antisubmarine helicopters, describing those in disagreement with her as being "enemies of Canada," strongly supporting the Charlottetown accord (and surrounding herself with the same unsuccessful strategists who had led the Yes campaign to disaster), pushing through the renewal of cruise-missile testing with little debate, and advising that she found it hard to relate to the average voter sitting in front of the television set in his undershirt drinking beer. Responding to widespread criticism about cuts in Via Rail service, she suggested: "You would have thought that we had engaged in a mass slaughter of the Canadian beaver."

Supporting Kim Campbell were Robert Stanfield, many representatives of Bay Street, much of the right-wing press, most of Ottawa's powerful lobbyists, Norm Atkins, and much of what remained of the "Big Blue Machine" in Ontario. Much of the federal Tory caucus, including Flora MacDonald, also backed Campbell.

Even before her decision to announce her candidacy, the media had decided that Kim Campbell would crush "yesterday's man," Jean Chrétien, in the election. For the media, in the days and weeks following the February 1993 announcement of Mulroney's resignation, Kim Campbell was bright, sophisticated, bilingual, refreshing, and appealing. I found this amazing, but I was delighted.

The spending limit for the Conservative leadership candidates was widely advertised as $900,000, but the limit had so many loopholes no one paid any attention to it. There was no question who were not "the enemies of Canada." The country's corporate elite chipped in with some $3-million for Campbell's leadership campaign.

After her election as leader and her swearing in as prime minister, for most of the next two months Campbell was even more the media's darling, receiving between seventy and seventy-five percent of all total mentions of party leaders on CBC and CTV television, and similar treatment in much of the print media. By early fall, she had the highest public-popularity figure of any prime minister in thirty years. Suddenly the moribund Conservatives had risen from the depths of unpopularity into a virtual tie with the Liberals in the public-opinion polls.

By June, the polls showed the National party at one percent. In a memo to the board and staff, I wrote: "I think that's great. If we're at one percent after only six months and the NDP after decades is at ten percent and the Reform party who have been in business for about seven years is also at ten percent, we're doing very well, especially considering that fewer than one-third of Canadians have ever heard of us."

Kim Campbell was going to "change the way we do politics." And so she did. It was the most dramatic and fastest crash-and-burn of any prime minister or major party leader in Canadian history. All the flaws I had seen in the Vancouver CBC studio gradually became apparent to voters and to the press. Gaffe followed gaffe, blunder followed blunder. When asked about her position regarding cuts to Canada's social programs, Campbell advised that an election campaign was "not the time . . . to get involved in a debate on very, very serious issues."

Campbell promised to throw herself "across the railway tracks" in defence of medicare. It was unnecessary; by this time the electoral train had already passed over her and the dissected remains of the Conservative party. She was prime minister for less than nineteen weeks and was defeated in her own Vancouver riding.

John Robert Colombo should consider including the following memorable Kim Campbell quote from a 1987 debate in the British Columbia legislature in his next book of quotations: "It's a great pity that there is paranoia about AIDs. I don't think AIDs is a particularly contagious disease, certainly not in the context of other things to which people may be exposed."

A Crusade Short of Time

DESPITE THE FACT that the National party could not issue tax receipts, we were now getting quite a few nice donations from individuals across the country. I made it clear that our complete donation list was open for examination to anyone.

At a press conference in Regina on May 26, 1993, I again challenged all political parties in Canada to open up their books to the public *before* the federal election.

Time was getting very short. If we were not as organized as we should have been, watching the supposedly slick, experienced, well-financed Tories was amazing. In late June former finance minister Don Mazankowski wrote to *Maclean's* quoting major international credit-rating agencies to the effect that Canada's debt problems had been grossly exaggerated. Three pages later in the magazine, Kim Campbell was quoted as labelling those who say the debt isn't a problem as "enemies of Canada."

The National party still had internal troubles. Early in June there was a destructive conference call in which Bill Loewen raged at Brian Smith, Derik Hodgson, and Daphne Kelgard, our policy chairperson. All three announced they were ready to quit. But on the plus side, many of our nominating meetings were being hotly contested. In one B.C. riding we had five people contesting a nomination, and in one Edmonton riding we had four. The candidates came to us from many different backgrounds. We had constituency associations formed in sixty-six ridings and more were being added to the list every week.

In early summer I began another cross-country tour. It was a great success with excellent crowds almost everywhere: eight hundred in Toronto, seven hundred in Winnipeg, six hundred in Edmonton, and nine hundred in Vancouver. As a result, we started, for really the first time, to receive some good press coverage. Meanwhile, more and more nominating meetings were taking place across the country, and I was very pleased by just how good most of our candidates were. But there was now *so* little time — only some seventy days before the election. Our membership had grown to over six thousand and was getting bigger every day, but now there was no more time to spend concentrating on new memberships; only the election counted.

As I crossed the country it was interesting to see two things that differentiated the National party from other parties. First, as I had hoped, our call for radical political reform and true democracy had attracted a very large number of outstanding young men and women. And second, about half our members had never belonged to a political party before. In the end, with so many things to be done so quickly, this was not in itself an asset, but it did mean that we had attracted a large number of Canadians who wanted to become formally involved in politics for the first time.

The summer campaigning was both exhausting and exhilarating. Whenever I felt tired or discouraged, the quality of the people I met immediately cheered me up. These were men and women not interested in patronage or government contracts, but people who loved their country and didn't want to see it disappear.

Like all parties, the National party attracted its share of unusual, sometimes weird, and sometimes unsavoury people. One man who worked his way into an important position of authority ending up walking away with a substantial amount of party funds and equipment. Another, we learned much later, had been accused of theft by the senior officers of another political party.

Almost half our members were former members of either the Liberals or the NDP, with a few from the Reform party and a few disgusted Tories ready to lynch Brian Mulroney.

In the middle of my tour someone leaked a trade-union-commissioned poll to us. Only eighteen percent of Canadians had even *heard* of the National party! And the election was on the horizon. The figures ranged from only six percent in Quebec to more than a quarter of those polled in Toronto and Western Canada.

On average I was giving three speeches a day, not to mention the press, radio, and television interviews, the nominating meetings, the conferences with local and regional party executives, the speeches to write. It was both fascinating and tiring.

I continued to receive complaints about the party's decision-making process. In a memo to the Election Planning committee in June I wrote:

> I hope that all three of you will remember to keep the board informed on a regular basis so they do not feel left out. I think this is very important. As you know, many of the board members felt they were not being consulted and . . . also felt that the party was not being run as democratically as it should be. That being the case, I think that the three of you should

report regularly to the board and from time to time consult them as may be required and at least once a month from now to the election. . . .

Prior to the June board-of-directors meeting I wrote to Bill Loewen and Brian Smith suggesting that Brian take over the party presidency on at least a temporary basis until elections could be held, and Loewen become either CEO or honorary chairman. I also wrote that

we must develop a hard-working democratic board, i.e., the board must be more than tokenism. . . . We must [put in place] reassuring methods to show . . . we intend to democratize the party's decision-making process and involve the board in this process.

. . . there is unfortunately a fairly widespread perspective that the party is being run undemocratically. This, of course, is exactly the opposite of both our goals and the true image we want to project. . . . The changes we need to make are not to be seen as only superficial.

In effect, a small group of executive members were making most of the key decisions. And our executive which was supposed to be comprised of eleven members, had shrunk — mostly because of resignations — to six. In any event, the constitution clearly indicated that it was to be the board of directors who were in charge of the party. As I said in a memo to executive and board members, and key party officials, "This is not a very impressive reflection of our constitution, or of democracy at work. I suggest that we must follow our interim constitution from now to the convention and that some means be undertaken to expand the board between now and the convention. Why not have the regions elect their representatives to the board?"

As each month went by, relations between Loewen and me deteriorated. A very tense board meeting was held in the Chelsea Inn in Toronto in mid-June. Soon after, Kathryn Barker resigned from the board. "I was disgusted. I was so angry," she said. For Arlette Sinquin, who I had hoped would be one of our best candidates, enough was enough. She left the Toronto meetings early and also resigned from the party. "I left because it was not being run in a democratic way

373

— not at all." Soon after the June board meeting, our two youngest founding members and our oldest founding member also resigned. So did one of our Vancouver founding members. According to Kathryn Barker, "The situation was bizarre. I'd served on lots of boards but I'd never seen anything like this before." Twice Kathryn resigned and twice I talked her into coming back. But she was dismayed. The idealistic, open, democratic party I had promised was turning out to be very different from her expectations. And mine. With the election expected in four months, it was a terrible situation. For the party to succeed it had to be a shining example of grassroots democracy at work. It was not. I hoped that after the election, to solve our problems, we could improve the constitution and hold truly democratic elections at our founding convention.

Blacked Out

WE WERE SURPRISED and disappointed in the summer of 1993 to read in the papers that I would not be allowed to participate in the televised leaders' debates. The CBC, CTV, and Global television networks had made the decision behind closed doors in an unannounced meeting with representatives of the Liberal, Conservative, New Democratic, Reform, and Bloc Québécois parties.

Our position was that it was highly arbitrary and probably illegal to exclude the leader of a party that was running candidates all across the country, and that any party running candidates in at least half the ridings across Canada should have been included in the debates. Moreover, all such parties should have been part of the negotiations about the debates, and such negotiations should not have taken place behind closed doors. Shutting us out of the televised debates and limiting us to only a few minutes of combined free and paid television- and radio-advertising time was punitive and undemocratic. Neither the Reform party nor the Bloc had official status in the House of Commons, so that argument could hardly be used to exclude us. Lucien Bouchard would take part in the English debate despite the fact that his party was running candidates only in Quebec, while Preston Manning would take part in the French debate despite the fact that Reform was running no candidates in Quebec! The Bloc, running only seventy-five candidates, would be in both debates, while the National party, running a minimum of 150 candidates, and with candidates in all ten provinces as well as Yukon, would not be allowed to take part in either one.

We received very strong editorial support on the issue. The Prince Edward Island *Evening Post* put it well in an editorial headed: "We need people like Mr. Hurtig." The editorial was typical of those in other papers:

> Things seem slightly out of whack here. On one hand, a leader whose party is dedicated to the break-up of Canada by pulling Quebec out of Confederation, is given a spot in national television debates.
>
> On the other hand, a fervent nationalist whose goal is to make Canada strong, is denied a place in the debates. No wonder Mel Hurtig is incredulous.
>
> The Alberta judge said a decision about who takes part in the debates is best left to broadcasters and politicians, not the courts. The judge is correct, but why was Mr. Hurtig forced to seek redress in the courts in the first place?
>
> The Bloc has a very real chance of winning the majority of seats in Quebec and holding the balance of power in a minority government. If this should happen the country will need leaders like Mr. Hurtig to guide us through some dangerous times. We need people like Mr. Hurtig to speak loud and clear about our country and not be muzzled like he is now.

Late in September the *Toronto Star* asked readers if they would "have preferred that Mel Hurtig, head of the new National party, be included in the leaders' TV debates." Eight-six percent said yes, fourteen percent said no.

Nevertheless, our legal challenges to my exclusion were not successful. Our lawyers contested the decision in three courts, beginning with the Alberta Queen's Bench, on the grounds of constitutional charter rights, violation of free-speech rights, and failure to provide equal treatment. In the end the judges decided that it was not a matter for the courts to decide. But for what it's worth, four months *after* the election, in a letter to one of our members, the secretary general of the Canadian Radio-television and Telecommunications

Commission wrote: "The Commission has received a number of complaints from various parties regarding the debates held on the CBC and other licensees and has come to the conclusion that the CBC did not fulfil its obligation as interpreted by the commission."

A bit late. However, I suppose there was at least one mitigating factor to consider: we were allowed the grand total of two minutes of free time on CBC Radio. Perversely, much to our astonishment, following the news of the television-debate exclusion, some of our candidates were not allowed to participate in local community election forums.

"Next Time for Sure!"

WHILE CHRÉTIEN AND Campbell were telling Canadians to trust them, I was saying: "Look, here are our policies. This is what we believe in and here's why." The entire election campaign seemed amazingly devoid of new ideas. Allan Fotheringham wrote:

> Jean Chrétien's major weapon so far (in the most important election in our history) is to break out a denim shirt that one of his image-doctors bought at the GAP, the better to shield his tired old persona.
>
> Preston Manning in a massive bit of retaliation, has changed his glasses, wears a sweatshirt and wanders about the stage with a mike in hand like some Phil Donahue from the steppes.
>
> The only person so far to keep his tie on is Mel Hurtig, which is appropriate since he is actually talking about the issues.

For months I had used every spare moment to put together a more detailed policy book for the media and for our candidates. By the time it was close to one hundred pages, I simply had no spare time left. I sent it off to Winnipeg, where it was to be produced, along with a request that they finish the last pages and fill in some missing numbers. *Jobs for All Canadians*, our plan for revamping the Canadian economy, came out in September but was almost completely ignored by the media. I was very disappointed. Where the Liberal Red Book was full of clichés, rhetoric, and vague promises, *Jobs* was a detailed 111-page document put together with the assistance and advice of some of Canada's best economists, tax experts, a large number of business-men and -women, and others. It squarely addressed many important issues facing the country and, in its detailed economic analysis, was head and shoulders above anything any other party produced in 1993. However, aside from our party members and those who attended our meetings, almost no one else heard about it.

Early in September someone broke into our Vancouver offices and stole computers, other communications equipment, and documents. The offices were left in a shambles. The election was less than two months away, so it was a major setback. (This was our second break-in; our Ottawa office had been vandalized during the summer.)

Our final total of 171 candidates was well beyond what we had hoped for when we began the party, especially since we had been organized for only a few months. (In 1988 the Reform party ran only seventy-two candidates, even though they had been at work for well over two years.)

By late September, the NDP was in freefall, down to only six percent in the polls, well behind the Reform party at ten percent.

Less than three weeks before the election, in the best column written about the National party, William Neville of the *Winnipeg Free Press* compared the Reform and National parties and concluded that "the National Party . . . is scarcely less reformist in arguing over-haul of our political processes, but instead of urging Canadians to dismantle government, it encourages them to take control of it as the means of regaining control of Canada."

Two weeks before the election I wrote to all our candidates: "Whatever happens in the election we'll soon begin planning for our first national convention and we'll take major steps to democratize the Party and refine the policy-making process and plan for new elections. I am very proud of all of you and very proud to be associated with such fine, dedicated and altruistic people."

A few days before the election we had an overflow crowd of 1,700 in Vancouver. Chrétien had spoken to some seven hundred in the same spot a few days before, and Preston Manning to some 1,100, both with great local and national media coverage. I had some populist and appealing policy announcements to make but alas, there was almost nothing in the media about our own successful and enthusiastic event. Our B.C. organizers were bitterly disappointed.

Election night was a disappointment for us as well, in that none of us was elected to Parliament. Reform went from one seat to fifty-two seats in the Commons, the NDP ended up with only seven percent support and nine seats, while the Bloc jumped from eight to fifty-four seats. Nevertheless, almost 200,000 Canadians voted for the National party, about the same number that had voted for the Reform party in the first election they contested in 1988. Considering that we had our first organizational meeting only ten months before the election, I was not dismayed by the results. This time we tried and failed. But just wait!

No one in Canada foresaw the annihilation of the Conservative party. Even close to the end of the campaign, the worst forecasts still thought that the Tories would capture at least seventy seats. But Kim Campbell had seemed on a self-destruct mission almost from the beginning. On April 29 she had issued a press release saying that she was "totally supportive of the government's economic direction first laid out by Michael Wilson and consistently followed since then." Campbell's rise and fall was quite remarkable. Looking back, I believe the media helped create her to a very large extent and then, realizing their mistake, reversed themselves with a vengeance. While Campbell's performance was a key factor in the destruction of the Conservative party, there were two other important factors The first was a pervasive, profound dislike for Mulroney and what he and his fellow Conservatives had done to Canada during the past nine years. The second was the splitting of the right-wing vote, particularly in Ontario. No one came remotely close to predicting that the Liberals would win ninety-eight of Ontario's ninety-nine seats, an unprecedented near sweep.

On election night I spoke to our disappointed members in Edmonton:

Tonight, all across our Country, there are *many thousands* of Canadians who have voted for a brand-new political party, *a party that didn't even exist a year ago!*

Tonight, in every single province, there are strong, proud, principled, dedicated National Party of Canada candidates and well-organized riding associations in place.

I have spoken to most of our 171 candidates during the past 48 hours. To a one, this is what they have said to me: "Mel, just *wait* till next time! We will begin preparing for the next election tomorrow morning."

In Edmonton Northwest I finished third behind the Liberal and Reform candidates, but ahead of the Conservative incumbent Murray Dorin and the NDP candidate.

The almost 200,000 votes the National party received across the country were more than the *combined* total for the Christian Heritage party, the Abolitionists, the Canada party, the Green party, the Libertarians, the Commonwealth party, and the Natural Law party; no great accomplishment, but a good start.

By the time of the election, our party had only some $2-million left to spend. The Liberals, Conservatives, and NDP, with few if any dissenting voices from their members or the media, had all supported legislation increasing allowable federal-election spending from $8-million to a whopping $21.6-million. Of course the $21.6-million was a limit on what they could *officially* spend during the actual campaign. In fact, all three parties had spent many millions before the election writ was dropped.

Officially the Conservatives spent $10.4-million, the Liberals $9.9-million, the NDP $7.4-million, the Reform party $1.5-million, the Natural Law party $3.4-million, and the National party $2.1-million. But these figures are very deceiving, representing only what the parties themselves spent *during* the election campaign. If candidate spending were to be included, the Conservative total would be some $24.4-million, the Liberal total $22.1-million, the Reform total $7.4-million, and the National $3-million. As well, if party spending in the weeks before the election writ was dropped were to be taken into account, the disparities would be much, much greater.

A few days after the election I wrote to all of our candidates:

> I have been very pleased by the enthusiastic and optimistic response I've heard from candidates all across the country during the last few days. As far as I am concerned, we're engaged in an important historical development that will have a major impact on the future of our country. Our journey has only begun!
>
> As to my own future, I am going to ask that our membership be polled. I think the democratic thing to do after an election is to ask the members whether they want to have a new Leader. The Constitution now calls for all members of the Party to be involved in such a decision, so we will have to do this by some sort of mail ballot.

(I was very proud that our party constitution made it mandatory that every member of the party would be able to vote in leadership elections, not just those who could afford to attend a convention.)

My hope from day one was that the Canadian public were fed up with the old-line parties and would vote for a party that stressed democratic reform, Canadian sovereignty, and a much fairer tax system. In the end, though, most of the protest vote went to a much better-organized, higher-profiled Reform party. Despite all of our efforts, only a minority of Canadians knew who we were and what we stood for. But there was one other key factor that prevented us from doing better at the polls. After the election people often stopped me on the street and said, essentially: "Mel, I want you to know I didn't vote for you this time, but I sure intend to next time. I just wanted to be damn sure we got those rotten bastards out before they destroyed the country." There was so much hatred for Mulroney and the Conservatives that people were determined to toss them out, and the best way to do that would be to vote for someone they thought was likely to win the riding: the Liberal or Reform candidate. But "next time for sure!" was something I heard again and again for many months after the election. At first I thought it was just people being nice, but then I began hearing exactly the same thing from our candidates all across the country.

"Next time for sure!"

The Beginning of the End

THERE WAS TO BE no next time. Month after month my relationship with Bill Loewen continued to deteriorate. It was a toss-up as to who disliked whom the most. Late in the campaign he had sent a television crew to Edmonton because he wanted me to record a commercial pushing his own economic theories. I took one look at the script and refused to do the commercial. Loewen was furious. I wrote to him after the election:

Re: economics — I had *great* trouble with your job creation theories. I did eventually talk to Bruce Wilkinson, Arthur Donner and Ian Stewart. They were all very negative about suggesting so many jobs could be created so quickly. I then consulted Fred Lazar and Abe Rotstein. They too were *very* negative. Sorry, Bill, but I cannot sell something I don't believe in. As I made clear to you several times, I think we should have shown more *moderate, gradually increasing* job growth and attribute it to our *package* of policies not just to your theories about the dollar and replacing foreign debt.

There had not been a single meeting of the party's board of directors for more than six months. Now a meeting was scheduled for Toronto in January.

Despite the problems, enthusiasm in the party remained very high. Members were looking forward to our founding convention, to an improved constitution, to the democratization of the party, and last, but not least, to getting to meet each other, in most cases for the first time. It seemed to me that our opportunities to continue to expand the party and to take our message to Canadians were excellent. After all, as I had predicted, there were now three conservative parties in Canada, and the NDP was dispirited and in disarray. "The future is ours if we work hard and plan properly," I wrote to our members.

By early January 1994, it had become clear there was no possible way I could work with Loewen in the future. I wrote Brian Smith a long detailed letter in which the situation was summed up in one sentence: "Simply put, life is far too short for me to have to go through another year fighting with Bill Loewen and going from crisis to crisis, virtually every month."

On January 10 my daughter Barbara was shot as she left her office in Vancouver after work. It was a random shooting by a nut, but it was a shock to all of us. Barbara was shot from behind at close range, and the bullet passed through her jacket, between her arm and her body, and out the front of her sweater. There was a flesh wound, but an inch either way and the damage could have been deadly. Barb had phoned and left a couple of messages on my answering machine, but I hadn't had a chance to play my messages back. I heard the news on the 7:00 a.m. CBC radio news as I was shaving the next morning. The meeting of the board was to take place two days later, but I decided not to attend in case I had to fly to Vancouver to be with my daughter.

At the meeting Loewen and the executive were requested to stand down and, after a bitter debate, agreed to do so. The board would be expanded and new elections would be held. The party office would be moved from Winnipeg to Ottawa, and a new executive would be elected at the next board meeting. Loewen angrily announced that he was leaving the party and resigning his party membership; he would return only "when Mel leaves."

At the February board meeting in Ottawa, a new executive was elected, headed by a new president, Cyril MacNeil, of Montreal. But Loewen had not left the party. A very angry millionaire showed up at the meeting with his lawyer in tow, and then he and several of his colleagues left the meeting, set up their own board and their own executive, and began legal action in an Ottawa court in an attempt to gain control of the party.

In the following weeks both boards hurled a steady stream of invective and accusations at each other via fax, mail, and long-distance conferences. Day by day the party was being torn apart, while the legal costs in meeting the Loewen-financed court action were escalating. From the reports I received, the only hope that the party might survive lay in the convention, if one were ever held. Both groups were at each other's throats with memos and letters faxed across the country referring to "malicious information," "bogus press releases," "expelled dissidents," "blatant attempts to take over the party," "lies and misrepresentations," "outrageous acts," "splinter groups," and similar invective.

There was one small problem — money. Loewen was in control of party funds. All membership fees and donations were going to Winnipeg. How could we plan and pay for a national convention? How could we even pay for a board-of-directors meeting? I arranged a bank loan of $20,000 to keep the party going until matters were resolved in court, and to allow the Vancouver convention committee to put a desposit down to reserve Canada Place for the June convention.

In March Loewen and his lawyer attempted to cancel the reservations for the founding convention, scheduled for the Trade and Convention Centre. The convention committee was outraged by Loewen's actions, and a court action was launched in Alberta alleging that Loewen's board had physically taken over the Ottawa headquarters and was "dealing" with the party's assets.

Loewen and his board lost their court case. When the Ontario Court of Justice decision was finally announced in April, we were elated. Perhaps a nightmare was coming to an end. At last we could get on with the job of building the party. The judge's fourteen-page decision was elegantly written, opening with: "The National Party of Canada is being rent by two factions, to use Lord Durham's phrase, 'warring in the bosom of a single' party. . . . Such a bifurcated party must be a daunting challenge to the most dedicated of members." A daunting challenge indeed! The party had been paralysed until the court case was resolved.

The press asked me to comment on the judge's decision. "It's a major victory for democracy and for grassroots politics," I said. "I'm tickled pink with the decision. The verdict virtually guarantees a very successful founding convention in Vancouver. Most of all, it ensures that the party will be in the hands of its members and that democracy will prevail in the party. It's unfortunate that we were forced into court, but we were optimistic from day one that justice would prevail."

Mr. Justice David McWilliam's decision rejected claims by Loewen's group and left the legitimate board in charge. According to the *Ottawa Citizen*, "Bickering over who controls the National Party was silenced by the court." "Hurtig regains control," read the headline in the *Winnipeg Free Press*.

All in all it was a disquieting experience. I did not want "control," but I did want a democratic party. With this in mind, I asked that the founding convention also become a leadership convention. I wrote to the board:

(1) I was elected Leader by our 45 founding members at our first meeting on November 21st, 1992. We now have over 10,000 members. They should be allowed their say re the leadership.

(2) In a democratic political party, the members should be able to vote on the leadership, the board, the executive, etc., on a regular basis — to be spelled out in our constitution.

(3) There should always be a vote after a federal election where the Party does not form the government.

(4) The Leader needs the endorsation of the members to reinforce his or her position, and of course must be prepared to be rejected by the members.

There had been some criticism of my performance as leader at the January board meeting, as was to be expected after the election and the bitter conflict with Loewen, and I very much wanted to give the membership an opportunity to accept or reject my performance. I offered my resignation to the February board meeting, but the board showed no inclination to stage a leadership convention. I felt I had no alternative but to submit my resignation. The board rejected it, saying: "Hurtig is the heart and soul of the National Party and the Executive believes that now, more than ever, Canada needs a party led by Mel Hurtig."

I had thought that after losing the long and expensive court case, Loewen would go away. It was not to be. All I could see was more conflict on the horizon. As a result, by late spring I had pretty well made up my mind not to seek election as leader. I would continue to work for the party, give speeches, attend fundraising dinners, do research, and help with policy, but the previous year and a half had been an experience I didn't wish to repeat.

Privately I informed the board of my decision. They would not hear of it. Soon letters and phone calls poured in from party officials and members asking me to stay on as leader and to stand for reelection at the convention. My wife, my children, and my close friends, who understood the situation, all urged me *not* to run for the leadership. The previous eighteen months had easily been the most difficult period of my life and it showed. While building the party and the campaign had been exciting and exhilarating, and most of the members were wonderful, dedicated men and women, the prospect of a continued conflict with Loewen held no appeal. But try as I might, the members would not let me resign.

In late May, just before the deadline, I agreed to run. If I was elected I would continue to help build the party, but there was no way I would lead the party into another federal election. There were at least four men and three women in the party who, in my opinion, would make intelligent, attractive, articulate, and energetic leaders. I would do my best to help build the party and then step aside so that one of them would be elected to take my place. But that was for the future. For now, the task was to once again fight off the challenge of Bill Loewen, who was preparing a slate to run against me as leader and for the executive and board positions.

The First and Last Convention

EVEN WITH ALL THE internal problems of the first few months of 1994, I remained optimistic about the party's future prospects. With the Liberals, Conservatives and Reform crowded to the right side of the political spectrum, it seemed to me that if we had a good founding convention in Vancouver, we could go on to occupy the centre-left with much success.

Despite a considerable amount of turmoil, the convention was successful in many ways. Members from more than a hundred constituencies representing every region of the country attended. To say that the debate was spirited and the elections hotly contested would be gross understatement. But members from Toronto met members from Vancouver for the first time, and members from Montreal met members from Edmonton and Calgary. A new and improved constitution was ratified, although it was obvious that sooner rather than later more work was needed to improve it.

The board of directors had opted for Maritime Telephone and Telegraph's "teledemocracy" proposal for voting for the leader, the president, and some key policy resolutions. I was sceptical about the proposal and was the only member of the board who didn't vote in favour. The cost was, in my opinion, prohibitive, probably in the neighbourhood of some $100,000. As a result, members across the country would be charged twenty dollars to vote during the convention. Twenty dollars was more than the cost of party membership. Moreover, many of our members could not afford to spend twenty dollars to vote. I felt that a simpler, less expensive, and more democratic choice would have been a mail ballot. As well, I was concerned about the technology; would it actually work as promised?

As I had predicted, the voting fee turned off many of our members, both on principle and for financial reasons. When advance voting registrations showed a disappointing total, a hasty, belated decision was made to allow all members to vote without a fee, and the constituencies were charged with collecting what they could after the convention. Few, if any, tried. The cost to the party of teledemocracy was just under $130,000.

Despite all these negatives, the National party did become the first federal political party to allow every member to vote for the leader and the party president. Voting was no longer exclusively reserved for delegates who could afford air fare, accommodation, and convention-registration costs.

Just before the convention, Bill Loewen distributed a long document, *The National Party of Canada: The First Fourteen Months*, in which he presented his version of the party's history, but neglected to mention that the Loewen board had lost its court challenge. The document was a harsh attack on me, clearly meant to sway convention voters. In the document, Loewen expressed his disappointment in my performance as party leader. The convention committee wrote him an open letter in response, part of which read:

> Standing for election yourself would have been a more appropriate vehicle through which to have made known your views on past political and administrative leadership as well as for your ideas on policy and party development.
>
> We . . . regret that you chose to stop your "history" just prior to the court case which you and others initiated in an attempt to take control of the National Party of Canada structures and resources. Honesty would then have compelled you to acknowledge that the Court ruled that there was no legal validity to the claims made by the petitioners who were required, by that decision, to return all Party property to the control of the legally-acknowledged Board. We feel compelled to request of the Board that the appropriate body investigate the method of distribution of this document to ensure that Party property in the form of Party mailing lists were not used.
>
> In closing, we wish to reiterate our disappointment that you would choose to circulate such a document on the eve of the founding convention of the Party. This can only be construed as a destructive act on a fledgling party.

And destructive it was. Brian Smith, who was not one of my supporters, called Loewen's document a "blatant, self-serving attempt to rewrite history . . . typically undemocratic . . . just another example of how, if you have the money, you can represent your version of events with little fear of being effectively countered."

The document had been sent out to party members across the country just before the voting, so I had no opportunity to respond except at the convention.

The press asked me to comment on Loewen's actions. "I think the mood of the members is clear," I said. "We've had enough. Let's get on with building the party."

When the votes were counted, I had received almost eighty percent support. Almost all of Loewen's candidates went down to defeat, including those contesting the party presidency and the positions of vice president and treasurer. "Hurtig sweeps back as National Party Leader," was the Canadian Press headline, and "Publisher's convincing victory climaxes a stormy two-day session," said the *Globe*.

Much to my pleasure, the convention and those voting by telephone soundly rejected, by a two-to-one margin, a proposal that the party accept donations from corporations and unions in the future. I proposed a resolution for consideration at the first meeting of the newly elected governing council:

> . . . given the fact the National Party of Canada has a policy of not accepting donations from corporations and trade unions, and given the fact the reform of democracy is a key priority for the Party, therefore it is inconsistent for the Party to accept unlimited donations from individuals.
>
> Therefore, be it resolved that the National Party of Canada will in the future limit donations from individuals to no more than $10,000 in any calendar year, and that this limit go into effect immediately.
>
> I wish to point out that $10,000 would amount to only one-third of one percent of a $3-million election campaign.

Three days after the convention I wrote to all members of the newly elected party council, which replaced the board of directors. "Democracy, democracy, democracy," I said. "We not only must run the party in a truly democratic manner, but we must be seen to be running the party in a democratic manner, as well. Yes, this creates a tremendous amount of extra work. But yes, it's what our members demand and expect and we can't let them down in this respect. Let's do our best to involve them in the decision-making process and to keep them well informed about what is happening in the party."

After the convention I was optimistic that at last the party's troubles were finally over and we could begin organizing and building across the country. I was wrong.

Grand Design and Failed Enterprise

IN JULY 1994 THE newly elected president of the party, Dan
Whetung of Victoria, phoned to tell me that an associate had
contacted the RCMP fraud squad and that a former party financial
official would probably be going to jail for theft of party funds.
Moreover, he claimed that a firm of forensic accountants had been
contacted in Vancouver, and that they were "quite familiar" with the
individual in question. I was stunned by these comments and was
unaware of any proof to substantiate his charges. Not long after, as
might be expected, the accusations created terrible turmoil in the party.

Soon after the convention, quite unknown to me, a seven-page
memo was faxed to Vancouver from Winnipeg. It contained serious
allegations about the honesty of one of the party's financial officials.
Then, some three weeks after the convention, a memo was circulated
"To the Leader, Officers, Regional Representatives and Members-at-
Large of the National Party of Canada," signed by the past president,
the past treasurer, the convention chairperson, and three other
members of the convention committee. The memo demanded that
Dan Whetung "be removed as President and expelled from the party"
and that other members "guilty of acts inconsistent with the aims,
objects, or ethics of the party" also be expelled and "measures . . .
taken to disband dissident organizations within the party."

Good grief! Not again. When I read the memo, I felt sick to my
stomach.

In late July party vice president Bill Stephenson and I wrote the
former official asking fourteen questions about the party's financial
situation, its revenue and expenditures, the availability of financial statements, the location of party funds, the status of accounts
payable, the situation regarding the legally required financial audit, the
disposition of funds received from Elections Canada, and a number of
other key questions. We requested a response in writing before the
coming executive meeting in Vancouver.

The party's new national executive met for the first time at the
Water Street Café in Vancouver's Gastown on August 12. After the
meeting, as I walked back to my hotel, I made the decision to resign.
Enough was enough. Once again the party was in chaos, and it
was not even two months since the convention. Because of the allegations of wrongdoing and suggestions of problems with the party's

finances, the president and vice president were at each other's throats, there were new two-way threats of legal action between two factions on the council, the past treasurer refused to present his financial report with the newly elected president present in the room and threatened to have work on the party audit suspended, and the newly elected treasurer resigned, and this was only part of the ugly chaos that developed in such a short period of time.

Kay and I drove up to Sechelt where I gave the annual Bruce Hutchison Memorial Lecture, and then we headed to Whistler to play golf for a few days. Just before I left for Sechelt, I was given a copy of a two-page letter from another party's constituency president to the British Columbia president of that party accusing our financial official of having misappropriated funds, along with a request that they should "initiate proceedings which will inform all members of our organization that he cannot be trusted with funds or to act with integrity in regard to handling official records of general meetings or of any party activities."

In my opinion there was only one solution: we must immediately employ a first-class forensic auditor to examine the National party's books. I called the most respected firm of forensic auditors in Vancouver and, to my dismay, was told by one of their senior partners that our financial official had indeed "been involved in lawsuits — at least one currently under way involving misallocation of funds." The same day, the other party's president made even worse accusations to me on the telephone.

On August 29 I wrote Dan Whetung an eight-page letter announcing my resignation and spelling out the reasons for my decision:

> After a great deal of thought and lengthy discussions with my wife, family and friends, I have decided to resign as leader of the National Party of Canada.
>
> Given the ludicrous events of the past few weeks, I doubt that you will be completely surprised by my decision.
>
> My resignation is effective immediately and will not, under any circumstances, be reconsidered.
>
> There are two principal reasons for my resignation. First, I simply cannot do my job properly because of the unfortunate and totally unanticipated events in the Party since the convention, and second, as you well know, I have been unable to

obtain satisfactory information about the financial affairs of the Party.

As you know, a long memo has been circulated making serious accusations relating to the integrity of a former senior officer of the Party. Apparently this memo prompted numerous enquiries by you and your associates in British Columbia. Subsequent correspondence and phone calls in response to your enquiries have proved worrisome, to say the least.

Unfortunately my worst fears have now been realized. As you are well aware, once again the Party is in disarray and once again controversy rages within the Executive, the Council and the membership.

The ideals of sovereignty, democracy and social justice that I proposed are now mired in a morass of charges relating to accusations about the integrity of the former senior officer mentioned and his handling of Party funds. Your colleagues in Vancouver have decided to circulate these accusations across the country.

For me, one of the most troubling aspects of this matter has been my own inability to obtain adequate financial information about the affairs of the Party, despite a sustained and determined effort to do so. Since you have copies of my correspondence in this connection, this will not be news to you. My letters, faxes, phone calls and messages to the person in question have gone unanswered. The financial information that has been provided has not been satisfactory so as to allow me to answer important questions that I have raised.

Obviously, when important questions about the Party finances from both the leader and the president go unanswered, a serious problem exists, a problem that would surely not be tolerated by any other political party.

If the Party gets its act together and resolves the problems it now faces, I would be happy to be of some assistance in the future, but not in the capacity of leader. I am today writing the Chief Electoral Officer advising him of my resignation.

By the end of September, there were once more two separate groups at full-scale war within the party, one led by the president and one by the vice president. According to the Canadian Press, "The captain has gone, the crew was fighting and the corps was in critical condition."

Corps or corpse? I thought.

My greatest regret was knowing I had let so many good people down. But the many nice letters and phone calls helped.

By early September, Dan Whetung had revoked the membership of the party's vice president, secretary, acting treasurer, and Toronto chairman, informing them that unless they turned over all party records and party property, further actions against them would be taken. A few days later Bill Stephenson, party vice president, announced that Whetung's membership in the party had been suspended "in the interest of protecting the party from further harm."

In a meeting of the council in September 1994, by an eight-to-four vote, a decision was made to dissolve the party. The press asked me for a statement:

> Thousands of dedicated Canadian men and women who tried to make the National Party of Canada a success are going to be bitterly disappointed by the news that the Executive of the Party has voted to put an end to the Party's existence.
>
> I share with them that disappointment. Some 200,000 voters supported the Party in the last federal election. Clearly, the Party has let them down.
>
> In sum we tried and lost. Better to have tried and lost than not to have tried at all. During the last 24 hours I have heard from Canadians in every province. Through the tears and recriminations there has been one common theme — "We won't give in — we've just begun to fight for our country."
>
> I think it's quite possible that some new entity may emerge from the ashes in the future. My own plans are to leave politics completely and begin work on two books that I have promised my publisher.

In September and October a number of board members asked me for my continuing involvement in decisions relating to the future of the party if it continued. I replied that I would not be involved unless a democratic, elected council was in charge with full representation as a result of regional elections, and unless the party commissioned a forensic audit of all 1994 revenue and expenditures.

About the same time, in a letter to all constituency presidents, dedicated nationalist Kim Stebner of Vancouver, who had taken over as interim party treasurer, advised that "over the last seven months this party has been forced to spend over $200,000 in legal fees."

Early in November Dan Whetung wrote to me asking if I would continue to be a member of the National party. I replied in part:

> The events since the end of August lead me (and many others) to despair. I hope I am wrong, but I believe the prospects for the Party have been destroyed by the vicious infighting, power struggles and by a few very self-centred men who care more about their own personal priorities than they do about the National Party and a sovereign, independent Canada in charge of its own destiny. . . .
>
> I very much like Winston Churchill's famous "Never give in" speech. I certainly have no intention of ever giving in to those who have been selling out our country. But my efforts in the future will not be directed towards the National Party.

For a new political party with a principal theme of honesty, integrity, openness, democratic reform, and grassroots decision-making to be mired in a vicious name-calling morass was an absurd situation. All political parties have terrible internal battles; for example, David Lewis versus the Waffle, Lucien Bouchard and Brian Mulroney, Dalton Camp and John Diefenbaker, John Turner and Jean Chrétien, Judy LaMarsh and Pierre Trudeau, the embarrassing internal battles in the Reform party. But for a brand-new party, one still in its infancy, such divisions were fatal.

For me personally, the National Party of Canada was both a marvellous experience and a nightmare. It was a fascinating adventure and a dreadful catastrophe. The party was full of wonderful, exciting, enthusiastic, altruistic, and patriotic men and women of all ages, and also some of the strangest characters I have ever encountered in public or private life. As Allan Fotheringham wrote of Ross Perot's August 1995 Dallas gathering: "Every screwball and government-hater and conspiracy-believer who could afford bus fare showed up in Dallas, pushing a Third Party." We had our share, too. A new party will inevitably attract the lonely, the disaffected, the angry, and the hopeful. We promised a lot and we gathered in a great many idealists and more than a few screwballs.

When I look back, there is no question in my mind whatsoever that had we started a new party back in 1985, instead of the Council of Canadians, today that party would be playing a major role in Canada's political system. We could have planned more slowly and more carefully, taken the time to develop a first-class constitution that would have avoided many of our problems. We could have avoided the rush decisions and built more gradually and more surely. But, as we all know, hindsight is always easy. We did what we did in 1992 and 1993 because many of us felt that another four or five years of continentalist right-wing government would lock us into an irreversible spiral.

VII

"LADIES AND GENTLEMEN"

Speaking of Speaking

FOR ALMOST THIRTY years I have spent a great deal of my time giving speeches across the country. I am now quite comfortable doing so, but this was not always the case. When I was twenty-nine, I became president of the Edmonton Art Gallery. I was so nervous about speaking in public that I would *never* agree to open a show. Invariably I would beg the vice president or some other gallery officer to take my place. I was nervous with good reason: I was a terrible speaker. And the most important reason I was a terrible speaker was that I was nervous.

Many people are terrified of public speaking. Even many very familiar entertainers (Alec Guinness, Barbra Streisand, Helen Hayes) suffered from stage fright. When I sat in on university classes, I rarely asked any questions. In a 1969 article for the *Toronto Star*, journalist Barry Westgate described me as "a man who is quiet and analytical."

Through the early 1970s I began receiving, on average, two or three speaking invitations from across Canada every day. They came from professional groups, trade unions, health-care organizations, teachers and students, academic organizations, universities and colleges, industry groups, and government bodies. In those years I didn't give a single speech where I wasn't quite on edge before the talk.

But it didn't take me long to figure a few things out. First, there was no way I could read a speech; when I tried I felt as if I was acting. Moreover, I lost eye contact with my audience, and that's fatal. So, what I did was this: I would often (but not always) write the speech out word for word, read it over a couple of times, then take a single page of lined letter-size paper, divide it vertically into four columns, then list the key words in order, paragraph by paragraph, top to bottom. This way I could speak directly to my audience but keep my thoughts in order with only an occasional glance at my sheet of paper.

By far the most helpful thing I learned was that if I could get my audience laughing at the beginning of my talk, I would relax and so would they. The real trick was, of course, to tell funny stories and tell them well. The best speeches I ever gave were those where I got my audience laughing so hard at the beginning of my talk that I started laughing, too. Most of my stories were from my own experiences, but I didn't hesitate to borrow from others.

One story I told was of a speech I made to a big convention in Vancouver. The man who introduced me had said: ". . . and among the books which Mr. Hurtig will publish this fall will be *The Diaries of Louis Riel*, including one of Riel's diaries never before translated into English." After my speech, a number of men and women gathered below the stage podium, asking questions, shaking my hand. Finally there was one woman remaining. Here is how the conversation went:

"Mr. Hurtig, that was a wonderful speech."

"Thank you very much."

"Mr. Hurtig, I'm a great fan of Louis Riel. I've read everything he's ever written. I'm just delighted you're publishing the diaries. I can hardly wait."

"That's great. We should have them out in September."

"Wonderful! Tell me, Mr. Hurtig, will Mr. Riel be making a national promotion tour for his book this fall?"

I also liked to tell the true story of the time I spoke to a big convention at the Hotel Vancouver. I went to bed just before eleven. Soon after, I was wakened by a knock on my door. I wrapped a towel around my waist and opened the door a crack. There stood a beautiful blond woman, wearing a black mink coat. "Hello," I said, wiping the sleep out of my eyes. "Hello, Mr. Hurtig. I heard your speech tonight and I thought it was marvellous. I'm a very passionate nationalist and I'd really like to meet you." So, to make a long story short, I sold her a membership in the Committee for an Independent Canada.

Another story I liked to tell was of how once, in Vancouver, Jack Webster was to introduce me at a high school in Langara. I did Jack's open-line radio show from the Georgia Hotel, and then we drove out to the school in his Saltspring Island four-wheel-drive. On the way he said: "Mel, you should know there hasn't been much publicity. We could have quite a small crowd." I said that was no problem, I'd spoken to small crowds before, but darned if Jack didn't say the same thing to me twice more before we got to the school.

When we arrived, there was no place to park. Every street was packed with cars. We got out a few blocks from the school and walked. But when we turned the corner we immediately realized why there were so many cars; there was a baseball game in progress and the bleachers were packed. We found the rear entrance to the school and walked down a long, dimly lit corridor. At last we found the rear stairs to the auditorium stage. Jack went up first and I followed. He headed straight for the drawn stage curtains and peeked out into the auditorium, then turned to me with a stricken look on his face. He motioned for me to come and have a look, which I did. I peeked out between the curtains into a big fully lit auditorium. There wasn't one single person in it. Not one! My speech was scheduled for eight o'clock, and it was now five after. I looked at Jack and he looked at me. Our CIC workers weren't even there!

Ten minutes later we discovered we were in the wrong school. When we got to the right school a few blocks away, an impatient and worried crowd of six hundred were waiting for us.

ONCE I WAS TO SPEAK to a Southwest Alberta teachers' convention in Lethbridge. My assistant, Rhonda, and my travel agent figured out that if I took the first Time Air flight out of Edmonton early in the morning and changed to another Time Air flight in Calgary, I could get there for my 9:30 a.m. keynote address. When we were directly over the University of Lethbridge, the pilot announced, "Ladies and gentlemen, we're about to land in Lethbridge. Please fasten your safety belts, put your seats in an upright position, fold the table in front of you into the seat ahead. We'll be landing in a couple of minutes." We were flying in a Fairchild F-27 with an overhead wing and big oval windows. I sat next to the window looking down at the university, then watched as the wheels folded down out of the wings above, then locked into position right opposite me only a few feet away. But then I could hardly believe my eyes. The wheel fell off. I watched it fall down and away behind us in horror, then quickly reached up and pushed the button for the stewardess.

"Pardon me, miss," I said, as we were rapidly descending, "but the left wheel has fallen off."

"Oh sure."

"Have a look yourself."

She leaned over me and looked out, then all the blood drained from her face. She lurched back two rows and called the cockpit.

"Captain. The left wheel has fallen off."

A pause, and then: "I'm *not* kidding! The left wheel has fallen off!" This time she said it loudly enough for everyone to hear.

We circled Lethbridge for more than forty-five minutes. All the while there was not a single word from the cockpit; from time to time the stewardess walked down the aisle, a smile frozen on her face. The man next to me clutched the armrests so firmly all his knuckles were white; I was sure he was going to have a heart attack. Finally the intercom came on. This was the entire message from the captain: "Ladies and gentlemen, we are returning to Calgary because the runways are longer there." Click.

When we got over Calgary, it was very reassuring indeed. We could look down and see all the fire trucks, ambulances, and police cars gathered on both sides of the runway. Gulp. Down and down we went until we hit the runway, spun, and stopped. No one was hurt.

On another occasion I spoke to a split-session teachers' convention in Toronto. My talk was at 9:00 a.m., there was a coffee break at 10:30, and then a different speaker. I did something I very rarely did: I told a very long complicated but very funny story at the beginning of my talk. The story took a good ten minutes to tell properly, but if you did it right, it was hilarious. I had my audience rolling in the aisles soon after I began and right through to the end of the story. Afterwards, I stayed for coffee and since I had some time before I had to head for Pearson International, I sat at the back of the auditorium to listen for a few minutes to the next speaker, a gentleman from New York. He was introduced to a nice round of applause, and then he immediately launched into exactly the same story I had told. Within seconds, the audience was convulsed with laughter. The speaker, thinking he was obviously doing a great job, continued on with much vigour. Soon the audience was falling out of their chairs, laughing not at the story but at the misfortune of the poor speaker.

I borrowed shamelessly from others for my openings. For example: Tommy Douglas was in Edmonton, attempting to fend off a boisterous heckler who kept yelling, "You're rotten!" throughout Douglas's speech. Finally Tommy stopped, pointed a finger and shouted back, "And you're drunk!" "Shoorr," said the drunk. "I'm drunk, but I'll be sober in the morning and you'll still be rotten!"

Then there were the great one liners, which I often paraphrased in my debates: Disraeli re: Gladstone on the difference between a misfortune and a calamity: "If John Crispo fell into Lake Ontario that would be a misfortune. If someone pulled him out that would be a calamity."

Or Richard Sheridan's comment when Prime Minister William Pitt entered the House of Commons: "There but for the grace of God goes God."

Or the story about a birthday party for Australian Prime Minister Malcolm Fraser, where a scantily dressed blonde emerged from a cake. The next day in the Commons, a Labour MP told the House: "This is the first time the prime minister has been successful in stimulating the private sector."

Once John Diefenbaker spoke at a high school graduation in rural Saskatchewan. It was a hot June day. Halfway through his speech the microphone stopped working. After a long delay, Dief tried again. "Can you hear me now?" Someone at the back shouted "No!" A man in the second row got up and yelled back: "Great, I'll trade you places."

I borrowed John Colombo's stories about seeing the highway sign "Historic site under construction" and the sign in the dry cleaner's window "Drop your pants here and receive immediate attention." I borrowed Peter Newman's stories about the research vessel that radioed down to the diver, "Surface immediately, the ship is sinking," and about the farmer he encountered when he became lost on a country road in Ontario. Newman asked the farmer, "Have you lived here all your life?" "Nope, not yet" came the reply. Then there was the query to a waiting speaker from the man who was to introduce him: "Do you want to speak now or shall we let them enjoy themselves a little longer?" My own worst line was when I suggested that if Duke Ellington had been a Canadian, the song would have been "Take the train, eh."

The most awful thing a speaker can do is to tell the wrong story to the wrong audience. I once told a story about Joe Clark to a convention of Conservative oilmen in Calgary; nobody laughed. Speaking to Calvin College, a conservative Christian school in Michigan, I told the story of the Earl of Sandwich saying to John Wilkes in the House of Commons: "You will either die on the gallows or of some terrible disease." And Wilkes replied: "That, sir, depends on whether I embrace your politics or your mistress."

I learned that I always gave my best speeches when I was very well prepared, well rested, and when I spoke on an empty stomach. Once I spoke to a dinner meeting in a legion basement hall in Southern

Ontario. As usual, I sipped on water while everyone ate. Then, just before I was due to speak, my favourite dessert, chocolate pie with whipped cream, was placed in front of me. I took my fork in hand, but then, somehow, willpower took over. The next morning I learned that more than a hundred people had been seriously poisoned, some hospitalized, by the chocolate pie.

It took me some time, but I became a good speaker. Early on I was criticized for being too "emotional." Then I was criticized for having too many statistics in my speeches. After a while, I got it close to right. Often I would use slides and a laser pointer or large charts to illustrate my talks. In universities I almost always used a blackboard. For me, the key thing was not only to know my material well, but also to really believe in the importance of my message. By far the best speeches I ever gave were with no lectern, with no notes, and a microphone clipped around my neck.

I think the worst speech I ever gave was to an electrical contractors' convention at the Sheraton Centre in Toronto. I had spoken the previous day in Victoria and arrived in Toronto late at night. At seven the next morning I got my wake-up call; my speech was at nine. One problem: I had left my electric razor in Victoria. I called the front desk; could they send me up an electric razor? "No problem, Mr. Hurtig. It'll be up in a few minutes." At eight I phoned again; where was my razor? "Sorry, Mr. Hurtig, we've been looking and looking but we can't find our electric razors — someone must be using them."

Well, then, could they send me up a regular razor, a blade, and shaving cream? "Sorry, Mr. Hurtig, but we don't have any." To compound matters, the gift shop would not be open until nine.

I hadn't used a blade to shave for more than thirty years; when-ever I was in the mountains or the bush I had just let my beard grow. When I finally got to the lower hall where I was to speak, twenty minutes late, there were patches of tissue all over my face and neck, and blood on my shoes and pants. The large crowd looked restless. The association president gave me a nice introduction, explained what had happened, and then tried to lower the microphone (he was quite tall) so I could speak. His attempts failed. He and others tried for a good ten minutes before calling the hotel for a replacement mike. By the time I got up to speak, it was almost ten o'clock and the audience had been sitting there for an hour. At least now the mike was in the right place, the blood had stopped oozing down my face, and I was ready to go. But wait — another small problem. The platform was composed of two joined sections, one side a good three inches higher than the others, and this was exactly where I had to stand to give my talk. I moved from foot to foot, side to side; nothing worked. I was terribly uncomfortable. I then told a very funny story that had brought down the house in Victoria the day before. Perhaps in my discomfort I may have left out a crucial line. Whatever. No one laughed. Perspiration broke out on my forehead. I then proceeded to give what surely must have been one of the worst speeches ever heard in Canada.

You are guaranteed a bad speech if you've become bored with your material. That happened to me twice, both times when I was giving too many speeches in too short a period. Once in Regina speaking to a co-op annual convention, halfway through my talk I suddenly realized I was putting them to sleep. I was able to salvage the evening by abandoning my topic and switching, just in time, to a passionate speech about the survival of Canada. Another time in Vancouver I gave a terrible speech to an alumni association for the simple reason that I was bone tired.

In the early 1970s one title I used quite often was "Who Are You and Where Are You Going?" The title referred to an amusing incident that occurred at the prime minister's residence at Harrington Lake near Ottawa when U.S. President Lyndon Johnson was visiting. In the middle of the night, Lester Pearson, dressed in pajamas, bathrobe, and slippers, was rudely accosted by an American Secret Service agent. He asked Pearson: "Who are you and where are you going?" Pearson responded: "I live here and I'm going to the bathroom."

I don't know how many hundreds of high schools I have spoken in, but it's a big number. I love speaking in high schools, especially the question-and-answer periods. I would get many letters after my talks. Here's a sample from Westlock, Alberta: "I can't tell you how much I loved your speech. Your enthusiasm and upbeat way of communication certainly blasted my mood at the time." "You gave some very valuable and interesting information." Your speech really boomed my interest in world affairs!" "You are a very intelligent and well-educated man. You also have the wit to match. Never change! I'll never forget how you 'woke' us up that day; Tuesday, May 12, 1987!"

It took me quite a while to feel comfortable on television, but it wasn't long before I understood its enormous power. Even if I appeared on some lacklustre midmorning "homemakers" show, the mail and telephone response was incredible. At first I was terrible on television, nervous, uncomfortable, never eyeballing the camera. But after watching tapes of myself that horrified me, I learned a few basic lessons such as looking right at the camera, smiling and laughing, using my hands, breathing deeply at the beginning while I was waiting for the red light on the camera to go on. In December 1991 I debated William F. Buckley, Jr., on his "Firing Line" show. I understood from the beginning that rather than getting into a big angry fight with him, the best tactic would be to laugh at his outrageous statements and to present my case with good humour. It worked. A correspondent from Vanier, Ontario, wrote me and said: "My wife and I saw you on 'Firing Line'. . . . He behaved like a buffoon, as I had never seen him do before. He lost a huge amount of respect and you gained a lot. You stuck to the facts; you were prepared: you didn't attack him (no matter how much he provoked you and played to the audience); we were proud of you and ashamed of him."

Of course, a great many people are nervous doing television. Poor Tom d'Aquino. He and Peter Lougheed debated Bob White and Maude Barlow on consecutive evenings on network television. The first night, perspiration was dripping from d'Aquino's nose and chin; he looked terrible. The next night there was no perspiration. How did he manage such an amazing turnaround? A year or so later I happened to be in the TV station's makeup studio, making small talk while my makeup was being applied. Could the makeup lady tell me any funny stories about her experiences? Yes, in fact, one came to mind immediately, about how they had to put deodorant on Tom d'Aquino's forehead to get him to stop dripping.

I usually did some four or five new speeches every year and modified them each month as circumstances or the audience required. I worked *hard* on these speeches.

In 1986 Walter Kaasa presented me with the Canadian Speech Communicators Association Speaker of the Year Award, which was first presented to John Diefenbaker in 1973, and later to Joey Smallwood, Chief Justice Samuel Freedman of Manitoba, and Grant MacEwan. The same year I received the Toastmasters International Award for Communications and Leadership. But probably the nicest reward of all was the thousands of letters and phone calls over the years from men, women, and young Canadians who appreciated and supported my message.

"Never Heard of Them . . .
They Must Be Canadian"

I N THE EARLY 1970S, teachers from across the country began asking
me to come to speak at their conventions. The more time I spent
talking with the teachers and students, the more disappointed I
became at the lack of Canadian content in the curriculum. In many
school libraries there were only a few Canadian books or magazines.
Most of the students I talked to knew very little about our country.

It seemed to me that somehow curriculum people and many
teachers had become preoccupied with methodology, forgetting to
keep course content in mind. The teachers' conventions I attended
most often had keynote speakers from the United States. The
seemingly obvious mandate to teach Canadian children about Canada
had somehow been discarded.

One school text I came across, *How People Live in Canada*, had a
big picture of Abraham Lincoln on the cover. Another book, this one
about hockey called *Fury on Ice*, ended with the dirty French-
Canadian centre getting a two-minute penalty, which allowed the
valiant American captain to score the winning goal. One grade-three
class in Edmonton learned that "our flag" consisted of thirteen red
and white stripes and fifty stars. Another class was assigned a paragraph to copy that ended: "Now we have 50 states. We are proud of
our country." A grade-eight class wrote essays about Robert E. Lee,
"one of our greatest generals." In Calgary a grade-four class dutifully
recorded that "our nation's birthday is on the fourth of July." Quizzes
concentrated on which was the highest mountain, the biggest lake,
the largest city, and so on, all in the United States. One American
high school text used in Manitoba advised students that Canada needs
the U.S. ten times more than the U.S. needs Canada. In one grade-
twelve class I visited in Charlottetown, of thirty students, only one
knew who Papineau was, only one could identify Samuel Hearne,
and only half could identify the name Wilfrid Laurier. In Calgary a
group of twenty-four grade-twelve students did an educational television show with me; only four knew who Laurier was; only one
could identify Palliser, and only one knew who Crowfoot was. After
one speech I gave complaining about the situation in Canadian
schools, the Canadian Press reporter wrote: "Mr. Hurtig said young

Canadians were learning all about Davey Crockett, but not about Simon Frazer." No editor caught the spelling error. Canadian kids knew all about Daniel Boone and George Washington; they rarely knew anything about David Thompson or Louis Riel. Some four hundred Ontario university students were asked to take a test given to landed immigrants before they received their citizenship. Seventy-six percent of the students could not name the governor general, eighty students identified Harold Wilson as a Canadian premier, while more than ninety percent could not name three provincial premiers. Most of the university students failed the test.

In 1971 students in political science at McMaster University in Hamilton went on strike because there was not enough Canadian content in their classes. Sixteen of the eighteen faculty members were not Canadians. The University of Alberta hired an American professor from Texas to teach high school teachers how to teach social studies.

By the mid-1970s, some ninety-five percent of all the texts used in elementary and high schools in Canada were produced by foreign publishers, mostly American, and at the postsecondary level it was ninety-two percent. Canadian librarians were asked in a survey, "What sources do you use to choose your books?" The four most-mentioned sources were *The American Library Association Journal*, the *Virginia Kirkus Service* (out of Chicago), *Time* magazine, and the *New York Times Book Review*.

About the same time, Lakehead University in Thunder Bay, with some nine thousand Indians and Métis living in the immediate area, had a graduate course in Black studies, but not a single course on Canadian Indians or Métis. The head of the sociology department at one major Canadian university was an American citizen as were twenty-five of the department's thirty-six members. When staff had to be reduced, five Canadians were let go.

Closer to home, Imperial Oil sent a speaker to a high school in Edmonton. After his talk, teachers phoned to tell me that the speaker told the students they mustn't be overly concerned with issues like foreign ownership. "Nationalists like to make a lot of noise," the speaker had said. Besides, "we shouldn't turn our back on the rest of the world."

After eight years of trying, *The Journal of Canadian Studies* finally was given a small grant from the Canada Council — $3,770. The same year, the council gave the *Canadian Journal of African Studies* a grant for $11,355. (About the same time, the RCMP decided to celebrate its anniversary with a cross-country pageant. The RCMP hired an American to write the show!)

In 1974 not one of the three professors teaching Canadian history at Simon Fraser University in Vancouver was a Canadian.

In my travels across the country the question I asked over and over again was: "How can we expect to survive as a country if, in the face of massive inundation of American culture, we fail to teach our own kids about our own history, culture, traditions, heroes, accomplishments, and values?" Across Canada provincial ministries of education, instead of insisting on texts with adequate Canadian content or developing curriculums with adequate Canadian content, simply allowed themselves to become dependent on foreign textbooks, almost all of them American. In a Reader's Digest "reading skill builder" used in elementary schools, Canadian youngsters learned that the American eagle is the "symbol of our proud freedom." In Nanaimo students read in their language text that the American forces defeated the British "and our flag had won its first victory." In Calgary students were asked in a test: "Who was the first president of our country?"

Seven months after Pauline Jewett was appointed president of Simon Fraser University, the senior faculty threatened to break her. She had vowed to restrict the hiring of American staff. Sixty percent of the faculty were non-Canadian, with Americans the highest percentage among them.

During the 1970s billions of dollars flowed out of Canada to purchase American films, film strips, books, and other educational material for use in Canadian schools.

One day in 1974, after visiting a high school in Ottawa and once again being disappointed by the lack of Canadian content in the curriculum, I decided to see if I could somehow give the Canadian educational establishment a jolt. What I set out to do became one of the most important things I had ever done. It took almost a year of planning, organization, distribution, and coordination, and cost some $5,000. Political scientist Larry Pratt helped, as did a large number of teachers in every province. In a March 22, 1975, article in the *Globe and Mail* I recounted how "in March of 1974 the Surrey-Langley chapter of the Committee for an Independent Canada conducted a 'Canadian Awareness Survey' of students in their last year of high school in six schools in and around Vancouver." I went on to document a shocking lack of knowledge about Canada. For instance, less than thirty percent could identify the BNA Act as Canada's Constitution — the Magna Carta, Declaration of Independence, and Bill of Rights were frequent answers; seventy-two percent could not name the premier of the province of Quebec; seventy-one percent could not name the capital of New Brunswick; asked to name *any* three Canadian authors, sixty-one percent were unable to do so.

My own survey was conducted in all ten provinces, the Northwest Territories, and Yukon. It was distributed to students in villages, towns, and all our major cities, in affluent and poor areas, in farm communities and urban suburbs. We worked very hard to obtain a true cross-section of students in their last year of high school all across Canada.

Here are some of those results: 63% were unable to name *any three* of Canada's prime ministers who held office since the end of the Second World War; 61% were unable to name the BNA Act as Canada's Constitution; the majority of students could not name the province or territories in which the Annapolis Valley, Athabasca River, Mackenzie River, or the Klondike are located; 66% were not able to name the Canadian who was awarded the Nobel Peace Prize in 1957; 89% could not identify Gabriel Dumont, 69% René Lévesque, 96% Emily Murphy, 92% Norman Bethune; given a list of eight names (Robert Frost, E.J. Pratt, Ernest Hemingway, Margaret Atwood, Al Purdy, T.S. Eliot, Margaret Laurence, and Morley Callaghan) and asked simply to circle the names of Canadians, 78% failed to select Pratt; 69% Atwood; 79% Purdy; 70% Laurence; and 51% Callaghan; 59% could not say into which ocean the Mackenzie River flows; about half had no idea why the War Measures Act was proclaimed in 1970; over a third of the students surveyed thought Imperial Oil, General Motors of Canada Ltd., Chrysler, and Shell were Canadian companies, and selected Harold Wilson as among the premiers of Canada's provinces.

Altogether, 62% of the students failed the questionnaire (that is, they scored under 50%). At the bottom of the last page of the questionnaire we asked for comments from the students. Here are a few representative comments: "I know more about American presidents than Canadian prime ministers!"; "I can't believe how ignorant I am about Canada"; "I could probably talk on the U.S. for many hours and yet maybe 10 minutes on Canada"; "I find that although I have almost completely finished Gr. 13 and with an honour standing each year, I am unable to answer a good 50% of your questions"; "If they want us to know these things why don't they teach them in school?"

My *Globe* article went on to criticize the educational establishment.

"If, when our kids leave school, they know very little about their country, where are they likely to pick it up? If they're not provided with an education that makes them *interested* in Canada, are they very likely to acquire it later? I am not suggesting the cultivation of isolationist, parochial, inward-looking schools. But I *am* suggesting that in a nation overwhelmed by American influence, and increasingly owned by Americans, we have a special obligation to our own children in our own schools. If they are supposed to be the decision-makers of the future, then surely we must equip them better than the results of this survey indicate."

Perhaps one of the student comments summed it up best: "Margaret Atwood, Margaret Laurence — never heard of them so they must be Canadian."

The response to the article was incredible. Ontario Premier John Robarts had breakfast with Eddie Goodman the morning the survey results appeared in the *Globe*. Robarts was furious. Goodman told me that he just about went through the roof of the Prince Arthur Room in the Park Plaza. Many newspapers across the country phoned for permission to reprint the survey results. Newspapers, magazines, and radio and TV stations did their own surveys. *Canadabooks* sent copies of the survey to every member of Parliament and every senator in Ottawa. I was inundated with letters expressing outrage at the lack of Canadian content in our schools from every region of the country. There were many mostly supportive letters from people in education.

One rather interesting development after the survey was published was the establishment of chairs of (wait for this) American Studies at Canadian universities. Four months after my survey, Val Sears of the *Toronto Star* reported the details of a memo from the U.S. Embassy in Ottawa to the State Department in Washington:

> The American Embassy in Ottawa has proposed that the government finance a professorship in American studies at Ottawa's Carleton University to offset a "negative image" of the United States on Canadian campuses. The memo says that the "traditional" arguments against the appointment of a U.S. professor — that there are too many already and that he would become the target for attacks by Canadian nationalists — are now irrelevant.
>
> The targets of the Canadian nationalist sentiments are not scholars of the first rank but those who have been judged as

third-rate academics by peers on both sides of the border. The nationalists' complaint is that preference in the third-rate academic category should go to the Canadian citizen.

So it was clear that it would be okay to hire "third-rate" Canadians.

Oil money was used to establish a chair of American studies at the University of Calgary, where no chair or department of Canadian studies existed.

I wish to make something clear in all of this. Yes, Canadian students must learn about the world about them; it's imperative that they do so. Yes, we should have good American and British and French professors, and others, in our postsecondary institutions. Many of them become Canadian citizens and are among the most patriotic and valuable people in the country. But somehow in Canada we have gone way too far in the opposite direction from patriotism. We have become a pale shadow of a country, lacking in understanding of our own roots, our own genesis, our own metamorphosis from colony to nation. By the 1970s, we were rapidly headed once again for colonial status. Myopia, money, and mesmerism allowed American culture to dominate even our schools.

In October 1993 a poll showed that the most popular of all politicians for Canadian teenagers was U.S. President George Bush. George Bush, for God's sake!

Peace, Order, and Bad Government

MANY OF MY SPEECHES, from the 1960s through the 1980s, dealt with peace and disarmament. Canada's Department of External Affairs continued to be comfortably preoccupied with the concept of "quiet diplomacy" and the idea that Canada had a special relationship that somehow provided us with both influence over American policy and special treatment. In reality, although External Affairs seemed oblivious to the obvious, any modest special treatment we may from time to time have received we paid for dearly with our adherence to U.S. foreign policy and in our colonial acceptance of the American buy-up of our industry and resources.

In the days of Lester Pearson, External Affairs regarded our primary role as that of a "helpful fixer" — a peacekeeping and, in a lesser way, a peacemaking nation. But during the height of the Cold War, Canada's ability to do anything constructive about the growing super-power confrontation and nuclear proliferation was sharply diminished by the perception and the reality of Canada's subservient position in its relations with the U.S. For example, for more than two decades Canada had followed the Americans in voting against China's admission to the United Nations, somehow managing to convince ourselves that the Chiang Kai-shek government in Taiwan was the legitimate represen-tative of the Chinese people.

In 1971, much to his credit and Richard Nixon's and Henry Kissinger's dismay (Canada beat the U.S.), Pierre Trudeau announced our recognition of the Beijing government. Washington was angry.

In 1969 I had published *Alliances and Illusions: Canada and the NATO-NORAD Question*, by Lewis Hertzman, John Warnock, and Thomas Hockin, with an introduction by Dalton Camp. In his intro-duction, Camp wrote: "It is an illusion bordering on fantasy to believe the United States will ever compromise its own judgement, or limit its response to crisis, because of either Canadian sensitivity or opinion." The same year I initiated a foreign and defence policy teach-in at the University of Alberta that drew a crowd of some two thousand students and faculty.

During the two years that I was the Liberal party's chairman of their task force on international affairs, the most important lesson I learned was something most other people already knew: there was often a huge gap between what politicians say and what they do. While the central thrust of Canadian foreign-policy commitment at the time was supposedly the reduction of international conflict, and while we were the twenty-seventh largest country in the world in terms of population, we were also the fifth-largest exporter of arms. On a per-capita basis, Canadians spent about ninety dollars for defence while contributing twenty cents to the United Nations.

I found it difficult to understand how we could work effectively for world peace and disarmament when we continued to permit the presence of nuclear weapons and continued to engage in large-scale research and development of chemical warfare. Moreover, in NATO we were completely silent about the oppressive military dictatorships in Greece and Portugal. At the same time, the history of the North American Air Defence Command (NORAD) clearly demonstrated that *all* the key decisions, without exceptions, were made in Washington, while the antiballistic missile system was some-how deemed not to even be a part of NORAD.

In September 1969 Prime Minister Trudeau and External Affairs Minister Mitchell Sharp visited Richard Nixon and Henry Kissinger in Washington. A few days later I met with Sharp in his office in Ottawa. During our meeting Sharp suggested that the most important role Canada could play in world affairs was to "not rock the boat." He also said that both he and the prime minister had come to the conclusion that Canada's major responsibility was to protect the American deterrent. I was astounded. This was certainly not what the Canadian public was being told. Only ten months earlier the Liberal Party of Canada's National Policy Conference in Ottawa had passed a resolution that said that "Canada's foreign policy is determined to a very large extent by the American domination of the Canadian economy. To be independent in world affairs, we must repatriate more control of our economy." The resolution had been fought vigorously by Mitchell Sharp and Paul Martin and much of the Liberal party's senior establishment, yet it passed by a large margin — 592 to 273. The rank and file of the party were well ahead of the government on the issue of Canadian independence.

In a Liberal policy paper I wrote that "Canada seems long ago to have lost the opportunity to have an independent foreign policy because our economy is now so susceptible to U.S. retaliation . . . or at least that's the way the politicians and mandarins and bureaucrats seem to believe."

With the Liberal party in so much trouble with the voters in 1972, Sharp surprised everyone with a proposal for "a third option" in our international commercial activities, which would allow Canada to become less vulnerable to the U.S. and facilitate the development of a long-overdue, more independent, national industrial strategy. Nothing came of the "third option" for two reasons. First, the Liberals were never really serious about such an alternative. Second, most of Canada's trade was conducted between parent American companies and their subsidiaries or related companies; this situation would never change as long as there was so much U.S. ownership and control of the Canadian economy.

The 1983 decision by Pierre Trudeau and his cabinet to allow cruise-missile testing in Canada, after massive pressure from Washington, discredited Trudeau in the eyes of many Canadians, including many Liberals, and somewhat diminished his international reputation.

Thereafter, when Trudeau urged the Americans to be less confrontational with the USSR, he was ignored even more than in the past.

The decision to test the cruise missile prompted an avalanche of letters and phone calls to members of Parliament and demonstrations across the country. For the Canadian public, the danger of a nuclear holocaust was very real, but for the Liberal government, threats from the White House were more important. If President Reagan wanted Canada to test cruise missiles, so it would be. Other NATO countries had declined American requests for cruise tests, but branch-plant Canada believed it had no such option.

In March of 1983 U.S. Ambassador Paul Robinson threatened Canada. According to a press report, "Robinson called opponents of the cruise missile a small, noisy minority with no understanding of the complexities of international politics. . . . 'I don't get exercised about people who march around with placards.'" (The "small minority" amounted to fifty-two percent of Canadians who opposed cruise testing.)

In September 1983 Pauline Jewett, who by then was the NDP's external affairs critic, and I debated the Liberal government's new defence minister, Jean-Jacques Blais, at an Operation Dismantle conference at the University of Ottawa. Time after time Pauline and I hammered Blais, making his arguments in support of cruise-missile testing look foolish. Nevertheless, when the session was over, Blais advised the *Ottawa Citizen* that the decision had been made "and that decision is not reversible."

That same year, I helped organize a conference at the University of Alberta relating to the nuclear-arms race. George Ignatieff, who was now chancellor of the University of Toronto, spoke on the subject "Canada and the Danger of Nuclear War" and strongly made the point that if Canada agreed to test cruise missiles, we would be playing a major role in the escalation of the nuclear-arms race rather than trying to contain its growth.

Ignatieff reminded his audience that both the USA and USSR had more than enough nuclear weapons to destroy the world many times over, and the time had come for Canada to clearly say *no* to further nuclear buildup.

Also the same year, I published *This Is the Way the World Will End*, by Harold Freeman, and I promptly proceeded to give away thousands of copies, carrying them with me wherever I went and mailing them out across the country. Soon after its publication, George Ignatieff wrote to me:

I congratulate you for publishing Freeman's book. . . . I have been working on this issue since 1946, when I went down to New York with General McNaughton to try to stop the horror described accurately in the book at the outset. . . .

Our own politicians and decision-makers, except for the NDP and some individuals like Roche and McRae, seem to be like somnambulists. This particularly applies to Trudeau, who knows better, but apparently gives in to the pressure of that small minority that wants "high-tech" sub-contracts from the American rearmament program.

In January 1984 I went to see Pierre Trudeau with the idea of establishing an institute at the University of Alberta whose goal would be to bring together Americans and people from the Soviet Union in an effort to deescalate tensions between the two superpowers. Nothing came of my proposal. Later in the year I helped bring Dr. Helen Caldicott to Edmonton. This time we drew over three thousand people to the University of Alberta. Montreal filmmaker Terri Nash's superb NFB film about Caldicott, *If You Love This Planet*, had won an Oscar and numerous other awards. She gave a marvellous speech. In my introduction I called Canada "a nuclear bowling alley between the USA and the USSR."

Around this time, I helped the National Peace Petition Caravan in its campaign for an end to cruise-missile testing in Canada, the declaration of Canada as a nuclear-weapons-free zone, the diversion of arms spending into the funding of human needs, and a free vote in Parliament on issues relating to nuclear proliferation. In November the new Conservative defence minister, Robert Coates, said he wouldn't try to keep the cruise-missile tests in Canada secret "unless the U.S. thinks the Canadian public should be kept in the dark."

Once again in 1986 a national Liberal policy convention enthusiastically passed resolutions calling for a cessation of cruise-missile testing, Canada's becoming a nuclear-weapons-free zone, support of a comprehensive test-ban treaty, and opposition to Ronald Reagan's strategic-defence initiative. However, no sooner had the resolutions passed in convention than the right wing and continentalists in the Liberal party began to put considerable pressure on Leader John Turner to ignore them. George Ignatieff, Dr. Brian Sproule, Robert Penner of the Canadian Peace Alliance, Joanne Miller of Project Ploughshares, and I went to see Turner, Lloyd Axworthy, and Allan

MacEachen in an attempt to convince the Liberals to hold the line and support their own party's convention resolutions. Unfortunately next to nothing resulted from the meetings.

The same year, a number of people in British Columbia organized a public inquiry in Nanaimo into the hazards of testing nuclear weapons and vessels in Canadian waters. American Los Angeles class attack submarines, carrying nuclear-armed Tomahawk cruise missiles, and other U.S. warships were regularly visiting Nanoose Bay for weapons testing. One submarine carried a potential explosive force equal to more than eighty percent of all the explosives used during the Second World War. Bishop Remi de Roo of Victoria and I were asked to serve as moderators at the two-day inquiry. I was most impressed by the structure of the inquiry, particularly its emphasis on citizen participation. When I returned to Edmonton, I made up my mind to have a broader inquiry related to nuclear proliferation, defence policy, international affairs, peacekeeping, and other matters relating to world peace and the threat of superpower nuclear confrontation. The True North Strong and Free? A Public Inquiry into Canadian Defence Policy and Nuclear Arms would be cosponsored by the Edmonton chapter of the Council of Canadians and by Physicians for Social Responsibility.

We started off planning a conference for only about three hundred people because we thought the $30 registration fee might inhibit attendance. But when word got out about our plans, the demand for advance tickets was so great we had to find a larger auditorium that would hold at least a thousand. It wasn't long before we realized that even that venue would be far too small.

Two months before, the inquiry registration stood at 2,700. By the time the conference began in November, an incredible 5,400 people had registered, including people who travelled to Edmonton from the Arctic, from Newfoundland, from six other provinces, and from the U.S.

The True North Strong and Free?, as we later explained in the introduction to our book about the conference, "was born out of concern and belief: a concern for a world caught in an arms race that threatens our survival and a belief that Canada can be a powerful force for international peace and that each of us has personal power to help realize Canada's role as a peace-making nation." Altogether, we had some two hundred volunteers who spent many long months preparing for the inquiry. I must mention at least a few: Brian Sproule,

John Sproule, Lois Hammond, Irene Clay, Brock Macdonald, Bill Stollery, Roberta Carey, and Ian and Elizabeth McBride. They were a superb team. Despite numerous attempts, we received no cooperation whatsoever from Joe Clark or anyone else in External Affairs until it became clear that thousands of Canadians would be attending the conference and that there would be a great deal of press coverage since many well-known Canadians would be participating.

Finally Joe Clark agreed to send Ralph Lysyshyn, director of the arms-control-and-disarmament division in External Affairs. Although he seemed quite nice and bright, he did not have the public presence of the other participants. On several occasions he refused to answer questions or answered in an evasive manner, drawing hisses and boos from the audience. Clearly the government had underestimated the requirements for the conference.

Altogether, the conference took ten months of organizing by many dedicated men and women and a great deal of fundraising. On the eve of the inquiry a national Angus Reid poll showed, by an overwhelming margin, that Canadians felt Brian Mulroney was too closely aligned with Ronald Reagan and American foreign policy, that Canadians believed the risk of a deadly nuclear war was a real threat, and that a nuclear war triggered by human or equipment error was a distinct possibility. By a two-to-one margin Canadians now opposed cruise-missile testing in Canada.

The two True North inquiry moderators were Bishop Remi de Roo and Jean Forest, former chancellor of the University of Alberta. The conference opened with Disarmament Ambassador Doug Roche issuing a strong plea for Canada to lead the way in a campaign to eradicate nuclear weapons. Next came Dr. Dorothy Goresky's startling description of the appalling consequences of the detonation of a single nuclear weapon. Then Lloyd Axworthy told the audience that Canada should avoid the entanglements of free trade with the United States so that we do not lose our independence.

David Suzuki received two standing ovations when he condemned the scientific establishment for becoming part of a system of "destruction and profit." Gwynne Dyer presented a passionate, logical rationale for Canada pulling out of the North Atlantic Treaty Organization. And I said that it was clear that "Canadians are increasingly concerned about the escalating arms race, the world buildup of nuclear weapons and delivery systems, and about the policies of the Canadian government."

Brigadier-General Don Macnamara, a Defence Department representative to the conference, proved to be intelligent, articulate, and quite amazed by the proceedings. "These five thousand people are not hostile to the military at all. But they do want to know much, much more than they know now. We have been given an absolutely outstanding, friendly, and hospitable reception here."

In the end the conference strongly supported resolutions calling for the international regulation of all cruise missiles, a worldwide nuclear-test moratorium, the establishment in Canada of an international centre designed to deescalate tensions between the superpowers, and opposition to Star Wars development. The resolution that received almost unanimous endorsement was that Canada should rescind the agreement with the United States for cruise-missile testing.

After the conference we widely distributed the resolutions that were passed and we published a paperback book, *The True North Strong and Free?*, containing all the papers presented at the inquiry. Brian Mulroney wrote to Lois Hammond and Irene Clay thanking them for the materials they had sent him. According to Mulroney, "Your writing to me is another indication that Canadians want their country to follow an independent, active, and internationalist approach to our foreign policy." Right. According to Doug Roche, "Nowhere across Canada, in the International Year of Peace, was the idea of properly preparing for peace so clearly and eloquently asserted than at the True North conference."

The mix of people at the conference was quite amazing: generals, ambassadors, cabinet ministers, MPs, business men and women, academics, university and high school students, teachers and professors, white-collar and blue-collar workers, professionals, farmers — an almost complete cross-section of the Canadian public. It was grass-roots democracy at work at its best. Without exception, there was spirited discussion at every session and long lineups at all the floor microphones. After it was all over Geoffrey Pearson wrote to me: "I congratulate you and the Doctors for putting together a remarkable conference which has clearly had repercussions in Ottawa."

Overall the television and press coverage was truly wonderful. But one paper, the *Los Angeles Times*, produced an extraordinarily warped account. In the words of Brian Sproule, the *Times* reporter "appeared to have been at a different conference than the one we attended. It is fascinating to see the spin at work, distorting an unusually thoughtful, civil, undemonstrative, intellectual and muted inquiry into a forum of 'arm-waving pronunciations about Canadian separation from the U.S.'"

By 1987, the Trudeau and Mulroney governments had signed almost four hundred different military agreements with the United States, a great many of them secret and most with little or no public debate. Some of these agreements, never disclosed, allowed the presence of U.S. nuclear weapons in Canada. Meanwhile, Canada did not vote for many of the two dozen disarmament resolutions passed in the United Nations' General Assembly, even voting against a motion calling for a USA-USSR nuclear freeze, a resolution that passed in the UN with a huge margin of support.

Our country had become so closely bound to U.S. defence policy that an American expert, William Kincade, warned that Canada "will become inevitably and inextricably tied into the U.S. nuclear strategy for North America, militarily and politically . . . [Canada's current position] removes any possibility of a credible independent role. Canada will become to the United States what Poland has been to the Soviets."

The suggestion from the continentalists has always been that a closer relationship with the United States would allow us more influence in shaping American foreign policy. This is, of course, nonsense. In fact, the reverse is true. The closer we have become, the more intertwined in defence-sharing agreements, the more we have been simply taken for granted.

During the Vietnam War Canada shipped billions of dollars of military supplies to the United States. In her book *Yankee Doodle Dandy* Marci McDonald writes about "hundreds of secret cooperation agreements" between Canada and the United States "for developing and testing potential atomic weaponry, plus Strategic Air Command plans" for "nuclear-armed B-52 bombers to disperse to the Canadian Forces airfield at Cold Lake, Alberta . . . a clear contravention of Ottawa's non-nuclear policy." In the words of retired Admiral Robert Falls, the former chief of the Canadian Defence Staff, "Canada is a nuclear colony of the United States."

Almost without exception — the invasions of Grenada and Nicaragua, the Gulf War, cruise-missile testing, the *Polar Sea* incursion — the Mulroney government either fully supported American policy or was so timid in its response that in effect there was no difference between support and opposition. Canada's once proud position as an independent nation in international affairs was now little more than an international joke.

A commonly heard assertion of peace activists is that if only a quarter of the sum spent annually for military purposes, *only a quarter*, were diverted, then almost all world poverty, homelessness, hunger, illiteracy, soil erosion, forest depletion, health-care deficiencies, water problems, and the like could be wiped out. Why not limit membership in such organizations as the World Trade Organization to countries that agree not to export arms? Yes, yes, I know, the Americans and Chinese and Russians and the French would object. But why don't we get together and outvote them? An independent Canada could lead the way in a worldwide conversion campaign with enormous potential to alleviate human suffering. But Canada the colony can lead no one anywhere.

ALL THESE ACTIVITIES afforded me the great pleasure of getting to know George and Alison Ignatieff, whom I first met in 1975. George was born in St. Petersburg, Russia, in 1913. He arrived in Canada at the age of fifteen, a poor immigrant, the family living in a cold-water flat in Montreal. His family background, his education, his environment, and his idealism led him to believe that public service was of the highest calling. Among his many diplomatic postings were service as Canada's ambassador to Yugoslavia, assistant under-secretary of state for External Affairs, and Canada's representative to NATO, the United Nations, the GATT, and the Disarmament Committee in Geneva. Alison Ignatieff was one of the most delightful women I have ever met. The sister of George Grant — author of *Lament for a Nation* — was at least as smart as her husband and every bit the dedicated nationalist.

George Ignatieff was charming, elegant, and very astute. When he was provost of Trinity College at the University of Toronto, he was asked if he would accept appointment as Canada's next governor general, and after conferring with Alison he agreed to do so. Soon after, George flew to Ottawa from Toronto along with Liberal cabinet minister Norman Cafik. On the plane, Cafik heartily congratulated Ignatieff on his impending appointment. Somehow the *Toronto Star* got the story and George's picture, and the announcement appeared the next day in the *Star*. The same day, Jim Coutts and at least one other cabinet minister told Ignatieff that it was "a done deal" and the official announcement would be made in a few days. George advised Trinity College and began to make the necessary arrangements.

Soon after, the Ignatieffs attended a banquet in Toronto where

George was told that Ed Schreyer was to be appointed governor general. The news would be released the next day. One of George's sons told me that he *never* saw his father react the way he did that evening and in the following days. He was devastated, not mainly for himself, but for the acute embarrassment the whole affair caused Alison. My own sources told me that Trudeau reversed the decision because an election was coming and votes would be needed in Western Canada. Without question, Ed Schreyer was a good man with a sound record, but the treatment of George Ignatieff was shameful political expediency at its worst.

After the True North conference, the headline in the *London Free Press* read: "Ex-diplomat unlikely star of nuclear conference." I don't know about the "unlikely," but George was certainly the star, receiving a long standing ovation for his articulate appeal for greater civilian control over military decisions and greater Canadian independence. Ignatieff described the inquiry as "easily the most important forum of its kind in a decade." Of the hundreds of letters we received, two samples speak for themselves: "I am 63 years old and have just returned from the most fulfilling weekend of my life," and from a fifteen-year-old student, "I have never in my small lifetime learned so much in one day."

I was very happy and very proud of what we had accomplished. In 1988 I received the Lester B. Pearson Man of the Year Peace Award, for which I was most grateful, but in truth it really should have gone to the superb team of men and women who had made the inquiry such a spectacular success.

Mountains and Valleys

MACLEAN'S MAGAZINE once asked me to write about my favourite holiday. Here is some of what I said:

The ingredients I require for a good holiday: Rocky Mountain air, good hiking trails, a place where there is no TV, no radio and no telephone, seclusion, one bottle of vermouth and several bottles of gin for before dinners, and a case of Scotch for after, an enormous open fireplace and a big suitcase full of old clothes and new books. Lastly, an old-fashioned bed — the kind you climb up onto and then roll down into, beneath the blankets and quilts, just after you've thrown the windows open. You do this last bit quickly because it's damn cold in the mountains after dark. And you lie there thinking about the people down east sweltering through the hot night.

Actually, if you were out hiking in the mountains all day, you didn't lie there thinking about anything for very long; usually you were fast asleep in a very few minutes. I love going to the Rockies best in either early summer or mid-fall when there are relatively few people around. Once I remember hiking with Kay and our friends the Sproules in to Mt. Assiniboine Lodge beginning at the reservoir just past Spray Lakes, twisting up twenty kilometres through Assiniboine Pass to the beautiful Lake Magog and the lodge. On the way back we were directed to take the Wonder Pass route. I asked, "Why do you call it Wonder Pass?" "You'll see," was the reply. And a true wonder it was! We started off through an Alpine meadow full of mountain flowers of every description and colour: Indian paintbrush, anemone, mountain heather, Alpine forget-me-nots, saxifrage, marigolds, and violets, to name just a few. Then we came to a high near-vertical cliff. Below us was a magnificent sight — the turquoise Marvel Lake and the beautiful long mountain valley. This trip out from Assiniboine down the rugged switchbacks was one of the loveliest mountain experiences of my life. It was August and very hot, around thirty Celsius. All day long on the long hike back to Brian's car, we saw only one other person. The heat and backpacks tired us, and we were glad to reach the car in the late afternoon. Then a splendid surprise. Brian had four bottles of ice-cold beer stored in a cooler in the trunk. It was the finest bottle of beer I ever drank.

A place I keep going back to every few years is Lake O'Hara in Yoho National Park, my favourite spot for hiking. The early mountaineering author and photographer W.D. Wilcox wrote: "In all the mountain wilderness the most complete picture of natural beauty is realized at O'Hara Lake." The lodge (elevation: 6,700 feet) is superb, and the fifty miles of hiking trails are marvellous, ranging from an easy stroll around the lake to the tough climbs to Wiwaxy Gap, All Soul's Prospect, Yukness Ledge, and the Grand View Prospect alpine routes. An exciting and dangerous trip that requires an experienced guide is up to Abbott's Pass and across the tops of glaciers to Lake

Louise. In front of the lodge is the beautiful Lake O'Hara, surrounded by high mountains: Huber, Lefroy, Victoria, and Hungabee, all painted by members of the Group of Seven, as well as Carl Runguis, Walter Phillips, A.C. Leighton, John Singer Sargent, and many other famous artists. O'Hara is very safe, but unfortunately the last time Kay and I were there, the day before our arrival, in a very rare incident, a grizzly attacked a party from Boston and seriously injured a man. So most of the trails were closed, but we were able to hike for a day with the park warden, who was searching for the grizzly.

Over the years I've had a fair number of encounters with bears, but none serious. Once, on the Banff Springs Hotel golf course, I hit a lucky drive, getting a big bounce off a curving road that put me into position to reach the green on a par-five hole with a good three wood. Just before I started my backswing, I took one final look at the green — and what I saw was a huge black bear charging like a racehorse towards me from about two hundred yards away. I stopped, panic-stricken, and yelled to my friend Don over on the far side of the fairway: "What should I do?" He replied: "What club have you got?" The bear's charge continued, my heart was in my throat, then suddenly he veered off about ten degrees and went by me like a tornado. My heart was pounding. I took an eight on the hole.

Because I was in the mountains frequently, I often asked experts what precautions against bears one should take. I knew all about singing, clapping hands, bells, "bear bangers," and generally making lots of noise, but what else? The great mountain man Bruno Engler observed that grizzly bears could not run downhill too quickly, something to keep in mind. When I told this to the widely respected Andy Russell, author of *Grizzly Country*, he almost fell on the floor laughing. So, Andy, what do *you* suggest? There was only one solution for a close face-to-face encounter: stand up straight, square yourself, chin held high, point at the bear, and speak to it like you would to a bad dog. When I ran into Bruno again a few months later, I told him of Russell's advice; he, too, almost fell on the floor laughing. "Are you kidding? You try that once and you'll never live to tell anyone about it."

I've had many great experiences hiking in the mountains, but unquestionably the worst was a sojourn to Skoki Lodge up across the opposite east side of the valley from Lake Louise. From the end of the Temple Fireroad up through Deception Pass, it's a good eleven kilometres with a couple of rather steep stretches. We had a prepaid reservation at the lodge for three days and looked forward to some great new hiking. Unfortunately somehow we believed we would be bused to the lodge. No way. So, Kay and I and my daughter Leslie headed up the mountain with (it's hard to believe) one big stuffed suitcase. Halfway up no one was talking. Then Kay, who was in the lead, made a wrong turn and we found ourselves, an hour and a half later, at a small lake in a dead-end canyon. Back we struggled, suitcase and all. Then, incredibly, we did it again, going around a mountain instead of turning left and proceeding straight to the lodge only two kilometres away.

It was the one and only time I had ever hiked in the mountains without a map and we paid dearly for it. With every step the suitcase became heavier. When we got to the lodge, the people there couldn't believe what they saw — three exhausted people and one big bloody heavy suitcase. On the plus side, however, the three days of hiking were great. On the downside, we got lost again! We were heading out, back down to the highway far below. Just as we were leaving the lodge, suitcase in tow, it was like a scene from a Hollywood movie. A handsome warden came riding towards us out of the trees, rifle at his side. "Folks, take good care. There's a mean grizzly on the loose in these parts." I saw Leslie go pale. The horse reared and then the warden was gone. Off we went, at a bit better pace since it was downhill. But once again we somehow made a wrong turn, and this time we were *really* lost. Hour after hour went by and the sun was beginning to sink behind the mountains. Great. Lost in the mountains, night is falling, and there's a mean grizzly in the area. Ahead of me was a steep loose-scree slope. I asked Leslie and Kay to wait while I tried to scale it to get some bearings. One small problem: for every three steps forward I slid back two. It took an hour to reach the crest of the ridge and I sat there exhausted. But there, far below, was the Fireroad that would take us back to our car. Although we now have great laughs about this little "adventure," for days afterwards I didn't speak to Kay and she didn't speak to me.

One thing you should know about Kay is that she is very competitive and very strong. On one trip to the Robson area with Stuart and Patricia Smith, we decided to leave the Smiths and head up to Berg Lake. Brian Patton, whose guidebook to the mountains is the bible for climbers and hikers, describes the twenty-kilometre, 2,600-foot altitude gain to Berg Lake as "brutal . . . a real grunt . . . allow seven to ten hours in." We left the Smiths at Kinney Lake intending to go up only to Emperor Falls. But Kay decided she wanted to see Berg Lake and wouldn't quit. There was no way I was going to admit to being tired. Up and up and around we went, until finally we reached the north slope of Mount Robson. We rested briefly at the lake in the dark shadows, listening in the solitary stillness to the sharp sounds of the glacier cracking high above the lake, then down we headed, finishing the two-way trip in just over ten hours. I've never been so tired in my entire life.

Different Shots and Different Thoughts

GOLF WAS EVEN MORE of a passion with me. I think it's fair to say that most people who don't play golf are totally mystified by the appeal the game has for those who get hooked. I was once convinced by a friend prior to a trip to England that if I read up on cricket and went to Lord's, I would find the game fascinating. I did read up on the game, I did go to Lord's, and after an hour I was ready to leave.

Some people claim golf was invented by the devil. There may be some validity to the claim. Of all the sports I have played over the years, golf is easily the most fun, the most difficult, the most satisfying, and the most aggravating. It's an impossible game to master, and it's unlike other sports in several important ways.

First, and perhaps foremost, golf has an excellent handicap system, which means you can play against someone much better than you or much worse than you, yet still have a splendid match that can go right down to the last putt on the eighteenth green. I know of no other sport that allows contestants of all different levels to compete against one another, or in teams, on a truly competitive basis. For example, if a middle-aged man with an average serve plays tennis against a tall twenty-year-old with a powerful serve, he's dead; there's no match at all. This factor alone is one of the reasons the popularity of golf has surged while that of tennis has remained comparatively static. The handicap system also makes golf a very sociable game. You meet and play with many different men and women and have great contests, despite vastly different skill levels.

The second aspect of golf that makes the game unique is all the thousands of wonderful courses, each one different, each one requiring different shots and different thoughts. Moreover, a great many courses are beautiful in themselves, with spectacular settings. I know of no other sport where the venue and challenges are so varied. For me, stepping up to the first tee of a new golf course is always exciting.

There is little doubt in my mind that golf is more difficult than most sports. While it's true that some great athletes are good golfers, most of them are not, yet most athletes in other sports love golf and work hard at it. The game has the darnedest way of playing tricks on you. One day the driver works like a miracle machine, but you hit your irons fat; the next day the irons consistently hit the green, but your putter is broken; the next day the putts fall in, but you leave the ball in the trap all day.

Once I'm on the golf course, I don't think about anything else. And if I'm in a good match, every shot is key and the game great fun. Mind you, the handicap system isn't always perfect. My guess is that some eighty-five percent of golfers punch their scores into the locker-room computer truthfully. But I suspect some five percent are "sandbaggers," that is, they have artificially high handicaps because they don't post all their low scores; perhaps another ten percent have artificially low handicaps, strictly because of ego. This last group usually loses a fair amount of change during the course of a year, and the sandbaggers tend to find fewer and fewer people to play with over the years.

After I got my right-handed bar mitzvah gift, I lived down at "Muni," the public golf course in the North Saskatchewan River valley just blocks from my home. We played as frequently as we could, finishing in the pitch-dark more often than not. Mind you, in Edmonton during the middle of the summer you can play till almost eleven at night. By the time I was nineteen, I was down to a five handicap and playing a fair amount of tournament golf. One of my best games was when I took the defending Alberta amateur champion, Neil Green, to the nineteenth hole in the first round of the provincial amateur championship.

Muni became so jam-packed (sometimes we sat in a car all night so we could be in line to book weekend tee-off times) that some of us moved to Riverside, the new public course. There I played at least once a week with Frank Willey, the pro at the club. One day Frank disappeared. His body was never found, but much blood was found around a power saw at a house that was under construction, and two men, including a friend of Frank's wife, were convicted of his murder.

Soon Riverside, too, became jam-packed. A few doors down from the fur store a man named Keith Smeltzer ran a men's clothing store. Keith also happened to be chairman of the membership committee of the Edmonton Golf and Country Club. My constant golf companion was Don Atkinson, and after a great deal of persuasion (Don was just getting married), I talked Don into applying with me to join the Country Club. Smeltzer agreed to sign our applications. About a month later I was sitting having dinner with my parents when I heard a car screech to a halt in front of the house, a car door slam, and someone running up the front sidewalk. Don burst into the house, arms waving, shouting, "We're in! We're in!" However, that afternoon I had received my cheque back in the mail from the Country Club. My application had been rejected.

This was the first time in my life when I was really affected by anti-Semitism. I was dumbfounded. I never for a moment had even thought about this as a potential problem in joining a golf club. I had been invited to the Country Club to play many times, and three of my regular golf companions played there.

A couple of years later I joined Windermere, a fine new private club on the outskirts of the city. It was an excellent "track" with lots of wonderful members. But one day Al Pyrch, who served on the board of the Edmonton Art Gallery with me, suggested I apply to join Mayfair Golf and Country Club, at the time the premier golf course in Edmonton. It was a superb course, minutes from my home and office, well maintained, and a good challenge. "Any Jewish members?" I asked. "No, no golf members, but one Jewish doctor is a social member," Al replied. "No way," I said. "I'm not going through that again." But Al was insistent. He enlisted Clarence Richards, a Mayfair member who also happened to be my old biology teacher and Edmonton's first regional book publisher, and they signed my application. I've now played at Mayfair for thirty-six years; it's a great club with lots of fine men and women golfers and a first-class staff. When I take friends from Toronto to the course for the first time I prepare them for an hour-long drive. But much to their astonishment, four minutes later we're in the locker room putting on our spikes.

While I was starting off as a bookseller, I had to give up golf for several years, and then my political activities made finding the time to play difficult. Nevertheless, I did manage to accumulate a pretty good collection of memories, including two hole-in-ones. My worst golf experience, by far, was playing in the pro-am preceding the Los Angeles Open at the famous Riviera golf club "Hogan's Alley." There were hundreds of spectators and half a dozen television cameras crowded around the first tee. My partner was American pro Scott

Hoch, and it was my honour. I hit some six inches behind the ball, which barely managed to roll off the tee into tall grass growing on a forty-five-degree downslope below the tee. I could barely see the ball. The second shot went all of twenty yards. I was mortified.

Probably the toughest hole in major tournament golf is the Road Hole, the infamous seventeenth at St. Andrews. Called every name in the book, it's a par four, averaging over 4.7 strokes in major championships, 461 yards long, a dogleg right to a difficult plateaued green, which is guarded by "the satanic crater," the Road Bunker. Japanese pro Tommy Nakajimi putted into the bunker and took four shots to get out during the 1978 British Open. Anyway, the only time I ever played St. Andrews I holed from the Road Bunker for a birdie. My Scottish caddie almost fainted.

(Not many people realize that a golf course has eighteen holes because St. Andrews, the home of The Royal and Ancient Golf Club, has eighteen holes. Fewer still realize that St. Andrews had twenty-two holes to begin with, and then, in 1764, it was reduced to eighteen.)

One of my fondest golf memories was playing once a year with my friend Bruce Willson and Kay and Nick Weslock at Glen Abbey. We always had great fun. I watched Nick (winner of a bagful of Canadian championships) consult a little black notebook from time to time, which resulted in Nick's writing one of our bestselling books, *Your Golf Bag Pro*, which I still maintain is one of the best golf-instruction books ever published.

Last year, after exactly fifty years of golf, I won my first two golf trophies, one for shooting 78 and tying for low gross in a tournament, which automatically won me low senior. After half a century of golf it was a great thrill.

I mentioned before that Kay is very competitive. That's like saying Ben Crenshaw knows how to putt. When Kay and I were married, she'd never played golf. Today she hits the ball farther than most of the men at our club and is certainly one of the best putters I have ever seen. On Canada Day, 1996, she aced the eleventh hole at Mayfair.

I hold one golf record no one will ever match. Playing golf in Edmonton in February is about as likely as spotting an alligator in Lake Louise. But on February 29, 1988, during an exceptionally mild spell and playing with Kay and my friend Bruno Chicchini, I eagled the eighteenth hole at Muni. No one will ever do that again on February 29.

VIII

The Dismantling
of Canada

From Nationalism to Nihilism

I N MANY INTERVIEWS over the years I was frequently asked what it was that made me become a Canadian nationalist. I had, at first, no answer to the question because I hadn't spent any time thinking about it. Moreover, it always seemed to me that in most other countries the idea of self-determination I believed in and the message I was delivering would hardly be classed as "nationalism."

But I did know this: the more I saw, the more research I did, the more I travelled to small towns and to big cities across the country, the angrier I became at the way Canada's business leaders and politicians were selling out the country, at the abysmal mismanagement of the Canadian economy, at the squandering of our natural resources, and the growing concentration of political and economic power in Canada in relatively few hands, both inside and increasingly outside our country.

In his 1972 book *Towards the Discovery of Canada*, Donald Creighton wrote that modern Canadian nationalism had its origin in the famous 1956 debate in Parliament over the trans-Canada pipeline. "Slowly but inexorably" Canada's economy and hence its politics were coming under American domination. For Creighton, while Canada subsequently did make occasional attempts at resisting the erosion of its independence, "The Canadian efforts were isolated and piecemeal, tentatively advanced, and hurriedly abandoned at the first sign of risk of retaliation." And in the ensuing years, the nationalists who tried to preserve Canadian independence "have been dismissed, or defeated, or repudiated." He went on:

The story of the Canadian national movement during the fifteen years that followed the pipeline debate is a dismal story, full of retreats and defeats and frustrations. The nationalists have had some good leaders, a copious and effective supply of statistical ammunition, a good deal of interest and some support from the press, and apparently a large and vocal following among the Canadian people. Yet they seem to have achieved virtually nothing. What has gone wrong? Why are the results so tragically disproportionate to the efforts expended? Was the Canadian nationalist movement doomed from the beginning? Or is its comparative failure up to now attributable to some vital defect in its strategy and tactics? Who are the principal opponents of Canadian nationalism? What are the reasons for their opposition and what forces can they bring to the attack?

For Creighton, part of the answer was clear: it was the powerful forces of continentalism, disguised as internationalism, that had prevailed in Canada. Yet, "it is imperialism, not nationalism, which poses the greatest threat [and] the imperialistic pull of the superpower is so great as to be almost irresistible; Canada has succumbed to it [and] become a dependent state of the American empire."

Throughout the seventies and early eighties we kept hearing from the right wing how the entire country was going to move to the United States: business must have lower taxes to match those in the U.S.; the petroleum industry had to have much better incentives and lower royalties and bigger government grants or they would move their rigs out of Canada; the doctors had to have higher incomes or they would move to the States; and so on and so on, ad infinitum. In 1992 I decided to check some numbers. What I discovered confirmed my suspicions. During the previous twenty-five years, some 356,000 Canadians had moved to the U.S., but some 358,000 Americans had immigrated to Canada. Moreover, as the Science Council of Canada demonstrated, Canada had a very large net gain when it came to the two-way movement of scientists.

While throughout Canadian history there have been periods of nationalism and periods of continentalism, in 1985 I wrote that it seemed strange to me that while there had been a fair amount written about Canadian nationalism, it was ironic that in the new era of powerful, overwhelming continentalism, there had never been a single book examining the powerful elite behind the move towards integration with the United States.

For many years I have been saying that even the term "continentalism" is sadly lacking in its description of the forces at work. The Spanish word *compradors* and the French word *vendus* seem far more appropriate. But Canadian political scientists, sociologists, and writers have come up with no similar descriptive nouns. Perhaps "integrationist" is an accurate word, but it lacks the power of contempt the genre deserves.

How does one identify a Canadian continentalist? It's easy. Almost without exception (though Conrad Black is one) they are always outwardly horrified by any suggestion that they might be so identified. "Who, me? No way! I've never met one and wouldn't know one if I did." As well, continentalists always talk in terms of foreign investment, but never ever about foreign ownership or foreign control. Nor will they ever say, when challenged to do so, just how much of the country they are prepared to see sold off. ("Well look, I'm a Canadian first, but you know we need the money.") A continentalist will always tell you how very beneficial foreign capital is to the Canadian standard of living but is rarely able to back up such a claim with facts and figures or able to refer to reputable studies which do so.

We all know that the word "nationalism" means many different things to many people. For the Canadian continentalists and compradors, the word is always preceded by a prefix, an adjective, a derogatory straw man set up to be immediately knocked down. It is inevitably "chauvinistic nationalism" or "ultra-nationalism" or "petty and narrow nationalism." Then there are all the other words: xenophobic, rabid, dangerous, rampant, hyper, and emotional. Chauvinistic? In 1973 in a speech in Kingston, I quoted the words of Jay Walz, head of the *New York Times* bureau in Ottawa: "Canadians are the least patriotic people on earth . . . certainly they are never guilty of chauvinism. . . . Unless action is taken, such empty Canadianism will collapse before the pressure of north-south trade and culture, making Americans out of Canadians whether they like it or not."

Canada-lasters? Anti-Canadians? Compradors? Whatever you call them, all have one thing in common: they are intensely hostile to Canadian nationalism yet at the same time somehow completely oblivious to the danger of Canada disappearing into one of the most flag-waving, nationalistic, chauvinistic nations the modern world has ever seen. On the surface it seems bizarre. But looking more deeply, there is a ready explanation. *Those who are selling off our country are profiting handsomely in the process.*

When George Grant's *Lament for a Nation* was published in 1965, the reviews were mixed; about a third were complimentary but many were outright hostile. "Exaggerated." "Too pessimistic by far!" Mordecai Richler reviewed the book in October 1965: "Canada, Grant concludes, is a satellite. Yes, of course, but its independence, it seems to me, was always illusory [and] to be a Canadian . . . I think, was to turn pinched backs on the most exciting events on the continent, and to be a party to one of the most foolish, unnecessary and artificial of frontiers." So, in one brief repugnant paragraph, Richler rejects the entire idea of Canada. So George Grant was right. So what?

In case there is any doubt about what the nature of Grant's message was, allow me to quote briefly:

> This lament mourns the end of Canada as a sovereign state
> . . . . The element necessary for our existence has passed
> away. Only nationalism could provide the political incentive
> for planning; only planning could restrain the victory of con-
> tinentalism . . . no such combination was possible, and
> therefore our nation was bound to disappear.
>
> Canada has ceased to be a nation, but its formal political
> existence will not end quickly. Our social and economic
> blending into the American empire will continue apace, but
> political union will probably be delayed.

Who was to blame? There was little doubt in Grant's mind: the elite, the establishment, money, power, the ruling classes, the wealthy, and the Liberal party. "The wealthy of Toronto and Montreal do not care about Canada. . . . They lost nothing essential to the principal of their lives in losing their country." For George Grant, the Conservatives had been the defenders of Canada. In Kenneth McNaught's 1965 review he wrote: "It is now beyond doubt that Conservatives, in recognizing the desperate need of a counter balance to the American continental pull, have always been the most nationalist of the two major parties. . . . Genuine Conservatives . . . were prepared to use government not just to guarantee free competition . . . but to limit private intrusion upon the public interest. They established a tradition of public enterprise in transportation, communication and power development."

It's a good thing George Grant died before the likes of Brian Mulroney, Michael Wilson, Ralph Klein, and Michael Harris transformed the Conservative party into an imitation of Reagan-omics, Thatcherism, and Barry Goldwater rolled into one. The reality is, in terms of nationalism and continentalism, there is little to distinguish the Conservative Party of Canada during the past two decades from the Liberals, and for the past twelve years there has been nothing of consequence; they are, in office, one and the same.

But the xenophobic, destructive, aggressive nationalism of Nazi Germany, the superpatriotic, flag-waving, chest-thumping, mass-culture-exporting nationalism of the United States, the cruel suppressive nationalism of the USSR, none of these for a moment remotely resembled nationalism in Canada. Nationalism in Canada made virtually every other developed nation in the world look like ultra-chauvinists and jingoists by comparison.

Canada must surely be unique in the entire world in that invariably, when you speak in favour of or in praise of your own country, the knee-jerk reaction of some corporate executive, business columnist, open-line caller, or politician is to say you are anti-American. One day in the 1970s Peter Newman was doing Jack Webster's show in Vancouver. In the course of his remarks, Newman said: "You know, I really love Canada." The switchboard lit up and the first caller was a woman. You could almost see her foaming at the mouth. "Oh, so you love Canada, eh? Well, tell us Mr. Smart-apple Newman, why are you so anti-American? Eh?"

There is a huge difference between being pro-Canadian and anti-American, between being un-American and automatically disliking Americans. The fact remains that most Canadians like most Americans, but most Canadians have no desire whatsoever to become Americans. This is not to say for a moment that from time to time the Americans are not scheming, subversive, aggressive, dictatorial, and demanding. But it has been our own Canadian leaders who have allowed them to be so successful.

Canadians have much to admire and much to dislike about the United States. We admire its technological development, its energy and innovative abilities, its sports heroes and novelists, its entrepreneurial skills, many of its films, and much of its music. But we do not admire its violence, its cruelty, its aggression, its arrogance, its stratification, its uncaring society. Whatever our likes or dislikes, if there is one common denominator for Canadian nationalists, on the left or on the right, it is a simple one: we do not want to be Americans. We want the freedom to decide our own standards and our own policies and our own future. Why? The answer, too, is simple: most of us believe that we can do better, that we can create a better society.

But living next door to a colossus creates big problems for the timid. In an article for *International Perspectives* I wrote: "The greatest irony is that even modest, hesitant moves by Canada to protect its own national interest have been regarded by many, on both sides of the border, as "nationalistic." When one considers the juxtaposition of the world's greatest, super-patriotic superpower next to the world's foremost branch-plant colony, cries of too much Canadian nationalism must surely be some giant cruel joke, except for the fact that so many poorly informed Americans and Canadians really believe it."

Whether it was the Committee for an Independent Canada, the Council of Canadians, or the National Party of Canada, the compradors always accused us of wanting to "build a wall around Canada" or wanting to "stop trading with other nations." Moreover, "The status quo won't do!" What utter nonsense.

During all those years I knew of no one who wanted to maintain the status quo. The status quo meant continuing to sell off more and more of the ownership and control of our country, continuing to be more and more vulnerable and at the mercy of decisions made in Washington, continuing to accept unneccessarily high rates of unemployment and a declining standard of living. As well, I cannot think of one person I worked closely with during the past thirty years who believed in aggressive, isolationist, or parochial nationalism. The nationalists I know are, without exception, men and women who have a deep and genuine love for their country, a strong belief in Canada's future possibilities, a respect for its traditions and values, a feeling of gratitude for their good fortune to be living here, and the realization that our ability to control our own future and the ability of future generations to influence their own welfare and destiny have been dramatically eroded.

Almost all of the many thousands of men and women I have worked with in the CIC, the COC, and the National party have been strong *internationalists*, people who believe that Canada should play a more active role in international organizations, people who are dedicated to world peace, to alleviating the suffering of the world's poor, people who completely reject isolationism.

But they are also people who reject the idea that you should sell everything you own to people in other countries, and they reject the idea that we do not have a responsibility to manage our resources properly for future generations. They believe that we Canadians should be much more self-reliant and more independent, that we should stand on our own feet and set our own goals, our own priorities, and establish our own national standards, policies, and values.

Simply put, when you live next door to the world's greatest super-power, an aggressive, nationalistic, militaristic industrial powerhouse and the greatest culture exporter the world has ever known, if you're not at least somewhat nationalistic your chances of survival are next to nil.

But Canadians have gone in exactly the opposite direction. We now are, in our public policies, the least nationalistic and the least patriotic developed nation on earth. This is not to say for a moment that most Canadians are not patriotic. Year after year public-opinion polls clearly show the contrary, that most Canadians have a deep love for their country. But inundated with American culture, Canada has rarely promoted its own heroes. The British colony evolved into a nation that did not even have control over its external relations for the first sixty-four years of its existence, its own flag for the first ninety-eight years, and did not have final control over its own con-stitution for its first 115 years. When Canada finally did gain its full independence, its political and business elites sold off the country. At the same time, the pervasive influence of American television became the most underestimated development in modern Canadian history. Travel across Canada and turn on television sets in Inuvik and Saskatoon, St. John's and Sudbury, to TV direct from the U.S., and you will understand how misplaced George Grant's faith was when he wrote optimistically: "Most helpful is that among the young . . . the desire for independence is greater than for many generations."

Not only is this statement pathetically untrue today, but most of our young people have no idea that Canada's independence is even an issue, let alone seriously threatened. The absence of large numbers of university, college, and high school students from the "great free-trade debate" and from the crucial 1988 election campaign showed that, while Grant's faith in the young was in error, his prophecy about Canada was not.

Just before the 1995 Quebec referendum, Léger and Léger asked Quebeckers the factors influencing their voting decisions. First (in a list of many choices) came "Pride in being a Quebecker." In second place was "Future of our children," and third was "Preserving social gains." But in Canada in recent years, pride in our country has dimin-ished as respect for politicians and government has plummeted. Now, more than at any time since the Great Depression, the future of our children is in grave doubt. Meanwhile, as many of us predicted a decade ago, rather than preserving our social gains we are rapidly losing them.

From the end of the Second World War to Brian Mulroney's election in September 1984, Canada vacillated between the two great tides that, since even before Confederation, dominated the struggles between the two polarities that have shaped our history and national destiny — nationalism and continentalism. Historian Bill Morton said that "nationalism may be a bad thing, but nihilism is worse." The globalized world of corporations in charge is in many way similar to the nineteenth-century world where greedy capitalists ran roughshod over society. Transnationals have only one allegiance and that is to their own bottom line. And their own bottom line can best be enhanced by the weakening of the nation-state.

I would much rather live in a world where the important decisions are made in a democratic public process by a majority of citizens than in a world where large corporations set the rules, standards, and values of society. Just as the FTA was falsely packaged and sold to the public as something for the public good, globalization has been packaged in a similar manner. Yes, trade is good; yes, communications are changing the world. Yes, by all means, let there be a free flow of information and ideas. But a borderless world without nations that is controlled by the big banks, the big oil companies, and other large transnational organizations will be a world that returns to the values of a feudal society, a world of the very wealthy few and the impoverished masses. During the past three decades, as world trade exploded, the poorest eighty percent of the world's population's share of GNP fell from thirty percent to seventeen percent, while the richest twenty percent of the world's population increased their share of world income from thirty times greater than the poorest to sixty times greater. Today the same process is under way *within* many nations. Humankind's slow but steady process towards egalitarianism is being reversed. The time has come for citizens to stop this retrogressive process and to take control of their societies.

So Much for Democracy

THE FEDERAL LIBERAL party, for as long as I can remember, has presented itself to the electorate as the party of the average Canadian. But in reality they are now and for the most part always have been a party where the power of big business dominates. From time to time there are exceptions to this rule, but they are temporary aberrations. The Foreign Investment Review Act and the National Energy Program were such deviations, as was John Turner's ardent opposition to the Free Trade Agreement. When a Liberal government veers to the left, it has nothing to do with political philosophy. Calgary historian David Bercuson put it well: "The one underlying philosophy that has marked successful Canadian governments and prime ministers from 1867 to now has been that they have no overriding philosophy."

With no philosophy, how can there be a vision of the nation? In his memoirs Keith Davey wrote: "Harry Truman's contention was perfectly correct and to paraphrase it: faced with the alternative of voting for a real Tory or a carbon-copy Tory, the Tory will vote for the real thing every time. Right-wing liberalism is a recipe for political disaster." Is it any wonder, then, that when the Liberals fought the 1993 federal election, they lied to the people of Canada about their intentions regarding free trade, Canada's social programs, the GST, cultural industries, the CBC, and more free votes in the House of Commons?

As for Chrétien, on the surface apparently the least philosophical prime minister in our history, a closer examination proves that he is indeed a man of the people, the people being the bankers, the transnationals, the Paul Desmaraises, and Bay Street. At the Aylmer conference Chrétien said that globalization "is simply a fact of life. We have to deal with reality [and] we cannot be isolated anymore."

Isolated? Only a very misinformed person or a functionary for a continentalist economic elite would use such an analogy.

The Paul Martin budgets have been closer to what one might have expected from a Preston Manning and the Reform party than anything emanating from the Liberal party of the past half century. Peter Newman called the 1995 budget "a dismantling of the federal structure. . . . Provincial capitals will thus gain the kind of fiscal autonomy Bouchard has long advocated for Quebec." Dalton Camp described it equally succinctly: "As a political document, it reveals the new order as counter-federalist, continentalist and callous in the bargain," and David Crane said: "Instead of building a new social system with the provinces . . . Martin seems to be saying that the government of Canada will no longer be a key player. The implications are profound."

Profound indeed! The dramatic reduction of the federal presence in Confederation, the continuing increases in provincial powers, the draconian cuts to social spending, the inevitable consequences of a national movement towards a U.S. style of widening inequality, and the Free Trade Agreement combine to tear away the remaining crumbling foundations of the nation.

When asked what he thought his father would feel about his 1995 budget, Martin replied: "I think he would say that he did what he had to do in his time, and I have done what I had to do in mine. And that, I think, is the definition of a Liberal."

William Thorsell was delighted with both Martin and Chrétien: "This crop of Liberals are conservatives indeed. . . . This orientation . . . should give enormous comfort to those who worried that Brian Mulroney's agenda might be derailed."

Some comfort.

For former trade minister Roy MacLaren, expanded, harmonized policies must be the new order. "Free trade is moving into domestic areas that were previously outside of international scrutiny or rules," meaning national standards, investment regulations, and intellectual property such as drug patent regulations, "a whole range of issues that hitherto were not part of the GATT practice." And what if nations wish to exert their sovereignty? According to Tom d'Aquino, "Business is not going to pay any attention to the rules because we are leaping over them."

So much for democracy.

In a recent conversation I asked Eric Kierans if he agreed that the Liberal government of millionaires Jean Chrétien and Paul Martin is the most continentalist Liberal government in Canadian history. His reply was tinged with sadness and brief: "They're going along dutifully giving the U.S. everything they ever wanted."

The Niche Colony

WRITING IN *SATURDAY NIGHT* magazine, *Globe and Mail* and now Southam columnist Andrew Coyne described Canada prior to the FTA as "one of the most protected economies in the developed world."

Protected? By 1974, Canada had more foreign ownership than the United States, Britain, Germany, France, Spain, Italy, and Japan combined. While Canadians had been debating the subject for two decades, the amount of foreign ownership in Canada had tripled. In my speeches there was another quote from American George Ball I liked to use, this one not so well-known: "How can a national government make an economic plan with any confidence if a board of directors, meeting in another country, can, by altering its pattern of purchases and production, affect in a major way that country's life?"

By the end of 1984, the year Brian Mulroney decided we should become "open for business," total foreign-controlled assets in Canada were just over $252-billion. By the time Mulroney left office in 1993, they had almost doubled, to $493-billion. All told, there were thirty-three industrial groups in Canada that were foreign-dominated from fifty-two to ninety-nine percent. In the U.S., Germany, and Japan, not one single industry group was foreign-controlled.

By 1993, the OECD was reporting that of all the major industrial nations, no other country was anywhere near as dependent as Canada on foreign-sourced parts and components. In Canada the ratio for foreign content of domestic sourcing was fifty percent. By comparison, in the U.S. there was thirteen percent foreign sourcing and in Japan only seven percent. The heavy degree of foreign ownership in Canada was the principal reason Canada purchased so much from outside the country.

Aside from the serious ramifications of balance of payments, lost tax revenue, and absence of recirculating profits, the real cost was hundreds of thousands of lost jobs. No wonder we had such constantly high unemployment. After the OECD report was published, I calculated that if Canada only had the same ratio of employment in manufacturing as the *average* of all the other twenty-three OECD nations, there would be an additional 603,000 Canadians employed in full-time, high-wage manufacturing. And, of course, manufacturing activity has a huge spinoff into all the other areas of the economy. The multiplier effect would create hundreds of thousands of additional jobs.

In short, if we were simply only an average nation among industrialized nations in this one respect alone, we could cut unemployment by more than half, reduce our external and internal deficits substantially, and dramatically cut unemployment insurance and welfare payments, and other burdensome social costs, not to mention our burgeoning debt-servicing costs. (One interesting exercise we engaged in was an annual examination of the *Financial Post 500*. By comparing sales figures with the number of employees, it was clear, year after year after year, that Canadian-controlled companies employed on average sixty to seven-five percent more men and women for every million dollars in sales than American firms operating in Canada.)

Since Brian Mulroney declared Canada "open for business," more than six thousand companies in Canada have been taken over by foreign corporations. More than eighty percent of the takeovers were completely unscreened. *Not one single takeover has been denied!* Less than eight percent of all new foreign direct investment has been for the establishment of new businesses in Canada; the rest has been for takeovers.

In one month that we examined, the companies taken over included corporations working in the following areas: computers, design, data processing, nursing homes, oil and gas exploration and production, hydraulic equipment, pressure gauges, investment services, paint products, sporting goods, amusement parks, high-performance lubricants, industrial tools, vending machines, direct mail, medical products, actuarial consulting, asphalt manufacturing, mobile communications, adhesives, fans and blowers and pumps, computer software, tunnels and pipelines, photocopying products, transportation services, homecare services, travel services, windows, fish farms, tobacco products, chair controls and bases, optical laboratory services, pharmaceuticals, apartment buildings, chemical testing, plastic manufacturing, bottled water, cranes, freight transportation, shaving systems, oil-field equipment, forestry equipment, health testing, insulation, hardware and garden products, telephone services, casinos, neon lighting, wood products, import/export trading, hazardous wastes, processed food, concrete, motion pictures, and engineering.

All in one month!

The political power of foreign corporations in Canada is much greater than even the very large percentages of foreign ownership and control indicate. Among the five hundred largest nonfinancial corporations in Canada, some forty percent are foreign-controlled. It's these huge transnationals that have become more and more successful in determining the course of public policy in Canada. IBM, General Motors, Imperial Oil, and Ford, among others, all enthusiastically pushed the FTA. Listen to the words of the president of Chrysler of Canada: "We'd better all fall in line with that trade agreement in a helluva hurry."

According to the former chairman of DuPont Canada, anti-free traders "often seem to think that you can't be pro-Canadian unless you are anti-American." And, "Why are some of our most ardent patriots and defenders of Canada the same people who have no faith in their fellow Canadians — especially the Canadians who happen to be in politics or business?"

No faith in their fellow Canadians in business? This is the same man who recently suggested Canadian corporations should appoint many more Americans to their boards of directors.

The Gray report said that foreign investment entering Canada brings with it cultural baggage. A branch-plant society produces branch-plant values, a branch-plant mass culture, and a branch-plant mentality. Moreover, it prevents men and women from speaking out about their concerns. Many letters I received over the years began with words like "Mr. Hurtig, I'm sorry not to sign my name to this letter, but I work for an American company. I thought I should write to you in support for your campaign to stop the foreign takeover of Canada." Often the letter would supply details of transfer-pricing activities, the blatant rejection of competitive domestic sourcing, and other activities of the foreign corporation.

Over the years what has constantly amazed me more than anything else is the oft-repeated, taken-for-granted claim that U.S. investment in Canada is necessary to support our standard of living. From the end of the Second World War to the end of 1995, Americans brought a net amount of some $23-billion into Canada. During the same years some $91-billion left Canada for the United States in profits alone. Yet, during the same period, the book value (that is, the lowest measurement) of American ownership of Canada increased by more than $98-billion. Canada "needs" more foreign direct investment like an alcoholic needs a truckload of gin.

In my speeches in the early 1970s I used to hold up a full-page Royal Bank of Canada ad from the *Wall Street Journal* headlined: "We Deliver Canada." The audience would always groan. The Toronto-Dominion Bank chipped in with its own ads proclaiming: "We're happy to be accused of un-Canadian activities." I wrote two governors of the Bank of Canada, Louis Rasminsky and Gerald Bouey, and three finance ministers, Jean Chrétien, Donald Macdonald, and Michael Wilson, asking them all the same question: "What percentage of loans made by Canada's chartered banks go to foreign-controlled firms either inside or outside Canada?" The answers were always the same: "I'm sorry, Mr. Hurtig, but the Department of Finance (Bank of Canada) does not keep information of that kind." Bouey wrote to me in 1971 that no agency of the government keeps track of such information. Today, twenty-five years later, the situation is even worse. In a number of astonishing moves, Ottawa has consciously set out to curtail information about foreign ownership and the activities of foreign corporations in Canada. The formerly excellent annual Corporations and Labour Union Returns Act (CALURA) report from Statistics Canada now no longer reveals the degree of foreign ownership, control, sales, and profits in a long list of Canadian industries. The Chrétien government recently closed down the valuable Petroleum Monitoring Agency, which tracked foreign control in the oil and gas business. Now the Liberal government has drastically weakened the mandatory reporting requirements of foreign corporations operating in this country.

By 1995, *every hour* of every day, seven days a week, for 365 days of the year, an average of $4.6-million left the country to pay for the foreign investment already in the country, a total outflow exceeding $40-billion. This figure does not include the business service costs directly associated with foreign ownership in Canada. Nor does it include the many billions of dollars in costs associated with purchases of goods from outside Canada due to intercorporate purchasing or transfer pricing.

While $40-billion left the country in 1995, foreign ownership of Canada grew by a record amount, over $20-billion, without counting the unknown growth of foreign ownership financed by foreign borrowing in Canada.

Few Canadians know it and none of the politicians in Ottawa ever talk about it, but the FTA has investment provisions (Article 1607) that allow Americans to continue to take over Canada, even if we decide that enough is enough and too much of Canada is already foreign-owned. Now, every day, foreign ownership is expanding into new areas of the Canadian economy. Harry Rosen tells us that soon all that will be left for Canadians in the retail industry will be "the possibility of becoming niche retailers." Niche retailers in a niche colonial country.

Massive foreign ownership is a growing fatal cancer for Canada, yet now in 1996 hardly anyone even mentions the subject, no federal or provincial politician, no editorial writer, no television or radio commentator. The topic has vanished from public consciousness.

The Power Behind the Throne

WHEN ANDRÉ OUELLET was Liberal minister of Consumer and Corporate Affairs in the 1970s, his department officials strongly recommended much tougher competition policies. But Marc Lalonde shut down all proposals of any consequence. Despite the fact that Canadian laws regarding competition, takeover, and merger were hopelessly weak and out-of-date, ("a travesty," in the words of one expert), even modest reforms were hijacked by the big-business lobby in Ottawa.

Under the Mulroney government, corporate concentration increased in all sectors. Canada's anticombines laws were largely ignored or weakened further. The two large airlines were allowed to buy up regional carriers from coast to coast, accumulating massive debt at high interest costs. Deregulation came also to the financial sector. The large and powerful banks, already highly oligopolistic and very profitable, were allowed to take over insurance companies, trust companies, and brokerage houses.

The level of corporate concentration in Canada makes a mockery of "market economics" or "free enterprise" theories. On the contrary, it reflects a shocking presence of powerful, dominant monopolies and oligopolies. But the same big-business barons who sold the people of Canada the idea that the FTA would be good for them because of the increased competition it would bring to the marketplace are the exact same people who have fought legislation in Canada that would produce laws to finally stop the appalling growing levels of corporate concentration in this country. Now the Bureau of Competition Policy is attempting to strengthen the scrutiny of takeovers. However, according to one member of the advisory panel that has been hard at work assisting the bureau, "the business representatives are screaming and hollering and belching in opposition" to any moves to make the word "competition" more meaningful. Moreover, the bureau is badly underfunded and many important cases are not brought forward because it simply does not have the resources to do so.

As in the case of foreign ownership, hardly anyone in Canada even mentions corporate concentration today. When was the last time you saw an editorial calling for tougher competition and antitrust laws? When was the last time you heard the great populist Preston Manning, the little-guy-of-the-people Jean Chrétien, Ralph Klein, or Mike Harris express concern about growing corporate concentration? Don't hold your breath.

By 1992 the top one-hundredth of one percent of all corporations controlled fifty-eight percent of all corporate assets in Canada. The top one percent of corporate enterprises controlled a staggering eighty-seven percent of all corporate assets. Since then the pace of corporate concentration has accelerated. Huge tax concessions to big corporations in Canada helped produce a situation whereby a very tiny number of corporations owned and controlled most of the country. Regardless of who is in power in Ottawa, these large corporations also control the political agenda. They fund the campaigns of and offer lavish resort havens for prime ministers. They put up most of the money for party-leadership candidates. Those who write the cheques write the laws.

Little wonder that corporate concentration is not a public issue in Canada. First, there is so much corporate concentration in the media (and this has worsened markedly in recent years) that it is highly unlikely that much of the media would be inclined to take a strong position on the subject. Year after year, when the annual report on corporate concentration was published by Statistics Canada, the print media either ignored or downplayed the information, startling as it often was, and inevitably the electronic media did likewise.

I very much doubt that any other developed country's competition rules would have allowed Ted Rogers to take over Maclean-Hunter, Conrad Black to take over control of Southam, or Black to take over the major newspapers in Saskatchewan. By early 1996, Conrad Black, Ken Thomson, and Paul Desmarais controlled eighty-one of the 104 daily newspapers in Canada! The Irvings controlled all five daily newspapers in New Brunswick, and Black all dailies in Saskatchewan, Newfoundland, and Prince Edward Island. What are the chances of one of these newspapers coming out against excessive corporate concentration in the media? Were Mulroney and Black on the same wavelength? Peter White, Black's longtime associate and partner, became Mulroney's principal secretary. What were the chances of a Conservative government stopping Black's increasing media control? Should Paul Desmarais want to increase his media assets, what are the chances of Jean Chrétien ever saying enough is enough? And what are the ramifications for public opinion in Canada? In the words of James Winter, professor of communication studies at the University of Windsor:

> Black's strong, neo-conservative political beliefs have led him to exert greater direct and indirect influence on his newspapers than has Ken Thomson, beginning with (but not limited to) those who are placed in positions of managerial power.
>
> David Radler, president of Hollinger, has, since the latest acquisitions, been espousing his belief in the editorial autonomy of local publishers — all of whom, of course, are appointed by Hollinger. This is the same David Radler who, three years ago in a less-guarded interview with Peter C. Newman, said, "I am ultimately the publisher of all of these papers, and if editors disagree with us, they should disagree with us when they're no longer in our employ."
>
> But perhaps what is *most* disturbing about "the Establishment Man," as Peter Newman labelled Conrad Black in his book of the same title, is Black's all-consuming quest, not only for newspapers and profits, but for political power. Newman quotes journalist Laurier LaPierre, Black's former teacher at Upper Canada College, as saying, "I don't think Conrad wants to be prime minister, but he really *does* want to be the power behind the throne and feels his money will buy him that."
>
> . . . Black's latest acquisitions should serve as a warning of the political consequences of our growing media monopoly. As John Bassett, publisher of the long defunct *Toronto Telegram*, once replied after being asked if he used his newspaper to push his own political views, "Of course. Why else would you want to own a newspaper?"

The situation in television is only marginally better. Right-wing Conservatives or conservatives now control almost ninety percent of private television revenue in Canada. And, of course, there is nothing they would like better than the shutdown of the CBC. Needless to say, the same people are major financial contributors to both the Liberal and Conservative parties, and more recently to the Reform party, as well.

Tearing Down a System

WHEN BRIAN MULRONEY campaigned for the leadership of the Conservative party in 1983, he promised that "a Conservative government would restore the original fifty-fifty split in medicare costs between the federal and provincial governments." Of course they did exactly the opposite, cutting back the federal government's share. By 1990, the federal share of total social spending in Canada had dropped to below forty percent.

By the broadest, most all-inclusive measurement of social programs, in 1983/84 federal social expenditures were 11.1 percent of GDP. Ten years later they had increased by less than one percentage point.

In 1985 I began giving speeches and writing articles warning against an impending assault against social spending led by big business. Eleven years later the assault has become an unrelenting war. Social spending in Canada, well below the average in the OECD and the European Union, is blamed for Canada's serious debt problem. Moreover, it is invariably compared only to social spending in the United States. The refrain has been unending: we spend too much on social programs — they're driving us into bankruptcy. But those leading the attack are once again exactly those who fervently promised us that the FTA would allow us to *strengthen* our social programs.

Among all the developed nations in the world, Canada is now thirteenth in social spending as a percentage of GDP. But for the likes of former Molson chief Mickey Cohen who years before helped mastermind huge federal tax breaks for the Reichmans and who presided over the majority sale of Molson to non-Canadians, there was little doubt about what we would have to do in terms of our social programs: "This isn't about cutting a little here or trimming a little bit there," Cohen said. "We'll have to go through a period when we're seriously going to have to lower our living standards."

Big business (and the Reform party) will never come right out and admit it, but they would like Canada to move much closer to the nonuniversal, two-tier, user-fee, private-insurance health system in the United States. So would Conservatives like Ralph Klein. Not only would this be tragic in human terms, but it would be an economic disaster. Health-care costs in the U.S. have been escalating at a much faster rate than those in Canada. From 1981 to 1991, health-care expenditures in Canada increased by 0.9 percent of total public spending. In the U.S. during the same period, costs jumped by almost three percent. In real terms, U.S. health-care costs have risen faster than in any other OECD nation, while the U.S. remains the only major developed nation without a comprehensive public-health-care scheme.

In 1993 the *New England Journal of Medicine* indicated that "adopting Canadian practices would save U.S. hospitals as much as $40-billion a year." In 1991 the same journal indicated that "reducing U.S. administrative costs to Canadian levels would save enough money to fund coverage for all uninsured and underinsured Americans." The total of uninsured and underinsured Americans is more than double Canada's entire population. Some ten million American children have no health-care coverage.

Perhaps a quote relating to a study that appeared in the *Journal of the American Medical Association* sums it up best: "In the U.S., the richer you are, the higher rate of bypass surgery. Would you want to live in a country where if you're poor, you don't get access to that surgery?" But that's exactly the kind of Canada our business elite and our Preston Mannings and Ralph Kleins are leading us to. In the United States almost half of eighteen- to twenty-nine-year-olds periodically avoid going to the doctor because they can't afford it. It's true that waiting lists in the U.S. tend to be somewhat shorter, but there's a very simple reason: poor people in the U.S. often can't afford the surgery, so they're not put on a waiting list. In *Jobs For All Canadians* I wrote:

> U.S. President Clinton has complained about a polio vaccine that costs almost $10 in the U.S. compared to $1.80 in the U.K. and 77 cents in Belgium. As a result only Bolivia and Haiti have lower rates of immunization. According to the U.S. president, drug profits in the U.S. are increasing at four times the profit rates for the average *Fortune 500* companies. Brian Mulroney and Michael Wilson have greatly helped that process by providing U.S. drug companies with substantially

extended patent protection in Canada which will unnecessarily cost Canadians billions of dollars.

In many U.S. states, one in six have no health-care coverage of any kind. Children often do not receive inoculations and pregnant mothers do not receive prenatal care. For those who do have private insurance, the costs are often staggering. As the *Edmonton Journal* recently reported: American grain farmer Gene Demars spoke from the heart when he told how his family's health insurance jumped from $3,300 annually in 1989 to $10,500 in 1992. "Our health insurance cost us more than our farmland . . ." When Demars' wife of 37 years had heart surgery in 1991, the hospital stay cost $34,000.

Universal social programs do not foster a have and have-not society. They are a reflection of a caring, compassionate community. Without universal social programs, a trend develops whereby segments of society resent payments to the underprivileged. Inevitably those most in need find their benefits eroded. And, equally important, universal social programs are *much* less costly to administer. But, while universality has many advantages, it *must* go hand in hand with a truly progressive tax system. Without such a system "the Wealthy Banker's Wife" becomes a reality. A progressive tax system will tax away a large portion of universal social-program benefits that go to those who do not require them.

Jeffrey Simpson summed the current situation in Canada up well in a *Globe and Mail* column: "While what has been called the 'glass tower elite' of traditional plutocrats . . . thrive in their enclaves of affluence and reinforce each other's complaints about the world — complaints echoed both by a braying press and *Poujadiste* tabloids — their world is increasingly divorced from the one lived by their fellow citizens." The elite promote the idea of privatized social services. The belief that removing social programs from the public sector would solve our economic problems is beyond comprehension. True, there would be cost savings for government, but for society as a whole the costs would rise substantially. If anyone tells you differently, ask them to look at the rapidly ballooning costs of health care in the U.S., now heading for 14 percent of GNP, whereas in Canada they have declined to under 10 percent.

Not for a moment am I suggesting that improvements cannot continue to be made in our social programs and in the delivery of health care. Other countries have programs that produce somewhat better results for lower costs. But the movement towards a two-tier American-style society is madness. Inevitably the have-nots will end up with vastly inferior and continually deteriorating health care and worsening living standards.

Before the impact of Bills C-22 and C-91, Canadian drug prices were already the highest or second highest of the G-7 nations. Now they top the costs for all industrialized nations and are the fastest-growing expense in the health-care system. It should come as no surprise that big foreign drug companies are major financial contributors to the Liberal and Conservative parties and their leadership candidates and were the largest contributors to the Yes side of the Charlottetown constitutional debate. Billions of dollars could be saved each year through the use of more generic drugs. Despite all the cries of the drug lobby, the big drug companies had an excellent return on capital before the Mulroney government's multibillion-dollar largesse.

Of course everything is relative. In 1993 one EH-101 helicopter (Brian Mulroney and Kim Campbell wanted to buy fifty and thirty-five respectively) cost some $117-million. Some half a million Canadians have cancer; some 62,000 will die of cancer in 1996, and over 129,000 new cases will be diagnosed. In 1993 we spent $68-million on cancer research in Canada.

Let us suppose that for the past decade Canada had adopted a less-rigid monetary policy, and interest charges on the public debt had been *only one percent lower*. The total savings in servicing the debt would have been $42-billion. With a different monetary policy, there would be no crisis today in medicare and other social-program funding or in the funding of postsecondary education. This said, by far the best way to relieve the strain on Canada's social programs is to have a full-employment policy that will supply jobs to many more Canadians.

Last year the C.D. Howe Institute, once again in keeping with their traditional role, produced a widely reported study saying that, rather than severely damaging Canada's social programs, the massive cuts in federal transfer payments to the provinces will "preserve and promote" our social safety net. If there was even a single snicker in the press, I missed it.

Much of what the political and economic elite backed in the Meech Lake agreement and in the Charlottetown accord will be accomplished without constitutional changes by the two Paul Martin budgets and their followups, which amount to a massive abandonment by the Chrétien government of national policies and standards. Gone will be the federal-provincial cost-sharing Canada Assistance Plan and Established Programs Financing for health care and postsecondary education. In their place will be a greatly reduced Canada Social Transfer with few national standards attached. The federal government's ability to ensure that the poor, the sick, the disabled, and others in need are the proper recipients of even the new reduced transfers will be either diminished or nonexistent. Instead of the Liberals' Red Book promises of improved social security, Canada's underprivileged will suffer. Instead of Paul Martin's promise that fairness would be "paramount," the 1995 budget was an attack on those underprivileged citizens, while dozens of tax loopholes, family trusts, and the like went unchallenged.

The BCNI-backed process of decentralization and reduced social spending in Canada has gone on with inadequate public debate. During the 1970s, transfers from Ottawa to other levels of government averaged 19.4 percent of federal spending; by 1993-94, they were down to some 16.5 percent and are now headed lower still. Reduced social funds from Ottawa will put enormous pressure on the provinces and municipalities. The 1.4 million children living in poverty in Canada will pay the heavy price for the terrible Liberal and Conservative mismanagement of the Canadian economy and the inevitable balkanization of social programs across the country.

Let us now turn to the words of longtime member of Parliament and former Liberal cabinet minister Warren Allmand, speaking about Martin's 1995 budget in the House of Commons:

> These proposals in the budget are completely contrary to what we said in the Red Book during the election campaign. They are completely contrary to what we said during the nine years in opposition. They are completely contrary to what we did when we were in government under Prime Minster Trudeau and Prime Minister Pearson.
>
> I am opposed to these provisions, first of all, because social programs in this country are not the cause of the deficit, so why are they being attacked in this bill whose goal it is to reduce the deficit?
>
> Second, I am opposed to these provisions in the budget and the budget bill because they will cause severe harm to those in need. They will widen the gap between rich and poor,

and in my view lead to social unrest and increased crime.

I regret I have to make these sorts of interventions in the House. However, I cannot contribute to tearing down a system that for my 29 years in the House I helped build up. I just cannot do it.

Because Allmand voted against the budget, Jean Chrétien fired him as chairman of the Commons justice committee.

Twisted Yardsticks and Broken Promises

PABLO NERUDA WROTE that "history is written by the conquerors." I would rephrase that for Canada's business press: "History is written by the compradors." Just as I am writing this chapter, a new edition of *Canadian Business* magazine advises that "measured by any objective yardstick, free trade has been a huge win for Canada." And in another article in the same magazine: "Quite simply, we've never depended so heavily on the U.S. or been so tied to its economy." And then: "For everyone who thought that free trade was the final stopping point in the economic integration of Canada and the U.S., think again. Sooner or later, both countries will probably wind up using a common currency."

For the *Globe and Mail*, there was never any doubt. From day one "Canada's National Newspaper" strongly supported the Mulroney government's "trade" plans. In December 1995 the paper closed the door on any further debate on the subject. The matter had been decided. Quoting an American study that analysed the agreement's first seven years as "an economic success," the *Globe* editorial page told its readers that the FTA and NAFTA are now "non-issues."

According to *Globe* editor-in-chief Bill Thorsell, the cumulative results of the FTA "make a mockery of the opposition to Mr. Mulroney's historic 1987 agreement with the United States." Moreover, "all Mr. Mulroney need do to prevail is to wait" for history to vindicate him.

It's interesting to note Thorsell's comments in the *Globe* in May 1990: "How can we explain such angst at a time when Canada's economy is still strong on its feet after seven years of healthy growth and the national government is secure with a second working majority?" He went on to say: "Some observers feel Canadians have developed a bad habit of hectoring and bitchiness akin to masochism." These words were written as the "economy still strong on its feet" was, in fact, plunging into a deep, devastating, protracted recession from which recovery has been feeble.

There's not much doubt about where the editor of Canada's most influential newspaper stands in his politics. The Tories and Reform should merge so that Preston Manning becomes prime minister, Thorsell advised the nation in June 1995, all this to be brokered by none other than Ralph Klein. But what else would we expect from Thorsell, the man who in 1993 rated Brian Mulroney as the best Canadian prime minister in the past thirty-five years?

In May 1996, after the Reform party embarrassments, Thorsell changed his mind. The only alternative to save the country, he wrote, "is the Charest Conservatives . . . the campaign to merge these parties . . . is doomed — nay, damned."

Now let us turn from the Thomson empire to that other kingpin of newspaper ownership in Canada, Conrad Black. Mr. Black is a great admirer of the U.S. and has moved his business headquarters to that country. About the same time that Black derided Canada's "most ill-considered of all . . . national initiatives, to show that we are more 'caring and compassionate' than the Americans," the Associated Press was reporting that "hunger is increasing in the United States . . . 301 out of every 1,000 children under 12 are hungry or at risk," and that the gap between rich and poor in the U.S. is growing even worse while the level of violence in the country continued to far surpass that of all the developed nations in the world. No doubt when Mr. Black travels to Washington, he doesn't get to spend much time in poor areas. The nation's capital is a place where over one-third of its residents receive public assistance, some fifty percent of schoolchildren fail to complete their schooling, and much of Washington, now the nation's number-one "murder city," is, in the words of The Economist, "a moonscape of devastated streets."

The often repeated line is that "Canada is a trading nation with a growing percentage of our gross domestic product derived from exports." However, huge increases in imports and other economic activities must be measured against the increased exports.

The business press constantly emphasizes Canada's exports. But let's take a closer look at the first seven years of the agreement (1989 to

1995) and see how the yardsticks of Statistics Canada, the Bank of Canada, the Department of Finance, and the OECD compare with what we read in our newspapers.

Let's compare the first seven years of the FTA with the seven years before the FTA was implemented (1982 to 1988). In the seven years before the FTA, real GDP growth increases in Canada totalled a healthy 23.6 percent. In the first seven years of the FTA, the GDP increases plummeted to less than half that level, a dismal 10.2 percent. Similarly, the total growth of employment in Canada fell from 12 percent all the way down to an anaemic 4.3 percent.

Looking specifically at merchandise trade, if one reads the *Globe*, the *Financial Post*, or even from time to time the business reports from the Southam Press, it is clear that the Free Trade Agreement has been a roaring success. For years headlines reported EXPORTS SOAR or EXPORTS PROPEL ECONOMY or MORE EXPORT RECORDS BROKEN. But a closer examination of the trade reality presents a vastly different picture. In the first seven years of the FTA, Canada's merchandise trade balance was a huge $27.2-billion lower than in the earlier seven-year period. *Lower!* Moreover, if the same comparisons are made in constant 1986 dollars, our merchandise trade balance is an enormous $60.6-billion lower, and a comparison of trade in goods and services combined presents an even more dismal picture.

In all of 1995 a pitiful total of 8,000 full-time jobs were created in Canada. During the past five years employment in the goods-producing sector of the Canadian economy has fallen by almost 300,000 jobs. Since the FTA was implemented, Canada's population grew by some 2.7 million, yet full-time employment is still back about where it was in 1989. During the first seven years of the FTA full-time employment in Canada grew at less than one-sixth the rate for the previous seven years.

Yes, yes, yes, our exports have grown. But while exports increased, jobs did not. And while exports increased, so did imports. And increasing imports wiped out thousands of jobs. While Canadian manufacturers increased their share of the U.S. market by some $4-billion (U.S.), the U.S. manufacturers' share of the Canadian market increased by greater than five times that amount. Thirty-one BCNI members responding to a survey indicated that they had reduced employment by 172,000 jobs, while thirteen members increased employment but only by 23,000 jobs. One need not speculate what the figures would be like if all BCNI members had responded to the survey. Statistics Canada also measures the number of Canadians employed by business in Canada. During the first seven years of the FTA this figure shrunk by a total of 310,000 jobs. As this is being written, a new survey indicates "Canadian blue-chip companies continue to slash jobs as if the recession never ended."

Throughout 1990, 1991, and 1992 we heard from Tory finance ministers Michael Wilson and Don Mazankowski, and their colleague Thomas d'Aquino, that Canada was caught in a "worldwide recession." While unemployment stood at 1.5 percent in Luxembourg and was up to 2.2 percent in Japan, 3.9 percent in Switzerland, 4 percent in Holland, 5 percent in Sweden, and had leaped to 7.4 percent in the United States and Germany, in Canada it stood at 11.3 percent, and in virtually every other key economic measurement Canada was at or near the bottom of the barrel. Of the world's twenty-four OECD industrialized nations, only Turkey had a smaller percentage of its workforce employed in industry.

The Mulroney government continued to blame the so-called "worldwide recession," but no other nation had deteriorating figures anywhere near as severe. In 1988, before free trade, Canada's unemployment rate stood at 7.8 percent, and the rate had been *declining* for five consecutive years. During the first seven years of the FTA our unemployment rate averaged 9.8 percent. By comparison, during the same years the average OECD unemployment rate was 7.3 percent. In 1995 Canada's unemployment rate of 9.5 percent was much higher than the G-7 average of 6.9 percent or the OECD average of 7.8 percent. When so-called "discouraged workers," who dropped out of the labour force, and involuntary part-time workers were added to the officially unemployed, Canada's combined rate was worse than most industrialized nations, and well in excess of the rates for countries such as the United States and Japan. According to Warren Jestin, the Bank of Nova Scotia's chief economist, "If Canada's labour force participation rate were the same today as at the start of the decade, the national jobless rate would be 13 percent."

For all the thirty years of the 1950s, 1960s, and 1970s, Canada's unemployment rate averaged only 5.3 percent. During those same years our export ratio to GDP was only a fraction of what it is today. Put another way, as our exports and imports soared, the growth rate of employment *declined* sharply. During the first seven years of the FTA, employment in manufacturing fell by almost 150,000 jobs. Now only some forty-five percent of the market for manufactured goods in Canada comes from domestic production, down from seventy-three percent in 1980.

One thing virtually all the economists promised us was that the FTA would improve Canadian competitiveness. In 1989 Canada was fourth overall in the annual World Competitiveness Report. By 1995 we had fallen all the way to between eighth and twelfth place, depending on whose study you believe. What, then, about productivity, also a promised winner by the FTA advocates? Since 1989, of all the G-7 nations, Canada is at the bottom of the barrel in its annual growth rates in productivity.

Not only did Canada do very poorly in employment compared with the pre-FTA period, it also did very poorly in growth compared with the other G-7, European Union, and OECD nations. In the seven years before the FTA, in real GDP increases, Canada outperformed every other OECD nation. But during the first seven years of the FTA, the G-7, EU, and OECD growth averages all exceeded Canada's by margins of forty to fifty percent.

Now let's look at how Canada fared compared with our FTA partner. Between 1982 and 1989 Canada's per-capita GDP had steadily climbed to some ninety percent of that in the U.S. By 1994 it had dropped all the way back to eighty percent and was headed lower.

One direct impact of the FTA has been record-breaking increases in the American ownership of Canada. From 1989 to 1995 American-controlled assets in this country grew by record amounts. Here are the extraordinary words of an *Ottawa Citizen* reporter after the high-tech SHL Systemhouse was taken over by an American company in 1995: "Investors, managers and employees are reluctantly accepting the fact that any Canadian company wanting to remain Canadian is doomed."

Of course it is true that we were promised that the FTA would bring big increases in overall investment in Canada. But even including the record-breaking foreign takeovers, the rate of growth in real gross fixed-capital formation in Canada has been a disaster. In the seven years before the FTA it grew on average at an annual rate of 3.9 percent. In the first seven years of the FTA it plunged to 1.3 percent. Let us now once again return to the wisdom of the *Globe and Mail*. Here are the closing words of an editorial from late last year: "By making ourselves attractive to outside investors we have made our own economy stronger and more prosperous. It is a lesson we should not forget." True. Like jumping off a bridge with a rope around our neck is a lesson we would not forget.

In a 1988 election speech Brian Mulroney promised that free trade would "create more jobs, especially for our young people, and put more money in the pockets of our workers." Moreover, the agreement would "assure our prosperity and well-being as Canadians." Probably one of our most important measures of the health of the economy is the measurement of annual changes in personal consumer spending. In the first seven years of the FTA the rate of increase in consumer spending fell by over fifty percent compared to the previous seven years. There is much irony in this. Advocates of the FTA constantly promoted the bountiful benefits the deal would bring consumers. But consumers without money to spend or who are fearful of losing their jobs don't spend very much.

Since the Free Trade Agreement came into effect, some 1.3 million more Canadians have been forced into poverty. By 1993, there were a dismaying 4.8 million Canadians living in poverty. One in seven Canadian children below the age of eighteen now lives in conditions of real, debilitating, humiliating poverty. For preschool-age children, the rate is now one in four. During the first seven years of the FTA, children living in families experiencing long-term unemployment increased by over fifty percent, and those in working-poor families by almost forty percent. Canada now has one of the highest rates of poor children among the industrialized countries.

In 1988 fewer than two million Canadians were forced to rely on welfare. By 1994, that figure had grown to more than three million. Is it any wonder? Today less than forty-five percent of those who are unemployed receive unemployment insurance benefits. In a list of nineteen top industrialized countries, Canada now ranks sixteenth in terms of UI benefits.

For some members of the Mulroney government, poverty was no big problem. Their answer was simple. All we had to do to reduce poverty was to adjust the poverty line. As one sardonic person noted in a letter to the *Globe*, if you adjust your bathroom scale, you can immediately lose weight.

With a help-wanted index well below the average before the FTA, with hundreds of thousands of Canadians forced to work at insecure, poorly paid part-time jobs, with hundreds of thousands more having exhausted their unemployment insurance benefits and forced to rely on welfare, and with a growing trend towards long-term unemployment, is it any wonder the domestic economy has stagnated, and the retail sector and its domestic suppliers have done so poorly?

Personal savings are another important economic indicator. In the seven years before the FTA these increased on average by more than 1.8 percent per year. By the end of 1995, personal savings in Canada were close to a twenty-five-year low. Since the relationship between savings and investment is direct, the implications for the future of the Canadian economy are ominous. So, too, are the implications for our overall standard of living.

Of course, there is one industry in Canada that has done very well indeed. In 1994 Canada's six big banks made a record profit of $4.3-billion. In 1995 our banks made profits of $5.2-billion. The banks' rate of return on share equity has far exceeded the return in the rest of the economy for the past six years. Meanwhile, it's interesting to compare the record bank profits with their record of loans to business in Canada since the FTA came into effect. During the seven years before the FTA, business credit in this country expanded at an annual rate of over eight percent. During the first seven years of the FTA the rate shrunk to barely one half of one percent! With high real-interest rates and the abandonment of reserve requirements, the banks have been laughing all the way to their directors' boardrooms. Currently the banks own some $80-billion in risk-free government bonds and treasury bills, which provide well over half of their annual profits.

In February 1986 Thomas d'Aquino, speaking to the Men's Canadian Club in Calgary, promised that as a result of a free-trade agreement "the incomes of Canadian households would rise. So would consumer spending and investment [and] jobs would grow." In a speech during the 1988 election campaign, Brian Mulroney promised that the FTA would "raise the living standards of all Canadians" and that the "extra money in your pocket will recycle through the economy." Real family income in Canada increased every year from 1984 on, peaking in 1989. Then it fell for four consecutive years. Today, in 1996, it is some $2,500 below the level of the first year of the FTA, a decline that Statistics Canada describes as "the largest and steepest" in the past forty years.

Is it any wonder, then, as household debt has increased every year and as real disposable income has declined by almost ten percent, that recent polls show deep pessimism among Canadians? One in three say they fear that they or a member of their family is in danger of losing their job. For many Canadians the recession has never ended, and most now believe that the younger generation will be worse off.

More Canadians than at any time since the Great Depression fear they will be plunged into poverty.

A dismal picture? Not at all according to Andrew Coyne, who writes that "the advantage of importing things is that it saves us having to make them ourselves." True, just as the advantage of losing your job is that you don't have to work.

In 1994 the export of goods and services as a percentage of GDP amounted to 33.2 percent while imports were 32.5 percent, for a net difference of 0.7 percent. But, as two Foreign Affairs studies have pointed out, if we consider the very large imported U.S. component in our exports, we actually have a merchandise trade *deficit* with the U.S. (amounting to some $4-billion in 1994). For example, "Our electrical and electronics industry in 1993 depended on imported inputs for almost 60% of its output and the transportation industry for 54%." Before the FTA went into effect, imports into Canada that became components of our exports amounted to fourteen percent. By 1992 they were thirty-two percent and rising. The difference between the two figures represented hundreds of thousands of lost jobs in Canada.

When Pierre Trudeau was elected prime minister in 1968, sixty-five percent of Canadian exports went to the United States, a figure considered to be a very dangerous overdependency. Today that figure has increased to eighty percent.

Southam columnist Don McGillivray put the consequences of such heavy reliance on one trading partner this way: "Canadians may as well resign themselves to being drawn ever closer into the American orbit. And the U.S. will continue to follow its own national interest rather than Canada's. Perhaps we'll eventually reach a time when we'll have to apply for membership in the U.S. just to get a say in our own destiny."

Were we ever a "closed" nation before the FTA? Nonsense. In 1985 Canada was second among all the largest OECD trading nations in per-capita exports, well ahead of such countries as Britain, Japan, Italy, the United States, and Australia. If one examines the economic history of England, Germany, and Japan, these nations grew strong as a result of their capacity to produce first for their own markets and then for export. In other words, they became strongly self-reliant well before they opened their domestic markets. In the words of *Atlantic Monthly* Washington editor James Fallows:

> If you make steel rather than just being able to buy it, you'll
> be better able to make machine tools. If you're able to make

machine tools, you'll be better able to make engines, robots, airplanes. If you're able to make engines and robots and airplanes, your children and grandchildren will be more likely to make advanced products and earn high incomes in the decades ahead.

The economies that have grown most impressively over the past generation from Germany to Thailand to Korea to Japan all certainly believe in competition . . . but it would be very hard to find a businessman or an official in these countries who would say, with a straight face, that their industries grew "automatically" or in a "natural" way.

Both England and Japan, on their way to prosperity, broke virtually every rule of trade in the protection of their own developing industries and their own domestic markets. Cheap imports were prohibited, state subsidies flowed to key industries until they became strong and competitive. Fallows continues: "America's economic history follows the same pattern. While American industry was developing, the country had no time for *laissez-faire*. After it had grown strong, the United States began preaching *laissez-faire* to the rest of the world and began to kid itself about its own history, believing its slogans about *laissez-faire* as the secret of its success."

In fact, for over 150 years after the American Revolution, the U.S. was a strongly protectionist nation. According to Abraham Lincoln, "I don't know much about the tariff . . . but I know this much. When we buy manufactured goods abroad, we get the goods and the foreigners get the money. When we buy the manufactured goods at home, we get both the goods and the money."

It's no great secret that the U.S. has had a national industrial strategy using the defence industry as a catalyst for economic development. Domestic production has been the number-one priority. Huge research grants and government contracts have been the norm, while high tariffs on lower-priced goods kept them out of the country until domestic industries became competitive.

The Americans invaded Canada five times. Canada fought back valiantly and survived. But the *welcomed* invasion of American ownership of the Canadian economy and the Free Trade Agreement are a deadly combination. The so-called trade agreement "window of opportunity" has turned out to be a trapdoor down into a cold dark cellar.

Often, after my speeches, people would ask me, "But what would the consequences be of cancelling the FTA and NAFTA?" My answer was always the same: "A higher standard of living and more freedom for Canadians."

For those of us accused by the continentalists of not being concerned about the welfare of poor Mexicans in our opposition to NAFTA, the subsequent collapse of the Mexican economy is ironic in the extreme. Not only has the standard of living there plummeted, but an impoverished Mexico is no longer in control of its own economy; Washington now calls the shots on all key economic decisions. The peso crisis and the trade agreement have combined to produce a devastating impact: a huge increase in poverty and unemployment, a huge decline in the average standard of living back to Third World levels, a big increase in the cost of living along with a similarly large drop in real wages, growing disparities between the very rich and all other Mexicans, plus large increases in crime and violence. Leading Mexican economist Carlos Heredia has said that "the trade agreements are the results of alliances that have been forged among the elites of Canada, the United States, and Mexico [and] the agreements are not beneficial to the majority of the population."

It's interesting to look back and see what has become of the three national leaders who negotiated and so enthusiastically promoted NAFTA. George Bush became one of the few single-term U.S. presidents in the twentieth century, soundly defeated by Bill Clinton in the 1992 election. Brian Mulroney's popularity plunged to the lowest levels since public-opinion polling began in Canada; he had no choice but to step down as leader of the Conservative party and as prime minister. Even today, years after his resignation, Mulroney is one of the most disliked men in Canada. And Carlos Salinas fled Mexico in disgrace, reviled and despised by his own people.

Not all of the economic devastation of the protracted deep recession in Canada and the feeble sputtering recovery can be traced back directly to the FTA. Some of our poor economic results can be tied to myopic monetary policy. Some have been caused by distorted tax policies. Some have been the result of growing foreign ownership and corporate concentration, and some have been caused by terrible fiscal planning. However, anyone who would deny that the FTA has been a key factor in our declining standard of living must be a blind ideologue.

Or, is it really simpler than that? Is it really greed rather than ideology that leads to deceit and to the deception of a nation?

The Death Knell of Culture

I AM VERY PROUD of what Hurtig Publishers was able to accomplish. Helped by our bestsellers and an excellent backlist, we grew to become the fourth-largest trade-book publisher in Canada and the largest anywhere in the country outside of Toronto. For three years we were number one in the country in total sales. I tried to publish books on subjects Canadians would want to read about — history, biography, politics, nature, books on aboriginal peoples, and the North — and beautiful books on photography and art. But most of all my desire was to publish books that would help make Canada an even better place to live.

At the same time as members of the Mulroney government were attacking me, they were constantly assuring Canadians that culture was not on the free-trade table, that Canada's cultural industries would not be affected, and that the government of Canada was committed to safeguarding the cultural interests of Canadians.

In January 1992 the same government announced policy changes that, according to Carol Martin writing in *Canadian Forum*, "could kill the cherished Canadian dream of a domestically controlled publishing industry." The policy changes drastically weakened the 1985 Baie Comeau policy that had been designed to increase Canadian ownership in book publishing. The Minister of Communications at the time was Perrin Beatty, whose political career has been a classic example of accommodation. While Tory Marcel Masse had earned some plaudits from Canadian cultural industries while in the Communications portfolio, Beatty's performance was greeted with dismay, similar to the reaction to his 1995 appointment to the presidency of the CBC.

Beatty and his officials discussed the book-publishing policy changes with U.S. officials in Washington and with American publishers before the changes were announced in Canada. We now know that whatever was said officially about culture not being on the tableas part of the Free Trade Agreement, there was the tacit understanding that the Mulroney government would act in such a way as to avoid major U.S. complaints about both the book-publishing industry and film policy.

While some seventy to seventy-five percent of the market for books in Canada is taken by foreign publishers, over eighty percent of all Canadian-authored books continue to be published by Canadian-owned houses. If Statistics Canada were able to accurately measure the direct imports of books into Canada, which it cannot, and if it properly classified the pseudo "Canadian" publishers that are really controlled from abroad, the foreign sector of the Canadian market would be well over seventy-five percent. The situation relating to book clubs and mass-market paperbacks is even worse. For many years Canadian content in book clubs operating in the Canadian market was a pitiful three or four percent, while for mass-market paperbacks it was a ridiculous two percent. Recently newspapers across Canada included in their weekend papers two large foreign book club advertising brochures. Both displayed a Canadian book prominently on the brochure cover. But on closer examination, the Canadian content was typical: for one it was three percent; for another less than seven percent out of 147 books offered.

The Liberal Red Book stated that culture "is the very essence of national identity, the bedrock of national sovereignty and national pride." Moreover, with globalization to contend with "Canada needs more than ever to commit itself to cultural development." And what have the Liberals done since their election? Aside from drastically cutting the budgets of the CBC and every other important cultural institution in the country, the Chrétien government has slashed its two key programs designed to assist Canadian book publishers by an astounding sixty-one percent. Moreover, policies designed to Canadianize the foreign-dominated industry have been abandoned. In the words of Ron Besse, president of Canada Publishing Corporation, "the government no longer wants to differentiate between Canadian and foreign publishers. They've opened the floodgates. . . . I really feel they don't give a damn anymore."

By April 1995, Avie Bennett, reacting to the massive cuts in federal-government assistance to the publishing industry, was very pessimistic. "In my view," he said, "it's tolling the death knell of Canadian publishing. . . . There won't be a publishing firm in this country that will not be in dire straits as a result of what they've done, and every company will be up for grabs or will go bankrupt, one or the other."

According to another of Canada's leading book publishers, who asked not to be identified, most of the bureaucrats in Ottawa simply had no understanding of how much damage the massive cuts would do to Canadian publishing. One of the key officials was clearly a continentalist who really didn't care, and another was a Francophone who viewed the industry through the eyes of the Quebec publishers (Quebec publishers don't have to compete with American books and do quite well). Another prominent Canadian publisher called the Chrétien government's actions "the most cynical betrayal in the history of book publishing in Canada. . . . They absolutely don't give a damn!" The impact of both federal and provincial cutbacks is enormous: far fewer new books will be published, fewer new writers will be published, and there will be even more staff layoffs and forced mergers. Most of all it means that many excellent Canadian books will never be published.

There is probably no better example of how inept bureaucrats, foreign lobbying, and weak cabinet ministers have damaged an industry than book publishing in Canada. Myopic government policy abandoned Canadian ownership as a goal and encouraged foreign publishers to do a better job publishing Canadian books. Wonderful. So, Doubleday published Pierre Berton's memoirs and many other bestselling Canadian authors are now published by foreign publishers. Even Maude Barlow's last book was published by HarperCollins and printed and bound in the U.S. By 1996, American publishers such as Random House were capturing more and more well-known Canadian authors.

This is a development I warned about many years ago. Canadian publishers such as Jack McClelland, Jack Stoddart, and Anna Porter, plus many small and medium-size houses, spent years producing Canadian books, encouraging and taking chances with new authors, often publishing new voices knowing full well they would lose money on a particular book or books, but also believing in the authors' futures. Now big foreign publishers are outbidding Canadian houses for the same authors. Year after year more bestselling writers are moving to non-Canadian houses. Well, of course, this is no doubt fine for those successful authors. But *who* will help develop the new Canadian writers of the future? If you think for a moment that publishing houses controlled in New York and London will do the job that needs to be done, you are seriously deluded.

When I recently described my interpretation of Ottawa's misguided strategy to Anna Porter, she said: "Mel, you're right. We're now being used as the farm teams." The impact of a publishing house losing a successful, well-known author goes well beyond the immediate loss of a book's sales and profits. Most good publishers use their revenue from their "stars" to help finance books by their lesser-known authors and their brand-new authors, so there's a serious multiplier effect.

Many major Canadian book publishers now feel that the agency system in Canada is doomed. Regardless of federal legislation to support agency arrangements, the power of the big American bookstore chains with the U.S. publishers is enough to force "open market" arrangements in Canada. Once that happens, the agency system will crumble, but Canadian publishers will still not be able to bid for the publishing rights for the overwhelming majority of foreign titles.

One well-known Canadian publisher believes that in the near future only half as many Canadian books will be published, and that at least thirty Canadian houses will disappear in the next few years. Meanwhile, American publishers are delighted; over half of all their book exports *to the entire world* go to Canada. Anna Porter is very pessimistic: "I don't see how it can get worse. My guess is that the Canadian publishing industry will be wiped out in ten years." Jeffrey Simpson puts it this way: "There cannot be another country in the world that makes it so difficult for domestic creators to find an audience."

And what about television? The average Canadian spends some four hours a day watching TV. That's two full months out of every year, or on average, a quarter of the entire time a person is awake. Some eighty percent of the television they watch is American (and more than ninety percent of the movies). As I mentioned before, everything is relative. A few days after Mulroney's government announced a $75-million cut in the CBC's funding, they also announced tax measures that reduced petroleum industry taxes by $578-million. When the Chrétien government chopped another $110-million of CBC money in Paul Martin's March 1996 budget, they also gave another $422-million in tax relief to the petroleum industry.

Alphonse Ouimet, former president of the CBC, wrote to me in 1985 and said that "the impact of American television on Canadians is so strong and pervasive that, when added to other pressures, there may soon be in practice no distinguishable cultural or characteristic differences left between the average Canadian and the average American. When this happens, and in my view we are already perilously close to it now, how long could Canada survive?"

I do not think that Gerald Caplan, co-chair of the 1985 Task Force on Broadcasting Policy, overstated the case when he said, in March 1996, "The Chrétien government doesn't give a damn about public broadcasting."

As almost everyone knows by now, culture was not really excluded from the FTA. In reality, no new cultural programs of any significance are possible without the likelihood of U.S. retaliation. But what was the use of "exempting" culture and then, in the face of the enormous forces of Americanization resulting from the FTA, cutting back cultural institutions, book publishing, the CBC, Telefilm Canada, and aid to artists? The Gotliebs and the Burneys and the Lougheeds who somehow thought that "culture" would be there to save the nation were hopelessly naïve.

A Dream of Canada

IN THE PREFACE TO *The Betrayal of Canada* I wrote: "The work and the dreams of generations of Canadians are being destroyed. The tragedy of Canada is that this is happening after we have done so very well. Compared with all other nations, we were probably the most fortunate people on earth. Our real standard of living, combined with the quality of life we have had, was unequalled. Our great potential for the future was the envy of the world."

Canada was transformed by the Second World War. We entered the war in 1939 having barely emerged from the Great Depression, badly battered and weakened, lacking confidence as a nation. During the war our transformation to one of the world's leading industrialized powers was truly remarkable. The nation became a beehive of activity while Canadian men and women here and overseas helped defeat the brutal Nazis and the Japanese, and helped defend freedom and justice for the good of all mankind.

Almost overnight the depression in Canada was gone; suddenly jobs were everywhere. With industrialization came innovation, exciting new products, new lifestyles, and a much higher overall standard of living. From the grinding poverty and bitter frustration of the long depression, within a few years Canadians had, on average, the second-highest standard of living in the world. A vital new spirit and a confident new culture reflected our new affluence, and a pride of accomplishment, determination, and optimism was found across the country. How well we had done! And the future surely could only be better.

Even though American films, magazines, books, and broadcasts largely ignored the fact that once again the U.S. had entered a world war years late, and even though the U.S. media portrayed the Second World War as essentially another glorious battle fought and won by Americans, we Canadians knew better. We knew about Dieppe and we knew about Dunkirk, just as we had known about Vimy Ridge and Passchendaele. What brave heroes we produced. What tragic losses we suffered. What glory we earned and what grief we endured.

And, how proud we were that we Canadians had asserted our presence in the defence of liberty as a strong sovereign nation, now firmly in control of our own future. Halfway through the century we began to think that Wilfrid Laurier had been right all along: the twentieth century would indeed belong to Canada. After all, look at how much we had accomplished in such a very short time! And look at all the enormous space and bountiful resources we had to work with, our abundant fresh water, our immense forests, our mines and minerals. And then in 1947 came Leduc Number One — oil and natural gas in amazing quantities, well beyond our wildest dreams.

Not only had we emerged from the Second World War as an economic powerhouse, but we also had become a truly independent nation, beholden to no one, controlled by no other country, in charge of our own future, and a widely respected presence in the world community of nations. From colony to nation, from political and economic dependence, a proud affluent young giant had emerged.

The tragedy of Canada is that we managed to squander away so much, so quickly. In the face of spectacular opportunity, we created truly miserable circumstances for millions of our fellow citizens and dismal prospects for the very existence of our country. With a vital, well-educated population and envied resources, we allowed inept politicians and greedy businessmen to create a subservient, drastically weakened economic colony.

Only four years after our exuberant centennial celebrations, the *Guardian* concluded an article entitled "Canada — economic colony" this way: "Some will recall that in George Orwell's novel *Nineteen Eighty-Four* the hero, Winston Smith, strives hard to maintain his identity and nothing in the novel comes equal to matching this need. But he is already doomed by the actions of past generations in creating the sort of society into which he is born. After a long period of brainwashing he makes the final submission of his own accord. One begins to wonder if Canada is a nation of Winston Smiths." In the same year the great literary critic Northrop Frye wrote in his preface to *The Bush Garden*: "Our country has shown a lack of will to resist its own disintegration. . . . Canada is practically the only country left in the world which is a pure colony, colonial in psychology as well as in mercantile economics."

Twenty-five years ago I read these comments with increasing anger, not at the authors, but at the politicians and business elite who had sold our country out and brought us to our knees. It wasn't long before I began to believe that perhaps, after all, George Grant, Donald Creighton, and Walter Gordon were right in their pessimistic appraisals of Canada's ability to survive. All three had come to the conclusion that it was already too late to save our beloved country. When I saw the final text of the Free Trade Agreement, it was quite clear to me that the dream of Canada would almost certainly disappear once and for all if the agreement was implemented and left in place for very long.

Soon after I entered public life, I became very tired of endless panel discussions about Canadian identity. And, I suspect, most Canadians shared my annoyance. Most of us knew well who we were and had known for many years. But somehow there developed a pre-occupation with asking questions most citizens in most countries wouldn't dream of having to ask. Most of us felt that a key aspect of our identity was straightforward: we Canadians were very fortunate to live in Canada, we could take advantage of our great good fortune and build on it, not squander it; we should value our heritage, be free to choose our own national values, and be free to decide how we developed our economy and our society. *That very freedom was our identity.* It was distinct, it was special, it was real.

Independence? Nationalism? Are these two words even the right words? I think not. The compradors and continentalists are fond of quoting Dr. Samuel Johnson's famous line "Patriotism is the last refuge of scoundrels." But is it? Johnson, among a long list of other illnesses, had Tourette's syndrome, one characteristic of which is uncontrollable vocalizations. James Boswell, in his *Life of Johnson*, recorded: "Patriotism having become one of our topics, Johnson suddenly uttered, in a strong determined tone, an apothegm, at which many will start: 'Patriotism is the last refuge of a scoundrel.' But let it be considered, that he did not mean a real and generous love of our country, but that pretended patriotism, which so many, in all ages and countries, have made a cloak for self-interest."

Canadians need not fear being patriotic. They do need to fear the scoundrels who tell them it is evil to do so, and they need to be wary of those who hide their selfish interests in a cloak of globalization.

Is there such a thing as the "national interest"? I certainly hope so, otherwise what's the use of having a nation? Can there really be a national interest in a country as big and diverse as Canada? Of course there can and it's easy to define. The national interest must primarily be the improvement of the welfare of the nation's citizens. It must encompass fairness and compassion. What is it that holds a nation together? Surely it must be a body of commonly shared moral values and principles based on social and economic justice.

Ultimately for the survival of Canada there can only be one solution: freedom to choose our own values and our own destiny, and that freedom can flow only from true democratic decision-making in our political and economic affairs. If I have learned one important thing over the past three or four decades, it is that such democratic decision-making is sadly lacking in Canada. Behind the facade of democracy lies entrenched, consolidated, dominating economic power.

As the Mulroney government did so often, the Chrétien government repeatedly mentions Canada's number-one rating in the United Nations Human Development Index. But the index is based on a relatively narrow range of measurements. Moreover, many of the qualities measured by the UN are a direct result of our benevolent social programs, which are now in the process of being downgraded and dismantled. The widespread impact of the recent reduction in federal social transfers will profoundly change Canada and move it increasingly closer to the American model.

The Chrétien government's social-policy changes and other plans now under discussion will change Canada in other important ways. In a nation already by far the most decentralized large developed nation in the world, as grasping, parochial, provincial premiers and provincial media stridently demand more and more transfers of power from the national government, the Chrétien government, as part of its Quebec strategy, is prepared to further weaken the national government and transfer yet more power to the provincial governments. A strong decentralist push has come not only from Chrétien and Paul Martin and the provincial premiers, but also from the right-wing think tanks and the conservative media beholden to the BCNI and the multinational business community that likes nothing better than a weak national government. What was once a national community of dreams is being replaced by an inept, weakened federal government whose vision of Canada seems to be a balkanized collection of decentralized states, a loose association of increasingly foreign-owned fiefdoms that will never survive American manifest destiny.

I have said very little in this book about Quebec. This is not because I am not terribly concerned about what has been happening, but rather because I intend to address the subject in some detail elsewhere in the near future. I will say this: the Quebec Liberals and the Chrétien government grossly mismanaged the referendum campaign in 1995. More of the same shoddy performance will certainly mean a shattered country. And those who believe that transferring more power to the province of Quebec will ever placate the separatists are as hopelessly naïve as those who believe more powers can be transferred to Quebec without transferring those same powers to other provinces. In 1996 new asymmetrical federalism has about as much chance of succeeding as the reintroduction of Meech Lake or the Charlottetown accord. This said, lest anyone think otherwise, I strongly support the protection of French language and culture in Quebec and official bilingualism in Canada.

During the last federal election I said I believed that if the Conservatives or the new continentalist Liberals were to win a majority government, then the dream of Canada would likely be over: "Already so close to the precipice, I think another four more years would push us over the edge."

Today the stark and simple question is quite clear. If we continue to abandon the important differences that have for so long distinguished us from the United States, why should there continue to be any demand for a separate country? The reality, of course, is that there will not be such a demand. Moreover, with increasing foreign ownership, balkanization, and the abandonment of national standards, at a certain point, even if the spirit and the desire are there, even if the assembled documentation and human misery are overwhelming, even in the face of a new Vietnam or a new Richard Nixon, even if the Canadian standard of living plummets and the anger of betrayal surges across the land, at a certain point the chance to turn things around will have passed us by forever.

Perhaps Canada will not disappear. Perhaps there will still be maps with a different colour on the top half of the North American continent. There could even still be a Maple Leaf flag. But the nation we are now in the process of becoming will be a nation essentially in name only — an economic, social, political, and cultural colony, a place not a country, a feeble remnant of a once proud nation.

How do Canadians feel about what is happening? The latest polls continue to show that, by an overwhelming margin, Canadians still love their country, still want to live here and nowhere else, still feel we have a distinct identity worth preserving. But for the first time in my memory, they also show something else.

Pollster Allan Gregg termed the annual *Maclean's*/CBC poll of 1996 "the blackest I have ever examined in twenty years of analysing poll results. . . . Canadians believe that virtually everything about Canada not only has got worse than it was in times past, but that we can expect continued deterioration [and] the aspects of Canadian life that have given us a common sense of purpose and character will exist — if at all — only as pale imitations of what they were. . . . As I look at these findings, I see very little cause for optimism that the public opinion fabric of the nation is strong enough to hold Canada together."

Today we are witnessing the tragic shattering of the Canadian dream and the virtual abandonment of the idea of a national community and national public philosophy. Across the country there is a pervasive feeling of helplessness and insecurity. As government increasingly acts as an agent of the large corporations, citizens are at the mercy of powerful interests they cannot combat. And all across the land it is the unfortunate, the underprivileged, who, in the growing absence of a sense of community and common good, bear the brunt of an abandonment of standards that would have been unheard of a generation ago. The "War on Poverty" has been transformed into a war against the poor.

Meanwhile, the four horsemen of the national eclipse, somehow ignored by our politicians and most of our journalists, continue to leave their deep imprint on our public policies and our freedom. Foreign ownership, corporate concentration, the FTA, and NAFTA — all led by our abysmally outdated, undemocratic electoral system — continue to gallop across the national landscape without restraint.

Donald Creighton asked *why*, given their good leaders, their bountiful documentation to back up their positions, plus "a large and vocal following among the Canadian people," have the results for Canadian nationalists been "so tragically disproportionate" and such "a dismal story, full of retreats and defeats and frustrations." Nothing could be clearer in my mind than that the overwhelming reason is the failure of Canadian nationalists to engage directly in politics. The nationalists in Canada have been defeated because they spent too much energy on a multitude of skirmishes without engaging in by far the most important battle — the battle for political power. Today, Canadian nationalists are without a political voice. While all across Canada there are millions of proud Canadians who yearn for a confident Canada in control of its own future, the Liberals, Conservatives, and Reform parties are all aggressive continentalists, and the federal NDP seems lost and dispirited.

William Neville wrote of the ill-fated National Party of Canada that "instead of urging Canadians to dismantle government, it encourages them to take control of it as a means of regaining control of Canada." The predominant political philosophy in Canada today is the dismantling of government. And don't the big transnational corporations and conglomerates love it! Instead, what is needed is for citizens to take control of government, for government to become a true manifestation of the will of the people. How far have we strayed from such an ideal? Let us go back more than 2,400 years to Pericles' funeral oration recounted in Thucydides' *History of the Peloponnesian War*. Compare the words of Pericles with Canada in 1996 and weep:

> Our constitution is called a democracy because power is in the hands not of a minority but of the whole people. When it is a question of settling private disputes, everyone is equal before the law; when it is a question of putting one person before another in positions of public responsibility, what counts is not membership of a particular class, but the actual ability which the man possesses. No one, so long as he has it in him to be of service to the state, is kept in political obscurity because of poverty.
>
> We give our obedience to those whom we put in positions of authority, and we obey the laws themselves, especially those which are for the protection of the oppressed.

Some say that people get the government they deserve. I don't believe this for a moment. I say we get the government the economic elite want us to have, and they are victorious because the system is of their design. There is no hope that they will ever want to change a political system based on money, for such a system works directly for their benefit. Martin Luther King said: "We know through painful experience that freedom is never voluntarily given by the oppressor." In Canada, freedom will never voluntarily be given by the economic and political elite. We will have to take it back ourselves.

Time after time the nationalists in Canada won the battles for public opinion — whether it was on the questions of foreign investment, cruise-missile testing, the Free Trade Agreement, or NAFTA — but time after time we lost the only battle that counts, the battle for power, the power to enact legislation.

Is there still hope for our beloved country? Yes, there is; we must never ever surrender to the selfish, the greedy, the deceitful compradors who would rob us of our birthright and destroy our nation.

Everything I know tells me there will soon be a widespread and growing revolt against an undemocratic world controlled by big corporations, and a backlash to attacks against the nation-state. The neoconservatives are already finding themselves under increasing unfavourable scrutiny. The pendulum of power may not be stuck; it could swing back. But it won't swing back by itself. In Canada it will *never* swing back unless many, many more men and women decide to become directly involved in federal politics. Every man and every woman *can* make a difference. The history of Canada has always been one of waves of continentalism and nationalism. True, today we are engulfed in an unprecedented massive tidal wave of neoconservative continentalism, but things *can* change.

Richard Gwyn has put it well: "Neoconservatism has just one serious flaw: It's unworkable. It's unworkable because it's inhuman. It's all about 'me, me, me' and to hell with caring and sharing. . . . At some point, in a repeat of the Great Depression, the economy will implode because too few people will have enough money to buy the goods being created by the wealthy. A backlash against neoconservatism thus is inevitable."

The backlash can and must turn into a political revolt. The public is now beginning to understand that the elite's neoconservative globalization propaganda represents a massive transfer of power and wealth from citizens and employees to corporations and the already wealthy. As this understanding broadens, the possibility for well-organized political action will increase.

Despite all of our serious problems, more than four out of five Canadians still believe that Canada has the best quality of life of any country in the world. And in 1995 a national poll showed that only three percent of Canadians would like to see Canada join the United States, the lowest such figure I can ever recall. This despite the fact that two out of three Canadians feel our country is in "deep trouble."

Many Canadian politicians and other public figures have been fond of saying that the price of being Canadian is a price worth paying. I always thought that such statements were nonsense. There is no price to pay. On the contrary, there is great good fortune to be had by remaining Canadian instead of dissolving forever into the American melting pot.

In June of 1990, after I had received an honorary degree from Concordia University, Hugh MacLennan wrote to me: "Thank you for sending me a copy of your superb address at Concordia. And thank you for all you have done for this country. . . . God bless you, dear old friend." A few months later, Hugh MacLennan was dead. In *Two Solitudes* he had written: "When you see this country for the first time, all of it, you say to yourself my God, is all of this ours?"

I have been very lucky in getting to know my country. I've stood on the tip of Cape Spear, the easternmost point in North America, and visited Old Crow, close to being the westernmost point in Canada. I've watched the air traffic control over the Atlantic Ocean from Gander and seen the thousands of puffins, hawks, and owls at the most spectacular bird sanctuary in North America, Cape St. Mary's in Newfoundland. I've flown across the Arctic from Prudhoe Bay to the east coast of Baffin Island, from Pangnirtung, Port Burwell, and Lake Harbour to Yellowknife and Whitehorse, up the Mackenzie River to Inuvik, Tuktoyuktuk, Banks Island, Sachs Harbour, Melville Island, Bathurst Island, Cambridge Bay, Resolute Bay, Coppermine . . . I've visited them all. And the more I saw of our country, the more I fell in love with it.

"My God," Hugh MacLennan asked, "is all of this ours?" Unfortunately the answer today is: "No, it no longer is, not by a long shot." Every day and every week and every month and every year, more and more of it disappears from our ownership and our control.

WHAT MAN OR WOMAN can look back on their life and objectively assess their own strengths and weaknesses, their accomplishments, their victories and defeats? Not me. Do I have many regrets? Not many, but there is one regret that is deep and fundamental, at the heart of a powerful profound feeling that I let so many people down who believed in me. Neruda wrote that "to have embodied hope for many men even for one minute is something unforgettable and profoundly touching." As I sorted through the stacks of archival boxes researching this book, and as I reread many of the thousands of letters from men and women across the country, it has been impossible not to feel a great sense of sadness for having failed so many who looked to me for inspiration and for leadership. Life is full of triumphs and defeats, and I have had a good share of both. Now I know that it took me far too long to understand the necessity of building a political alternative; the disaster of the hurried, stillborn National party is a profound inescapable failure, regardless of where the blame might lie.

While my political "career" must surely be deemed a failure, I know I did not fail in raising expectations, in promising hope, in teaching involvement, in defining genuine alternatives, and in discomforting the powerful.

What is the ultimate purpose of a nation? Surely it must be to do whatever it can to improve the standard of living of its citizens, to ensure that justice prevails, and that freedom is maximized. It has been said that you can judge a country by how it treats its underprivileged. Given the widespread poverty we now have in Canada, surely we grievously fail this test. For such a comparatively wealthy country to allow so many of its children to live in poverty is a situation that should never be tolerated. In 1988 fewer than one millon Canadians had to rely on food banks. Today that number is approaching four million, and some forty percent of these are children. What can one say about a wealthy society that has produced such misery and not only tolerates it, but whose elite largely ignores it? What can one say of our political leaders who never even mention it?

Let me end by returning to Pericles, with a modest amount of editing:

> The man who can most truly be accounted brave is he who best knows the meaning of what is sweet in life and what is terrible, and then goes out undeterred to meet what is to come.
>
> Fix your eyes every day on what was the greatness of our country . . . fall in love with her. When you remember her greatness, then reflect that what made her great were men and

women with a spirit of adventure who knew their duty, who were ashamed to fall below a certain standard. If they ever failed in an enterprise, they made up their minds that at any rate their nation should not find their courage lacking to her, and they gave to her the best contribution that they could.

And finally . . .

Make up your minds that happiness depends on being free, and freedom depends on being courageous.

Epilogue

IN THE PAST TWO YEARS my life has changed dramatically. For the first time I now have the time to read as much as I want to, to listen to new music, to try to learn how to paint, to take the dogs for long walks every day in the river valley. My new life is tranquil, reflective, and inquiring. The freedom I now have is quite unlike anything I have experienced before. Except for what I see happening to my country (and that's a very big exception), I am happy and content and my conscience is clear.

There has been one constant in my life; the more I have read and the more I have learned, the more I have understood how much more there is to read and to learn. Now I can read the important writers I missed before: Cervantes, Dante, Montaigne, and so many others. Meanwhile, I have been overwhelmed by the startling talent of Alice Munro, and of Cormac McCarthy; the latter's *All the Pretty Horses* is surely one of the finest American novels of all time. While I continue to spend most mornings in my den doing my political and economic reading and research, for the first time since I was a teenager my schedule is almost entirely my own and I can indulge myself in the hedonistic reading of poetry, history, short stories, biography that I have had comparatively little time for since my days as a bookseller.

George Steiner has said that as one grows older music plays an increasingly important role in one's life. I have been in love with music since I was nineteen. Now, for really the first time, I have the chance to properly appreciate my collection and enjoy new pleasures: Mahler, Bruckner, Gorecki, as well as Jann Arden and Jane Siberry and so many other marvellous Canadian artists. And now for the very first time, I am beginning to learn a bit about the history and the structure of music.

Perhaps the biggest change in my life is time. I have been so very, very busy over the years. Now time goes by much more slowly; what an extraordinary luxurious pleasure this is. What an indulgence. How pleasant to have the time to contemplate in solitude. I will write more in the future, give a few speeches every year, travel, golf, and hike in the mountains, but now there is time for all this. Missing is the pressure, the urgent deadlines, the burden of crucial business decisions, the tension of public life.

Next to our children, our home is our greatest treasure. We live in a beautiful old three-storey log house set high into the side of the hill overlooking the valley of the North Saskatchewan River and the golf course and the parks I grew up on. Outside our back door are plateaus of lawn and rose and rock gardens. In the summer we watch the spectacular, tumultuous late-afternoon and evening thunderstorms come rolling and erupting down the valley. A few yards away from our fence a family of five red foxes has established residence. At night the coyotes come up the valley and serenade us and spook the dogs. We have a multitude of other regular visitors: deer, skunks, pheasants, rabbits, squirrels, many different birds, and even from time to time a peregrine falcon.

In the spring the yard sits below an almost solid canopy of pink and white blossoms. For much of the year the house is hidden by trees: Manitoba maples, lilacs, willows, pines, birch trees, hawthorn, apple trees, elms, spruce, honeysuckle, silver maple, Russian olive, pear, and poplar. In the garden are yellow day lilies, blue delphiniums, scarlet poppies, peonies, tiger lilies, hollyhocks, valerians, lady's mantle, petunias, snapdragons, impatiens, and a wide variety of other beautiful flowers. Below the house are a multitude of wildflowers, a tangle of thick caraganas, thistle, and purpleweed. On the side of the house and the pergola that overlooks the garden are clematis vines, Virginia creepers, and grapevines.

Our living room, overlooking the valley, is two storeys high with a beautiful exposed-beam ceiling and a superb stone fireplace. Throughout the year the varied light in the room is a source of constant pleasure. Late in the day the entire room turns golden as the logs reflect the low sun. The house is snug and warm in winter, cool in summer, an extraordinarily cosy and comfortable place to live, with a dozen different decks, porches, nooks, and crannies in which to hide away and read or reflect.

What great pleasure Kay and I have had from our two dogs, Oliver and Victoria. Oliver is a magnificent German shepherd with a huge vocabulary, easily the most intelligent and most affectionate dog I have ever owned. He is also a fierce guard dog, determined to defend our property against every mailman, delivery boy, or stranger who dares approach. One bitterly cold winter night, Kay, Oliver, and I found a little white dog shivering in a snowbank on the Victoria Golf Course near the Groat Bridge. She was starving and terrified of people; obviously someone had abused and abandoned her. After months of trying, we finally convinced her that she could trust us. Little Victoria now is a loving, integral part of the family, who mimics Oliver in everything and follows me wherever I go.

The North Saskatchewan River makes a number of S-turns inside the city limits, and the city fathers years ago were wise enough to preserve most of the wide river valley for parks, golf courses, hiking and ski trails, bicycle paths, and now a large number of excellent off-leash areas. Walking with the dogs at Buena Vista or Terwilliger parks is like being in the middle of the country. The trails and meadows are beautiful, the people friendly, and the dogs are in heaven.

My four beautiful daughters were very close to their mother. They were devastated by Eileen's death from cancer in 1990. Today my girls are strong, intelligent, thoughtful, loving women, with all the fine characteristics a father could ever hope for. Best of all, Barbara, Gillian, Jane, and Leslie are all truly nice people. Barbara and her husband, Barry, produced my grandson, Max, four years ago. (Kay is away ahead of me with five adoring and adorable grandchildren.)

Kay is a loving wife, a superb cook, and a great companion, constantly steering me to good books, good movies, and good wine.

THIS BOOK WILL BE published almost exactly forty years from the day I opened my tiny bookstore. What fun I've had. What great adventures. What truly wonderful people I've had the pleasure of knowing. And what abundant joy I've had and, sometimes, what great sadness. I know that I certainly didn't succeed at everything I tried, but I also know that I always tried my very best.

The following poem, "Ithaca," by Constantine Cavafy, was read at

Walter Gordon's funeral. I can't imagine how I could do much better in summing things up myself, no matter how hard I tried.

> When you start on your journey to Ithaca,
> then pray that the road is long,
> full of adventure, full of knowledge.
> Do not fear the Lestrygonians
> and the Cyclopes and the angry Poseidon.
> You will never meet such as these on your path,
> If your thoughts remain lofty, if a fine
> emotion touches your body and your spirit.
> You will never meet the Lestrygonians,
> the Cyclopes and the fierce Poseidon,
> if you do not carry them within your soul,
> if your soul does not raise them up before you.

> Then pray that the road is long.
> That the summer mornings are many,
> that you will enter ports seen for the first time
> with such pleasure, with such joy!
> Stop at Phoenician markets,
> and purchase fine merchandise,
> mother-of-pearl and corals, amber and ebony,
> and pleasurable perfumes of all kinds,
> buy as many pleasurable perfumes as you can;
> visit hosts of Egyptian cities,
> to learn and learn from those who have knowledge.

> Always keep Ithaca fixed in your mind.
> To arrive there is your ultimate goal.
> But do not hurry the voyage at all.
> It is better to let it last for long years;
> and even to anchor at the isle when you are old,
> rich with all that you have gained on the way,
> not expecting that Ithaca will offer you riches.

EPILOGUE

Ithaca has given you the beautiful voyage.
Without her you would never have taken the road.
But she has nothing more to give you.

And if you find her poor, Ithaca has not defrauded you.
With the great wisdom you have gained, with so much experience,
you must surely have understood by then what Ithacas mean.

Index